Business Communication in a Changing World

Business Communication in a Changing World

ROY BERKO
George Washington University

ANDREW WOLVIN
University of Maryland

REBECCA RAY
Merrill Lynch & Co., Inc.

Bedford/St. Martin's
Boston ◆ New York

Sponsoring editor: Suzanne Phelps Weir
Editorial assistant: Hanna Shin
Manager, publishing services: Emily Berleth
Publishing services associate: Meryl Perrin
Production supervisor: Scott Lavelle
Project management: Books By Design, Inc.
Photo research: Books By Design, Inc.
Cover design: Evelyn Horovicz
Cover art: Rebecca Rüegger

Library of Congress Catalog Card Number: 95-73247

Manufactured in the United States of America.

6   5   4   3   2
h   g   f   e   d

For information, write:
Bedford/St. Martin's
75 Arlington Street
Boston, MA 02116
(617-426-7440)

ISBN: 0-312-13395-2

Photo Credits:
Page 3, Dave Bartruff/Stock, Boston; Page 37, Spencer Grant/Stock, Boston; Page
59, Hazel Hankin/Stock, Boston; Page 103, Robert A. Isaacs/Photo Researchers;
Page 121, Gale Zucker/Stock, Boston; Page 135, Miro Vintoniv/Stock, Boston;
Page 154, O'Leary/Tony Stone Images; Page 203, Frank Siteman/Stock, Boston;
Page 237, Matthew Boroski/Stock, Boston; Page 270, Blair Seitz/Photo

Brief Contents

Contents   vii

Preface   xvii

Chapter 1   The Business of Communication   1

Chapter 2   Communication Ethics in Business Settings   31

Chapter 3   Verbal Communication   54

Chapter 4   Nonverbal Communication   76

Chapter 5   Listening   111

Chapter 6   Managing Self-Communication   131

Chapter 7   Managing Communication with Others   153

Chapter 8   Interviewing   190

Chapter 9   Group Communication: Characteristics
of Business Groups   231

Chapter 10   Group Communication: Participating
in Business Groups   266

Chapter 11   Public Speaking: The Purposes and Types
of Business Speeches   291

Chapter 12   Public Speaking: Preparing the Business
Speech   307

Chapter 13   Public Speaking: Presenting the Business
Speech   333

Chapter 14   Written Business Communication   344

Glossary   367

Index   387

Meet the Authors   395

Contents

Preface   xvii

Chapter ❶ The Business of Communication   1

VIGNETTE   1

THE CHANGING NATURE OF TODAY'S BUSINESS ORGANIZATION   2
COMMUNICATION IN TODAY'S CHANGING BUSINESS ORGANIZATION   6
THE PROCESS OF COMMUNICATION   8
    Components of the Communication System   8
    Communication Models   8
BUSINESS COMMUNICATION VARIABLES   12
    Organizational Culture   12   Organizational Climate   12
    Organizational Channels   13   Organizational Networks   16
    Organizational Functions   18
IMPROVING BUSINESS COMMUNICATION   19
    Planned Business Communication   19   Prepared Business
    Communication   20   Responsive Business Communication   21
    Appropriate Business Communication   22   Coordinated Business
    Communication   24   Quality Business Communication   25

IN SUMMARY   26
BUSINESS COMMUNICATION IN PRACTICE   26
DIVERSITY SIMULATION   26
NOTES   27

Chapter ❷ Communication Ethics in Business Settings   31

VIGNETTE   31

THE ETHICAL DILEMMA   32
ETHICS AND BUSINESS   32
ETHICS DEFINED   33

BUSINESS ETHICS DEFINED   34

ETHICAL PRACTICES IN BUSINESS   35

    Capitalism and Ethics   36   Changes in Ethical Awareness   36

    Corporate Responsibility   36

FEATURE INTERVIEW: Joyce Hauser   39

USING ETHICS   39

USING ETHICS IN BUSINESS COMMUNICATION   43

SAMPLE SPEECH: "Principles for Managing in a Time of Change:
  A CEO's Perspective"   44

IN SUMMARY   **51**

BUSINESS COMMUNICATION IN PRACTICE   **51**

SIMULATIONS   **51**

NOTES   **52**

Chapter ❸ Verbal Communication   54

VIGNETTE   **54**

LANGUAGE DEFINED   55

DIALECTS   56

    Standard American English   57   Nonstandard Dialects   58

PRINCIPLES OF LANGUAGE MEANING   60

LANGUAGE PROBLEMS IN COMMUNICATING   61

    Assumption   61   Clarity   62   Concreteness   63

    Fact versus Inference   64

DIFFERENCES BETWEEN WRITTEN AND SPOKEN LANGUAGE   65

FEMALE-MALE LANGUAGE AND COMMUNICATION   66

    The Sexism of Standard American English   66   Male and Female

    Language Usage   67

FEATURE INTERVIEW: Deborah Borisoff   69

INTERCULTURAL IMPLICATIONS OF LANGUAGE USAGE   71

IMPLICATIONS OF LANGUAGE USAGE AND BUSINESS   72

IN SUMMARY   **73**

BUSINESS COMMUNICATION IN PRACTICE   **73**

NOTES   **74**

Chapter ④ Nonverbal Communication 76

VIGNETTE **76**

SOURCES OF NONVERBAL COMMUNICATION 78
IMPORTANCE OF NONVERBAL COMMUNICATION IN BUSINESS 79
VERBAL-NONVERBAL RELATIONSHIPS 80
    Substituting Relationship of Nonverbal to Verbal 80
    Complementing Relationship of Nonverbal to Verbal 80
    Regulating Relationship of Nonverbal to Verbal 80
    Conflicting Relationship of Nonverbal to Verbal 80
READING NONVERBAL COMMUNICATION 81
CATEGORIES OF NONVERBAL COMMUNICATION 81
    Kinesics 82
FEATURE INTERVIEW: Richard Urban 87
    Vocal Cues 88   Proxemics 89   Physical Characteristics 92
    Artifacts 93   Aesthetics 96   Chronemics 99
CULTURE AND NONVERBAL COMMUNICATION 100
    Greetings 102   Conversations 102   Gestures 103
    Time 104   Business Settings 104
DEALING WITH NONVERBAL COMMUNICATION 105

IN SUMMARY **107**
BUSINESS COMMUNICATION IN PRACTICE **107**
NOTES **108**

Chapter ⑤ Listening 111

VIGNETTE **111**

LISTENING IN THE BUSINESS ORGANIZATION 112
    Levels of Organizational Listening 112   The Organizational
    Listening Environment 113   Listening and Business Success 114
FEATURE INTERVIEW: Sean Greenwood 115
THE LISTENING PROCESS 115
    Motivation 116   Receiving 116   Attention 116

Perception 117   Interest 117   Interpretation 117
Responding 118   Storage 118   Feedback 118
THE GOALS OF LISTENING 119
Listening for Discrimination 119   Listening for
Comprehension 120   Listening for Therapeutic Value 120
Listening for Critical Evaluation 120   Listening for
Appreciation 122
OBSTACLES TO EFFECTIVE LISTENING 122
Physiological Interference 122   Lack of Motivation 123
Negative Self-Concept 123   Lack of Understanding 123
Lack of Preparation 124
IMPROVING LISTENING 125

IN SUMMARY 128
BUSINESS COMMUNICATION IN PRACTICE 128
NOTES 129

Chapter ❻ Managing Self-Communication 131

VIGNETTE 131

THE DIMENSIONS OF INTRAPERSONAL COMMUNICATION 132
Psychological Dimension of Intrapersonal Communication 132
Physiological Dimension of Intrapersonal Communication 134
Cognitive Dimension of Intrapersonal Communication 140
Affective Dimension of Intrapersonal Communication 141
THE COMMUNICATOR SELF 143
Self-Concept 144
FEATURE INTERVIEW: Linda Eaton 145
Self-Identities 145   Self-Talk 146
IMPROVING INTRAPERSONAL COMMUNICATION 146

IN SUMMARY 148
BUSINESS COMMUNICATION IN PRACTICE 149
NOTES 151

Chapter ❼ Managing Communication with Others   153

VIGNETTE   **153**

SELF-DISCLOSURE   155
INTERPERSONAL RELATIONSHIPS IN THE ORGANIZATION   156
INTERPERSONAL SKILLS IN THE BUSINESS ENVIRONMENT   158
 Using the Telephone   158 Using Voice Mail Systems   160
MANAGEMENT-EMPLOYEE RELATIONSHIPS   161
 Criticizing   163 Handling Grievances   164
 Dealing with Difficult Personalities   165 Directing   167
 Job Training   170
CONFLICT AND CONFLICT RESOLUTION   170
 Conflict in the Work Environment   171 Conflict Resolution   172
SEXUAL HARASSMENT   180
 Sexual Harassment Defined   181 Communicating about Sexual
 Harassment   182

IN SUMMARY   **183**
BUSINESS COMMUNICATION IN PRACTICE   **184**
DIVERSITY SIMULATION   **185, 186**
NOTES   **188**

Chapter ❽ Interviewing   190

VIGNETTE   **190**

STRUCTURING THE INTERVIEW   191
 The Opening of an Interview   191 The Body of an Interview   193
 The Closing of an Interview   195
TYPES OF INTERNAL BUSINESS INTERVIEWS   195
 The Informative Interview   195 The Problem-Solving
 Interview   197 The Counseling Interview   198
 The Persuasive Interview   199 The Employment Interview   199
FEATURE INTERVIEW: Scott Brandt   217
 The Performance Appraisal   218 The Reprimanding Interview   223

TYPES OF EXTERNAL BUSINESS INTERVIEWS 224
    The Press Conference 224   The Talk Show Interview 225

IN SUMMARY **226**
BUSINESS COMMUNICATION IN PRACTICE **226**
DIVERSITY SIMULATION **227**
NOTES **228**

Chapter ❾ Group Communication: Characteristics of Business Groups 231

VIGNETTE **231**

GROUPS DEFINED 232
GROUP VERSUS INDIVIDUAL ACTIONS 233
    Advantages of Groups 233   Disadvantages of Groups 233
TYPES OF GROUPS 234
    Work Teams 235   Committees 236
    Media-Conferences 236   Focus Groups 238
    Public Meetings 238   Town Meetings 239
GROUP OPERATIONS 239
    Group Norming 239   Group Storming 240
    Group Conforming 243   Group Performing 243
    Group Adjourning 245
MAKING GROUP DECISIONS 245
    Formulating an Agenda 246   Voting 249
    Decision Making 250
THE GROUP SETTING 255
    Seating Choice 256   Table Configuration 256
    The Effect of the Physical Environment 257
CULTURAL DIFFERENCES IN GROUPS 257
    Cultures and Groups 258   Cultural Attitudes toward Group
    Procedures 258   Cultural Contrasts in Procedural Structure 259
    Cultural Contrast of the Role of Information 260
MALE AND FEMALE ROLES IN GROUPS 261

IN SUMMARY **262**
BUSINESS COMMUNICATION IN PRACTICE **262**
NOTES **263**

Chapter ⑩ Group Communication: Participating in Business Groups 266

VIGNETTE **266**

THE PARTICIPANT   267
    Responsibilities of Group Members   267   Communicating
as a Group Member   269
FEATURE INTERVIEW: Barbara G. Rosenthal   273
    Roles of Group Members   274   Communication Networks   275
Dealing with Difficult Group Members   277
LEADERS AND LEADERSHIP   279
    Types of Leaders   280   Patterns of Leader/Leadership
Emergence   282   Why People Desire to Be Leaders   283
Responsibilities of Leaders   284   The Leader as
Communicator   285   Effective Leadership Questioning   286

IN SUMMARY   **287**
BUSINESS COMMUNICATION IN PRACTICE   **287**
DIVERSITY SIMULATION   **288**
NOTES   **290**

Chapter ⑪ Public Speaking: The Purposes and Types of Business Speeches 291

VIGNETTE **291**

PUBLIC SPEAKING DEFINED   292
INFORMATIVE SPEAKING IN BUSINESS   293
    Types of Informative Speeches   293   Characteristics of
Informative Speeches   294
PERSUASIVE SPEAKING IN BUSINESS   295
    Goals of Persuasive Speaking   296   Persuasive Strategies   296
FEATURE INTERVIEW: Robert Goldberg   299
SPECIAL OCCASION SPEECHES   300
    Speech of Introduction   300   Speech of Welcome   300
Speech of Presentation   301   Speech of Acceptance   301

After-Dinner Speech   301   The Motivational Speech   302
The Sales Speech   302   Question-and-Answer Sessions   302

IN SUMMARY   305
BUSINESS COMMUNICATION IN PRACTICE   305
NOTES   306

Chapter ⑫ Public Speaking: Preparing the Business Speech   307

VIGNETTE   307

COMPONENTS OF ANALYSIS   308
Prior Analysis   309   Process Analysis   312
Post-Speech Analysis   313
DEVELOPING THE SPEECH   313
Sources of Information   313   Supporting Material   315
Vehicles for Presenting Supporting Material   318
STRUCTURING THE MESSAGE   321
The Introduction   321   The Central Idea   323
The Body   323   The Conclusion   325
SAMPLE SPEECHES   326
Sample Speech to Inform   326   Sample Speech to Persuade   328

IN SUMMARY   330
BUSINESS COMMUNICATION IN PRACTICE   330
NOTES   332

Chapter ⑬ Public Speaking: Presenting the Business Speech   333

VIGNETTE   333

MODES OF PRESENTATION   334
Impromptu Presentation   334   Extemporaneous Presentation   335
Manuscript Presentation   335   Memorized Presentation   335
THE PHYSICAL ELEMENTS OF A SPEECH   335
Physical Presentation   336   Oral Presentation   337

PUBLIC SPEAKING ANXIETY   339

IN SUMMARY   **341**
BUSINESS COMMUNICATION IN PRACTICE   **342**
NOTES   **343**

Chapter ⑭ Written Business Communication   344

VIGNETTE   **344**

THE IMPORTANCE OF EFFECTIVE BUSINESS WRITING   345
THE WRITING PROCESS   346
FEATURE INTERVIEW: Penni E. Fromm   348

Preparing to Write the Document   349   Writing "Do's"
and "Don'ts"   350

ORGANIZATIONAL PATTERNS FOR COMMON DOCUMENTS   351

The Internal Memorandum   352   The External Letter   352
The Project Status Report   352   The Executive Summary   355
The Sales Proposal   355   The Resume and Cover Letter   355
The Minutes of a Meeting   357

THE ABC'S OF LANGUAGE   357
ENHANCING THE DOCUMENT'S IMAGE   359

Stationery   360   Layout and Format   360

ELECTRONIC MAIL AT THE WORKPLACE   360

Speed versus Accuracy   361   Privacy Concerns   361
Etiquette   361

ANALYZING THE WRITTEN DOCUMENT   363

IN SUMMARY   **365**
BUSINESS COMMUNICATION IN PRACTICE   **366**
NOTES   **366**

Glossary   267

Index   387

Meet the Authors   395

Preface

When confronted with taking a business communication course, students may not realize the immense value of possessing communication competencies. They may ask such questions as these: Isn't knowing the theories and concepts of the field of business all I need to succeed in the corporate setting? Is communication really important for a career in business?

Knowing the theories and concepts of the field of commerce is important, but communication skills will probably be the basis for a businessperson's success or failure. A recent study, for example, indicates that the two most important factors in current business hiring decisions are attitude and communication skills.[1] Other investigations suggest that specific skills needed to be successful in the corporate world include an understanding of and skills in decision making, intrapersonal communication, listening, interpersonal communication, interviewing, group communication, public speaking, and business writing.[2]

The topics in *Business Communication in a Changing World* have been arranged so that students first learn about the field of communication and the role of communication in business settings. The foundational understandings are further examined by investigating ethical communication, listening, and verbal and nonverbal signal systems. The learner as a personal and other-centered communicator in interactions, interviews, and meetings is then explored. Investigating the communicator as a public speaker and a writer completes the study. During this analysis such factors as the roles of culture, gender, and the changing nature of today's business organization are central to the discussion.

Business Communication in a Changing World is intended for use in business communication courses. The approach, the language, the examples, the format, and the emphasis on oral communication with the inclusion of written communication attempt to address what it takes to become a successful business communicator. Each area is grounded in the research base of the field. Because chapters are not interlinking, they can be used in an order that parallels the philosophy of the instructor.

We have tried to portray the most accurate and meaningful picture of the world of work by making the coverage practical. Features have been incorporated that should make learning both interesting and relevant. We have included an abundance of real business examples and references, factual scenarios from the world of work, interviews with professionals on a range of job-related topics, actual world simulations to be used to apply the strategies presented, and experiential activities to allow for practice of the skills and knowledge being acquired.

The world of business is ever changing. The altering demographics of the United States, the extension of business into a global market, the shift of the Northern American business from manufacturing to service . . . all of these factors have been confronted. Attention is given to such diverse topics as culture, harassment, conflict resolution, dealing with difficult people, the role of self concept, gender communication, and dealing with communication anxiety.

We hope that *Business Communication in a Changing World* assists the reader in becoming a successful businessperson—successful because she or he is an effective communicator.

We appreciate the valuable comments and suggestions of the following people, who kindly reviewed this manuscript: Joan W. Aitken, University of Missouri at Kansas City; Ellen Bonaguro, Ithaca College; Virginia W. Cooper, Old Dominion University; Jody Culp, MBR Consulting; Marianne Dainton, Lasalle University; Lynn Harter, University of Nebraska at Lincoln; Lawrence W. Hugenberg, Youngstown State University; Paula Krivonos, California State University; Melanie S. Mason, University of Nebraska at Kearney; Marian McLeod, Trenton State University; Frank Joseph Routman, Case Western Reserve University; Kristi Schaller, Georgia State University; Stuart M. Schrader, Indiana University/Purdue University at Indianapolis; Rebecca Soper, North Carolina State University; Margaret Underwood, Western Kentucky University; and Paula Yerty, Des Moines Area Community College.

Roy Berko
Andrew Wolvin
Rebecca Ray

● ● ● Notes ● ● ●

1. David Binko, "Technology in the Classroom," an oral comment made during a workshop given at Prince George's Community College, August 25, 1995, as transcribed by Marlene Cohen.

2. William Brock, *What Work Requires of Schools: A SCANS Report for America 2000* (Washington, DC: U.S. Department of Labor, June 1991), p. 15. Also see Isa Engleberg and Diana Wynn, "DACUM: A National Data Base Justifying the Study of Speech Communication," *Journal of the Association for Communication Administrators,* January 1995.Etiquette   361

Business Communication in a Changing World

The Business of Communication

CHAPTER
1

EXPECTED OUTCOMES

After completing this chapter, you should be able to:

- Understand that communication in an organization is highly complex.
- Recognize how the changing nature of organizations impacts their communications.
- Be familiar with current initiatives of quality and re-engineering as they influence organizational communication.
- Be able to identify the linear, interactive, and transactional processes of communication.
- Know that an organization's communication is modified by its culture, climate, communication channels, and communicators—at the executive, managerial, supervisory, and employee levels.

When my lawyer called to say that the final approval had come through on my purchase of an existing fast food franchise, I was excited and nervous. I always wanted to run my own business. I soon realized, however, that with opportunities come challenges. The staff had been very comfortable with the previous owner, so they weren't particularly open to change. They tested my authority. The counter help started to wander in late. The assistant managers didn't seem to have much enthusiasm. Customers complained of waiting in long lines. I was overwhelmed. Ironically, while all this was going on, I received a questionnaire from my college's business school asking me to evaluate my education. I wrote only one comment on the form: "Why didn't you include courses in communication in my degree program? All my problems right now are communication problems, and I'm not equipped to handle them!"

"The importance of communication in business cannot be overstated. By means of communication, a business receives and conveys information, transmits instructions and suggestions, and practices motivation and persuasion. Communication is the lifeblood of the organization and the means by which management gets things done."[1] The ever-changing challenges and methods of adapting to those challenges have a direct effect on the ways in which today's businesses and their representatives communicate.

The Changing Nature of Today's Business Organization

In the United States today, business organizations are caught in a frantic race to recoup the competitive edge of productivity, which many believe has been lost to Japanese industry. As a result, management specialists are concerned with determining just what can be done to restore quality. "The reality is that quality is essential to survival," so American manufacturing and service industries are trying everything from "statistical measurement of manufacturing processes to answering the phone on the first ring."[2]

As today's organizations strive to be competitive in the global marketplace, they are changing their nature and scope. A management expert suggests that "the typical business will be knowledge-based, an organization composed largely of specialists who direct and discipline their own performance through an organized feedback from colleagues, customers, and headquarters."[3]

The flattening-out of the organizational structure of many American corporations is accelerated by considerable downsizing. As the marketplace grows more competitive and the economy more precarious, many companies have found it necessary to reduce the levels of management and consequently ask fewer people to do more of the work. These changes necessitate communicative strategies for maintaining morale, ensuring open lines of communication, and creating new interactive patterns. A survey of corporate executives revealed that 94 percent had taken their companies through some form of downsizing or reorganization, and 66 percent predicted that the pace of corporate change would continue or accelerate in the near future.[4]

The trend toward downsizing has resulted in leaner, less hierarchical organizations, with fewer employees. These flatter organizations offer new challenges to managers and employees alike. Research suggests that American workers would like to become more involved in organizational decision making, but they do not perceive that employers are willing to share that power in the workplace. One survey suggested that the workers did not think they could do a better job in running the company, but they were "motivated to work harder when management listened to their suggestions."[5] Other management analysts have determined that, to achieve excellence, employees will need to become "self-leaders." As a result, managers will have to provide workers with "the autonomy and responsibility to be more in charge of themselves"; they will need to give up the managerial need for external control and authority.[6]

The structural changes required of American organizations are accompanied by dramatic shifts in the composition of the workforce. The increasing globalization of the economy has led to significant internationalization of many companies. Foreign companies invest in American business and industry. The European Community, the North American Free Trade Agreement, and the Asian Pacific Economic Group link countries and companies into a highly interdependent global economy. The end of the Cold War offers increased trade possibilities with Eastern Europe. All of these changes necessitate communication adjustments as different languages and cultural styles clash and meld.

As the American population becomes more internationalized, people from all over the world join the personnel rosters of companies throughout the

As American business organizations have become increasingly internationalized and diversified, organizations have been required to conduct much of their business overseas, dealing with international clients and customers.

United States. And diversification continues to be a personnel goal of most organizations. Today, women and other traditionally underrepresented groups have unparalleled opportunities in the workforce. White males are no longer the majority in American business; women and minorities make up at least 52 percent of the workers.[7] It is predicted that by the year 2000 women will make up approximately 46 percent of the workforce while African Americans, Hispanics, and other minorities will comprise more than 15 percent.[8] These changing workplace demographics necessitate greater understandings in order to avoid tension and conflict as individuals from different cultural groups learn to adapt to each other and to their often unfamiliar communication styles.

People in the workplace do not represent the only major change that companies face. The very nature of work itself has changed radically in the past few decades. As America has moved from an industrial nation to an information society, the work people do looks very different from the work of a previ-

---

Rank Ordering of Oral/Interpersonal Competencies as Perceived by Business Professionals

COMPETENCY	RANK
Listens effectively	1
Uses the telephone and intercom effectively	2
Maintains eye contact	3
Asks appropriate questions	4
Uses voice effectively for emphasis (speed, pitch, volume)	5
Uses appropriate tone of voice—conversational or formal	6
Establishes rapport with the audience	7
Organizes presentations effectively	8
Conducts/participates effectively in interviews	9
Uses appropriate techniques in making oral presentations	10
Is poised; controls nervousness	11
Uses proper interviewing techniques	12
Uses appropriate body actions in interpersonal oral communication	13
Objectively presents information in oral reports	14
Analyzes the audience before, during, and after an oral report	15
Uses audiovisual aids effectively	16

Source: Karen K. Waner, "Business Communication Competencies Needed by Employees as Perceived by Business Faculty and Business Professionals," *Business Communication Quarterly* 58:4 (December 1995): 52.

ous generation. It is predicted that people who entered the workforce in 1980 or later will experience as many as five to seven job changes and three to five career changes during their working lives. Opportunities in small business far outpace placements in large corporations. While the push for quality drives most companies, productivity and accountability continue to be the main concerns of managers who must orchestrate the work and the personnel.[9]

The phenomenal change in the workplace extends to the communication systems as well. Business has left the industrial age and entered the information age, to such an extent that at least half of the people in today's workforce process information of one type or another as their primary job task.[10] Consequently, electronic channels of communication now play a dominant role in how people communicate at work. Telephones and computers can make communication both more and less efficient and effective, depending upon how the systems are used. "In short," concludes one analyst, "how we communicate is changing how we work."[11]

Rank Ordering of Other Business Communication Competencies as Perceived by Business Professionals

COMPETENCY	RANK
Applies ethics, morals, and values in business situations to determine socially responsible actions	1
Understands personal values and shows sensitivity to the values of others	2
Uses principles of time management to organize work efficiently	3
Assesses own needs and behavior; locates outside sources of information to improve knowledge and skills	4
Collects, classifies, and analyzes information about business situations; uses creative thinking in developing solutions; selects effective solutions	5
Exhibits leadership by influencing and persuading	6
Plans, conducts, and follows up meetings effectively	7
Knows the importance of feedback in the communication cycle	8
Uses appropriate data-analysis tools to solve strategic and operational management problems effectively	9
Applies knowledge of intercultural differences to communication situations	10
Applies knowledge of demographic diversity to communication situations	11

Source: Karen K. Waner, "Business Communication Competencies Needed by Employees as Perceived by Business Faculty and Business Professionals," *Business Communication Quarterly* 58:4 (December 1995): 53.

Communication in Today's Changing Business Organization

As a consequence of the changes in the scope and composition of the American corporation, organizations have found themselves caught up in communication problems for which they are not prepared. These problems extend to both external and internal communication. **External communication** refers to relations with customers, stockholders, regulatory agencies, and others outside the organization. **Internal communication** refers to the flow of messages within a network of individuals and groups inside the company. A Ford Motor Company official, recognizing how critical communication is to the business of any organization, stresses that communication "should be at the top of the list of skills developed by every careerist who wants to get anywhere near the top of most any institution in this country."[12]

The critical need for effective communication in the organization is evidenced by the fact that people in business organizations spend an overwhelming amount of time communicating. About half of an executive's time is spent in listening.[13] The average manager spends between 50 and 90 percent of his or her time communicating by one means or another.[14] First-line managers may spend as much as 60 percent of their time in communication.[15]

Not only is the amount of time spent communicating a concern, but the effectiveness of an individual or even an entire corporation may be directly affected by communicative skills. In a survey of personnel officers, 85 percent indicated that an applicant's chances of success in their companies depend on the applicant's ability to communicate effectively.[16] Another study revealed that in the most productive departments of an organization, every worker spoke highly of the communication skills of the department head, while in the least productive departments only 26 percent of the workers rated the boss as a highly skilled communicator.[17] And the major source of a company's loss of labor grievance cases has been found to be the poor communication abilities of management while handling discipline and discharge problems of their workers.[18]

A landmark study identified factors that contribute to excellence in corporations.[19] Many of the excellence factors center on good communication. Listening to the customer, for example, was one of the keys to achieving corporate excellence. Another was encouraging employee participation in the company's decision-making processes. The principle of "Management By Wandering Around" was also observed as an important communication strategy. Instead of hiding away in an office dealing with paperwork, the effective manager has to be out and about, interacting with workers and with customers, to determine how the organization can best respond to their needs.

This view of corporate excellence has paved the way for today's corporate emphasis on achieving quality. The drive for delivering quality goods and services took shape as the **Total Quality Management** approach, adopted by many Japanese firms after World War II.[20] The major principles of Total Quality Management (TQM) are the importance of listening, the focus on the customer, the empowerment of employees to make decisions and deal with problems as they arise, and the use of as much statistical data as possible in order to make informed decisions.[21]

The use of the quality metaphor to enable corporations to reach levels of excellence has led others to adopt re-engineering as a strategy. **Re-engineering** calls for organizations to assess the processes and functions by which they do business and to redesign those processes and functions in order to better accomplish the improvements necessary in the cost, quality, service, and speed of the organization.[22] Re-engineering requires radical restructuring of the way an organization does its business, and much of that entails dealing with its communication systems as well.

The stress on corporate excellence and quality through re-engineering and Total Quality Management positions communication skills as a major key to organizational effectiveness. Most business executives and business analysts have come to recognize how central communication is to the very survival of their organizations. "In the 1990s and beyond," observe management specialists, "we will need more leaders at all levels in our organizations who can communicate effectively to influence and direct others' behavior toward improving performance. In such efforts, the communication skills of first-line supervisors and informal group leaders can be as crucial as the CEO's communication competence."[23]

One organization that prides itself on competent communication is the Walt Disney Company. The Disney theme park organization emphasizes communication from management to employee (known as a "cast member" in the Disney structure), from employee to guest, and from employee to management. The cast communications department at Disney has recognized that "(1) Disney views itself as essentially a communications company, and (2) it believes that over 90% of all organizational problems stem from a lack of communication."[24]

While competent communication can be an excellent device for improving problems, some people believe that it can be a "quick fix" for all the problems that a business faces. Unfortunately, communication is not simple. Indeed, it may be one of the most complex of all human behaviors. With this understanding of the changing nature of today's world of business, and the resulting need for effective communication, let's examine what communication is.

Take Charge of Communication

Who's in charge of communication where you work?

We don't mean just news releases and dealing with the media. We mean all those things that take place in the company that affect the way people feel about where they work and about how to communicate.

A study done by the Oechsli Institute, Greensboro, N.C., asked 1,500 managers, sales managers and administrative staff what two changes they would make in their company.

Ninety-one percent responded: "Improve communication."

Sixty-four percent said that nothing happens when feedback is received from employees.

With all the buzzwords in management, one constant remains: Just about every company should study all of its communication and come up with ways to improve it.

–Don Bagin

The Process of Communication

The process of communication occurs in a split-second sequence. A person receives the stimulus (the information) that has been sent, attends to it, perceives it, interprets it, and responds to it in some way.

COMPONENTS OF THE COMMUNICATION SYSTEM

The sending and receiving of information occurs through sensory channels—sight, sound, touch, smell, and taste. Much of the communication in a business organization utilizes the speaking and listening modes (sight and sound).

During the average workday people spend a great deal of time interacting as speakers and listeners in meetings, conversations, telephone conferences, formal interviews, briefings, and speech presentations. Early research on communication time reveals that about 45 percent of the typical worker's communication time is spent in listening; about 30 percent in speaking; 15 percent in reading; and only 9 percent in writing.[25]

COMMUNICATION MODELS

One way to understand the communication process is to examine its component parts and how they operate in relationship to each other. An early view of the communication process—and one still in use—describes a **sender** (the person who devises or **encodes** the message) sending a **message** (the information the sender devises for the other person to achieve some **purpose,** the goal of the communication) through a **channel** (the medium the speaker chooses, such as talking on the telephone, using electronic mail) to a **receiver** (the person who takes in and **decodes,** clarifies, the message). Also part of this communication equation is a **context** (the characteristics of the situation in which the communication takes place, such as the physical environment and the other people present). These elements may be illustrated by the linear process model (Figure 1.1).

Linear Model of Communication

The **linear process model of communication** illustrates that communication flows in one direction, from a sender to a receiver, and that there is one context that describes the communication situation for both the sender and receiver. In the field of business the linear model is used when a speech is given, a message is left on voice mail, or a videotape is made to send out to

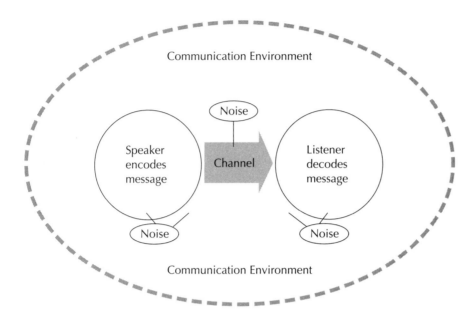

Communication Environment

Noise

Speaker encodes message

Channel

Listener decodes message

Noise

Noise

Communication Environment

FIGURE 1.1
Linear Process Model

convey the annual message from the company president to the employees at offices around the globe. In all these cases a one-way mode of message conveyance is being used.

Interactive Model of Communication

Communication is often more than just sending and receiving messages. Sometimes, communication is more effective if the sender gets some information from the receiver and is able to adjust the message if the intent has not been conveyed and received. **Feedback** in communication is the process of sending information about the effect of a message. The original speaker uses this information to adjust her or his message if the feedback indicates that there has been a problem in gaining the intent of the message. The adjustment to the message is referred to as **adaptation.** For example, a salesperson, noting that her message received either a blank stare and/or raised eyebrows, could offer some new examples to clarify her message. Adding feedback and adaptation (recognizing that senders and receivers occupy different contexts) changes communication from a linear process that flows from sender to receiver to an interactive process, one that flows from sender to receiver, then receiver to sender, and so on. The **interactive**

process model of communication changes the linear model to reflect the additional elements—feedback and adaptation (Figure 1.2).

Examine this conversation, which illustrates sending, receiving, feedback and adaptation, as a process that continues until the communicator accomplishes his/her goal.

LING: Maria, please hand me that sheet of paper on the desk.
(*Maria assumes she knows which sheet Ling is talking about and hands Ling a sheet of paper.*)
LING: Not that one, the yellow one.
(*Maria puts her hand on a yellow sheet of paper.*)
MARIA: This one?
LING: Not that one, the yellow one with the words "order form" on top.
(*Maria hands Ling the desired paper.*)
LING: Thank you.

Transactional Model of Communication

To get another view of human communication, we need to examine yet another model. Communication may be more than one person sending a message to another person, and more than having a single person responsible for

FIGURE 1.2
Interactive Process Model

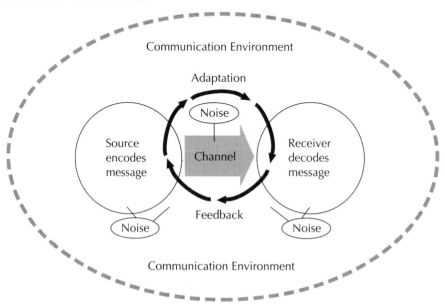

receiving the feedback of a receiver and adapting the message until the sender's goal is accomplished.

When messages are simultaneously sent and received, people cannot be classified as "senders" or "receivers," but only as *communicators*, simultaneous senders and receivers. Adding this characteristic to the definition of communication changes it from an interactional to a transactive process. The **transactive process model of communication** illustrates that any characteristic of the communication process affects and is affected by the others (Figure 1.3). This can be seen whenever two or more people simultaneously exchange ideas, for example, when a supervisor and a member of her work team discuss how to alter the pattern of accomplishing a task:

OMAR: (source) says, "I think we need to alter the voice mail message."

SHAWAYNE: (receiver/source) nods her head up and down in agreement as Omar is speaking and says, "That's a good idea."

OMAR: (receiver/source) says, "I'm glad you agree," while

SHAWAYNE: (receiver/source) picks up the telephone handle and dials 770, the code number needed for changing the message . . . while

OMAR: (source) says, "What should the new message say?" as

FIGURE 1.3
Transactive Process Model

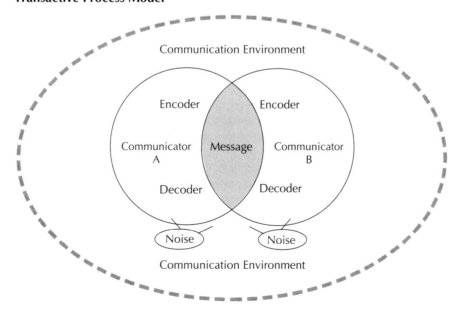

SHAWAYNE: (receiver/source) puts down receiver and says, "Why don't you give me about five minutes, and I'll write something up for both of us to check over." . . . as

OMAR: (receiver/sender) turns and goes to his desk as he says, "Good idea."

Throughout the transaction, Omar and Shawayne were simultaneously sending and receiving (encoding and decoding) verbal and nonverbal messages.

Business Communication Variables

Because communication is such an involved, complicated human process, there are no simple recipes or prescriptions for solving problems that arise within the complexities of the communication system. Effective communicators, however, are effective because they are aware of the variables in the communication process and use those factors to analyze and reinforce or adjust their communication.

Communication variables in the world of business are an organization's climate, culture, communication channels, networks, and functions.

ORGANIZATIONAL CULTURE

One of the key variables that affects communication in the modern organization is the organization's **culture,** the company's traditions, rituals, values, history, interactions, and norms. The culture is what makes an organization unique and gives it a distinctive personality. Communication analysts have come to appreciate how much the communication process shapes that culture and keeps it alive. People in an organization share stories about that organization, creating rituals, heroes, values, and communication networks that give the group their corporate identity and sense of connection to the group.[26] Indeed, communication has been identified as the major ingredient for building and maintaining strong organizational cultures: "The companies and organizations that do the best job thinking through what they are all about, deciding how and to whom these central messages should be communicated and executing the communication plan in a quality way, invariably build a strong sense of esprit within their own organization and among the many constituents they serve."[27]

ORGANIZATIONAL CLIMATE

The corporate culture shapes the organizational climate of any particular group. The organizational **climate** can be identified as the general atmosphere of supportiveness or defensiveness that people feel within the group. The use of the organization's communication channels can determine the extent to which workers feel comfortable in an open, supportive atmosphere. A study of managers revealed that a supportive climate that offers a worker a sense of self-worth and importance usually occurs in organizations where (1) there is mutual trust and confidence, (2) superiors exhibit a willingness to help subordinates with job and personal matters, (3) managers are approachable and honest about company policies and procedures, and (4) managers are willing to give credit to subordinates' accomplishments and ideas.[28]

The communication climate of an organization also is influenced by the communication channels that an organization utilizes. **Internal channels** are those within the organization. **External channels** are those outside the organization, for example, with the organization's various publics. An organization must use effectively both **internal channels** and **external channels**.

ORGANIZATIONAL CHANNELS

Internal communication channels develop both within departments and between departments. **Intradepartmental communication,** communication between department members, centers on such matters as setting a time by which a project is to be accomplished, disseminating operating information to field personnel, generating proposals for new or improved methods or prod-

---

Tuning In to the Grapevine

There's a fine line between the grapevine and the "rumor mill." If you're seen as a gossip, your reputation could suffer.

To stay away from gossip—and still keep in touch with the grapevine:

● *Don't talk about—or listen to—negative or personal rumors. Say: "I don't want to know about that." Or: Use body language that communicates you're not interested. Examples: Give the cold shoulder, continue working on a project or make a phone call.*

● *Don't pass on any information that is unclear. Only pass on positive information.*

● *Be careful who you tell. Tell only those who will do the right thing with the information. Example: If you know someone is getting a promotion, tell a coworker who may be interested in applying for the vacated position.*

● *Monitor your reasons for passing on information. Don't spread bad news about a person you dislike—or guess the outcomes of situations where you have something to gain. The intent—not the content—determines if the message is mere gossip or part of the grapevine.*

Source: Personal Report for the Professional Secretary, 1101 King St., Ste. 411, Alexandria, VA 22314.

ucts, providing instructions, updating procedures, and conducting evaluations. **Interdepartmental communication,** the communication between departments, may extend to the discussion of policy changes or various projects. One of the keys to the successful implementation of Total Quality Management has been the creation of **cross-functional work teams,** which bring together people from several departments to communicate with each other to problem solve or create new products or participate in new marketing initiatives.

In addition to the formal internal channels used by people in organizations, all organizational members make use of **informal communication channels**. This type of communication originates spontaneously outside of the formal channels and is the natural response to the need for social interaction and for information. While much of the research on organizational communication has focused on the formal structures, little is known about the informal channels, except that these channels may be the most significant in accomplishing the business of the organization.

The major informal channel is the **grapevine,** the gossip and news that spreads information from person to person. The grapevine carries news quickly and can serve as a safety valve. If an executive has to communicate bad news to employees, for instance, it may be productive to first "leak" that news into the grapevine so that people are prepared to receive the message. The grapevine also is the means by which rumors are spread, and such innuendo and misinformation can be damaging to people and organizations alike. Consequently, "with all the uncertainty, volatility and downsizing that have come with more competitive times, understanding and tapping into the grapevine are essential for survival" for managers and employees alike.[29]

Several years ago, Eastern Airlines was facing financial uncertainty and employee unrest. A revealing study at the time indicates that the airline was experiencing an organizational crisis. The study demonstrates the value of open internal communication channels. Interviews with and questionnaires administered to Eastern's pilots led the analyst to conclude that solid internal communication is critical in times of corporate crisis. It was determined that corporate communicators need to provide employees (1) credible messages from top level management; (2) as possible, assurances of job security; and (3) forums for effective feedback.[30]

External channels extend to sharing information with stockholders, customers, vendors, financial institutions, supplemental groups, media audiences, legislators, and government agencies. An organization often finds that it must reach many different publics, requiring different message strategies and even different channels to most effectively reach these different groups. American businesses tend to rely on public relations specialists for handling the external channels.

Corporate advertising is a major external channel for most companies. **Advertising** is designed to capture consumers' attention and persuade them to purchase and use the product. Advertising campaigns that are most successful occur over an extended period of time and build up consumer loyalty to the company and its products. Procter & Gamble, for instance, stresses loyalty to Tide laundry detergent. "Advertising is the lifeblood of our brands," observes Procter & Gamble's Chief Executive Officer.[31] "We use advertising to tell consumers what our brands stand for," adds Procter & Gamble's Executive Vice President, "and to show them why and how our brands will meet their needs. We know it works."[32]

A survey of U.S. and Canadian industrial organizations identified the communication channels that employees used as sources of current information and indicated which information sources were preferred.[33] The results reveal the prominent roles that the grapevine and the immediate supervisor play in an organization's communication (Figure 1.4).

FIGURE 1.4
Major Sources of Organizational Information

RANK	INFORMATION SOURCE	PERCENT OF EMPLOYEES USING THIS SOURCE	PREFERENCE RANK
1	Immediate supervisor	55.1%	1
2	Grapevine	39.8%	15
3	Employee handbook/ other references	32.0%	4
4	Bulletin board(s)	31.5%	9
5	Small group meetings	28.1%	2
6	Regular general employee publication	27.9%	6
7	Annual business report to employees	24.6%	7
8	Regular local employee publication	20.2%	8
9	Mass meetings	15.9%	11
10	Union	13.2%	13
11	Orientation program	12.5%	5
12	Top executives	11.7%	3
13	Audio-visual programs	10.2%	12
14	Mass media	9.7%	14
15	Upward communication programs	9.0%	10

ORGANIZATIONAL NETWORKS

Clearly, the complexity of an organization's communication is revealed in the way the organization uses its communication channels. Communication is an integral part of the management functions of planning, organizing, leading, and evaluating. Increasingly, managers are encouraged to "open up the lines of communication between management and workers, so both sides can benefit from gripes and recommendations."[34] The Pitney Bowes manufacturing firm has established yearly meetings between workers and corporate executives to facilitate communication. The company's vice president characterizes the meetings as an effective way to use the interpersonal communication channel: "Management listens to employee recommendations and acts upon them."[35]

One of the key responsibilities of management is planning the policies and procedures to be utilized in the company. The most typical method of approaching the planning function in American corporations is the **top-down process**. In the top-down approach, individuals who have been given the upper-level decision-making responsibilities determine the policies and procedures and inform those on the next level of these decisions and strategies for carrying out the decisions. The information and orders continue to proceed down through the organization, usually through a predetermined organizational flowchart until they reach the level at which they are to be carried out. Messages that typically are carried through the downward communication channels include job instructions, job rationale, procedures and practices, and organizational goals.[36]

The top-down communication process reflects the hierarchical, bureaucratic approach to conducting business. The decision-making authority in the top-down organization is vested in those with the power and responsibility for managing the various functions of the organization. The result is a very linear communication system with little if any attention to feedback and input from the workers who ultimately must carry out the decisions given to them.

The changing nature of the American workforce, however, has led many organizations to explore a **bottom-up communication process,** a system that is one of the cornerstones of Swedish and Japanese industries. In a bottom-up organization, workers are empowered to make decisions and provide input in the process. This communication approach is based on the concept that change and initiative within an organization should come from those closest to the problem. Messages carried through the upward communication channels may include what subordinates are doing; unsolved work problems; suggestions for improvements; and how subordinates think and feel about the organization, its work, and its people.[37]

Communicating Better at Work

by Frank Grazian & Don Bagin

Employees often show concern about the quality and quantity of communication at work.

Some claim that management gives only lip service to open communication but does little to really communicate with them.

Others contend their organizations believe that posting notices on bulletin boards and sending out memos provide adequate communication.

Still others say they receive vague instructions that are difficult to follow.

Ineffective communication often results in poor cooperation and coordination, lower productivity, undercurrents of tension, gossip and rumors, and increased turnover and absenteeism.

Experience shows there are many ways managers can improve internal communication. Here are some things they should do:

● Understand *that communication is a two-way street. It involves giving information and getting feedback from employees. It isn't finished when information is given.*

● Put more *emphasis on face-to-face communication with employees. Don't rely mainly on bulletin boards, memos and other written communication.*

● Ask themselves, *each time they give an instruction, if the message is clear. Most vagueness is caused by failing to be specific. Example: Don't just tell an employee to "show more interest" in his or her work. If an employee spends too much time chatting with others, be specific about it.*

● View information *as "service to" employees and not "power over" them.*

● Listen to *employees; show respect for them when they speak. They'll feel part of the team and will tend to be more dedicated and productive. One way: Ask questions to show interest and clarify points.*

● Don't just *talk open-door policy. Practice it by walking around and talking to employees. Allow people to disagree and to come up with new ideas.*

● Conduct one-on-one *meetings. Ask each employee to tell the manager how the manager can help the employee do a better job. Then share those things employees can do to help the manager do a better job.*

● Prepare publications *frequently. Emphasize current issues that employees care about; don't substitute quarterly "prettier" publications for substantive, up-to-date ones.*

● Concentrate *on building credibility with employees. Managers who lack credibility and fail to create a climate of trust and openness aren't believed—no matter how hard they try to communicate.*

ORGANIZATIONAL FUNCTIONS

The bottom-up communication system results in participative management. It is consistent with the efforts of many organizations today to be quality-based, utilizing principles of Total Quality Management to empower workers to make decisions and solve problems at every level. Japanese management practices have served as good models for implementing such a system. **Quality Circles**, in which a group of workers doing similar work were put together to meet on a regular basis to identify and analyze work-related problems and recommend solutions to management, served as a forerunner of today's quality-based work teams, which are self-managing groups, sometimes crossing departmental or functional lines. They are assigned the task of implementing the decisions they have recommended to management.

The use of upward communication requires that managers be willing to receive the communication and to respond to it. An organization that has not previously utilized participative decision making must orient its personnel to gain their trust and confidence before workers will be willing to participate. The group/team basis for much of the decision making also requires that the atmosphere of competition that is so prevalent in organizations be muted so that a cooperative spirit can evolve. The advantage, however, is that empowered employees will feel a much greater sense of control over and commitment to the work they do.

A bottom-up organization is based on an organizational culture that values people, their ideas, and their work. Such a communication process can eliminate the cynical view that managers must keep their workers in line and serve as the stern parents. One management specialist has described the bottom-up management philosophy: "You can keep good people longer and you can increase productivity, if you demonstrate clearly to them that you sincerely want their help and that you appreciate and reward those who willingly and thoughtfully bring their ideas and suggestions to you."[38]

While many North American companies seem to be far from the implementation of real upward communication structures, it is significant that some are trying out what can be termed a **horizontal organizational structure.** The focus of this type of organization is on core processes such as new-product development rather than on departments, permitting people to communicate across functions instead of through prescribed, controlled channels. The foundation for the horizontal corporation is the team and the focus is on customer satisfaction so that the work of the company is flattened out by combining related tasks. Information, then, is communicated *across* rather than up and down the organization: "The knowledge worker analyzes it, and technology moves it quickly across the corporation instead of up and down, speeding up and improving decision-making."[39]

Just as managers have communication functions, so too do employees who also need communication competencies in order to do their work effectively. Work skills that all employees must possess have been identified by the U.S. Department of Labor. The foundation for many of these skills is communication:

- *Basic skills:* Reading, writing, mathematical computation and reasoning, listening, and speaking.
- *Thinking skills:* Creative thinking, making decisions, solving problems, using imagination, knowing how to learn, and reasoning.
- *Personal qualities:* Individual responsibility as well as self-esteem, sociability, self-management, and integrity.[40]

People are among the major variables that affect the communication outcomes of any organization. The organization that has trained communicators equipped with skills in speaking and listening will find that the investment in that training can pay off considerably. If executives, managers, supervisors, and employees are prepared to communicate, they will be able to use the communication channels and control for the communication variables.

To reach the necessary level of ability, the organization's personnel need to have sufficient information about the communication process and functions within their organization. And, just as importantly, everyone in the organization must value communication as a significant part of accomplishing the company's goals.

Improving Business Communication

Recognizing how central the complex process of communication is to the business organization, many companies utilize key strategies for ensuring that they communicate effectively both internally and externally. Effective business communication results from organizational communication that is planned, prepared, responsive, appropriate, coordinated, and quality-based.

PLANNED BUSINESS COMMUNICATION

Because communication is so central and so complex, a company should not leave the process to happenstance. Just as an organization establishes a clear mission and goals, so too should its communication be grounded in clearly established goals and objectives. The communication plans should incorporate both the internal and external channels and connect them in an integrated approach. Companies have come to realize, for example, that all employees who interact with the public play an important role in the external communication of the organization. As a result, it can be useful to establish a communication plan that establishes the policy of supporting employees as "ambassadors" to the public or publics of the organization.

One of the first highly developed communication plans was prepared by Honeywell Corporation. The mission statement of Honeywell's communication department illustrates the company's commitment to an organized, structured approach to communicating: "The Corporate Communications Department exists to express and clarify the position and resulting identity of Honeywell to people inside and outside the company."[41]

Organizations today increasingly are likely to face public relations crises. Press scrutiny and the instantaneous nature of news broadcasting make it difficult for most companies to "hide" their disasters, as evidenced by experiences such as the tampered bottles of Tylenol that lead to several deaths, and Exxon Corporation's *Valdez* tanker grounding, in which gallons of oil leaked into Alaskan waters. As a result, careful planning for external communication during a crisis has become essential. Rather than responding after the fact, most corporations have put together **crisis communication plans** to enable them to better manage the bad news. Mobil Corporation, for example, provides a thorough guide for handling news media and public relations during an emergency. "A well-thought-out plan for handling the press not only can prevent loss of valuable goodwill, but also can be a positive means for increasing it."[42]

PREPARED BUSINESS COMMUNICATION

Effective communication results from careful preparation of executives, managers, supervisors, and employees to use the communication channels. This preparation within the company is especially significant in light of the scant preparation in speaking and listening that people receive prior to entering the workforce. Because so little attention is paid to speaking and listening education in schools and colleges, corporations have had to pick up the responsibility for ensuring that their personnel are able to speak and listen effectively. A survey of American industries revealed that 75 percent provide specific training in leadership; 74 percent in performance appraisals; 70 percent in interpersonal skills; 69 percent in team-building and in listening skills; 65 percent in problem-solving; 63 percent in conducting meetings; and 59 percent in public speaking/presentation skills.[43]

A U.S. Department of Labor study determined that companies that invest in training programs and treat employees as valuable assets are more profitable than those that continue to avoid "empowering" their workers. Motorola, for example, estimates that it earns $30 for every one dollar invested in employee training.[44]

Information Access
at Whirlpool

Whirlpool needed a way to reach not only its field representatives but also its consumer base. Salespeople needed pricing information, inventory updates, information on competitor promotions—and they needed that when they needed it, not when it was convenient for the home office to send out weekly notices. Often, sales reps needed to access information during a sales call. The solution was to equip each sales representative in the field with a laptop computer through which they could download product information, inventory updates, special pricing incentives, and new video clips from the home office's mainframe computer. Not only was access time greatly reduced, but information could be customized to the prospective client's situation and wrapped into the presentation being made to the client right on the spot. Whirlpool designed an interactive sales presentation with full-motion video clips of Whirlpool commercials and other promotional materials—a dramatic way to compare their products with those of their competitors. The result was a more polished, professional sales force and increased sales.

RESPONSIVE BUSINESS COMMUNICATION

The organization that communicates effectively has established a responsive communication system. All employees must be empowered to make decisions and to handle problems without bureaucratic delay. The hierarchical nature of most organizations works against this responsiveness, although forward-thinking companies have acquired more responsive ways of solving problems and meeting needs for customers and employees alike.

Most modern organizations are experiencing tremendous change. Internal and external pressures have necessitated flexibility and adaptation to changes in missions, economic realities, and the workforce itself. People often are uncomfortable with change, so managers today have to facilitate employees' responses to change as painlessly as possible.

The rapid changes in **communication technology,** electronic media, further challenges organizations, for technology offers benefits and drawbacks. Sophisticated computer systems enable employees to send e-mail messages around the world at no or limited cost, to conduct video conferences, and to transmit spreadsheet files between internal offices. Telephone technology provides almost unlimited opportunities for voice messages. "Technology is not only changing the way organizations conduct business," observes one communication technology management specialist, "it is altering relationships and communication among employees."[45]

But such technology is not always positively perceived. Companies that program their telephone systems with long messages offering "menu" choices for accessing information or leaving messages run the risk of alienating their callers. Voice mail has become so pervasive that only 25 percent of all business calls have been found to make it to the intended party on the first attempt![46]

Companies also rely on telephone technology for conducting meetings. Nations Bank, for instance, relies on audioconferencing and videoconferencing to hold management meetings. The system "allows the company's management to remain productive while maintaining contact with their people around the country," reducing both travel costs and wasted travel time.[47] The bank's videoconferencing facilities are used 140 hours each month, while the audioconferencing is used a million minutes a month. The company finds that the decrease in travel costs and increase in managerial productivity far outweigh the high costs of the system.[48] Not everyone agrees with this mode of conducting business. One critic states, "I want to close a deal, I'm going to interpret the slightest change in the movement of your eyebrow to tell whether the last offer I made is getting through. If I don't get that signal, it's much too dangerous to use a videoconference, especially if my competitor takes the time to fly out."[49]

Some companies have established toll-free hotlines to communicate directly with customers. Indeed, some retailers such as Lands' End, Harry and David's, and J. Crew rely on the effective use of the telephone to conduct their sales. A study of hotline callers revealed that most found the experience was responsive and satisfying.[50]

Telephone technology also enables some workers to work at home and use telephone, fax, and e-mail facilities to send their work in to the office. Compaq Computer Corporation closed its sales offices and set up the members of the sales force to work out of their homes—a move that helped Compaq cut costs and double revenue in less than three years.[51] It is estimated that by the end of 1995 there were 9.24 million **telecommuters,** individuals who are employed by a company and do all or part of their work at home. This represents a 10 percent growth over such employees in 1994.[52]

As companies struggle to find ways to cope with the ever-increasing amount of information required to conduct business today, the strategic use of computer databases to manage that information has challenged managers. To provide users with friendly access to computerized information, IBM has developed information catalogs, and Hallmark Cards has established full-time information guides in each business unit.

APPROPRIATE BUSINESS COMMUNICATION

As American business organizations have become increasingly internationalized and diversified, organizations have been required to conduct much of their business overseas, dealing with international clients and customers and exporting goods and services on a regular basis. At the same time, foreign business and industry have become much more "Americanized" as they acquire and work with American production and businesspeople. In addition to the globalization of the workplace, American organizations are experiencing significant diversification of the workforce.

To communicate effectively with such a diverse group of coworkers and customers, it is important that one understand cultural differences and adapt to them. Cultures are based on different values, customs, languages, and world views. Consequently, in order to operate effectively in a multicultural workplace and in international markets it is imperative to be aware of the social, business, and cultural rules—the **protocols**—of the cultures in which you will be operating.

Some generalizations can be made about cultural differences that can affect your business success. For example, when North Americans talk face-to-face, they tend to want to maintain a moderate distance between each other. People in other cultures, such as many Arabic cultures, communicate physically much closer together. Others, like the Germans and the English, tend to want even more space than North Americans. Likewise, negotiation methods

Diversity in the Corporate Setting

Without question, the changing nature of our society will impact the corporate workplace. Also without question, that change will continue to make the corporate setting a dynamic, exciting, and challenging environment. When we look at workplace diversity, it is tempting to think only in terms of racial or sexual differences. To really embrace diversity, we need to broaden the scope to include religious and affectional preferences, physical ability, age, educational background, regional differences, and a host of other factors. Some of these factors, while perhaps not as obvious to the casual observer, make a tremendous difference in the way workers interact with colleagues, make career choices, serve on teams, and approach the working world.

In order to become a truly diverse workplace, and to capitalize on the benefits of having a diverse workplace, we must move beyond simply identifying the differences and identify common ground and common purpose. Loden and Rosener, in Workforce America!, make a powerful case for the value of a diverse workforce, especially in the years to come. They offer a way to view the communication styles of others as a way to understand communication among diverse groups, not by splitting people along group lines but rather by looking at the specific behaviors and recognizing where that behavior is situated on a continuum. Perhaps this can be a starting reference point for separating the behavior from the individual and his or her cultural trappings. Perhaps from this vantage point we can look toward commonalities, for as Abraham Lincoln wrote many years ago, "a house divided against itself cannot stand."

vary greatly. People in Arabic cultures are accustomed to bargaining for goods and services, while those in some Asian cultures prefer to negotiate through an intermediary. Some cultures prefer to negotiate with teams who then go back for final approval, whereas North Americans generally come to negotiations empowered to make the deal. In some Asian and Arab cultures, giving gifts is an important part of conducting business. And people in many parts of the world prefer to spend time establishing a personal relationship before getting down to business—a difficult dimension for North Americans, who are accustomed to conducting business at a fast pace.[53]

As U.S. business and industry continue to internationalize and diversify, the communicator who knows his or her culture *and* the culture of the other communicator will be able to use this information to function more effectively in today's business world. It is a matter of appropriateness—of adapting one's verbal and nonverbal behaviors and messages to the other communicator. The appropriate communicator should make these adaptations at every level. Pepsico, for instance, had to adapt their former Pepsi slogan, "Come Alive," for the international market. Too many cultures translated the slogan literally as stepping up out of the grave! General Motors retired one of its auto names because of poor sales of the model in the southwestern U.S., Mexico, and South America: the company belatedly realized that the name had a negative notation since a derivation of "Nova" means "no go" in Spanish.

Because of the increasing diversity in the workplace and the problems resulting from intercultural problems, companies such as IBM, Digital Equipment Corporation, Motorola, and Xerox have developed systematic plans for communicating to employees and managers about matters related to diversity.[54]

COORDINATED BUSINESS COMMUNICATION

To deal with rapid change and diversity, many companies are finding that coordinating the internal and the external communication functions can best be facilitated by creating a **corporate communication department.** Bank of America's communication department offers a good example. The department is responsible for numerous activities, including generating news releases about the bank; training bank executives for television interviews; speechwriting for the president and members of the managing committee; preparing position papers on important bank issues; training employees to express their needs, concerns, and problems to management; developing plain language standards for customer forms; facilitating teamwork and problem-solving by providing meeting management training; publishing instructional materials; producing consumer education films; preparing speeches for speakers on request; preparing briefing packages about overseas visits for senior manage-

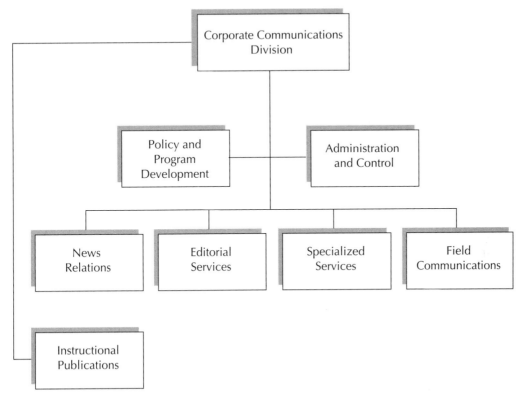

FIGURE 1.5
Model of Corporate Flow of Information

ment; developing a multimedia program for high schools; and developing patterns for speech programs for overseas management. To meet these objectives, the department is organized in levels, as illustrated in Figure 1.5.[55]

QUALITY BUSINESS COMMUNICATION

Just as a company's communication system must be planned, prepared, and responsive, so too must it be quality-driven and consistent with the quality goals of the rest of the organization. The payoff for attention to the company's communication functions can be considerable. GM's effort to "promote teamwork, partnerships and two-way communication is to improve our relationships with external, as well as internal, constituencies. GM is making a concerted effort to be more sensitive and responsive to how others view us. This involves both taking the time to tell our side of the story, and also making accommodations in the interests of building relationships."[56]

• • • In Summary • • •

As today's organizations strive to be competitive in the global marketplace, as the American population becomes more internationalized, and as the nature of work itself has undergone radical change, the importance of communication to business cannot be overstated. Businesses communicate externally with customers, stockholders, regulatory agencies, and other publics; and, internally, with personnel interacting with each other in top-down bottom-up systems. Communication is a complex process that can be represented by the linear process, interactive, and transactive models.

═══ Business Communication in Practice ═══

1. Make an appointment to talk with a personnel manager of a company. Discuss the major communication problems that the company has experienced and how the company has attempted to deal with these problems. Report back to the class on your findings.
2. Secure permission to spend a day in a business observing how its employees communicate. Note how the company's communication is influenced by how it uses its communication channels, by its corporate culture, by its communication climate, by its communication technology, and by its communicators at all levels within the organization. Report back to the class on your findings.

═══ Diversity Simulation ═══

Directions: Read the following scenarios. In a small group, determine what the individual viewpoint might be and how he or she would be likely to respond. What would be the goal of each of the individuals involved? What would be the barriers to effective communication? What can be done to resolve this situation? With what moral obligations?

Optional assignment: Research the laws on discrimination as they pertain to race and age. Do either of these scenarios fall within the legal restriction on discrimination?

1. Karen Sung, a Korean American, is an analyst at an investment banking firm. She is a part of a very tight-knit unit of analysts. There is a great deal of camaraderie among the members of the group. With such long hours and high stress, they joke and tease to ease the pressure. Managers and junior professionals often interact and come to know each other on fairly familiar terms. The managing director often shows appreciation for a job well done by taking the group out for pizza since they are often too junior

in rank to attend the formal closing dinner at the end of a deal. Karen wants to be a part of this team but just doesn't feel that she belongs. She is always cooperative when someone asks her to help out but she just can't "let loose" like the others. Having come to this country four years ago, she has trouble understanding American slang even though her formal English is excellent. She often misses the point of jokes and is very embarrassed by the sexual banter. She is often hesitant to disturb others from their busy schedules when she has questions about the projects she is working on. Once, she made a large mistake when trying to establish the value of a company about to offer stock to the public for the first time on the New York Stock Exchange because she did not want to ask questions and show that she did not know. She knows that others think she is "standoffish" and "prudish" and she feels bad about not being a part of the group. She opts out of group gatherings because she feels that she cannot respond quickly enough to the conversation. Her manager, Elizabeth, told her during the performance appraisal that she should work harder to integrate with the staff and to "lighten up." Karen was so humiliated and embarrassed by the feedback that she couldn't begin to explain herself. What should Karen do? What could her colleagues do?

2. Joseph O'Hare, age 55, has been employed at a graphics design firm for more than thirty years, working his way up from general office staff worker to assistant designer. He is well thought of and is the kind of person who goes out of his way to make the office run smoothly and make people comfortable. When he saw the posting for the new CAD (computer-assisted design) position, he decided to apply. Although the position would not pay more than he is currently making, Joseph saw the chance for additional growth, responsibilities, and career advancement. Joseph did not get the job but someone he supervises did—Mike, a colleague with only one year of experience. Joseph went to the owner, Margaret, and asked why he did not get the job. Margaret was evasive and implied that Mike had a good background and would be with the company for a long time. "Besides," Margaret told him, "you do an excellent job and would be difficult to replace." Margaret asked why Joseph would want to "bother going through all that trouble and stress of a major training program." She ended by saying, "At your age, I'd like to just rest on my laurels and take it easy." Joseph wonders what he should do about this situation.

• • • Notes • • •

1. S. B. Rosenblatt, T. R. Cheatham, and J. T. Watt, *Communication in Business* (Englewood Cliffs, NJ: Prentice Hall, 1976).
2. Cindy Skrzycki, "The Quest for the Best: U.S. Firms Turn to Quality as Competitive Tool," *The Washington Post* (October 2, 1988), H2.

3. Peter F. Drucker, "The Coming of the New Organization," *Harvard Business Review* (January–February 1988): 45.
4. Frank Swoboda, "The Case for Corporate Downsizing Goes Global," *The Washington Post* (April 9, 1995), H5.
5. Frank Swoboda, "For Most Workers, Sharing Power Is Just an Olympian Ideal," *The Washington Post* (June 25, 1995), H5.
6. Charles C. Manz and Henry P. Sims, Jr., *Superleadership* (New York: Prentice Hall, 1989), p. 8.
7. "America's Workforce Is Changing Dramatically," brochure for "Valuing Diversity Training" (San Francisco: Copeland Griggs Productions, 1989).
8. William B. Johnston and Arnold H. Packer, *Workforce 2000* (Indianapolis, IN: Hudson Institute, 1987), pp. 85, 89.
9. Morris R. Schectman, *Working without a Net: How to Survive and Thrive in Today's High Risk Business World* (New York: Prentice Hall, 1995).
10. Gerald M. Goldhaber, *Organizational Communication* (Dubuque, IA: Brown, 1990), p. 4.
11. Marc Heqet, "E-Mail Spins a New Web at Work," *Training* (August 1995): 54.
12. Cf. Linda L. Putnam, "Role Functions and Role Conflicts of Communication Trainers," *Journal of Business Communication* (Fall 1979): 371.
13. *Effective Communication on the Job* (New York: American Management Association, 1963), p. 110.
14. Ibid., 60.
15. Ibid., 15.
16. James Melohlov, Paul Popp, and Michael Porte, "Communication: A View from Inside of Business," *Journal of Business Communication* 11 (1974): 53–59.
17. *Effective Communication on the Job*, 114.
18. Ibid., 203.
19. Thomas Peters and Robert Waterman, Jr., *In Search of Excellence* (New York: Harper and Row, 1982), pp. 13–17.
20. W. Edwards Deming, *Quality, Productivity and Competitive Position* (Cambridge: MIT Center for Advanced Engineering Study, 1982).
21. Thomas Tuttle, "What Is Total Quality?" *The Maryland Workplace* 11 (1989): 1, 4, 5, 7.
22. Michael Hammer and James Champy, *Reengineering the Corporation* (New York: Harper Business, 1993).
23. Allan D. Frank and Judi Brownell, "Preface," *Communication and Behavior for Improved Performance: 2 + 2 = 5* (New York: Holt, Rinehart, and Winston, 1989), p. vii.
24. Paul L. Blocklyn, "Making Magic: The Disney Approach to People Management," *Personnel* (December 1988): 32.
25. Paul T. Rankin, "Listening Ability: Its Importance, Measurement and Development," *Chicago Schools Journal* 12 (1930): 177–179.
26. T. E. Deal and A. A. Kennedy, *Corporate Cultures: The Rites and Rituals of Corporate Life* (Reading, MA: Addison-Wesley, 1982). See, too, John C. Meyer, "Tell Me a Story: Eliciting Organizational Values from Narratives," *Communication Quarterly* 43 (Spring 1995): 210–224.

27. Allan Kennedy, "Back-Yard Conversations: New Tools for Quality Conversations," *Communication World* (November 1984): 26.
28. Rensis Likert, *The Human Organization: Its Management and Values* (New York: McGraw-Hill, 1967).
29. Robert L. Dilenschneider, "Cultivating the Corporate Grapevine," *The New York Times* (July 2, 1995), F13.
30. Martha Saunders, "Eastern's Employee Communication Crisis: A Case Study," *Public Relations Review*, 33–44.
31. "P&G Brands: Winning the World's Consumers," *Winning the World's Consumers* (Cincinnati: Procter & Gamble, 1994), p. 7.
32. Ibid.
33. A study of internal communication channels conducted by the International Association of Business Communicators and the New York consulting firm Towers, Perrin, Forster and Crosby.
34. Sylvia Porter, "Your Money's Worth," *The Washington Post* (September 22, 1981), D9.
35. Ibid.
36. Daniel Katz and Robert Kahn, *The Social Psychology of Organization* (New York: Wiley, 1966).
37. Earl Planty and William Machaver, "Upward Communications: A Project in Executive Development," *Personnel* 28 (1952): 304–318.
38. Charles C. Vance, "How to Encourage Upward Communication from Your Employees," *Association Management* 28 (May 1976): 59.
39. Rahul Jacob, "The Struggle to Create an Organization for the 21st Century," *Fortune* 131 (April 3, 1995): 91.
40. *What Work Requires of Schools* (Washington, DC: U.S. Department of Labor, 1991), p. 15.
41. *Honeywell 1988 Communications Plan* (Minneapolis, MN: Honeywell Corporation, 1988), 10.
42. *Mobil Guide for News Media & Public Relations during Emergencies*, p. 1.
43. "Who's Learning What?" *Training* (October 1994): 49.
44. "Odd Jobs," *The Washington Post* (June 11, 1995), H6.
45. Sandra E. O'Connell, "Human Communication in the High Tech Office," in Gerald M. Goldhaber and George A. Barnett (eds.), *Handbook of Organizational Communication* (Norwood, NJ: Ablex, 1988), p. 479.
46. Steven Pearlstein, "Corporate Voice Mail Puts Productivity on the Line," *The Washington Post* (June 15, 1995), B1, B13.
47. Ross Weiland, "Staying In Touch," *Performance* (June 1995): 42.
48. Ibid.
49. Fleming Meeks, "What Kind of Computer Will You Wear?" *Forbes* (August 14, 1995): 158.
50. Charles L. Martin and Denise T. Smart, "Consumer Experiences Calling Toll-Free Corporate Hotlines," *Journal of Business Communication* 31 (1994): 195–212.
51. Arno Penzias, "New Paths to Success," *Fortune* (June 12, 1995), 90–94.
52. Jackie Spinner, "Out of Sight and into Faxes and E-Mail," *The Washington Post Washington Business* (June 26, 1995), 5.

53. See Larry A. Samovar and Richard E. Porter, *Communication between Cultures* (Belmont, CA: Wadsworth, 1991), pp. 236–243.
54. "American Express Financial Advisors Complete a Benchmarking Study," *The Washington Post* (May 7, 1995), "The Diversity Challenge" supplement, p. 14.
55. Information and chart provided by Bank of America.
56. John F. Smith, President's Letter, *General Motors Public Interest Report*, 1994, p. 1.

Communication Ethics in Business Settings

EXPECTED OUTCOMES

After completing this chapter, you should be able to:

- Define and explain the concept of ethics.
- Explain why the morality of businesses has come under strong scrutiny.
- Explain and illustrate how people should ethically perform within given business structures.
- Explain why organizations should act ethically.

One busy Friday afternoon, I was madly dashing around the small restaurant where I worked as a waitress. The usual lunch crowd invaded the place. The other waitress and the busboy, who were supposed to work the shift with me, both called in sick. I took all the orders as quickly as possible, while at the same time I cleared tables as they became unoccupied. Not long after the rush began, Bob, the store manager, arrived. Bob noticed the large crowd and pulled me over and said that as customers finished their meals I should just collect their money and put it in the cash register without entering the transaction through the key pad. He also told me not to worry about filling out my tip report. He said he'd enter the tickets into the cash register and prove the cash later in the afternoon. Silently, I wondered if I should comply with his order or take the time to do the job right. Since Bob had taken over as manager, there had been some questions from the owner about perceived shortages of money based on our volume of business. Bob had told us several times in the past not to worry about entering transactions through the key pad.

I f at least part of the rationale and purpose of business (some would say the whole of it) is its contribution to the well-being of society, then the ethics of business and the kinds of value judgments the business community makes ought to be similar to those governing personal and social situations in general. Unfortunately, the morality of both people and businesses today has come under strong question.

The Ethical Dilemma

In recent years, scandals seem to have become a growth industry. We read about them in tabloids and pulp newspapers available at the checkout counter of supermarkets. Television blares the news of defense contractors bilking the Pentagon, banks laundering cash for suspected criminals, and rogue stock and bond traders at well-known brokerage firms who were involved in insider trading. Corporate embezzlement schemes, toxic waste dumping, insider trading, influence peddling, ill-manufactured products, and industrial espionage are heralded on the front pages, as are stories reflecting a growing crisis of conscience in the United States in general, and corporate America specifically. This situation is compounded by a multiethnic and transglobal marketplace where ethical decisions are complex and constrained by cultural rules and morés.

A recent study shows that many U.S. workers act unethically. Workers have identified specific unethical actions in which their coworkers have participated. These include lying to superiors, 56 percent; falsifying records, 41 percent; office theft, 35 percent; sexual harassment, 35 percent; alcohol and drug abuse, 31 percent; and conflict of interest, 31 percent.[1]

With so many signs of unethical behavior, one may wonder if ethics has any place in the business world. Has the term "business ethics" become a contradiction? Or, perhaps, has the word "ethics" come to mean one thing within a business context and another in personal life?

Ethics and Business

In the free-enterprise system, it is generally assumed that commerce and industry exist to make money. "In this age of satellite communications and computerized manufacturing, the competition isn't just the shop down the street. It's shops all over the world. Making money is hard, and so is resisting the temptation to make it any way you can."[2] Businesspeople operate under enormous pressures. Employees are pushed to increase sales to clients, managers are urged to cut costs, stockholders demand higher profits, top-level management imposes pressures, upwardly mobile families want more of the finer things of life. These economic pressures leave their mark on many corporate consciences, often creating a difficult atmosphere for encouraging ethical behavior.

Defenders of capitalism emphasize that the system allows individual freedom and individual choice. The defenders contend that under this system individuals are free to act as they wish so long as they do no harm to others. The people may use their money as they choose and register their preferences in their purchases.

The second basic feature of the system is that each person entering into a transaction seeks to achieve personal goals or ends. A transaction is considered to be fair or just if both parties enter the transaction with appropriate knowledge and if they enter it freely.[3] Those who espouse that attitude believe that each person is responsible for doing what he or she thinks is in his or her best interest, as producers, sellers, or consumers. They also believe that there has not been much change in the ethical system of businesses and industries; rather, they note that now consumer groups and regulatory agencies are keeping better track of fraud and deception, and the press is much more vigilant. They contend that such scrutiny makes citizens more aware of unethical actions, an awareness heightened by such movements as affirmative action, environmental concerns, and efforts directed against sexual harassment.[4]

Ethics Defined

To understand ethics, we must understand that it is part of an ongoing philosophical enterprise. Philosophy, in its broadest meaning, is a systematic attempt to make sense out of our individual and collective experience. We do this through analysis—investigating actions and thoughts in detail to determine the meaning of terms, the validity of arguments, and the nature and status of presuppositions by discerning their components. Next, we synthesize by constructing a unified view, which brings together all the parts of our experiences as intelligibly as possible.[5]

The word ethics comes from the Greek word ethos, meaning custom and character. "**Ethics** can be defined as a systematic attempt, through the use of reason, to make sense of our individual and social moral experience in such a way as to determine the rules which govern human conduct and the values worth pursuing in life."[6] Ethics is not just something practiced by individuals: it is a value shared by society as a whole. Customs and characteristics pervade society—individuals, families, media, government, and business and industry.

An important aspect of any ethical system is the role of truth and lies. The theoretical societal rule regarding lying is not to lie. However, the reality of lying is extremely complex. There are many kinds of lies, from the white lie in which small untruths are told to spare another's feelings, to the big lies told to protect national security or other major areas of concern. "Probably most Americans accept white lies as a necessary evil. Without them, everyday life would have considerably rougher edges."[7] "But the edges of those 'acceptable' untruths are easily blurred, and there is a huge middle range of falsehoods that Americans have traditionally viewed as unjustifiable: lies of expediency or cowardice; lies that give the liar an advantage he would not otherwise have, such as inflating credentials to get a job; lies that allow the evasion of responsibility—perhaps laying the blame on others—and lies that manipulate others to achieve the liar's goal."[8]

Business Ethics Defined

In dealing with ethics, U.S. business finds itself coming to grips with general philosophical concepts applied to the free-enterprise system. The theory of business ethics attempts to describe how people should act within given business structures; it is a practical discipline with practical importance. The application of business ethics can help people approach moral problems in business more systematically and with better tools than they might have otherwise. In addition, it can help people see issues they might normally ignore, and can impel businesspeople to make changes that they might otherwise not be moved to make. However, business ethics will not change business practices unless those engaged in the practices that need moral change wish to change them.[9]

Historically, the country's initial mandate to business was rather simple. People wanted products and services to be as plentiful, good, and cheap as possible. As problems developed, laws were introduced to regulate working conditions, protect children, prevent monopolistic practices, and preserve the environment. The regulations frequently represented moral concerns on the part of the people: "A business may ignore the moral demands of a whole society since it is part of that society and dependent on it at the same time that it serves it."[10]

The question of businesses and the ethics they practice, therefore, is essentially a question of personal ethics, based on both values instilled in the individual and the environmental background of the individual. (See Figure 2.1.) Personal ambition greatly distorts sound judgment in such matters, as does the overriding quest for corporate sales and profits. Should individuals in manage-

Percentage of workers who say these ethical
infractions are committed by co-workers:

Lying to supervisors	**56%**
Falsifying records	**41%**
Office theft	**35%**
Sexual harassment	**35%**
Alcohol and drug abuse	**31%**
Conflict of interest	**31%**

Source: Ethics Resource Center survey

FIGURE 2.1
The Unethical Worker

ment positions always tell the truth even when sales and the resulting profits are going to be impaired? Should they alert the public to possible dangers to the environment, health, and safety caused by the production of possible hazardous products? Are they obligated to share information that may never be known unless someone blows the whistle on the wrongdoing or wrongdoers? For example, should businesspeople be required to come to the public with information about toxic waste dumping, nuclear meltdowns, and dangerous products?

Given the lack of moral considerations in many decisions within the business community, it has been proposed that the basic line for businesses should be based on the ethical principle of utilitarianism. The **ethical principle of utilitarianism** states that an action is right or good if it contributes to the well-being of society in general. Historically, the concern of the opponents to utilitarianism is that it does not adequately consider the rights of individuals. However, with the safeguards provided by civil rights legislation during the past twenty-five years, the time may have come to apply this principle to current ethical abuses in business, much as it was used to correct abuses against industrial workers in nineteenth-century England.[11]

Ethical Practices in Business

An investigation of the topic of ethics in business centers on such issues as whether capitalism encourages immoral acts, whether ethical practices have changed, and the nature of corporate responsibility.

CAPITALISM AND ETHICS

Some critics of capitalism charge that this system encourages unethical behavior, rewarding selfishness, dishonesty, and greed. They contend that as long as we accept the cliché that "the business of business is business" and accept the premise that creating profits is paramount in the system, then individuals and organizations will do whatever they must to gain those profits even if it includes immoral or unethical acts.

CHANGES IN ETHICAL AWARENESS

Has there been a breakdown in business ethics? Some theorists believe that while there has been a great deal of negative publicity concerning the breakdown of ethics in the business environment, there has been little change in the practices of industry regarding ethical actions. As stated by one expert, "Overall, I don't see any evidence of a sharp decline in corporate ethics. Rather I believe our expectations for corporate behavior have risen."[12]

This view is further developed by the belief that because of questionable business practices and events such as Whitewater and the savings and loan scandals, the media have conducted more investigative reporting. This can be seen by observing the number of national television shows that center on exposing businesses and corporations whose actions are questionable, as well as the number of local news stations that have employed investigative reporters.

In addition, citizens' groups and consumer advocates have alerted the general public to their rights and responsibilities regarding such matters as safety, product defects, and environmental protection.

CORPORATE RESPONSIBILITY

The bottom-line statement in corporate responsibility should be that corporations should act in a "moral" fashion. But who decides what is "moral" and is it always practical to act that way? And is it sufficient to know what is morally required? American business is faced with more competition than ever before, in all industries. Can business nurture ethical behavior in such a cutthroat environment?

Can U.S. corporations compete on a worldwide level when their competitors are not governed by the same ethical standards? "In some countries, you have to pay someone before you can conduct business. They call it 'baksheesh'—which means a gift of money as a favor or reward—this payment is an accepted custom."[13] In U.S. society, we view baksheesh as unethical because we believe that paying to do business corrupts honest competition. A few years ago, a clamor arose when several American companies admitted to

Consumer groups are much more vigilant today, making citizens more aware of unethical actions.

paying bribes abroad. The companies claimed that these payments were a way of life in some countries, that they couldn't compete unless they went along.[14] Are our corporations expected to compete in the world market by world ethics or by American ethics? Whether dishonest business behavior is as old as humankind or whether it is fueled by our fast-paced, self-centered society, the issue of business ethics is real, and lasting solutions must come from within the business community.

Ethics is a new frontier for the business community. Traditionally ethics has been concerned with individuals and their actions. It is generally accepted that, ultimately, a corporation does not make moral decisions, but individuals within that organization make choices. Individuals make those decisions in keeping with their moral and ethical strengths or weaknesses—their truthfulness or lack of truthfulness, honesty or lack of honesty, and integrity or lack of integrity. Individualism notwithstanding, corporations are responsible for the decisions that are made by their representatives. Increasingly, organizations are recognizing that they must be concerned not only about the behavior of individuals, but also about the values that permeate the organizations.[15] "Corporations may limit the legal accountability of the persons who are incorporated, but insofar as they are simply a union of persons they still retain the ethical accountability of individuals."[16]

What is the business community doing about this dilemma? Corporations are implementing organizational codes of ethics, developing ethics training programs for executives and employees, evaluating and monitoring the organization's ethics, establishing ethics hotlines, conducting ethics audits, and employing ombudsmen to oversee a corporation's ethics. This is not an isolated pattern. "Ninety percent of Fortune 500 companies require employees to subscribe to a code of ethics. Such organizations as Union Carbide, Boeing, McDonnell Douglas, and Chemical Bank have set up programs to help employees deal with ethical conflicts."[17] A national teleconference on business ethics involving most of the major corporations was held recently. Colleges and universities also have accepted the challenge. "Eighty-five percent of all U.S. business schools offer courses in business ethics."[18]

This awareness of ethical accountability is making corporations accept responsibility for their actions. For example, when several people died after taking contaminated Tylenol capsules, Johnson & Johnson, the manufacturer, withdrew the product from the market and incurred a hefty financial loss. "The firm was helped to make this ethically correct, but economically difficult decision through its institutionalized ethics program. The corporate culture allowed someone to use the word 'safety' even if it meant a loss of millions in the short run."[19] It was not long, however, before Johnson & Johnson recaptured market share, a testament to the loyalty of consumers who felt the corporation had acted responsibly.

Corporations also are beginning to insist on employee accountability. "Distortion of credentials by applicants for all levels of employment has increased substantially."[20] In an effort to weed out potential problem employees, many companies have tightened the screening process of job applicants. Fortune 500 corporations are increasing their background checks for entry-level and executive position applicants.[21]

Many corporations also have instituted employment civil rights and responsibilities programs. These programs are often based on the belief that employees are entitled to certain types of treatment regardless of race, sex, sexual orientation, or age, and that each employee has a moral right to be treated like a human being. On the job, employees have the right to equality of treatment and the right of privacy. However, with these rights come obligations. Employees are obligated not to lie, not to spread false information, and not to abuse or harass others, sexually or otherwise. They are obligated to fulfill the terms of their contracts.[22]

Some organizations have even encouraged a form of internal whistle-blowing as part of their procedure. Traditionally, **whistle-blowing** has meant disclosing to some governmental agency, news reporter, or media personnel information about actions or conditions within a firm that are either illegal or harmful to the public or that may cause harm to consumers of the firm's products or services. Because the consequences of whistle-blowing are often disastrous, such action is not to be undertaken lightly. The general attitude about whistle-blowing has been that it is justifiable if "the issue on which an employee intends to disclose information to the public concerns the infliction of serious harm on the public in general or on some members of it. The more serious the harm, the more serious the obligation."[23] In some instances, employers have set up a procedure through which problems of the organization are discussed in groups, where employees are encouraged to share their views about the company's problems or problems with its product or services. In this way, the matter can be dealt with and corrected internally instead of becoming a public scandal. Auto manufacturers, such as Ford, have turned to this system with positive results.

Using Ethics

Even in these days of questioning authority and time-honored traditions, there appears to be a truism concerning ethics: "We are not a perfect society. But that doesn't mean our society values unethical conduct. Ethical conduct is the norm—the custom."[24] Understanding your personal ethical system helps you make sound judgments, bring meaning to your life, and fulfill personal, professional, and social responsibilities.

ASTD Code of Ethics

The ASTD Code of Ethics provides guidance to members to be self-managed human resource development professionals. Clients and employers should expect from ASTD members the highest possible standards of personal integrity, professional competence, sound judgment and discretion. Developed by the profession for the profession, the ASTD Code of Ethics is the Society's public declaration of its members' obligations to themselves, their profession and society.

I strive to . . .

- Recognize the rights and dignities of each individual.
- Develop human potential.
- Provide my employer, clients, and learners with the highest level quality education, training, and development.
- Comply with all copyright laws and the laws and regulations governing my position.
- Keep informed of pertinent knowledge and competence in the human resource field.
- Maintain confidentiality and integrity in the practice of my profession.
- Support my peers and to avoid conduct which impedes their practicing their profession.
- Conduct myself in an ethical and honest manner.
- Improve the public understanding of human resource development and management.
- Fairly and accurately represent my human resource development/human resource management credentials, qualifications, experience and ability.
- Contribute to the continuing growth of the Society and its members.

Source: American Society of Training and Development, Alexandria, VA.

Although no universally accepted code of ethics exists, certain forces drive the way an individual applies ethics. Consider these forces:

- *Each moral choice we make has repercussions for ourselves as well as for others.* For example, if you are working for a small business and the owner is not writing receipts for all of the sales and is taking the money for himself/herself, thus avoiding having to pay taxes on the income, what is your course of action? If you decide to report the incident, it is likely the owner will be arrested and you will lose your job, thus affecting both you and your employer.
- *We must recognize ethical issues if we are to act on them.* "Recognition of ethical issues is an imperative for acting on them. Unlike other questions

where we may decide on an answer without there being any requisite commitment of action, such as whether or not one product tastes better than another, ethical issues, since they involve human and societal well-being in a fundamental way, necessarily involve commitment and action as part of their resolution."[25]

When we are aware that we are making ethical judgments, we can start to identify hidden assumptions and determine whether or not there are reasonable grounds for making a judgment or for reaching a conclusion. For example, you can make the decision to report your money-pocketing employer for not acting ethically only if you are aware that this action is illegal and unethical.

- *We must recognize that being moral is in our best interest.* Without totally understanding the intricacies of the matter, most people know the right thing to do. However, people often need the encouragement to be moral. If we accept the idea that we ought to be moral because we want to live in a certain kind of society and that society must be protected, then it is in our own best interest to be moral. "Thus, a person who reports that an employer is marketing an unsafe product is both acting morally and acting in his own self-interest in that he is contributing to the well-being of society, and in that his own well-being is inextricably interwoven with the well-being of society."[26] Consequently, a person who has determined to act morally in his or her own self-interest would find it difficult not to report the tax-evading owner.

- *We must develop analytical skills.* People need to examine and make distinctions among concepts that center on ethical principles and moral rules. We need to understand how we reach conclusions and the consequences of our decisions. Basic ethical analysis takes three steps: (a) understanding what is happening; (b) determining whether or not the action is moral or immoral (using personal criteria); and (c) deciding if an action should be taken, and, if so, what the appropriate action should be. "This is not to say that analysis can always provide a clear-cut answer to what is moral. Some moral issues, such as abortion, are so complex as to divide even professional philosophers. However, this is not the case with the vast majority of issues that arise in business ethics. These are issues for which, for the most part, ethical analysis can help determine the moral status and thus guide us to appropriate ethical action."[27]

- *We must elicit a sense of moral responsibility.* Believing something is not the same as acting on that belief. Actions, not intentions, are the real issue. Believing that your employer is performing an immoral act and taking action to curb that unethical conduct are two different issues. "The major problem in business ethics is, in fact, not determining what is right and wrong, but increasing the awareness of ethical issues and developing a tendency to act in a morally responsible way."[28]

International Association of Business Communicators

The Code of Ethics of the International Association of Business Communicators (as revised in 1995) provides guidelines for IABC members and other communication professionals. The code covers communication and information dissemination, standards of conduct, confidentiality and disclosure, and professionalism.

1. *Professional communicators uphold the credibility and dignity of their profession by practicing honest, candid and timely communication and by fostering the free flow of essential information in accord with the public interest.*
2. *Professional communicators disseminate accurate information and promptly correct any erroneous communication for which they may be responsible.*
3. *Professional communicators understand and support the principles of free speech, freedom of assembly, and access to an open marketplace of ideas; and, act accordingly.*
4. *Professional communicators are sensitive to cultural values and beliefs and engage in fair and balanced communication activities that foster and encourage mutual understanding.*
5. *Professional communicators refrain from taking part in any undertaking which the communicator considers to be unethical.*
6. *Professional communicators obey laws and public policies governing their professional activities and are sensitive to the spirit of all laws and regulations and, should any law or public policy be violated, for whatever reason, act promptly to correct the situation.*
7. *Professional communicators give credit for unique expressions borrowed from others and identify the sources and purposes of all information affecting the welfare of others.*
8. *Professional communicators protect confidential information, and at the same time, comply with all legal requirements for the disclosure of information affecting the welfare of others.*
9. *Professional communicators do not use confidential information gained as a result of professional activities for personal benefit and do not represent conflicting or competing interests without written consent of those involved.*
10. *Professional communicators do not accept undisclosed gifts or payments for professional services from anyone other than a client or employer.*
11. *Professional communicators do not guarantee results that are beyond the power of the practitioner to deliver.*
12. *Professional communicators are honest not only with others but also, and most importantly, with themselves as individuals; for a professional communicator seeks the truth and speaks that truth first to the self.*

- *Ethical certainty is usually not possible.* "Ethical certainty is not always possible. However, you can avoid the chaos and despair of subjectivity. If you thoughtfully arrive at some ethical principles that make sense to you and apply these principles in a logical and consistent way to ethical situations, then you can bring coherency to your decision making."[29] If you know how you reached your conclusion and accept that the system or method was logical to you, then there is consistency and coherence to your decision making.[30]

Using Ethics in Business Communication

It is widely believed that communicators should be ethical and that their ethical quality needs to be consistent. Unfortunately, this consistency is not always the case. An individual may be scrupulously ethical in personal relationships or activities. For example, a person who might not cheat or lie when playing in the weekly bridge game or in a golf match may knowingly make false or misleading statements to gain an advantage in a business situation; and that person might do so with a sense of pride and satisfaction because of the gains to be made, with none of the pangs of conscience that normally accompany personal moral deviations.

Ethical communicators are regarded as those who have a strong sense of moral awareness and a high degree of personal integrity. Although some problems may have more than one moral solution, and no single definition of morality exists, an ethical speaker generally possesses certain qualities:

- Speaks with sincerity.
- Does not knowingly expose an audience to falsehoods or half-truths that cause significant harm.
- Does not deliberately alter the truth.
- Presents the truth as he or she understands it.
- Raises the listeners' level of expertise by supplying necessary facts, definitions, descriptions, and substantiating information.
- Conveys a message that is free from mental and physical coercion; a message that does not compel someone to take an action against his or her will.
- Does not fabricate statistics or other information intended to serve as proof of a contention or belief.
- Gives credit to the source of information and does not present information as original when it is not.[31]

"The line between appropriate and inappropriate behavior is often fuzzy, and what is considered acceptable in one company may not be in another."[32] However, to help resolve ethical dilemmas, apply the Ethics Litmus Test, by asking yourself these questions:

1. Does your course of action seem logical, responsible and legal?
2. How will your decision affect others? Where will it lead you?
3. Will you think well of yourself when you think back on your decision?
4. How would the person you most admire handle the situation?
5. What would your friends and family think about your decision?[33]

The ethical listener takes seriously the responsibility for communicating. Just as we enjoy freedom of speech, our freedom to listen is based on the obligation to provide a fair hearing of the message and then to analyze carefully the strength of that message. "The importance of truthfulness is fundamental to the whole area of ethics in communications. Confidence cannot be easily restored once it is lost."[34] Corporate executives are speaking out on this issue, as illustrated in the speech, "Principles for Managing in a Time of Change: A CEO's Perspective."

SAMPLE SPEECH

Principles for Managing in a Time of Change: A CEO's Perspective

Remarks by: **Daniel P. Tulley**
Chairman and Chief Executive Officer
Merrill Lynch & Co., Inc.

Distinguished Speaker Series **Harvard Business School**
October 19, 1994

Thank you. It's a great pleasure to be here. In preparing for today, I wondered what I could tell Harvard Business School students that they haven't already heard. I found myself leafing through a little booklet we put out about the history of Merrill Lynch and staring at some astonishing facts.

In the year 1942, our firm had $9 million in revenues, compared with $16.6 billion last year. In 1942, our earnings were $200,000; last year, they were $1.4 billion. I couldn't help thinking that while we predicted and anticipated change, the magnitude of that change surprised us—and still surprises us every day.

The one constant in our world is change, so I think the most important thing I can talk about is the need to manage change—and to be on the leading edge when that change occurs.

What it takes to steer an organization through a period of change and growth comes down to some basic principles. Peter Drucker, the great management thinker, describes this process very well. He says that every management, everyone in business, has to do the same things.

First, you have to assess the environment and understand the demographics, as well as everything else affecting the environment. Then, you have to prepare a plan—a road map that will get you from here to there.

The next step separates good management from mediocre management, and it's where the quality of leadership is most important. You have to implement the plan, which means having the guts to pull the trigger.

Jack Welch, the Chairman of General Electric, has written a book that has a title with which I totally agree. It is called *Control Your Own Destiny, Or Someone Else Will*. I beg you to control not only your own destinies but your time as well, because if you don't, someone will come along and fill the vacuum for you.

The corporate graveyard is littered with the bones of companies that were slow to respond to a changing environment—companies that were comfortable, content and smug in their own sense of security.

In his classic, *Marketing Myopia*, Harvard Professor Ted Levitt noted that the railroads woke too late to the fact that their business was not just laying track and operating locomotives. They never defined their business in broader terms.

They never recognized, as Ted Levitt said, that they were really in the larger business of transportation. It wasn't that people wanted to travel or ship freight *by rail*. They just wanted to get themselves or their goods from New York to Chicago or wherever. And so the railroads failed to anticipate the impact of the automobile, the airlines and the trucking industry.

More recently, we've seen the auto companies, banks, technology companies, the entertainment and insurance businesses—in fact, one industry after another—scrambling to catch up with a changing environment.

I can identify with their predicament. We in the financial world got a rude awakening sooner than most others. Our world was altered with a bang on "May Day" back in 1975, when the old practice of fixed commissions was ended. A lot of firms that saw their job as simply selling stocks and bonds were swept away, as were others that counted on high fixed commissions to cover the costs of research and other services.

At Merrill Lynch, we embrace the change. We set out to reinvent both our company and our industry, and I think we've succeeded. We transformed Merrill Lynch by building what was essentially a retail network into an investment banking powerhouse, in the process creating a unique dual franchise.

One key advantage was our basic company doctrine of putting the client's interests first. This had been drilled into us from the beginning by our founder, Charles E. Merrill. And when we talk about putting the client's interests first, we don't mean it merely as a matter of law and compliance, or as a slogan. We mean it as *an attitude* and a way of life.

We made a searching examination of what our clients really wanted and discovered that it wasn't just stocks and bonds. It was tailoring service to our clients' individual needs, whether they were investors or issuers of securities. It was creative advice and the ability to access complex global capital markets. It was a broad array of services to help clients raise and manage capital.

Thanks to the persistence of memory, a lot of people—even some who teach here at Harvard—still think of us as "The Thundering Herd," the firm that "brought Wall Street to Main Street." Back in the 1920s, 1930s and 1940s, we were known as the largest American "wirehouse," and the term stuck. But that was a long time ago. Meanwhile, Merrill Lynch has gone from Main Street to being a powerful presence in the global markets, with offices in 31 countries.

I've mentioned that we predicted and anticipated change without really appreciating the magnitude of change. Ten years ago, we developed a strategic plan. We said that by the year 2000 we wanted 20 percent of our revenues to come from outside the U.S. In 1993, a third of our revenues came from outside the U.S., and our estimate now is that, by the year 2000, 50 percent of our revenues will come from outside the U.S.—and, again, that may be too conservative.

We've redefined our role. Whether we are serving corporations, governments or individuals, we want to be their trusted financial advisor.

In 1975, Donald T. Regan, our Chairman at the time, put out a memorandum saying that because of May Day, we had to do things differently. He said, we'll no longer be just a selling organization, but rather a marketing, client-oriented company. And, he said, Tully here is going to be our Director of Marketing.

I don't think Don knew what *marketing* meant. I certainly didn't. I went to the library to study the subject, and that's where I came across *Marketing Myopia* and Ted Levitt. Of all the things I have learned in my 40 years in business, the little bit I told you about Peter Drucker and what I am going to say about Ted Levitt have been the guiding principles that have helped me achieve whatever success I have had.

Professor Levitt talks about the differences between selling and marketing. Selling starts off with the needs of the seller, whatever is in his bagful of goods or services. The seller starts off each day with what he has to sell, not what the clients want to buy. It's a very important distinction. Marketing focuses on the buyer—on the demand side of the equation, not the supply side.

Sales organizations focus on the transaction. If they have hula hoops to sell, they want to sell as many hula hoops as they can; whereas marketing organizations focus on relationships, on recurring and repeat transactions. Again, they try to define their business in broader terms.

Sales organizations think short term; marketers think long term. Sales organizations are strictly out for volume and revenues; whereas marketing organizations segment the marketplace. They are more concerned with profitability.

And, as you learn in your case studies here, in a true marketing company the product is a consequence of the marketing effort, not vice versa. It's a lesson all of you should carry from the classroom to the boardroom. Marketing people start out by asking, "What does the buyer want? What does the buyer need? What does the buyer want to accomplish, and how can we help them do that?"

In the mid-1970s, we did a tremendous amount of research, which showed us what clients really wanted: convenience, a full array of products and services, plus expert advice and guidance. In turn, this led us to develop the Cash Management Account®, perhaps the most revolutionary product in the history of financial services. It combined investments, check-writing, low-cost credit, high-yielding money market funds and credit cards—all in one convenient account. And using the same approach with our institutional clients, we developed LYONs®, MITTS®, PRIDES℠ and a whole assortment of client-focused derivative products. We never would have hit on any of these products if we'd remained a narrow, product-oriented sales organization. We've only succeeded by thinking from the client's perspective.

More and more, I find CEOs talking not about products but about what kind of value they can add for their customers. In our case, adding value meant knowing the intricacies of the international markets so we could provide the best advice to clients, whose interests are increasingly global.

Today, we have $548 billion in assets entrusted to us by our clients. In the last few years, the international portion of that has gone from about 2 percent to 10 percent, and at the turn of the century it will be 20 percent. By the year 2000, we predict that $548 billion will reach $1 trillion, so we expect to have $200 billion invested outside the United States.

We launched our expansion into the capital markets in 1978 with our acquisition of White, Weld, and later, A. G. Becker. The other major investment banking houses built their businesses over generations; we've done it in 16 years! In effect, we've built a whole new firm—a global leader in every major market—in less than one generation. We may not be the Methuselah of investment banking, but we certainly are the firm with the most momentum, energy and recent success.

We committed the resources. We took the risks. We restructured our organization. And today, we have been the leading global underwriter of debt and equity securities for nearly six years.

On a personal note, I've seen my career go from helping high-net-worth individuals plan their estates and retirement packages to advising the People's Republic of China, the Republic of Italy, Daimler-Benz, Blockbuster Entertainment, United Airlines and many more. But the most exciting thing about all these clients is that they represent long-term relationships, and also the successful realization of our global strategy.

Because of the markets' increasing size and complexity, we became persuaded that the global financial markets soon would be dominated by a handful of mega-firms. We were determined to be one of them, using our established distribution strength to help build our investment banking strength, and then using each to reinforce the other.

When we talk about the unique dual franchise in individual and institutional markets, it's more than a slogan. It's a strategy. The word "synergy" has badly been tarnished by overuse, so I try to avoid it. But one business area *does* augment the other. Our powerful institutional distribution network is complemented by our Private Client network. Together, they provide a ready market for the underwritings of our corporate, sovereign and municipal clients. And the perspective we gain benefits each of them.

We're not perfect, but we've learned from our mistakes. One thing we did right in the 1980s was to return to our core businesses—even as we expanded their definition and reach. We renewed our determination to do only what we do best, and to be the best at what we do—by which I mean being the premier provider of solutions to our clients' financial needs.

We've imposed disciplined cost controls and built a risk management system that has insulated us well from financial disasters. We strengthened our corporate governance—an important issue—by linking compensation to the performance of our entire firm. We did this by making share ownership an important component of compensation, especially for senior management.

In addition, we've worked hard at flattening our organization, following the old rule that the way to get people to act responsibly is to give them responsibility, including the responsibility for working as a team.

General Colin Powell tells a story about a young second lieutenant, very determined to get ahead, who goes to his hero and role model, the general, and says, "General, I admire you more than anyone else in the world. How can I become like you?"

And the general says, "Well, son, you've obviously got to work hard." The lieutenant says, "Yes, sir, I'll work very hard."

And the general says, "Well, you also have to study hard." "Oh, yes, sir, I'll study hard."

The general says, "You have to be loyal." "Oh, yes, sir, I will, I will, I will."

"And you've got to love what you do, of course." "Yes, sir. I will. But sir, is that how I'll become a general like you?"

The general says, "No, son. That's how you'll become a first lieutenant. Getting to become a general depends entirely on how well you can work with other people."

As I've learned over the years, it's amazing what you can accomplish when you don't care who gets the credit. I'm not just talking about deliberately giving others the credit as a tactical gesture. I mean knowing in your heart, mind and soul that you really don't deserve all the credit, and, therefore, you give it to others.

For generals, CEOs—and, in fact, any manager—the key to working with other people is a clear understanding of the core values that define the organization. Some cynics say that values don't matter. I have to tell you that they're wrong! Everything flows from values. That's why our company put enormous effort into formulating what we call the "Merrill Lynch Principles." These Principles aren't new. They've been part of Merrill Lynch from the very beginning, and, I daresay, they are common to every successful organization. Ours are:

- Client Focus
- Respect for the Individual
- Teamwork
- Responsible Citizenship
- Integrity

They sound simple, but, in fact, they embrace a lot.

Client Focus means not only being the "trusted advisor" but also earning that trust. It means determining what's best for the client in the long term, not what's best for ourselves in the short term.

Respect for the Individual means respect for every person, whether a client, shareholder, colleague or the person who empties the wastebaskets—everyone!

Teamwork means working together for a seamless integration of services. And it's not just the people in the trenches who have to practice teamwork. It's even more important at the corporate level.

Responsible Citizenship is essential because we're part of a larger community, with a duty to give something back. Wherever you go, you will see Merrill Lynch people giving something back to their communities.

And *Integrity* is where it all starts—and ends. It is vital in every business, but especially in ours. We deal with enormous amounts of other people's money, as well as our own. Integrity is the foundation of trust, and trust has to be earned over time. You may have noticed our company tag line, "A

Tradition of Trust." Those words didn't come easily. We've worked at them: "A Tradition of Trust."

And we've also seen that while it takes a long time to build up trust, companies can squander it in seconds. Other companies work hard to improve their Return on Equity and Return on Assets. At Merrill Lynch, we also care about those things, but we care more about our "R-O-I," our *Return on Integrity*, because we view Integrity as our most important corporate asset.

We're proud to be at the top of the league tables, but we are even prouder that we've never made a different kind of list—the best-seller list—in books like *Den of Thieves, Liar's Poker* and *Burning Down the House.* These were books about the ethical excesses of Wall Street in the 1980s, but they were not about Merrill Lynch.

The future of our company demands that we be visionary as well as ethical, that we think less about what we are now than about what we are becoming. I give a little talk at our training sessions, and I always tell our new recruits to take the ferry out to the Statue of Liberty and look back at the Merrill Lynch building. I say to them, "I want you to look back—not at what Merrill Lynch is, but at what Merrill Lynch can and should be."

Forty years ago, the typical volume on the New York Stock Exchange was less than two million shares a day. Now, it's 200 million or 250 million shares—and that's on a slow day and doesn't include the massive volume on the NASDAQ. A large transaction 40 years ago was $1 million. Recently, our firm completed a $4 billion transaction in three core currencies for a single client, the Republic of Italy. Five to ten years from now, our young people will be doing trillion-dollar transactions.

The numbers will keep changing, but the principles and values never, never change. Unlike financial markets, these principles are fixed. As Voltaire said, "There is only one morality, as there is only one geometry." And the great principles are also common to successful organizations everywhere. As the Chairman of Korea's Samsung Group wrote to his employees: "Only organizations which contribute to mankind will last; those organizations which lack humanism and morality can never become premier companies and will not endure."

You'll be entering the business world at a time when market economies are germinating, sprouting, blossoming all over the world. The need for capital is going to be enormous. The need for know-how in raising and using capital, and at the same time protecting the investors who provide it, will be equally great.

I envy you the challenge. I envy you the opportunity. There's no place I'd rather be right now than in your shoes, looking ahead to the possibilities of the 21st Century.

Thank you very much.

● ● ● In Summary ● ● ●

The theory of business ethics attempts to describe how people should act within given business structures; it is a practical discipline with practical importance. Many believe that the bottom-line statement in corporate responsibility is that corporations should act morally. In an attempt to develop and follow ethical values, corporations are starting to insist on employee accountability and have instituted employment civil rights and responsibilities programs.

═══ Business Communication in Practice ═══

1. Do you believe businesses can be both ethical and profitable? Should anything get in the way of businesses making money?
2. Should a person doing business in a foreign country carry on business in the manner of that country, even if it is contrary to American ethical standards?

═══ Simulations ═══

Directions: Each member of the class should determine what he or she would do in each of the following situations. The class will then be broken down into groups of three to five students. Each student will reveal her or his answer to each question and explain the reason for this stand. The group will try to reach consensus (general agreement) on a single answer for each situation.

1. You are working for a corporation located on a river that is the source of drinking water for a town located downstream. You become aware that toxic chemical waste is being dumped into the river in such a way that the source of the waste will go undetected.
2. You are the accountant for a small firm. You have been called before a governmental investigative panel and asked whether you are aware that the owner of the company is taking sales income from the business without recording it. You know it has happened. You will probably receive a jail sentence for being an accomplice if you admit the crime.
3. You suspect your friend and coworker John has taken approximately $600 in office supplies from the corporation for which you work to use in a home business. You are called into the manager's office and asked if you know anything about the depletion of the supplies inventory. The manager confides that he thinks John, a fellow worker, has been stealing them.
4. You are dissatisfied with your present job. You have applied for a position with another company. You are called for an interview. You are told

you must appear next Tuesday if you are to be considered. You will have to miss a day of work to go to the interview. You have no personal days off remaining. You don't want your present employer to know you are looking for another position because she would probably fire you.

5. A co-employee tells you in strict confidence that he has AIDS. You are employed in a high-risk health-care facility where it is possible for the employees to prick themselves with needles in the process of doing experiments, possibly contaminating the end product that is injected into patient's bodies and perhaps leading to patients being contaminated with the AIDS virus. On your monthly report, you are asked to reveal any information you have about possible health risks.

6. You are a lawyer. You are aware that your witness, a member of the executive board of the firm supplying 80 percent of your business, is lying during cross-examination.

7. A member of your firm has found a way to enter a competitor's computer operations. This allows you, if you so desire, to ascertain the competitor's bids on jobs that you both desire, in advance of the submission date. A large contract is up for bid. You and your competitor are the finalists for the job.

• • • Notes • • •

1. "The Unethical Worker," *USA Today* (October 18, 1995), B1.
2. Leila Zogby, "Business Ethics—The Answers Lie Within," *Piedmont Airlines Magazine* (May 1988): 22.
3. R. T. DeGeorge, *Business Ethics* (New York: Macmillan, 1982), p. 130.
4. "A Nation of Liars," *U.S. News and World Report*, (February 23, 1987): 54–57.
5. DeGeorge, 10–11.
6. Ibid., 12.
7. "A Nation of Liars," 54.
8. Ibid.
9. DeGeorge, 15.
10. Ibid., 7–8.
11. Taken from a personal interview with Charles Buckalew, Professor of Philosophy and Ethics, Lorain County Community College, Elyria, Ohio, January 12, 1989.
12. Charles S. McCoy, *Senior Fellow of Trinity Church's Center for Ethics and Corporate Policy*, New York, as quoted in Zogby, 119.
13. M. Euel Wade, Jr., "The Lantern of Ethics," a speech given at the University of Georgia, Athens, GA, November 5, 1987.
14. Ibid.
15. McCoy.
16. Buckalew.
17. Wade.
18. Jeffrey Baruch and Elizabeth Nicol, "Teaching Ethics in Business School," *Collegiate News and Views* (Fall 1980): 5.

19. Zogby, 122.
20. Ibid.
21. Ibid.
22. DeGeorge.
23. Ibid.
24. Wade.
25. Buckalew.
26. Ibid.
27. Ibid.
28. Ibid.
29. Ibid.
30. Ibid., and "Applied Ethics: A Strategy for Fostering Professional Responsibility," *Carnegie Quarterly* 28 (Spring/Summer 1980): 3–4.
31. Thomas Nelson, *Ethics in Speech Communication* (Indianapolis, IN: Bobbs-Merrill, 1966), p. 139.
32. Jacquelyn Lynn, "A Matter of Principle," *Entrepreneur* (August, 1995): 59.
33. Ibid.
34. Ibid.

Verbal Communication

EXPECTED OUTCOMES

After completing this chapter, you should be able to:

- Explain the importance of language in communication.
- Indicate the difference between standard and nonstandard dialects.
- Explain the basic principles that describe language and its meanings.
- Clarify the misunderstandings in communicative messages that may be based on making assumptions, not being clear, failing to be concrete, using inference for fact, and not understanding the differences between written and oral language.
- Identify some of the factors that constitute the difference between male and female language usage.

I am the only male employee in the public relations office of my company. Shortly after I was hired, a meeting was called to re-examine the procedures used to divide the workload of the office. Nadine, the director of public relations, presided at the session. It seemed to me that the meeting went on forever as the women kept making sure that everyone's opinions were heard. They also talked at length about the implications and fairness of the procedures. As far as I was concerned, this was a simple matter. Why didn't we just list the jobs, decide who would do what, and be out of there? Finally, Nadine said, "Do we all then want to go along with the plan?" I blurted out, "Why are you asking that question? We all just said we agreed!" All of the women looked at me quizzically. Later in the day, Sarah, the woman who has been acting as my mentor, asked why I had become so angry. I said there was a lot of time wasted and when Nadine asked whether we should go ahead, I had had it. Sarah laughed and said,

"Did you think she was asking a question? No, she was saying a decision had been reached." I replied, "She asked a question—that's not a statement." Sarah then said, "You don't know much about how women tend to communicate, do you?"

The world as you know it today would not be possible without language. Language enables you to express yourself and to elicit responses from other people. Language is a social tool through which you interact with others.[1] Language is central to your communication. Language is central to the operation of any business.

Beyond the personal and social level, the civility of a society as a whole often depends on the sophistication of the language spoken in that society. Because language is how we think as well as how we communicate, the more complex the language, the more likely it is that the participants in that society can accurately describe, explain, and develop concepts, and invent new ideas. Describing, explaining, developing concepts, and inventing new ideas are the very basis of the world of business and businesspersons. Language is the tool by which they send, receive, and think about their activities.

When you speak, you usually intend to communicate to your listener. Often, however, the result of spoken language is not understanding, but conflict and confusion. This is not the fault of the language; language is imprecise because what the sender means may not be what the receiver understands. In communication there are no mistakes, only outcomes. If, for example, you use the word "powerful" to describe a new idea that a coworker has proposed, that person might take the word to mean "it's a good idea." A supervisor might assume that you indicated the proposed idea is too strong and, therefore, not good. A third person might think that you were being sarcastic and were putting the idea down, rejecting it. Which of the receivers is correct? Only you know what you really meant. The others are interpreting based on their use of the language, or making assumptions about your use of the terms based on past experiences with you and the language you use.

Language Defined

Language is the structure system of symbols that catalog the objects, events, and relations in the world. Languages use syntax (grammar rules) and semantics (words) to set up a structure for making sense of what is said, heard, written, or read.[2]

Because language is symbolic and rule-based, the study of language involves the study of meanings—the meanings of speech sounds used as arbitrary symbols and agreed-upon markings that divide the symbols into groups. The arbitrary symbols in English are the twenty-six letters of the alphabet. These letters are combined to create words. For example, the letters *b u s i n e s s* have been grouped together to represent an organization that carries on a form of activity that supplies commodities or services. Any combination of letters could have been assigned to represent that meaning; however, those eight letters were selected.

The markings that have been agreed upon to divide the symbols into groups are called punctuation. Thus, a sentence, a unit of speech consisting of a meaningful arrangement of words, may be indicated by the use of a period at the end of the group of words. For example, a period marks the end of the sentence, "The business is a success because it made a profit last year." Other marking symbols in our language include the comma, question mark, colon, and semicolon. Each has a specific purpose in helping the reader understand the language presented in written form. Though not as readily apparent, you also punctuate as you speak. As you speak, you stop and breathe at the end of sentences, raise your voice at the end of questions, and pause briefly to set off ideas in a series. These actions are verbal punctuation marks. Though this sounds quite basic, think of how hard it often is to say exactly what you mean, of how many misunderstandings are based on pausing at the wrong place in a sentence. Think of how difficult it often is to differentiate between sarcasm and a statement of belief.

Your level of thinking depends greatly on your language competence; therefore, the more developed your language skills are, the more advanced you will be in processing information. Because speech is habitual, automatic, and ingrained, the major factors influencing language learning are your physical ability to do so, and the influences that have surrounded you. Individuals born with normally functioning senses (such as the eyes, ears, and mouth) and cortex (the section of the brain where communication is processed) learn language in a fairly standard way. As a child you were spoken to or overheard others speaking. Eventually, you absorbed the symbols of your society and started to use the language. How proficient you have become is based on a combination of your biological instruments, the amount and quality of the language that surrounded and continues to surround you, and your ability to practice the language.

Dialects

A **dialect** is a social or regional variation of a language. A dialect is represented by both the words that are used and the way they are pronounced. Over long periods of time, dialects may develop into separate language. For instance, French, Italian, and Spanish were original dialects of Latin.[3]

Hundreds of dialects are used in the United States. Each dialect is an equally viable, linguistically sophisticated mode with the potential for expressiveness. The only difference among the dialects lies in the situation in which each is most appropriately used.[4]

STANDARD AMERICAN ENGLISH

Standard American English (SAE) is generally accepted as the most common dialect of English spoken in the United States by professionals and is generally perceived to be the most credible in the world of business.[5] There are many Americans, however, who speak regional forms of English that are the norm for their areas of the country, which are acceptable in the world of business in those areas.

Why is Standard American English generally the dialect of choice in business? Linguistic analysis can ascertain the norm or standard of usage in any given language community. "A dialect is regarded as standard when it has acquired such prestige that its use is considered essential to professional performance for social and economic advancement. . . . Nonstandard dialects are viewed as lacking this prestige."[6] Note that in this context the term nonstandard does not mean substandard but simply means "different from the standard."

Linguists tend to agree that three basic reasons explain why a society should have a single dialect.[7]

1. *A standard dialect serves the social function of binding people together and creates a common bond for interaction and identification for society members.* By the same token, it can create an "in-group" and exclude other groups.
2. *Individuals having influence and responsibility will be able to communicate clearly to those whom they influence.* Since Standard American English is the medium used in communicative environments such as business, industry, and government, it is the form both the employer and employee are expected to use in order to communicate with others.
3. *There must be a common means of technique and learning.* A language mismatch causes misunderstanding and learning problems.

These reasons are often given by people who advocate the passage of legislation in the U.S. to make English the national language. This legislation, if passed, would mean that businesses would write product directions only in English, professional licensure testing would be given only in English, and work rules would be posted only in English. The movement advocating such laws, called **English Only,** is controversial because it appears to some that passage of such an act would marginalize those who are residents of the U.S.

but who do not speak English. This concept is based on the idea that since you develop your self-concept and belief systems from your culture, and a major part of culture is language, denying a person her or his language is like denying him or her a personal identity.[8]

NONSTANDARD DIALECTS

Some nonstandard dialects are the results of self-desired immigration by people from various countries where languages other than English were spoken. Others stem from the languages of people who came to this country as indentured laborers or slaves. In some instances dialects evolved as a means of expression with a familiar foreign language framework. For instance, Spanglish (a blending of English and Spanish) and Yiddish (a blending of English with a Germanic-based dialect spoken by many Jews in Western European countries) are foreign language deviations. Dialects also arise when a learner in a subcultural group is isolated from users of the standard dialect. Such an example in the United States would be the Appalachian dialect, which evolved because individuals living in the mountainous areas of West Virginia had only sporadic contact with mainstream Americans. Dialects may be regional, reflecting speech patterns developed in a geographic area, such as "down-eastern" of Maine, the "drawl" of Texas, and that of the Brooklynite or the Bostonian.

All language systems are perfectly adequate for communication within the group by the members of the group. We learn the dialect we have been exposed to and use the dialect common to those with whom we identify. For example, many African Americans speak what is known as **Ebonics, Black English,** or **African American Vernacular English (AAVE).**[9] This language system has highly consistent grammar, pronunciation, lexicon, and stylistic features that comprise the first language variety learned by many lower- and working-class African Americans in their home settings and used with family and friends.

Problems may emerge when the speaker of a dialect attempts to interact with others using the dominant language. Racism, for example, is often characterized by a negative response to users of nonstandard dialects. It is based on the assumption that such persons are inherently inferior to users of the standard form.[10]

Research has shown that there are social and professional disadvantages of speaking some dialects in business situations. "The speaker must come to grips with a dilemma: if he or she is to succeed in this society, she or he must cultivate the complementary use of Standard American English in situations in which it is to his/her advantage to do so."[11] But the nonstandard speaker must also be aware that intradialect alienation may occur when the minority mem-

In the multilingual U.S. society, businesses have become aware of the need to adapt their messages to a variety of potential clients.

ber chooses to reject a "native" dialect in favor of the standard dialect. Such a person may be described in her or his own subsociety "putting on airs," and may become a victim of alienation from the rest of the community who uses the nonstandard dialect.[12]

Businesses are often concerned about hiring individuals who speak in nonstandard dialects if those persons will be interacting with the general public. Conversely, some individuals are hired specifically because they speak a language other than English or use a nonstandard dialect. U.S.-based businesses have found that the ever-expanding number of non-native American speakers who purchase and request services from their companies requires individuals on staff who speak languages other than English. In addition, they have come to recognize that having individuals on their staff who speak nonstandard dialects may allow prospective customers to feel closer to salespeople, managers, and service people.

Some individuals learn to be **language switchers**—selecting the appropriate dialect or language to use in various situations. If a front desk person in a hotel confronts a customer in English, and the person responds in French, the employee should switch to French if she knows it. As for dialect, the same may take place. For example, a woman raised in Cajun Louisiana spoke a nonstandard English dialect with a Cajun French influence. Some of her pronunciation, words, and sentence structure were based in traditional old French. She decided that to "make it" in the business world, she needed to learn SAE. Now, in business contexts, she speaks SAE. When she goes home to visit family and friends, she uses the Cajun dialect of her childhood.

Principles of Language Meaning

The basic principles that describe language and its meanings include these:

1. *Meanings are found in people, not in the symbols of a message.* Words have no meaning in and of themselves; they take on meaning only as individuals assign meaning to the combination of letters. Therefore, two people from different backgrounds may decode a symbol in different ways. For example, when meeting with British businesspeople, a U.S. company's representative suggested "tabling" an item he wanted to postpone. However, the British individual discussed it immediately, because "tabling" means the opposite in British English from its meaning in American English.

2. *Meanings are learned.* Meanings are functions of personal experience. As we learn our language, imitating how those around us use the language, we also learn the meaning of symbols. For example, you probably would describe a computer as "an electronic appliance that enables you to perform efficiently a great many tasks." How do you know that? In all likelihood, someone either showed you a computer and said, "This is a computer." Or someone asked you to go the computer and then pointed at it and described it if you didn't understand the request. Someone somehow shared the meaning of the word with you, and you acquired the symbolic meaning. This is how most of your native language was learned.

3. *We learn words and acquire their meanings by perceiving new words in relation to other words, objects, or perceptions for which we already have meanings.* In other words, we build meaning upon meaning. If, for example, you didn't know what a computer was, the description of the computer would have little meaning.

4. *People can have similar meanings for words only if they have had similar experiences, or can anticipate similar experiences.* As two people communicate, they will understand each other only if they can agree on the

meaning of the terms being used. The Pepsi Cola Bottling Company learned this lesson in attempting to use the advertising slogan, "Come alive, you're in the Pepsi generation," when marketing Pepsi in China. The Chinese reacted with dismay because the phrase translated as "Pepsi brings your ancestors back from the dead."[13] If you are new to the world of investment banking, you may think an "MD" is a doctor, rather than a managing director. Unless you are involved with electronics or computers, you might think that "UPS" is a package delivery service, not an "uninterrupted power supply."

5. *To give meanings, or to change meanings, you must pair the meanings with identifications for which there are already understandings.* Basically, if you want someone to understand you, then you must use language that person understands or clarify by using definitions or examples that are part of his/her background.

Language Problems in Communicating

The major language problems that cause misunderstandings in communicative messages are making assumptions, not being clear, failing to be concrete, using inference for fact, and not understanding the differences between written and oral language.

ASSUMPTION

Some people think assumptively. The assumption is that when they tell a listener something, they have given a message to the listener that has been received and understood. This is not always true. The receiver must receive and decode the message and then translate what has been sent according to the intent of the sender.

The sender may be incorrect in assuming that the receiver can or will gain the intent of the message. First, the receiver may not be listening effectively. The listener may be daydreaming or not paying attention. Second, the listener may not want to receive the message. For example, if there is a negative relationship between the sender and receiver, the receiver may not want to listen to what the sender has to say. Third, biases may stop the receiver from decoding the implied meaning of the message. For example, if the sender is discussing the positive effects of changing the equal opportunity hiring practices of a business and the receiver has strong racial or ethnic biases, the message

---

Two Words That Persuade

Two key words will make you more persuasive. The words: *"if"* and *"then."*

Whether you're trying to sell a car or an idea, the message that works is "If you will take this action, then you will get this reward."

The next time you're planning to try to persuade someone, think about using these two words to get what you want.

Source: *Overcoming Resistance,* by Jerald M. Jellison. Simon & Schuster, 1230 Avenue of the Americas, New York, NY 10020

will probably not receive a fair hearing. Finally, the very nature of language affects sender-receiver clarity. Different people perceive messages in various ways depending on their backgrounds. For example, if an accountant is attempting to explain certain aspects of the financial status of the company to a new employee who has little accounting training or experience, the employee may not understand the technical terms used.

CLARITY

Clarity, making something clear and understandable, is key to effective communication. To ensure clarity, the sender should be certain that the receiver will be able to grasp the intent of the information. Comprehension is more readily achieved if the language used is not beyond the receiver's understanding. In addition, it is necessary to add details and use examples.

When adding details, the sender should include all information necessary for comprehension. For example, notice how in this series of statements the addition of details makes each statement clearer than the preceding one:

George bought his own business.
Yesterday, George bought his own business.
Yesterday, George bought his own insurance practice.
Yesterday, George bought his own Nationwide Insurance Agency.
Yesterday, George bought his own Nationwide Insurance Agency in Baltimore, Maryland.

A clear communicator uses understandable terms rather than abstract ones. Experts in a particular field, for example, often forget that others are not knowledgeable in that activity's terminology. Accountants may use "number talk" that is beyond the average person. Computer experts have incorporated "computer talk" into our language in ways that confuse many people. Unless you are familiar with computers you may be unable to decode such terms as graphical-user interface, reboot, and shareware, all of which are supposed to be user-friendly.

Businesses have become aware of the need to familiarize clients with their messages. For example, since 1987, Ford Motor customers are finding in the glove boxes of their new Ford, Lincoln, and Mercury cars a "plain English" version of the company's *Warranty Information Booklet*. Designed to be easy to use and to understand, the booklet was part of Ford's campaign to rewrite the company's documents in straightforward language. The company's previous booklet stated, "CLAIMS PROCEDURE To obtain service under the Emissions Performance Warranty, take the vehicle to a Ford Motor Company dealer as soon as possible after it fails an I/M test along with the documentation showing the vehicle failed an EPA-approved emissions test." The rewritten booklet states, "How do you get service under the Emissions Performance

Warranty? To get service under this warranty, take your car to a Ford Motor Company dealer as soon as possible after it has failed an EPA-approved test. Be sure to bring along the document that shows your car failed the test."[14]

Some businesses intentionally confound rather than clarify by using terms that seem to mean one thing when, in fact, they may be understood to mean something else. Or they use terms that are so unclear that there is no way to understand. For example, in describing a possible dangerous meltdown at a nuclear plant, a company referred to it as an "unscheduled event." A business announced that it was giving its employees a "salary adjustment" in order to soften the shareholder's potential negative reaction to employee raises that might reduce shareholder's dividends. A business contract to sell shovels called "displacement instruments" to the Pentagon indicated that the cost would be $85. The same shovel was sold commercially for $9.95. Clarity is the result of using simple understandable language. Ethics guide the honest word choices meant to illuminate ambiguity that may be persuasive but not necessarily ethical.

CONCRETENESS

Concreteness means being specific rather than abstract, being real rather than artificial. Concrete language attempts to describe specific experiences and behaviors. In order to develop concreteness, one needs to add details to a general statement. For example, rather than making the general statement "Sarah did well on the job last year," use a statement that is more concrete, such as "Sarah did well on the job last year, which is evidenced by her increased sales and the award she received for having the highest customer courtesy ratings." Instead of the general statement "I had a good time at the company awards banquet," a concrete statement would be "I had a good time at the company's awards banquet because most of my friends were there, the food was delicious, and the keynote speaker talked about my favorite subject—salesmanship!"

A concrete communicator should be aware of the difference between concrete and abstract terms, commonly referred to as denotations and connotations. The dictionary meaning of **denotation** is "referential meaning; the objective or descriptive meaning of a word."[15] The term refers to words that have specific meanings. Business examples of denotative terms, words that have a concrete dictionary definition, include computer, file folder, debit, and advertisement. **Connotation** means "the feeling or emotional aspects of a word's meaning, generally viewed as consisting of the subjectivity and evaluation. For example, the good-bad, strong-weak, fast-slow dimension or the associations of a term."[16] Examples of connotative words used in business would include quality, integrity, valuable, ethical, and efficient. These words all need clarifications and examples for the receiver to understand the user's intent.

Use These Powerful Words

To lead prospects to a "yes" in your sales presentation, try this three-phase questioning technique:

- ***Phase one.*** *Ask a question based on the soft word "feel." Example: "How do you feel about the current business situation?" Most people will respond because it's a neutral question that's easy to answer.*
- ***Phase two.*** *Ask a question using the more definitive word "think." Example: "Do you think this would work better than what you now use?" People are more reluctant to answer this kind of question. But once they do, they'll firmly defend what they've said.*
- ***Phase three.*** *Get prospects to take a stand by prefacing a question with the more definite and specific "In your opinion." Example: "In your opinion, is this the best product to solve the problem?" A "yes" means they've decided to buy. And they'll defend and justify that decision rather than change it.*

Source: *Advanced Selling Strategies,* by Brian Tracy, cited in *Sales & Marketing Management,* 335 Park Ave. S., New York, NY 10010.

FACT VERSUS INFERENCE

A **fact** is that which has been proven, usually through scientific investigation, or has been deemed true because of long-term acceptance. Examples of factual statements are "Fourth quarter earnings were up 14 percent" and "While president of the Chrysler Corporation, Lee Iacocca was the organization's television spokesman." A **factual statement** is "a statement made after observation that is limited to what has been observed."[17]

Inference is the passing from one judgment to another, or from a belief or cognition to a judgment. An example of an inference is "Because pollution causes public health hazards, any business that is convicted of any type of polluting should be closed down." The speaker bases the final statement on a leap of belief based on the original statement.

An **inferential statement** is "a statement that can be made by anyone, is not limited to the observed, and can be made at any time and about any time (past, present, or future)."[18] An inferential statement caused Sears's, Roebuck and Company to experience a crisis when the company's commission and quota system in its auto centers was the subject of a government investigation by the California Consumer Affairs Department. Before the case could be handled, questions started to arise over the quality of Sears's service.[19] No fact was presented, only inference. In order to counteract the negative publicity, Sears became proactive and counteracted the potential crisis with advertisements stating the facts.

Unfortunately, in communication some people use factual and inferential

TABLE 3.1 Differences between Factual Statements and Inferential Statements[20]

FACTUAL STATEMENTS	INFERENTIAL STATEMENTS
1. may be made only after observation	1. may be made at any time
2. are limited to what has been observed	2. go beyond what has been observed
3. may be made only by the observer	3. may be made by anyone
4. may only be about the past or the present	4. may be about any time—past, present, or future
5. approach certainty	5. involve varying degrees of probability
6. are subject to verifiable standards	6. are not subject to verifiable standards

statements interchangeably. If this practice is intentional, it is, of course, unethical. However, sometimes it is done naively, with no intention to confuse or underhandedly convince the receiver. Listeners must always be aware of the possibility of inference being passed along as fact. Ethical and responsible speakers who are aware of the difference between fact and inference will introduce inferential statements with identifying phases, such as "I believe," or "I think," or "It seems to me."

Understanding the difference between factual and inferential statements can help you acknowledge when you or someone else is making a statement of fact or of inference. However, one type of statement is not necessarily better than the other. "We need both types of statements; both are useful, both are important. The problem arises when we treat one type of statement as if it were the other. Specifically, the problem arises when we treat an inferential statement as if it were a factual statement."[21] Table 3.1 illustrates the differences between factual and inferential statements.

Differences between Written and Spoken Language

"For many people in the world today, language still exists only in its spoken form. Writing is a way of representing something that could be spoken. Writing is therefore a secondary way of representing language; it is not an alternative way. Written forms cannot exist apart from the spoken forms on which they are based; spoken forms can exist whether or not they are written. This is not intended to deny the usefulness of writing. It is simply intended to emphasize the proper relationship between speaking and writing."[22]

Written and spoken languages are meant to accomplish the same goals—

to develop ideas, inform, and persuade. However, the styles of written language and spoken language are not the same because one is meant to be read and the other to be heard. These differences are found in both the semantics and the syntax.

Spoken language is aimed at immediate understanding. The listener must be able to grasp ideas as they are presented. The receiver has no opportunity to go back and reexamine the material, as he or she may have when reading.

Research shows that spoken language uses significantly more personal references, more personal pronouns of the first-person and second-person singular and plural (I, we, us, you), shorter thought units, more word repetition, more monosyllabic words, and more familiar words.[23]

Female-Male Language and Communication[24]

During the last decade American business experienced a change. Women have been entering the workforce at levels equal to or exceeding those of men. Before the increase in the number of women executives, male language patterns dominated the upper echelons of most organizations. Women were present, but often in secretarial or low-level administrative jobs. The influx of women has prompted the investigation of an important aspect of business interaction—female-male communication and language.

An analysis of female-male language involves several facets. A major consideration is whether or not Standard American English is, in fact, sexist. Other aspects are how males and females use language and how usage affects the business and organization participant.

THE SEXISM OF STANDARD AMERICAN ENGLISH

Psychologists believe that roles are patterns of expectation by the self and others about appropriate behavior of an individual in a given social setting. Those roles are learned by means of our symbolic interactions, through which we also acquire the norms of culture and society. They are defined in the language of the society and once we acquire them, we believe in them.[25]

If language reinforces the concept that there are certain male roles, and other females roles, and if you think of people only in terms of he and him, then you assume certain things about yourself and others. If the assumption is that males are dominant and females are subordinate—because the pronoun "he" is used to refer to all people including all leaders and influential people—then males learn to play dominant roles and females submissive roles. If the assumption is that all executives, lawyers, and computer programmers are male, and that nurses and secretaries are female, then a child quickly learns both prescribed and proscribed roles.

For many years, English was a sexist language. It ignored women by referring to all individuals as him, defined women by specific roles, and put women in categories that differed from those attainable by males.

"The masculine-gender pronouns that eighteenth century grammarians used when they set up the rules of grammar did not reflect a belief that masculine pronouns could refer to both sexes. They reflected the cultural reality that males dominated society."[26] The word sexism was coined in the 1970s with the growth of a women's liberation movement whose goal was to achieve equal rights for women. An important part of this movement was the desire to change language by recognizing the equality of women. The attempt was not always met with agreement and admiration. In 1972, *Time* magazine referred to the national attempt to remove sexist references from the language as "Ms-guided."[27] Proponents of nonsexist terms were booed and assured that they can't legislate language change. In spite of the negativism, "In the past decade there has been a mini-reformation of the language that has surpassed the expectations even of many feminists."[28] By the mid-1970s neuter terms such as firefighter (fireman), camera operator (cameraman), and humanity (mankind) started to replace sex-specific terms. These terms still may not be the language of the majority, but they have become common where they once seemed awkward. Interestingly enough, though it is hard to prove that it is the result of the movement to change language, there has been an increase in the number of females fighting fires, serving as police officers, and repairing telephone lines.

Major linguistic sources have acknowledged the sexism of our language and have taken actions to change it. *The Associated Press Stylebook*, the guide used by many newspapers, now offers such warnings as "copy should not express surprise that an attractive woman can be professionally accomplished, as in: 'Mary Smith doesn't look the part but she's an authority on . . .'"[29]

"The current movement for language change has been in process for nearly two decades. There is some consensus about acceptable changes, but no full agreement among people outside of the academic world about the effects of 'he/man' language and women's self-esteem and on men's perceptions of women exists."[30] It is generally accepted, however, that language can affect learning, career development, and personal well-being.

MALE AND FEMALE LANGUAGE USAGE

Do men and women use language differently? The answer, according to numerous communication researchers, is a resounding yes. However, as in any generalization, it must be kept in mind that there are both men and women

---

How to Boss Words Around

In "A Woman's Guide to the Language of Success," Phyliss Mindell lays out a grammar of power for ambitious readers who haven't yet learned to boss words around.

For her, the forbidden "F" word is "feel," and an addiction to "I" signals indecision. Skip the "touchy-feely" syntax, she advises, and head for the real subject. People who say, "I (think) (guess) (feel) we need more time," are perceived as uncertain; people who say, "We need more time," or even, "More time is needed," are not.

She also considers "silly big words" a weakness, along with all things long-winded. Say "idea" and not "conceptualization," she advises. Keep it short. Be concise. Use strong verbs. Don't over-modify. (Ditch "very.")

who defy the research findings and act out of the identified norm patterns. Therefore, use generalized conclusions as guidelines for awareness, and do not accept them as all-inclusive statements that describe every man or woman.

"Many casualties in the war between the sexes result from a failure to realize that men and women actually speak different languages."[31] Communication between men and women sometimes can border on cross-cultural exchange. Some people have gone so far as to say that conversation between men and women is as different as talk between people from two different countries. "Men and women use language to contrary purposes and effect."[32] Some research has shown that women tend to use language to create intimacy and connection, and men use language to preserve their independence and negotiate their status.

How do these differences develop? Even in the same culture, such as the United States, the society expects different things from girls and boys and teaches them those differences. Language gender differences are observed in children as young as age three.[33] Boys tend to play in large groups that are hierarchically structured: there is a leader and/or there is a competition for leadership; there are winners and losers in the games they play; and there are complex rules. The emphasis is on skill and who is best. This dynamic traditionally has carried over into the business world, where men work in groups, report to a boss or leader, and strive to be winners in the competition with each other and different firms. Girls play in small groups or pairs and usually have a best friend. Intimacy is the key. Everyone gets a turn, there are usually no winners and losers, and they are not expected to boast about successes. Thus, when women enter the workplace they often find themselves at odds with the competitive, rule-oriented, leader-dominated structure.

Boys and girls talk to their peers differently. Girls generally don't give orders; rather, they express their preferences as suggestions. Boys say, "Gimme that!" and "Get out of here!" Girls say, "Can we do this?" and "How about doing that?" In the working world, the norms tend to be those that have been set by the business leaders—traditionally men—and, therefore, women may find themselves being judged according to male expectations.

Both male and female styles are valid in their own ways. Misunderstandings arise because the styles are different. While some women may wish to talk about their problems, share the information with others, and seek advice, some men may prefer to shake off the problems and be done with it. Research shows some generalized differences between the communicative styles of men and women. These generalizations are not to be taken as "always" factors. As with all research, they indicate trends. You may not act as these generalizations suggest, nor may the people with whom you work, but you may not be representative of the broader population. Regarding language usage:[34]

Business Professionals Share Their Views

Profile: Deborah Borisoff, business consultant in gender communication and professor of speech and interpersonal communication, New York University.

Does language have an effect on men and women in the business world?

Although the doors to business presumably are open equally to women and men, certain words used when hiring, and in the workplace, still privilege male sex-trait stereotypes.

Can you provide an example that illustrates this privilege?

One of my students recently interviewed for a position on Wall Street and was asked during the interview, "Can you be vicious?" He responded by relating how karate lessons as a child enabled him to beat up the school bully. The group of men interviewing him were delighted with his response and hired him. If we think about how differently boys and girls are socialized, it would be hard to imagine how a woman candidate might respond to the same question.

May language have an effect other than in the hiring arena?

Another student related that at a company board meeting, she expressed strong feelings about one of the topics. A male colleague told her to calm down and not get so "emotional." The term "emotional" when applied to a woman often is associated with being out of control and is seldom applied to men who demonstrate strong views.

What are the implications of these examples?

We need to think about how we can change the connotation of certain words or expressions as they apply to men and women in the workplace.

Men are *likely* to:

- use more obscene expressions and expletives
- use more commanding language
- use dominant language
- include content that deals primarily with tasks
- use competitive and sports-oriented language
- use language that treats people as part of a team or a system
- make direct assumptions more often than ask questions
- use words like "can" and "will" rather than indirect forms such as "might"
- use terms that refer to self more than to the listener
- focus on goals, plans, or accomplishments rather than anxiety, doubts, or personal limitations
- use nonstandard speech for emphasis
- use words that confront the listener if necessary

Women are *likely* to:

- be more grammatically correct
- use more prosocial language ("language that displays behavior that benefits others rather than the person performing the behaviors and may even involve personal risk or loss")[35]
- use more submissive language
- turn statements into questions or make them indirect statements
- use tentative phrases such as "I guess" or "Don't you think?"
- emphasize feelings and relationships
- focus on identity and relating more than on the physical and technical features of task achievement
- use terms of endearment like "honey" and "sweetie"
- react with respect for, or deference to, the listener
- allow options other than their own
- use indirect verb forms such as might or would more than can or will
- make few bold assertions
- qualify statements with adjectives or adverbs such as very, kind of, possibly, or
- use standard speech and rarely use nonstandard or taboo words

How to Communicate Effectively without Succumbing to "Rightspeak"

By Cheryl A. Godfrey

Look at the cultural context behind your words. Start by considering whether your point, not just your word choice, is discriminating or dehumanizing. Also consider if your words may be based on hurtful ideas of which you were not aware.

For example, a physically challenged person may tell you that she or he hates the word "handicapped" because it evolved from the image of people with disabilities begging in the streets with their caps in their hands. Using that word keeps the image alive.

The best way to tell whether your point hurts people who are different from you is to listen to a person who has a different perspective. All people have perspectives that grow out of their individual circumstances, whether we grew up poor, female, African-American, Jewish, or end up physically challenged (as many of us one day will).

Change hurtful language. If we find that our words show ignorance, exclude or devalue someone, we benefit from changing those words.

If, however, we find that words express exactly what we mean and that the only persons challenging them are overzealous fair housing groups, we should not change our words merely to avoid being criticized. Groups who find the words "spectacular view" hurtful are forgetting that it is not a sin to acknowledge that some people are sighted and would enjoy a view.

An examination of a specific business instance will help show the differences between the way males and females tend to use language.

Consider this situation: A formal research document is to be sent to another company. The course of action is being discussed. A woman might say, "Don't you think it would be better to send them an executive summary first?" It would not be unusual for a male to follow her statement by stating, "Send the summary." Others at the meeting would come away, therefore, with the impression that it was the man's idea because the woman never really directed the action.

If the first speaker was a man, he would probably say, "Send the executive summary first."[36] The validity of this example, of course, is dependent upon the people involved and their following the norms as revealed by research.

It will be interesting to see if future research shows a change in the traditional language use of the sexes as a result of the competitive nature of business and industry, the increase in the number of women in the boardroom, and the evolving role of women.

Intercultural Implications of Language Usage

With the ever-expanding internationalization of the business market, it is wise for businesspeople to be aware of some principles of language usage. Some principles that a U.S. businessperson should be aware of in order to reduce the chance of unintentional slips include these:[37]

- *Avoid sarcasm.* Standard American English has many double meaning words. In addition, tonal variations often change the meaning of words. These nuances often lack meaning to non-native speakers. A non-native speaking American computer programmer whose machine had gone down the day before had lost half of the program he was writing. He became confused when his boss said, "Wonderful! You just made my day."
- *Use specific, nonidiomatic action verbs, if possible.* For example, avoid telling a client that you have ordered a car for his transportation, and the "driver will pick him up."
- *Pause while speaking.* Don't be afraid of silence. North Americans think they have to talk all the time, but people from other cultures are used to silence. Japanese businesspeople can't understand how North Americans can talk and think at the same time!
- *Idioms can be confusing.* Be aware that people whose first language is not English tend to take terms literally. An employer told a woman non-native North American speaker, "Touch base at 11:30." At 11:20 the woman asked a coworker if she knew where the base was. Was it inside or outside?

Tips for Overcoming Cultural Language Barriers

• **When you ask if a foreigner understands you, don't automatically take yes for an answer.**
   Example: *A Chinese businessperson will say he understands you rather than offend you by saying you haven't been clear. It's better to ask a question that clearly indicates whether you've been understood.*

• **Use your best grammar.** *Chances are, it's what your counterparts have learned.*

• **Confine yourself to the simplest words in the English language**—*the ones that foreigners learn first.*

• **Recap and rephrase your ideas.** *Then pause for a second or two after expressing major points.*

• **Use specific, nonidiomatic action verbs, if it is possible.**
   Example: *"Ride" the bus, instead of "take" the bus.*

• **Speak directly to the other businessperson if you are using an interpreter**—*not the interpreter. And don't interrupt an interpreter, even when you think he/she is spending too much time clarifying a point. Take responsibility for misunderstandings—even when they are the interpreter's fault.*

• **Ask another company to translate back into English** *if you have doubts about a written translation that you've paid a company to do in a foreign language.*

• **Prepare more than you normally do for a presentation.** *When you try to wing it, there's a greater chance of using slang or forgetting a formality you have learned.*

- *Questions to the presenter are almost impossible for people from some cultures.* People from other cultures may not ask questions for two reasons: They don't want to look stupid in front of their colleagues. And it is conceivable that you might not know the answer, and then you would "lose face" or be embarrassed in front of others.
- *Avoid humor.* Humor doesn't translate well. Humor is often based on plays on words and when the information is taken literally, rather than figuratively, it isn't funny.

Implications of Language Usage and Business

Language is a fundamental part of communication, and is therefore an important part of business. In order to be effective in their careers, businesspeople must use language effectively. Employee promotions are often based on communication skills. Sales and service stem from communication. Studies show that as much as 92 percent of a chief executive's time and 60 percent of first-line managers' time is spent communicating.[38] However, much of this time is wasted time if the communicators do not have a command of their language.

• • •   In Summary   • • •

Language, the structure system of symbols, is used to describe, explain, develop concepts, and invent new ideas. It is the very basis of the world of business and businesspersons. The major language problems that cause misunderstandings in communicative messages are making assumptions, not being clear, failing to be concrete, using inference for fact, and not understanding the differences between written and oral language. Written and spoken languages are meant to accomplish the same goals; however, the styles of written language and spoken language are not the same because one is meant to be read and the other to be heard. These differences are found in both the semantics and the syntax. Culture has an effect on language, including the communication between men and women.

Business Communication in Practice

1. Find an article, advertisement, or employment announcement that is sexist. Rewrite the piece to eliminate the sexism.
2. Adjust these phrases and sentences so they are gender-free:
   a. mankind
   b. the common man
   c. The average student is worried about his grades.
   d. mailman
   e. As a teacher, he is faced daily with the problem of paperwork.
   f. Each student will do better if he has a voice in the decision.
   g. authoress
   h. male nurse
   i. The class interviewed Chief Justice Rehnquist and Mrs. Ginsberg, one of the woman Supreme Court justices.
3. Research gender communication. Give a three-minute speech on some research finding concerning male communication tendencies, female communication tendencies, or the conflict between male and female tendencies in the workplace. As a resource guide, consider Lois Einhorn, "Oral and Written Style: An Examination of Differences," *Southern Speech Communication Journal* 43 (Spring 1973): 306.
4. Read any of the sources on male and female communication listed in note 24 of this chapter. Prepare either a short paper or a speech on one of

these subjects: (a) the relationship of male or female success (or failure) in business based on language use; (b) the potential of conflict in the business environment due to male-female language differences; (c) women's continuing difficulties picking up and issuing power cues at work; (d) male-female language differences as the possible cause of perceived harassment by males in the workplace.

••• Notes •••

1. Blaine Goss, *Processing Communication* (Belmont, CA: Wadsworth, 1982), p. 55.
2. Joseph DeVito, *The Communication Handbook: A Dictionary* (New York: Harper and Row, 1986), p. 176.
3. Ibid., 94–95.
4. Delorese Tomlinson, "Bi-Dialectism: Solution for American Minority Members," *The Speech Teacher* 24 (September 1975): 234.
5. Ibid., 232.
6. Charles Harpole, "Eric Report: Nonstandard Speech," *The Speech Teacher* 24 (September 1975): 226.
7. Tomlinson, 234.
8. Ibid., 232.
9. For an extensive discussion of Black English, sometimes called Ebonics, see Michael Hecht, Mary Jane Collier, and Sidney Ribeau, *African American Communication: Ethnic Identity and Cultural Interpretation* (Newbury Park, CA: Sage Publications, 1993). For a discussion of African American Vernacular English see Arnetha F. Ball, "Expository Writing Patterns of African American Students," *English Journal* (January 1996): 27–36.
10. Tomlinson, 232.
11. Ibid., 233.
12. Ibid., 235.
13. Carol Kinsey Gorman, "The New International Communication Essentials," *Boardroom Reports* (March 15, 1995): 11.
14. Lee Gray, "Ford Offers a Readable Warranty Booklet," *Simply Stated . . . In Business* 18 (March 1987).
15. DeVito, 93.
16. Ibid., 76.
17. Ibid., 113.
18. Ibid., 155.
19. Ann Carney and Amy Jorden, "Prepare for Business-Related Crises," *Public Relations Journal* (August 1993): 34.
20. DeVito, 113.
21. Ibid., 113.
22. B. L. Pearson, *Introduction to Linguistic Concepts* (New York: Alfred A. Knopf, 1977).
23. Lois Einhorn, "Oral and Written Style: An Examination of Differences," *Southern Speech Communication Journal* 43 (Spring 1973): 306.
24. For discussions of female-male language and communication see Julia Wood, *Gender Lives: Communication, Gender, and Culture* (Belmont, CA: Wadsworth, 1994);

Wendy Simonds, *Women and Self-Help Culture: Reading between the Lines* (New Brunswick, NJ: Rutgers University Press, 1992); Karen A. Foss and Sonja K. Foss, *Women Speak: The Eloquence of Women's Lives* (Prospect Heights, IL: Waveland Press, 1994); Linda A. M. Perry, Lynn H. Turner, and Helen M. Sterk, *Constructing and Reconstructing Gender: The Links among Communication, Language, and Gender* (Albany: State University of New York Press, 1992); Barbara Bates, *Communication and the Sexes* (New York: Harper and Row, 1988); Deborah Tannen, *You Just Don't Understand* (New York: Morrow, 1990); Phyliss Mindell, *A Women's Guide to the Language of Success* (New York: Prentice Hall, 1995).

25. Roy Berko, Andrew Wolvin, and Darlyn Wolvin, *Communication: A Social and Career Focus*, 6th ed. (Boston: Houghton Mifflin, 1995), p. 206.

26. Carolyn Bocella Bagin, "Are All Men Equal? The Generic Dilemma," *Simply Stated* 62 (January 1986): 1.

27. Mary Schnuch, "This Ms-Guided Language Succeeds," *Atlanta Constitution* 9 (August 1983): 3B.

28. Ibid.

29. Dr. Jerie McArthur, as quoted in "Garble Gap: Men, Women Just Don't Talk the Same Language," *Cleveland Plain Dealer* (March 31, 1984) B1.

30. Barbara Bates, *Communication and the Sexes* (New York: Harper and Row, 1988), p. 102.

31. Dr. Lillian Glass, as quoted in "Garble Gap: Men, Women Just Don't Talk the Same Language," *Cleveland Plain Dealer* (March 31, 1984) B1.

32. Alfie Kohn, "Girl Talk, Guy Talk," *Psychology Today* (February 1988): 65.

33. Deborah Tannen, *You Just Don't Understand* (New York: Morrow, 1990), pp. 43–44.

34. Bates, 95.

35. DeVito, 240.

36. McArthur, B4.

37. The material in this section is based on the ideas of Carol Kinsey Gorman, Kinsey Consulting Services, and Marcy Huber, president of the Center of Language Training.

38. "Career Readiness: Perceptions of Business Communication" (Faculty Development Improvement Grant, Youngstown State University, n.d.), p. 1.

Nonverbal Communication

EXPECTED OUTCOMES

After completing this chapter, you should be able to:

- Understand that people communicate simultaneously at verbal and nonverbal levels.
- Define nonverbal communication.
- List and explain the categories of nonverbal communication.
- Realize that every culture has its own body language.
- Understand the role of nonverbal communication as it relates to business.

I am a recent hire in an accounting firm. There are two accountants assigned to working in a room about twelve feet square. The desks are arranged facing each other in the center of the room. This means that every time I look up, I am directly facing the other worker, only separated by the width of the two desks. She is a very nice person, but each time we make eye contact, she starts to talk about her husband and children and other employees. She has been very helpful in aiding me to learn about the job and the company, but I'm not getting my work done because of all the extraneous "talk time." I wish there were a way to discourage the talking without hurting her feelings. I wonder if repositioning the desks would help?

In the field of business we are constantly communicating both verbally and nonverbally. Verbal communication consists of the words we use; **nonverbal communication** is all message sending and receiving not manifested by words, spoken or written. "Nonverbal communication involves all those nonverbal stimuli in a communication setting that are generated by both the source and his or her use of the environment and that have potential message value for the source or receiver."[1] "Our clothes, jewelry, facial expressions, the hundreds of movements we can make; where and how we touch people; our gaze and eye contact; vocal behaviors such as laughter; and our use of time, space, and silence are just some of the behaviors we engage in that serve as messages."[2]

"Individuals are not aware of most of their own nonverbal behavior, which is enacted mindlessly, spontaneously, and unconsciously."[3] You are communicating nonverbally even though you may not be totally aware of the nonverbal messages you are sending and receiving. In contrast to verbal dialogue, however, there is no dictionary for understanding the rules.

One expert in the field hypothesized that "more than two-thirds of oral communication is actually nonverbal or communication dominated by the visual clues."[4] Still the experts suggest that, statistically, 35 percent of the social meaning of a message is carried verbally, while more than 65 percent is conveyed nonverbally.[5]

Why, then, are many people unaware of the impact of nonverbal communication? "Most people are unaccustomed to paying attention to their bodies when speaking, and they will frequently send out a huge array of neutral or flatly contradictory signals."[6] In addition, much nonverbal communication is beyond our level of actual awareness, both as senders and receivers. For example, how aware are you of what your hands are doing while you speak, or the position of your body, or the way you are walking? Do you really pay attention to the exact pitch or volume of your voice, or where your eyes are looking? Individuals may be very selective about the words they speak, but scarcely think about what they are doing with their bodies. Yet, each person is as responsible for his or her nonverbal actions as for the words used.

Actions speak louder than words, and nowhere is this more evident than in the way nonverbal communication can make or break a negotiation or business transaction. It's generally recognized that people who know how to read and use body language are more effective than those who do not.

Recently, the study of nonverbal communication not only has been recognized but has become very important in business and industry. "Companies such as IBM and AT&T are teaching their salespeople, negotiators and managers to make judgments based on nonverbal communication."[7]

The interest in nonverbal communication is a response to several widespread trends. One is the increasing diversity of the workplace. Men and women, including people from different countries and cultures, may use the

---

Test Yourself on Nonverbal Communication

Here is a quiz, based on solid research, that will test your knowledge of nonverbal communication. Just answer "true" or "false."

1. *Women are more sensitive to nonverbal cues—especially facial cues—and they transmit more accurate nonverbal cues than others.*

2. *When contradictory messages are sent through both verbal and nonverbal channels, most adults see the nonverbal message as more accurate.*

3. *People with low self-esteem use more eye contact when receiving negative messages than when receiving positive ones, while those with high self-esteem do just the opposite in each case.*

4. *When people are conjuring up a lie their pupils tend to become smaller. However, when they tell the lie, their pupils tend to dilate.*

5. *The three nonverbal cues an interviewer remembers most about a job applicant are gestures, posture, and handshake.*

Answers: *1. true, 2. true, 3. true, 4. true, 5. false—interviewers remember eye contact, appearance, and facial expressions.*

Source: NVC: Nonverbal Communication Studies and Applications, by Mark L. Hickson III and Don W. Stacks, Wm. C. Brown Communications Inc., 2460 Kerper Blvd., Dubuque, IA 52001.

---

same gestures to mean different things. For example, when a woman nods her head up and down it usually means, "Continue" or "Go on, I'm listening." On the other hand, a man making the same gesture is likely saying, "I agree." Same nonverbal gesture, different meaning.[8] Globalization is another impetus. People from different cultures are often confused by each other's nonverbal communication.

Sources of Nonverbal Communication

Neurolinguistic programming is an "attempt to codify and synthesize the insights of linguistics, body language, and cybernetics (the study of communication systems)."[9] The results of neurolinguistic studies have shown that we acquire our nonverbal communication patterns from hereditary and environmental influences.

Hereditarily, we respond to and communicate in various situations with such physical responses as eye blinks, facial expressions, and body tightening. A pebble hits the window as you are driving; you duck. A loud sound is heard; you may tighten up your body. Your boss says something that irritates or embarrasses you; your teeth may clench or you immediately look down at the floor. These are all examples of inherited neurological reactions. Your body performs certain impulsive acts in order to convey messages to you.

People learn body language "the same way they learn spoken language— by observing and imitating people around them as they're growing up."[10] An individual's ethnic background, social class, and lifestyle all affect communication, both verbally and nonverbally. Regional, class, and ethnic patterns of body behavior are learned in childhood and persist throughout life. All people, therefore, do not learn the same body language clues. Just as with verbal communication, differences in interpretation of nonverbal language may result from differences in background. These differences can lead to communicative problems in coding and decoding messages.

Importance of Nonverbal Communication in Business

Very few of us realize how much we depend on nonverbal clues in our everyday life as well as in our business contacts. "Nonverbal communication signals to members of our own group what kind of person we are, how we feel about others, how we'll fit into and work with a group, whether we're assured or anxious, the degree to which we feel comfortable with the standards of our own culture, as well as deeply significant feelings about the self, including the state of our own psyche."[11] We are what we communicate. Because much of it is beyond our level of awareness, what we communicate nonverbally often signals our real self, what we really think and feel, and what we do or don't want from others.

In the world of business we are responsible for persuading, instructing, and working with others. These functions are accomplished through effectively understanding and using the best possible means of verbal and nonverbal communication.

Often it does not take long to accept or reject a person and what he or she says. Much positive or negative reaction is based on such nonverbal influences as clothing, physical appearance, gesture patterns, use of space, facial expressions, and vocal animation. Because within the business environment such factors as being hired, retaining a job, fulfilling a job description, and achieving promotions result from communication skills, learning to read and use nonverbal as well as verbal signs is of great importance to the present or prospective business practitioner.

Verbal-Nonverbal Relationships

The relationship between verbal and nonverbal communication exists on many levels.[12] Nonverbal communication can substitute for, complement, regulate, and conflict with verbal communication.

SUBSTITUTING RELATIONSHIP OF NONVERBAL TO VERBAL

Nonverbal language can take the place of verbal messages, and thus create a substituting relationship. With facial and body expressions, you can nod agreement or disagreement, point to an individual and gesture for that person to leave, or show disgust without sending a single verbal message.

COMPLEMENTING RELATIONSHIP OF NONVERBAL TO VERBAL

Nonverbal and verbal messages may serve in a complementing relationship. As you give someone verbal directions, you can accompany each verbal signal with a gesture. You say, "Stand up," as your hand moves upward, and continue with "Go down the hall; turn left. It's the second office on your right," as you point toward the door, gesture to the left and then to the right.

REGULATING RELATIONSHIP OF NONVERBAL TO VERBAL

Nonverbal communication can also indicate some control over the verbal, thus creating a regulating relationship. Your boss might say, "Sit down," while she points to a straightback chair that is in front of you, while she goes behind the desk to a larger swivel chair that suggests status. Her desk creates a barrier between you, which sets the tone of formality for the conversation you are about to have.

CONFLICTING RELATIONSHIP OF NONVERBAL TO VERBAL

One of the most important relationships between verbal and nonverbal language occurs when there is a conflicting relationship between the two. There are times when what a person says with her or his body makes a lie out of what she or he is saying.

When verbal and nonverbal behavior conflict, the nonverbal is probably the more accurate. Through the socializing process, we have learned to manipulate words. Because the nonverbal gestures and behaviors tend to be closer to our real emotional level of feelings, we often have difficulty controlling them. It is difficult to stop your face from flushing when you are embarrassed, or your voice from quivering when you are nervous or increasing in pitch as you become angry. You may say, "I'm interested," but tapping your fingers and looking away from the sales representative often signals the real message.

Novice students of nonverbal communication tend to read too much into a basic cue such as crossed arms. Multiple cues generally provide a more accurate message. For instance, crossed arms, plus crossed legs, plus lack of eye contact, plus a set jaw, are more convincing proof of a closed mind than one gesture alone.[13] In attempting to assign meaning to nonverbal signs, remember that, as with verbal symbols, the meaning is in the communicator and not in the sign itself. Be aware also that an isolated sign may be meaningless and that the source of the sign must be considered. Thus, looking at clusters and seeking congruency are important aspects of interpreting nonverbal communication.

Reading Nonverbal Communication

In reading nonverbal communication, it is imperative to be aware of clusters and congruency. **Clusters** are groups of gestures. When an individual becomes angry, for example, his arms might tighten across the chest, the body becomes stiff, the jaw sets, and the eyes narrow. Each of these gestures in and of itself may be meaningless; however, as they cluster together they have significance. In addition, it is essential to be aware of a person's past patterns in order to recognize when there has been a change in the individual. It is through **congruency** (consistency of past patterns to present actions) that we can tell the boss is having a bad day or that something is bothering a coworker. By taking into consideration the way an individual has acted in the past and comparing it with present patterns, we can attempt to read his or her nonverbal communication.

Not only must we be aware of clusters and congruency, but consideration also should be given to cultural differences that affect interpretations.

Categories of Nonverbal Communication

Nonverbal communication can best be described in terms of certain categories. These nonverbal categories are kinesics, vocal cues, proxemics, physical characteristics, artifacts, aesthetics, and chronemics.

KINESICS

Kinesics refers to body language, the physical action used by a communicator. Individuals express attitudes and emotions by the way they stand or sit. For example, a participant in a business conference who slouches in a chair may be communicating boredom or disinterest.

Movement

We communicate physically through movement, eye behavior, and facial expression. While talking you move your hands, your feet, or your head. Observe yourself and others during a conversation, a business meeting, or while speaking on the phone. You will probably note that you are gesturing or using your hands (pointing, waving, playing with a pen), or moving your feet or legs. It is interesting to note that "even people born blind move their hands when they talk, although they've never seen anyone do it."[14] When people listen they nod their heads, nod vigorously if they agree, smile when they are pleased, look skeptical by raising an eyebrow or pulling down the corners of the mouth when they have reservations about what is said. They shift positions or look at their watches if they want to end the conversation.[15] It is not at all uncommon for individuals to imitate the behavior of those who are in charge. Employees may unconsciously fall into step when walking with an employer or superior, cross their legs if the boss does, or even synchronize breathing with a supervisor.

Gestures

Four nonverbal gesture classifications have been defined by researchers: emblems, illustrators, affect displays, and regulators.[16]

Emblems Emblems are gestures that have a direct verbal translation or dictionary definition within a specific societal group. For example, extending the pointing finger upward means one. That same gesture, placed so that the finger touches the lips, means "shh" or be quiet. In many cultures, a horizontal nod of the head means yes, while a vertical nod of the head means no. On the floor of the New York Stock Exchange an entire series of emblems are used to identify transactions, directions, and costs.

　　Emblems vary according to cultures. In fact, the same emblem may vary in meaning according in different settings. For example, "in Northern America making a circle with one's thumb and index finger while extending the others is emblematic of the word 'ok'; in Japan and Korea it signifies money ('okane'); and among Arabs this gesture is usually accompanied by a baring of teeth, and together they signify extreme hostility."[17]

Nonverbal Communication in the Speaking Setting

While all nonverbal cues should be viewed in relation to other cues and no one cue means the same for all people at all times, some nonverbal cues can fairly consistently indicate the feelings and attitudes of listeners. Here are some common examples.

Listeners . . .	to express . . .
rub hands together; maintain good eye contact; keep hands visible; lean bodies forward; or rest their chins on the palms of their hands	willingness to listen.
smile frequently; unbutton jackets; maintain good eye contact; keep hands and fingers still; or uncross arms and legs	friendly feelings.
nod; smile; or touch someone's shoulder	approval.
stare; interrupt; or speak out of turn	disrespect.
clean their glasses; chew on pens or pencils; or pour a glass of water	procrastination.
cross arms across chest; cross legs	defensiveness.
"steeple" fingers; hold coat lapels; interrupt; sit with hands behind the head; point to another person with finger; or cross leg over arm of another chair	superiority.
rhythmically tap or move hands or feet; doodle	boredom.
raise head; shift posture so that they no longer stand facing the person spoken to; or stand up or gather personal belongings	interaction is finished.

Illustrators Illustrators are gestures that accompany speech and help enhance the words being spoken. Gestures are used to point, show spatial relationships, or draw an imaginary path. For example, a speaker might say, "The RAM upgrade was about the size of a quarter," while at the same time forming a circle with her thumb and forefinger, enclosing a circle about the size of a quarter.

Affect Displays Affect displays are facial configurations that show emotions such as happiness or sadness. Pouting, winking, or raising or lowering the eyelids and eyebrows are examples of affect displays. Posture, gait, and gestures, for example, also express emotion and thus are also a source of affect display. We often read a person's moods by watching affect displays.

Regulators Regulators are nonverbal acts that maintain and control the back-and-forth nature of speaking and listening between individuals. Regulators include head nods, body shifts, and eye movements. These actions encourage and discourage speakers to continue or stop interacting. In addition, regulators can encourage or discourage individuals from getting closer based on such factors as a person backing away as you come near, creating a barrier with crossed arms, or focusing elsewhere with a body turned sideways. Seating positions may indicate that you are open for conversation if you shift into an alert position with your eyes directed at the speaker, or show boredom if you slump in the chair. Finger tapping, foot bouncing, and staring off into space are other examples of regulators.

Eye Behavior

One of the most potent elements in body language is eye behavior. Because the eye is an extension of the brain, it reacts as no other part of the body. It has been ascertained that the pupil of the eye is an excellent indicator of how people respond to various situations. When a person is interested in something, the pupils will tend to dilate (get larger); if the response is a negative one, they will tend to contract (get smaller). The theory of **pupilometrics** purports that people can't control the response of their eyes; therefore, it is possible to detect whether or not a person is lying through a sophisticated use of the theory.[18]

An individual's eye behavior depends on his or her culture. Every group has its own patterns. Most Americans find a normal eye glance of three to ten seconds comfortable. An overlong look—a stare—may signal affection, hostility, disrespect, a threat, or an insult. For Koreans, direct eye contact among unequals connotes competition, constituting an inappropriate form of behavior. In Nigeria, and much of Africa, people often choose not to maintain eye contact while they are listening to another person. The Chinese, Indonesians, and many Latin Americans will lower their eyes as a sign of defense, believing that too much eye contact is a sign of bad manners. Arabs, on the other hand, look directly into the eyes of their communication partner, and do so for long periods.[19]

A culture's male-female relationships also determine customs of eye contact and gaze. In many Asian and Arab cultures, it is considered taboo for women to look straight into men's eyes. Most men, therefore, will not stare directly at women. However, in France and Italy men stare at women in public. In America, prolonged stares of men at men is often a part of the homosexual culture and is perceived as a signal of interest. Heterosexual males in American society tend to participate in extended gazes only when they are combatants and are trying to stare each other down. The Native American Navajo tribe dislikes unbroken eye contact so strongly that they have incorporated it into their creation myth.[20] "Differences in use of eye contact also characterize communication between African Americans and white Americans. When speaking, African Americans use much more continuous eye contact then do whites, yet the reverse is true when listening. Whites make more continuous eye contact when they are listening than do African Americans."[21]

In business or other situations, a person's eye contact can be improved by following three basic rules:[22]

1. To establish a closer relationship with a business or social acquaintance, hold his or her gaze as long as possible as you meet, say hello, and pass.
2. To end a business or social conversation, stop looking at the other person, especially if you are the dominant one in the relationship.
3. If you want to create a warm business or social relationship with a person of the opposite sex, but are not interested sexually, limit the amount of time you look into that person's eyes while listening or talking.

The effectiveness of these behaviors depends on your ability to assimilate them into your daily patterns so that they become a natural part of your communicative repertoire. Furthermore, you can use them with more assurance if the other person is from the same cultural background.

Facial Expression

Some nonverbal communication specialists believe that the face is the most expressive channel of nonverbal communication.[23] Because we subconsciously express our inner feelings through involuntary facial movements, our face, along with vocal tone, may well be the key to understanding the emotional content of a message. Some facial expressions appear to be universal. Worldwide, a smile means happiness, and facial expressions are similar for the emotions of anger, fear, surprise, contempt, and sadness.

If the face is so expressive, why do we often fail to pick up the clues? A major problem arises because most of the time people do not closely watch each other's faces. Often, we are so concerned with the other's words, or with what we are saying, that we fail to notice what others are doing.

Touch

Touch[24] is a form of intimate behavior that includes holding and caressing.[25] Many touching patterns are based on background. Touching comes naturally to many people; for others it is difficult to give or receive hugs. If you came from an environment where people hugged each other freely, touched each other while speaking, and frequently put arms around each other, then you probably give and receive touches easily. If your family's practice was more "hands off," then odds are you feel uncomfortable touching or being touched. Of all the senses, only touch has the power to communicate depth, form, texture, and warmth. Although it is the simplest and most direct way of relating, studies show that even the most casual touch can have profound emotional effects.[26]

In business situations, the right touch can make a big difference. A simple pat on the back or shoulder can show approval, give reassurance, or emphasize a point. Touch can help diffuse tense work situations by conveying more understanding than words can accomplish. Used incorrectly, however, touch can be perceived as an invasion of privacy, a sexual come-on, or a reminder of superiority. There are some who believe that all touching has sexual overtones and is part of power plays. To touch or not to touch becomes a delicate situation in business. In general, the best policy in the workplace is "Don't touch," for the potential for misunderstanding is too great. In a business office, any contact that suggests personal, romantic, or even friendly involvement should be avoided.

In reality, some touching is inevitable in every workplace. At times of happiness, such as when someone gets a promotion, there may be a natural tendency to touch. When meeting new employees or greeting associates in the workplace, a firm handshake is still expected. However, increased sensitivity to power and control, and a rise in sexual harassment lawsuits, suggest that in a business context you might be well advised to moderate tendencies you might have to touch others. Aside from the sexual or power overtones, some people are raised in cultures that consider touching private communication. Many Americans, as well as those from other parts of the world, consider touch a private matter and find touching in any environment highly uncomfortable. Caution is especially important in jobs where the business protocol is conservative and formal. Although hugging and kissing are acceptable in artistic and show business environments, for example, major corporate offices are not usually the place for informality.

Profile: Richard Urban, award-winning real estate agent, Pardoe Realty, Washington, DC.

What is the role of nonverbal communication in real estate sales?

When you are working with customers, there are two nonverbal elements that a good salesperson is aware of: clients' facial expressions and the amount of time they spend in each room and at the property, in general. In facial expression, there is a certain smile that they get that indicates that their internal buttons have been turned on. Sometimes they try to hide it, but it is impossible to fake. Their pleasure or lack of pleasure shines through. As for time, the longer they spend in a house, the more they like it. If they rush through, the message is, "I don't like this at all." If they are interested in a property, they will tend to linger and stare at certain features.

What are the enticements that help sell a residence?

There are three nonverbal enticements: light, pedestrian flow, vistas.

Light: Windows, sunlight, views, and vistas make for positive energy. People like to feel positive in their environments.

Pedestrian flow: Customers look for easy open flow, circles of movement, and want few barriers so they can have an ease of navigation from place to place.

Vistas: People like to look out into space. They like to see nature such as trees, light, and sky.

Reading Kinesics

If movement, eye behavior, facial expression, and vocal cues are so central to communication, why do many of us miss the messages being sent by others? Here are some possible reasons:[27]

1. You don't look. We often are so involved in what we have to say, or in listening to the words of others, that we don't pay much attention to what others are doing.
2. It takes training to read the signs. With little or no understanding of the channels and basic meanings of nonverbal signs, you may find that you simply do not understand the message a person is sending.
3. Different people feel emotions differently and for varying amounts of time. Each of us has different environments and heredity; therefore, we may respond differently to the same stimuli. Some people are quick to show emotion; others build to the display of feelings slowly. We tend to read others' actions based on our personal experiences and reactions. Once we realize that looking for congruency is important, we often are better able to key in on the meanings of others.

4. People try to hide certain emotions or change them. Have you ever found yourself in a situation where you didn't want someone else to know how you really felt? Sometimes we want to mask our emotions from others so they can't tell what we feel. If the other person is not really alert to our actions, he or she may miss the slight cues we give.
5. We don't care. Our world is very complex. Many of us are so self-centered that we don't really pay much attention to what others are doing or saying. Unless we believe that it will affect us, we may not make the effort to communicate fully.
6. It takes time, effort, concentration, knowledge, and understanding to break the communication code, and you may be unable to combine all of these in order to figure out what is being communicated. In addition, because many kinesic signs are not clearly defined, the receiver may simply be unable to read them.

VOCAL CUES

Vocal cues encompass paralanguage, hesitations, pauses, laughter, and the way these affect our verbal signs as well as what they represent in and of themselves.

Paralanguage

Paralanguage, sometimes called **vocalics,** refers to all the vocal sounds except the word itself.[28] The vocal quality communicates nonverbally to the listening ear, conveying vocal stridency, harshness, and even vocal tension. The quality of the voice provides clues as to the emotional state of the speaker. These perceptions of feelings can affect the flow of communication. An employee who has a tense vocal quality, for instance, may be perceived as a worker under pressure who is having difficulty handling the workload.

Hesitations, Pauses, Laughter

Hesitations, pauses, and laughter also affect a message. People who are unsure of themselves may stammer, stop, or frequently pause within a sentence. They also may use nonwords and meaningless phrases to fill in these voids. Words and phrases such as "etcetera," "you know," and "and stuff like that" are typical of meaningless vocalized pauses that indicate a lack of idea development. They are almost always accompanied by body shifts, facial flushes, breaking of eye contact, and looking at the floor or ceiling.

Laughter can show enjoyment, but inappropriate laughter can indicate anxiety or awkwardness about the situation. A person trying to hide discomfort may giggle at the wrong time and when the situation is not really funny. Much like a flushed face, laughter often indicates uneasiness.

PROXEMICS

Another nonverbal category is **proxemics,** how people use the dimensions of space and environment. Each of us has an invisible bubble of space around us, which contracts and expands based on cultural background, emotional state, and the activity we are performing. In addition, such dimensions as demographic features (sex and race), relations between people, the interaction setting, the topic or subject matter under discussion, physical impairments of the communicators, and heat and humidity affect our perceptions and use of space.

Personal Space

In U.S. culture, each person's bubble of personal space seems to contract and expand around four main zones.[29]

Intimate zone refers to a space from direct physical contact to a distance of eighteen inches. We allow close friends, certain family members, or those with whom we are in love within the intimate zone. We may allow them to touch us—the highest level of personal intimacy. A spouse or lover may be allowed to enter our personal space. On the other hand, a boss who leans over your shoulder while you are trying to write a report, or puts a hand on your shoulder while talking to you, will probably cause you to feel uncomfortable and make you pull away. The boss has invaded your intimate space while not being on intimate terms with you and has made you uncomfortable.

Personal zone is the space most Americans feel comfortable with when they are with individuals whom they know but with whom they do not have intimate relationships. We prefer this distance when talking to others. Officially, the zone is one-and-a-half to four feet. Persons who get closer than that will usually cause you to pull back unless your relationship with them is intimate. If this doesn't work you will probably attempt to place some barrier between you and the other person, such as a chair or a desk. You might cross your arms in front of you, or, if you are holding an attaché case, notebook, or purse, you might put that in front of your body to shield yourself. If you feel uncomfortable or find yourself backing away from someone, do a quick reading to see if the person is too close. If so, you might alert the person to the fact that she or he is invading your territory. In a business setting, invasion of territory often occurs in an unconscious effort to get close to and share ideas and information with the other person. Some individuals do not realize that this causes discomfort in others.

Social zone is a distance of four to twelve feet. This space is reserved for strangers or those with whom you don't have an intimate or personal relationship. You employ this area during business transactions or exchanges, for example, with a sales clerk or a new client.

Public zone is a distance of more than twelve feet. When you give speeches or present reports you are generally in the public zone. You keep distances from those with whom you have no relationship at all. As you develop a relationship you allow the person to get closer.

You can often tell if your relationship with a person has changed by how close you allow him or her to get to you. If a fellow employee moves into your personal space and you do not feel uncomfortable, that individual may have gained the stature of personal relationship. If you allow someone to touch you or get very close, it may indicate that you have developed an intimate relationship with that person. However, if you no longer want to be very close to a person who has been allowed to invade your intimate zone in the past, it may indicate that your feelings for that person have changed—based either on a short-term action (having an argument, being insulted by what was said), or on long-term relationships (being fired).

When a person is angry or under stress, his or her bubble of space may expand, causing the need for more space. Notice how, if you are at work and you have to get some job done in a short period of time, you don't want anyone near you. If a fellow employee irritates you, you might move away quickly, get out of his or her territory, or demand that the person leave your work area. Your need for more room increases as you feel boxed-in, emotionally or physically.

As with the interpretations of other nonverbal cues, Americans must recognize that these dimensions of personal space are characteristic of cultural space in the United States. Businesspersons conducting business in other countries often report on totally different uses of space by the people with whom they come in contact.

Privacy Space

People have privacy space needs as well as personal space needs. If people are denied privacy, they feel deprived of something that is very basic to them. "A person's privacy is a sense of himself, and any business that doesn't recognize the need for employees to have that identity is making a mistake that can cost millions in lost productivity."[30] "People who don't feel that they have any say in their space are reduced to childlike status. Productivity fails. It bothers workers. Whether they're conscious of it or not, they need a space where they can establish their separateness."[31] In most business settings, special efforts are made to ensure privacy space for those in management positions; however, often little effort is made to protect the privacy of the workers. In the office the workers usually have little control over about where they sit, with whom they sit, or with whom they must converse. In many cases no provision is even made for a personal space as small as a desk drawer or a locker.

If you do have a specified space, giving it some definition of individuality is important to establish a feeling of privacy. Personalizing the space with photos, postcards, prints, or plants says that the space is yours.

Spatial Arrangements in Business

While many workers have little control over the physical space in which they work, it is important to realize that spatial factors, such as how the furniture is arranged, can affect efficiency and operation for an office or meeting. Using a rectangular table, for instance, with the group leader at the head of the table will usually lead to a much more formal atmosphere and less interaction among people than if they are seated around a circular table.

Workers' desks that face each other (Figure 4.1) will lead to much more worker interaction than a side-by-side arrangement (Figure 4.2), because the individuals will find it easier to talk to each other head-on than if they have to turn toward each other each time they wish to converse. Placing the workers with their backs to each other (Figure 4.3) will lead to even less communication. But productivity might increase in this case if there is a spatial distance between the workers that will necessitate their shouting, or turning completely around, in order to converse.

FIGURE 4.1
Face-to-Face Desk Arrangement

FIGURE 4.2
Side-by-Side Desk Arrangement

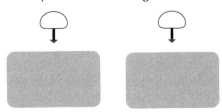

FIGURE 4.3
Back-to-Back Desk Arrangement

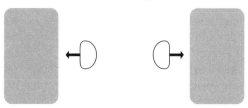

In planning an office, the furniture arrangement should be considered. In addition, placement of plants, lamps, and large decorative objects can result in encouraging or discouraging interactions. If they block the views of employees from each other, they will discourage interaction. If they do not block, then interaction is encouraged because they communicate warmth and personality. Consider the purpose. If you are young and in a position that requires giving orders to more mature staffers, you might want a formal office decor in order to establish your authority. If you want to increase the appearance of openness and equality with your coworkers you might choose a more open furniture arrangement with chairs facing each other, or place your desk against a wall so that when you speak to others you are facing them without a barrier between you and the others as your communicate.

PHYSICAL CHARACTERISTICS

Physical characteristics, such as physique, general attractiveness, body and breath odors, height, weight, and hair and skin color communicate information about an individual. Whether we like it or not, or are aware of it or not, such factors as outer beauty and physical attractiveness/unattractiveness play an influential role in determining responses for a broad range of communicative encounters.[32]

A study of college graduates revealed that men 6 feet 2 inches tall or taller received starting salaries 12.4 percent higher than equally qualified men who stood 6 feet or less.[33] Although short women may be positively looked upon as being "petite," they are not immune from prejudice in the job market. "Those women 5 feet 3 inches or less earn measurably less than their taller female classmates."[34] "Personnel managers, given equally qualified applicants, tend to hire the taller ones first."[35]

The conclusion that can be reached from the studies concerning physical characteristics and their effects on hiring and salary is that often people are hired by image, that is, because of looks rather than ability. If this is true, what can individuals do to counteract the prejudice?[36] (1) Precede face-to-face meetings with a variety of introductory techniques, such as telephone calls, letters, and having a mutual acquaintance talk about you to the employer. All of this should help form a first impression that is not based on how you look. If a strong enough impression is formed, how you look matters little. (2) When introductory techniques cannot be used, work to create a good impression.[37] Such factors as proper selection of clothing, being well prepared, and being well qualified can certainly help.

ARTIFACTS

Artifacts refers to the clothing that a person wears, and also to makeup, eyeglasses, and beauty aids, all of which convey messages. Clothing is an extension of personality. A person's choice of clothing reveals information about that person's character.

When you step into a room, even though no one in the room knows you or has seen you before, the others will make many decisions about you based solely on your appearance. Think about your own experiences. What was your first impression of your instructor? If you have gone for a job interview, how did you perceive the person interviewing you? How many of these conclusions were based on the interviewer's clothing and grooming patterns?

Clothing

The way you dress and the image you present can contribute to success or failure in business. Clothing is so important for businesspeople that top-level businesspeople and some individuals seeking corporate positions hire "image consultants" to aid them in picking out their clothing. A leading image consultant, who has made a career of telling business executives (male and female) how to dress, keys in on which colors to choose, styles to select, and image to present. His premise is that if you want to be the president of the corporation, then you must dress like the president of the corporation.[38] "Companies pay as much as $2,000 a day to teach grooming techniques to employees."[39]

Clothing is so important in industry that 65 to 75 percent of the companies in the United States have a dress code in order to ensure that the "corporate image" is kept intact.[40] It's important to study the industry you're in, its image, and the image of your company in making clothing selections.[41] Many times new employees believe that they can change the image of the company that has hired them. Such attempts have been made, but few have worked. Businesses and industry tend to be conservative and slow to change. "What's acceptable in business will not be influenced from the bottom."[42]

What is considered acceptable attire in the business world? At present, the

How Casual?

If your organization allows a casual day or casual dress, be sure not to err in the direction of being "too casual."

Casual doesn't mean a sweatshirt and torn jeans. It also doesn't mean "sloppy."

See if there's an official policy on the subject and follow it. If not, check with some managers to get their interpretation of what's acceptable.

When in doubt, dress more conservatively rather than too casually.

Source: 501(c)(3) Monthly Letter, P.O. Box 192, Atlantic, IA 50022.

man who wants to package himself for success in a business career should stick to traditional clothing. Historically, "the business-suit class arose in 19th-century Europe, after the industrial revolution took hold as a professional and managerial costume idealizing sedentary power."[43] That image still holds. In general, men should wear suits (gray or navy), simple, tasteful jewelry, white shirts with straight or button-down collars, wing-tipped black or dark brown laced shoes, over-the-calf socks (preferably black), ties should touch the belt buckle, and shirt sleeves should remain buttoned.[44] "A double-breasted suit transmits more authority than a single-breasted suit."[45]

The generally recommended women's business uniform consists of a tailored skirted suit and complementary blouse or conservatively cut dress. The blouse should be basic and simply cut. Wardrobe consultants advise that a woman at any level who wants to move up should not wear a sweater or vest without a jacket. Shoes should be plain pumps, in a dark color (blue, black, deep brown, or gray), with closed toe and $1\frac{1}{2}$-inch heel. Research shows that the hairstyle is one area where a businesswoman has some leeway. Hair length should be medium or shoulder length; hair should lie neatly, and not be excessively curly or wavy. Jewelry (except very cheap pieces) is acceptable but less is better.[46] While there is no question that women have a greater range of colors to choose from than men, care should be taken to select those within a fairly conservative palette.

In spite of the heavy emphasis on corporate clothing, there have been some major changes in its definition. Retailers report that sales of men's suits have declined in recent years. They credit the change of attitude toward the "corporate look" as the reason. Casual dress in the workplace, a trend that bubbled up from California's Silicon Valley, is part of the dress-down trend in some companies. These organizations allow, or even encourage, employees to wear jeans and other casual clothing.[47] Companies such as Alcoa, Southwest Airlines, Coca-Cola, Progressive Insurance, and American Express have all gone to a relaxed atmosphere.[48] A survey indicates that 74 percent of employers allow casual dress, with dress-down Fridays the most popular policy.[49]

The trend toward more casual clothing in the workplace has brought about changes in clothing marketing. Clothing makers are targeting employers in an aggressive bid to cash in on casual dress policies. Wolverine World Wide, makers of Hush Puppies shoes, sends to major companies videos and guides to dressing down in the workplace. Levi Strauss, maker of Dockers pants, has distributed 42,000 copies of A Guide to Casual Businesswear to Human Resource managers.[50]

Casual clothing does not appear to be a trend that will quickly go away. A semiotician, who studies linguistic and other signs and symbols, predicts, "the only types of offices that will be viable are those that are going to be less formal and hierarchic—those that allow more creativity in order to get the job done. That means getting rid of the rigid, fixed rules like dress codes."[51] In addition, another factor has made casual dress popular with management. "Casual dress policies can be offered as a benefit in an era when so many other benefits are being trimmed."[52]

Another new trend is workplace uniforms. They are seen not only at fast food restaurants, but also on bank officers, travel agents, and runners at the stock exchange. The trend started with Century 21 gold-blazered real estate agents, and it has expanded.[53]

Be aware, however, that although some companies have gone to casualness, this is not the general rule. Many companies, especially banks and law firms, discourage the casual look because it might suggest that their employees lack dignity. This is especially true of companies dealing in foreign markets where the business suit is still very much the corporate garb.[54]

When it comes to clothing for job interviews, casual is definitely not in. Though loafers and sweaters are replacing pumps and pin stripes in the corporate wardrobe, "the interview outfit has changed little during the last decade."[55] A director of placement states, "We're telling students to err on the side of conservatism. For women a dark blue suit, cream-colored shirts, hems on skirts should be at the knees. For men, a dark blue suit, white shirt and red tie is the way to go. In a sense, a job interview is like any other ceremony that requires a costume. The rule still holds that you want to dress two levels above the job you are interviewing for. It shows a courtesy, that you think the people who are interviewing you are important and that you are not just running across the street for a pack of gum."[56] In addition, for recent college grads, "Grown-up clothes also help young candidates look the part."

Cosmetics, Jewelry, and Other Artifacts

Other artifacts that can convey information are cosmetics, badges, tattoos, and jewelry. We can reach conclusions about an individual based on how that person uses lipstick, eye shadow, eyeliner, and other makeup, for example. In general, the business environment demands subtle use of cosmetics. As with makeup, conservative jewelry that does not hinder the work process is recommended. Large earrings can interfere with telephoning. Cuff links that get caught on instruments, bracelets that make noise and get in the way, and rings that snag fabrics are negative artifact factors. Wearing sunglasses with dark lenses or tinted-lens glasses effectively cuts off visual contact and may cause frustration on the part of the fellow workers who can't see your eyes and, therefore, have difficulty reading your moods and eye shifts.

Though the exact role of clothing and other artifacts is still unknown, we do know that they communicate messages about us and influence others' responses to us.

AESTHETICS

Aesthetics factors such as music, light, and color have an effect on us. Our moods are altered by soft and slow music and the beat of the music, the brightness or dullness of the lighting, and intensity or calmness of colors.

Behavioral kinesiology (BK) is a scientific field based on the notion that every major muscle of the body relates to an organ. All the organs in our body are affected by a proportion of the music and other aesthetics that we are exposed to daily.[57] In testing over 20,000 records, researchers have discovered that rock music has a subliminal "stopped" quality that causes the listener subconsciously to come to a halt at the end of each measure. This has a weakening effect on the body. This is only one of the many conclusions that suggests that businesses must consider carefully the music, the lighting, and the colors they select for the office and retail environment.

Music

While walking through a supermarket, you subconsciously pace yourself in time to the music being played. During the day the music often has a slow, wandering sound, while near closing time the beat speeds up and you march right out of the store. Office environments can also be altered by the type of music played.

The inclusion of music in the work environment has received endorsement by unions as well as general researchers: "Music is a friend of labor for it lightens the task by refreshing the nerves and spirit of workers."[58] Music can serve as an environmental aid because it has the ability to soothe emotions and give a psychological lift to employees. The use of background music helps people cope with routine tasks, helps keep them alert in the job and wary of safety hazards, and reduces fatigue.

Specifically, the findings regarding music are:[59]

1. Performance was significantly better when music was used as a background rather than motor noise or silence.
2. Visual tasks were performed better when radio broadcasts were piped into work areas than when people worked in silence.
3. There was an 18 percent improvement in mental tasks and a 17 percent improvement in assembly tasks when music was used in the background.
4. Music has a significant effect on muscular activity, which increases or diminishes according to the music being played.
5. Music reduces the number of errors in routine office work up to as much as 37 percent.

6. In a routine office work situation, productivity increased 8 percent and late attendance dropped by 36 percent after the introduction of a planned background music program.

Lighting

People are affected by the amount of light in their environment. Bright lights stimulate, low-level lights soothe, colored lights create moods, and constantly changing lights (such as at discos and other places of entertainment) create psychological excitement. In businesses, careful thought should be given to lighting, both natural and artificial (lighting fixtures and lamps). Designers and architects like to use skylights and extensive windows in public buildings and offices. Natural lighting is recognized as a valuable part of the work environment.

One of the most important environmental factors is natural light. If employees work in a natural environment or have access to a natural environment, they are stimulated and feel more positive. Anything that gives employees an emotional lift, such as natural light, is important in a business. Proper light can bring about greater productivity, better work quality, reduced fatigue and eyestrain, and increased morale. Special consideration should be given to task lighting in business environments. Studies show that all areas of an office need not have identical illumination. Only work areas requiring high light quality should be so illuminated. Other areas should be lit according to their needs.[55]

Business experts now recommend that staff members who spend most of their time in the office should be given prime views with natural light. In turn, supervisors and managers who spend less time in their offices should be given side offices without views and windows.[60] Those who spend a great deal of time looking at the computer screen derive great benefit from looking out a window and focusing on distant objects, thereby reducing eyestrain. Putting workers' needs above the special privileges given to executives breaks down the traditional concept in American business of the power associated with the number and size of windows in an office. However, it probably is in the best interest of the organization to rethink such traditional views based on the research concerning the effects of lighting in the workplace.

Color

Do you feel differently when you sit in a room that is predominantly red than you do in a room that is light blue? Is there meaning to the phrases "red hot," "feeling blue," and "green with envy"? Researchers in the field of color psychology believe that colors do make moods. While there are different cultural attitudes toward color, it is a significant and an influential element in personality.[61] Some basic principles about colors are: colors have symbolic meaning, and colors selected for business environments have an effect on the workers.

The colors that surround us induce feelings within us; they carry specific messages. The colors red and orange are associated with excitement, stimulation, and aggression; blue and green are associated with calm, security, and peace; black, brown, and gray suggest melancholy, sadness, and depression; yellow can stimulate cheer, gaiety, and fun; and purple is associated with dignity, royalty, and sadness. Pleasant hues have been rank-ordered by preference: blue, green, purple, red, and yellow.[62] The most arousing color is red, followed by orange, yellow, violet, blue, and green.[63]

Early research revealed certain colors can be classified as "beautiful" and "ugly." Blue, yellow, yellow-green, and orange were identified by test subjects as beautiful colors, while white, black, and brown were considered ugly.[64] What are the implications of this classification? Children tested in "beautifully" colored rooms scored higher on tests than children in "ugly" colored rooms.[65] This can be applied to the work environment by assuming that individuals in "beautifully" colored environments will tend to do better work than those in "ugly" environments.

The knowledge that red makes one nervous[66] suggests that offices and other workstations should not be predominantly red. Several years ago when brightly colored red and electric blue typewriters were produced by IBM, office designers picked up the trend and decorated offices in these hues, resulting in higher levels of stress on the part of workers. Most electrical equipment is presently being produced in calming colors, gray or buff tones.

Office colors for walls, floor coverings, draperies, and furniture must be chosen carefully as these are the surroundings in which workers spend their time. If that surrounding causes stress, the result will be less productive time use than if the individual is comfortable in the work area. Walls, ceilings, and reflective surfaces should be light, soft colors; floors and carpets may be darker. Moods are created by the colors chosen. Blue, green, and violet are associated with serenity or coolness and can help create a calm, relaxed mood. Warm colors such as red, orange, or yellow can suggest cheerful and friendly atmospheres, if that is what is desired.[67]

Large work areas can be made to look smaller by breaking them into different colors. This allows workers to identify with their own environment, thus ensuring security and a sense of personal space.

"A time interval spent before a warm color is perceived as shorter than that spent before a cool color." This finding suggests that if employees are surrounded by warm colors (pink, yellow, mellow blue), time will pass more quickly for them. Knowing that large size often frightens some people, painting large pieces of machinery the same as the background colors of the environment will make the machinery appear less obvious and therefore less threatening.

CHRONEMICS

Chronemics, the use of time, is another important communicator. Remember, actual clock time varies among individuals, as does their biological clock time. Some people are **hyperkinetic**—they can't sit still, their bodies are always in action, they operate on fast time. Others are **hypokinetic**—their bodies operate slowly, they operate on slow time, they seem to take forever.

In most instances, in the United States to be "on time" usually means five minutes early. Other cultures often do not adhere to this time pattern. In Switzerland, as the saying goes, you can set your watch by the trains. The Swiss demand and expect exact promptness. In Japan, to be on time usually means to be early to show respect for your host. In Mexico and many South American countries people tend to be rather lax, by U.S. standards, in their promptness.

The theory of action chains may explain why people of different cultures and racial and ethnic backgrounds have difficulty dealing with each other's use of time. "An **action chain** is a behavioral sequence with two or more participating organisms, in which there are standard steps for reaching a goal. If you leave out one of the steps, the chain is broken, and you have to start all over again."[68] Applying this theory to time use suggests that different perceptions of time use could well break the chain of operation. This difference is important in the business environment. If a personnel manager expects a prospective employee to arrive on time (by American time standards), and the individual arrives late, then the flow of steps leading to possible hiring may be broken. Or if a businessperson from Mexico arrives late for an appointment with a Japanese businessperson, the flow of events may also be halted. American businesspeople have to learn, for example, when dealing with people from Arab cultures in the Mediterranean, that they are operating in a slow action chain culture. "In the Middle East, if you aren't willing to take the time to sit down and have coffee with people, you have a problem. You must learn to wait and not be too eager to talk business."[69] "When negotiating with the Japanese, Americans like to get right down to business. They were socialized to believe that 'time is money.' They can accept about 15 minutes of small talk about the weather, their trip, and baseball, but more than that becomes unreasonable. The Japanese, on the other hand, want to get to know their business counterparts. They feel that the best way to do this is to have long conversations with Americans about a wide variety of topics."[70]

Culture and Nonverbal Communication

Every culture has its own body language, and children absorb its nuances along with spoken language as they grow up.[71] Because of cultural differences, a person's sex, ethnic background, social class, and personal style all influence body language. The person who is truly bilingual (speaks more than one language fluently) is also bilingual in body language.

Whenever there is a great cultural distance between two people, problems are bound to arise from the differences in behavior and expectations. People of Northern European heritage—English, Scandinavians, Germans, Swiss—tend to avoid personal contact and need more space around themselves. They also tend to show less outward emotion. Those whose heritage is Italian, French, Spanish, Russian, Latin American, or Arabic tend to like close personal contact and to show much more outward emotion. Thus, when you are working with a woman of Norwegian descent, for example, she might seem "standoffish" because of the way in which she was raised, which makes her quite shy by U.S. standards. Meanwhile, a coworker of Israeli descent might seem pushy because of her open communication style based on her having been encouraged to speak up and defend herself.[72]

Naturally, American persons refer to normative American behavior as the basis for sending and decoding nonverbal messages, while those from other cultures use different perceptions. For example, adult male North Americans feel comfortable with a distance of arm's length to about four feet apart for private conversation. South Americans like to stand much closer. An American and an Arab are not compatible in their space habits, as the Arabs thrive on close contact and long, direct eye contact.[73] North Americans basically look another person in the eye when they are speaking, occasionally glancing away. A Puerto Rican female invariably lowers her eyes as a sign of respect and obedience when she is being questioned by someone in authority. These cultural differences could lead an American of Arab descent, for example, to interpret a Puerto Rican American's answering of interview questions as dishonest because she is not looking him or her in the eye.

Knowledge of cultural differences in nonverbal communication is extremely important in business. We must consider not only international cultures **co-cultures,** but also cultures from our diverse backgrounds in the U.S., for example, English Americans, Mexican Americans, African Americans. An experience of U.S. steel company representatives who were negotiating with a group of Chinese government representatives for a trade agreement illustrates the problem of cross-cultural misreading. All through the discussions the Chinese kept smiling and nodding their heads, seemingly in agreement with

Did You Want a Waiter or a Dog?

To underscore the complexity of cross-cultural communication and the need to be aware of the often vast differences in meaning, research points to varying interpretations of non-verbal communication. Because communication involves more than the spoken word, especially "high context" cultures throughout the world, international managers must also be wary of inappropriate hand and arm gestures and facial expressions. Use of gestures can be embarrassing or even result in costly errors. Some dangerous signs to keep in mind:

Calling a Waiter
In the United States, a common way to call a waiter is to point upward with the forefinger. In Asia, a raised forefinger is used to call a dog or other animal. To get attention from a Japanese waiter, extend the arm upward, palm down, and flutter the fingers. In Africa, knock on the table. In the Middle East, clap your hands.

Insults
In Arab countries, to show the soles of your shoes is an insult. Also an Arab may insult a person by holding his hand in front of the person's face.

A-okay Gesture
In the United States, using the index finger and the thumb to form an "o" while extending the rest of the fingers is a gesture meaning okay or fine. In Japan, however, the same gesture means money. Nodding your head in agreement if a Japanese uses this sign during your discussion could mean you are expected to give him some cash. And in Brazil the same gesture is considered a seductive sign to a woman and an insult to a man.

Patting a Child on the Head
In Western cultures, adults often pat children on the head as a sign of affection. In Malaysia and other Islamic countries, however, the head is considered to be the center of intellectual and spiritual powers, and should not be touched.

Eye Contact
In Western and Arab cultures, prolonged eye contact with a person is acceptable. In Japan, on the other hand, holding the gaze of another person is considered rude. The Japanese generally focus on a person's neck or tie knot.

Handshake and Touching
In most countries, the handshake is an acceptable form of greeting. In the Middle East and other Islamic countries, however, the left hand is considered the toilet hand and is thought to be unclean. Only the right hand should be used for touching.

Scratching the Head
In most Western countries, scratching the head is interpreted as lack of understanding or noncomprehension. To the Japanese, it indicates anger.

Indicating "No"
In most parts of the world, shaking the head left and right is the most common way to indicate "no". But among the Arabs, in parts of Greece, Yugoslavia, Bulgaria, and Turkey, a person says "no" by tossing the head to the side, sometimes clicking the tongue at the same time. In Japan, "no" can also be said by moving the right hand back and forth.

Agreement
In addition to saying yes, Africans will hold an open palm perpendicular to the ground and pound it with the other fist to emphasize "agreed." Arabs will clasp their hands together, forefingers pointing outward, to indicate agreement.

Goodbye
In most countries, goodbye is achieved by waving the vertical hand. But in many Eastern countries, including parts of China, India, Pakistan, Burma and Malaysia, the palm is extended upwards and moved towards oneself and may be confused for hello. In Italy, the right hand is sometimes extended, palm up, as the hand is opened and closed.

everything the U.S. company's negotiators were saying. But after the talks were ended, the Chinese, instead of cheerfully signing the agreement, said, "Now we seem to be in real trouble on several points." What the Americans learned later was that the Chinese, in smiling and nodding, really meant, "We hear you" or "We understand what you are saying," and not, "We agree with you."[74]

Specific nonverbal behaviors can directly affect business relationships between Americans and individuals from other cultures.[75] A knowledge of these may save some embarrassing moments and loss of business.

GREETINGS

Americans commonly shake hands when they are introduced and when they part. This pattern also exists in Europe, but handshaking is not the custom worldwide. In parts of South America a slight bow is a courteous gesture of greeting. An Asian person who has to leave a gathering will usually bow before departing, communicating apology. In some Mediterranean, Arab, and South American countries, men embrace as a common form of greeting. Some Muslims might not want to touch the hand of a non-Muslim, but might put their hand to their heart as a gesture of taking the person to heart. U.S. etiquette suggests that in same-sex greetings, the person of more power, or the woman in cross-sex situations, should extend the handshake first in business situations.

CONVERSATIONS

An educated person from England will tend to lift the chin slightly when conversing. To an American businessperson, this may be perceived as snobbery. In the United States this behavior might indeed be snobbery, but for the English it shows poise and signifies a polite gesture. In conversation with Arabs, raising the eyebrows indicates a negative reaction, not surprise as in this country.

British and Arabic businesspeople practice rigorous eye contact as they speak. This practice is so intense on the part of the Arabs that it may make their American counterparts uncomfortable. Arabs pay a great deal of attention to eye movements, as they believe the eyes are the mirrors of the soul. Sometimes, U.S. businesspeople are surprised when they go to a formal meeting and carry on negotiations with an Arab wearing dark glasses. This practice may be fairly common, because the Arab may not want you to be aware of what his eyes are doing or that he is studying you.

Americans commonly shake hands when they are introduced, while an Asian person will usually bow. Often these customs blend together in an attempt to show respect toward the other person and his/her culture.

GESTURES

Americans sometimes perceive strong emotional displays, especially vigorous gesturing, as too emotional, immature, or vulgar. However, many Southern Europeans, Arabs, and South Americans use frequent and energetic gestures. In business dealings with people from those areas, the absence of strong gestures might be considered suspect, as it shows an abnormal pattern of movement.

TIME

The use of time is one of the most frequently misinterpreted nonverbal signs. Serious misunderstandings can result unless the individuals are aware of their differences of perception. Such differences may include how preparation is done, when engagements such as meetings are to begin and end, and the period of time negotiations should take.

Cultures organize time in one of two ways: either monochronic (M-time) or polychronic (P-time). M-time is characteristic of people from Germany, Austria, Switzerland, and America. These people tend to think of time as something fixed in nature—something linear, segmented, and manageable, something not to be wasted. Phrases used in these cultures are "saving time," "losing time," and "killing time." P-time cultures deal with time holistically and place great credibility in what is happening right now. "Arabs, Native Hawaiians, Africans, Spaniards, Portuguese, Greeks and Mexicans emphasize people more than schedules. They do not perceive appointments as iron-clad commitments and therefore often break them."[76] (See Figure 5.4.)

Americans are trained to be efficient and take pride in efficiency. We properly prepare in advance for a meeting, a speech, or a business contact. We have a special relationship with time—we spend it, waste it, save it, or divide it. We tend to prepare for business conferences, interviews, and meetings because it is the efficient thing to do. But if we expect this same efficiency of individuals from other cultures, we may be disappointed. Moreover, we may become angry because others do not show us "respect." If an associate from Mexico, Malaysia, or Kuwait seems unprepared for a scheduled session, it is not necessarily disrespectful. People in these cultures tend to operate in an action chain that does not stress prior preparation. The Arab action chain toward business tends to center on getting to know a person, interacting with him or her, meeting again after the social interaction, and then dealing with business matters. Americans, driven by the clock, want to meet, settle the issue, and complete the deal.

Americans and others in the Western world generally regard the clock with respect. An appointment is set, and tardiness is a serious breach of respect. This is not the pattern, for example, in much of Mexico, South America, or the Caribbean. Americans dealing in some countries quickly learn to ask if the scheduled meeting is to be "American" time or "local" time.

BUSINESS SETTINGS

Americans tend to conduct major business meetings in an office. The typical U.S. business executive keeps the desk between him or her and the other person. This arrangement would offend many Latin Americans who feel uncomfortable with the barrier between the participants. Seating positions at a table hold great significance for many Asians. Because Asians may believe that whoever sits at the head of the table is in charge, they will feel uncomfortable, or may refuse to sit at a rectangular or square table. A circular table is much preferred.

Americans tend to be casual regarding dealing in rooms with opened doors. If you are negotiating with a German, you would be wise to close the door. In general, Germans find an open door or entering without asking permission to be the height of rudeness. Arabs, however, are likely to feel uncomfortable in a private, enclosed office. They are used to dealing in open areas, often with observers present. American businesspeople are often upset by media coverage at "private" conferences, while Arabs often accept the media as part of the acceptable audience.

Obviously, you cannot be expected to know the cultural patterns of all countries. And it must be remembered that there are exceptions to these generalizations about the people from various cultures. Not all people from a culture act in exactly the same way. It would be wise, however, to approach all interactions with sensitivity to the nonverbal and verbal responses of others. If your work assignments include international interactions, whether in that country or in the United States, find out about the basic greeting, time, space, and meeting setting patterns.

Dealing with Nonverbal Communication

Knowing about nonverbal communication immediately prepares an individual to be a better sender and receiver of messages. By paying attention to what you and others are doing, you become a more effective communicator. You must learn to listen with your eyes as well as with your ears to messages sent and received. Here are some guidelines regarding specific ways to improve nonverbal sending and receiving.

1. Some specialists think that women have a more difficult time assimilating business leadership roles because traditionally corporate values and behavior patterns have been male. Recommendations for women entering the corporate ladder are to adopt an open, straightforward style that coincides with both male and female behavior traits. Women should not attempt to nonverbally imitate men. The most successful women know

how to maintain their professionalism without losing their femininity. They do this, for example, by allowing themselves to be warmer and more responsive than most men, while at the same time keeping their distance, and not smiling too much.

2. Pay attention to first impressions. For example, be aware of whether you are evaluating a person on the basis of physical appearance or artifacts. Also be aware that others are judging you on the first impression you give.

3. Maintain eye contact. Use the eye patterns of your own society, remembering that those from other cultures may not be using the same code.

4. Make your words and nonverbal signals consistent. Most people aren't very good actors and have trouble faking nonverbal signs that do not agree with the verbal.

5. Don't violate people's sense of personal space. Evaluate whether your relationship with another person is intimate, personal, social, or public. Moving too close and inappropriate touching could lead to negative perceptions. If the person you are talking to pulls away, or starts backing up, you may be too close. Also, be aware that individuals from different cultures use space in different ways and what may be negative to you may be positive to them.

6. Pay attention to your tone of voice. Your vocal and physical presentation can be a personal clue to your feelings and your meaning. You also should listen to how other people are vocally sending messages, as well as the words they are speaking.

7. Examine your posture and walk. Walk and posture convey messages of your attitude, interest, and attentiveness. Monitor your body use to avoid giving negative cues, for example, boredom or rejection of a speaker's proposal.

8. Be aware of how inanimate objects affect communication. Do you find yourself looking at your wristwatch during a sales call? You might be subconsciously telling yourself that you want to leave. Is there a desk between you and a prospective buyer? It is probably creating a barrier to personal involvement. Are the chairs in a position that leads to open conversation if that is desired? All of these are inanimate objects that can affect your communication with others.

9. Be aware of the way you dress. Much of your impression, and therefore your effectiveness as a business communicator, depends upon the image you create. Your clothing is an important part of that image. Much time and effort has been spent in analyzing clothing and how it affects your self-image as well as others' perceptions of you. Are you sending the image you want to convey? Are you aware of the way others' nonverbal behavior affects you in your relationships?

• • • In Summary • • •

Nonverbal communication is all message sending and receiving that is not manifested by words, spoken or written. Every culture has its own nonverbal language. Very few of us realize how much we depend on nonverbal clues in everyday life as well as in business contacts. The relationship between verbal and nonverbal communication exists on many levels. The principal nonverbal categories are kinesics (body language), vocal cues (paralanguage, pause, laughter), proxemics (space), physical characteristics (physical attractiveness, body shape, size, skin color), artifacts (clothes, makeup, eyeglasses, jewelry), aesthetics (music, light, color), and chronemics (time).

═══ Business Communication in Practice ═══

1. Topics for discussion:
   a. "Every culture has its own body language." Identify some cultural pattern that you, a friend, or someone you have observed at a place of work has that is unique to your culture (e.g., time use, hand use, vocal excitement or control).
   b. Name a job interview situation in which you have been involved that was affected by your clothing, grooming, or physical appearance.
   c. Why do you think most people are not aware of the nonverbal messages they send and receive at work?
   d. "People learn body language the same way they learn spoken language—by observing and imitating people around them as they're growing up." Identify several nonverbal mannerisms you have that are like those of people you came in contact with during early childhood. Be prepared to share two of them with your classmates.
   e. Do you agree with the image consultant's observations that were discussed in this chapter concerning dressing for success? React to the clothing requirements for men and women.
   f. What effect do specific colors have on you? Be prepared to give specific examples.
   g. Have you experienced any personal difficulties because of action chains? If so, be prepared to describe them.
2. Interview someone in business, preferably someone who is responsible for hiring, evaluating, or supervision. Find out what effect clothing and physical appearance have on the organization's practices. (OR) Interview a businessperson who deals with physical factors of an organization (construction, decoration, office assignment, and use of work space). Find out what problems arise due to these environmental factors.

3. Carry on a conversation with someone while both of you are standing. Without being obvious, continue to move closer to the person as you speak. What happens? Try this activity with a first-generation Arab, Israeli, or an Asian person. Do they react the same way? Discuss your results as they pertain to this chapter's section on space invasion.

4. Dress in your best clothes and go shopping in several stores. Then go shopping in similar stores while dressed in old grubby clothing. Discuss in class the differences in treatment, based on this chapter's explanation of artifacts.

5. The class will be divided into pairs. Engage in a conversation with one other person, changing positions as described here. Spend two minutes in each position: (1) opposite the other and within three feet; (2) opposite each other but with chairs placed at an angle; and (3) side by side. Note how these variations alter your feelings, interaction, and productivity.[76] Discuss your reactions.

● ● ● Notes ● ● ●

1. Larry A. Samovar and Richard E. Porter, *Communication between Cultures,* 2d ed. (Belmont, CA: Wadsworth, 1995), p. 182.
2. Ibid., 186.
3. Peter Andersen, "Explaining Intercultural Differences in Nonverbal Communication," in Larry A. Samovar and Richard E. Porter (eds.), *Intercultural Communication: A Reader,* 7th ed. (Belmont, CA: Wadsworth, 1994), p. 229.
4. Based on the work of Arnold G. Abrams.
5. Ray Birdwhistell, *Kinesics and Context* (New York: Ballantine Books, 1972).
6. Based on the studies of Norm Jorgensen (communication consultant), James Gray (image consultant), and Nancy Henley (body politics lecturer).
7. Mark Hendricks, "More Than Words," *Entrepreneur* (August 1995): 54.
8. Ibid.
9. Daniel Goleman, "People Who Read People," *Psychology Today* (July 1979): 69.
10. Edward Hall and Mildred Hall, "The Sounds of Silence," *Playboy* (June 1971): 204.
11. Ibid., 206.
12. Samovar and Porter, 183–184.
13. Hendricks, 56.
14. Norbert Freedman, Director, Clinical Behavioral Unit at Downstate Medical Center, Brooklyn, New York, n.d.
15. Hall and Hall, 139.
16. For an in-depth discussion of speech-independent gestures, see Mark L. Knapp and Judith A. Hall, *Nonverbal Communication in Human Interaction,* 3d ed. (Ft. Worth, TX: Holt, Rinehart, and Winston, 1992), pp. 198–207.
17. Samovar and Porter, 191.
18. Edward T. Hall interviewed by Kenneth Friedman, "Learning the Arabs' Silent Languages," *Psychology Today* (August 1979): 45–54.

19. Based on Min Sun Kim, "A Comparative Analysis of Nonverbal Expression as Portrayed by Korean and American Print-Media Advertising," *Howard Journal of Communications* 3 (1992): 321, and William V. Ruch, *International Handbook of Corporate Communication* (Jefferson, NC: McFarland, 1989), pp. 166–167.
20. Samovar and Porter, 194–195.
21. Ibid., 195. For an in-depth explanation of African American nonverbal patterns see Michael L. Hecht, Mary Jane Collier, and Sidney A. Ribeau, *African American Communication: Ethnic Identity and Cultural Interpretation* (Newbury Park, CA: Sage, 1993), p. 102.
22. Knapp and Hall, 310.
23. Knapp and Hall, 284–286. For an in-depth discussion of the effect of the face on human communication, see Stella Ting-Toomey, *The Challenge of Facework* (Albany: State University of New York Press, 1994), and Knapp and Hall, Chapter 7.
24. For an in-depth understanding of the influence of touch see Stanley E. Jones, *The Right Touch: Understanding and Using the Language of Physical Contact* (Creskill, NJ: Hampton Press, 1994).
25. For an in-depth discussion of the effects of touching behavior on human communication, see Knapp and Hall, Chapter 6.
26. Don Oldenburg, "The Touchy Topic of Hugging," *The Washington Post* (February 11, 1985), B5.
27. Based on the concepts of Gerald Volgenaur.
28. Samovar and Porter, 200.
29. Ibid., 201.
30. For an expanded discussion of territory, see Knapp and Hall, 149–154.
31. Based on the work of C. Frederick John.
32. Ibid.
33. Janice Munson, "Clothes Make the Job," *Cleveland Plain Dealer* (February 27, 1978), B2.
34. Knapp and Hall, 113.
35. Based on a study by Saul Feldman.
36. Based on the research of Lawrence Rosenfeld.
37. Ibid.
38. John Malloy, *Dress for Success* (New York: Warner Books, 1993).
39. Jeanne Marie Laskas, "Executive Grooming 101," *The Washington Post Magazine* (November 15, 1992): 16.
40. Munson.
41. Ibid.
42. Based on the work of William Thourlby.
43. Teri Agins, "Breaking Out of the Gray Flannel Suit," *The Wall Street Journal* (March 23, 1992): B1.
44. Malloy.
45. Laskas, 30.
46. John T. Malloy, *The Woman's Dress for Success Book* (New York: Warner Books, 1987).
47. Judy Mann, "Dress Less for Success," *The Washington Post* (June 9, 1995): E3.
48. Agins.

49. Ellen Neuborne, "Casual-Clothing Makers Make Pitch to Offices," *USA Today* (February 7, 1995): B1.
50. Ibid.
51. Marshall Blonsky, as quoted in Agins.
52. Neuborne.
53. Elizabeth Snead, "Casual Look Suits Today's Businessmen," *USA Today* (August 13, 1993), D1.
54. Ibid.
55. Jennifer Steinhauer, "It's 'The Gap' Once You're Hired, But Job Hunters Must Spiff It Up: Interview Suits Are Still Navy after All These Years," *The New York Times* (April 2, 1995): 13.
56. Ibid.
57. Patricia McCormick, "Rock Music Can Weaken Muscles," *Elyria Chronicle-Telegram*, Sunday Magazine (January 12, 1979), 15.
58. Report from the Department of Productivity, Melbourne, Victoria, Australia, n.d.
59. Ibid.
60. "Work Environment: Its Design and Implications," *Personnel Journal* (January 1981).
61. Hall and Hall, "The Sounds of Silence," 12.
62. Albert Mehrabian, *Public Places and Private Spaces* (New York: Basic Books, 1976).
63. Ibid.
64. Ibid.
65. Based on the work of H. Wong and W. Brown.
66. Deborah T. Sharpe, *The Psychology of Color and Design* (Chicago: Nelson-Hall, 1974), p. 85.
67. David J. Hyslop, "Physical Environment in the Office," *The Changing Office Environment* (v: National Business Education Association, 1980), 127.
68. Edward T. Hall as interviewed by Kenneth Friedman.
69. Ibid.
70. Richard Brislin, *Understanding Culture's Influence on Behavior* (Ft. Worth, TX: Harcourt Brace, 1993), p. 211.
71. Agins, 33. In addition, for an in-depth investigation of culture and body language see William Gudykunst and Young Yun Kim, *Communication with Strangers,* 2nd ed. (New York: McGraw-Hill, 1992), pp. 32–35, 172–188.
72. Hall and Hall, "The Sounds of Silence," 140.
73. Davis, "Body Language," 130.
74. John Koha, "Body Signs," *Cleveland Plain Dealer* (December 15, 1976), 8F.
75. Based on Larry Samovar and Richard Porter; Knapp and Hall; Gudykunst and Young.
76. Samovar and Porter, 208.

CHAPTER 5

Listening

EXPECTED OUTCOMES

After completing this chapter, you should be able to:

- Identify the major role that listening plays in business organizations.
- Understand the complex process of receiving, attending to, interpreting, and responding to messages.
- Know when you are listening for discrimination, comprehension, therapeutic response, critical analysis, or appreciation of messages.
- Learn how to overcome listening obstacles and develop your own plan for improved listening behavior.
- Recognize that there is no "quick fix" for improved listening in the organization.

I had spent most of last week preparing the final report for senior management. The project examined every angle concerning moving into Pacific Rim markets. I was very proud of the thoroughness of my work. I was shocked, therefore, when a half-hour after I dropped off the report, the manager appeared in the office and said, "I can't believe that the most important element of this report is missing. I told you that the analysis had to include a comparison with Latin American markets so that a decision can be based on a choice between the two. I can't take this to the steering committee. This isn't what I asked for." I couldn't remember him asking for that information, and I didn't have any notes to refer back to in order to determine whether he had asked for that specific information.

Listening in the Business Organization

In American business, effective listening is recognized as a principal means to improved productivity. "Listening was judged to be one of the super critical skills needed by people for organizational success."[1] Poor listening can be costly: "With more than 100 million workers in this country, a simple $10 mistake by each of them, as a result of poor listening, would add up to a cost of a billion dollars. And most people make numerous listening mistakes every week."[2]

Recognition of the significant role of listening in the organization is highly warranted. American workers spend a great deal of time listening. It has been estimated that adults spend as much as 42.1 percent of their communication time listening, in contrast to 31.9 percent speaking, 15 percent reading, and 11 percent writing.[3] Results from professional, technical, administrative, and clerical people in a research and development laboratory revealed that 50 percent to 80 percent of the workday is spent in communicating—primarily in speaking and listening.[4]

LEVELS OF ORGANIZATIONAL LISTENING

Listening is important at all levels of an organization. Within any given working day, an individual may be required to listen to the boss, fellow employees, peers, customers, suppliers, stockholders, community leaders, professional education groups, labor unions and leaders, government officials, and communication media.[5] Eight listening situations that impact the productivity of any organization are:

1. Salespeople listening to customers and prospects.
2. Customer service representatives listening to customer complaints and problems.
3. Managers and supervisors listening to subordinate problems, suggestions, and solutions.
4. Group members listening for mutual understanding in order to coordinate their efforts.
5. Employees feeling valuable as individuals and as workers because they have someone to listen to them.
6. Employees listening to suggestions of those involved in producing and receiving goods or services in order to improve the quality.
7. All persons in the organization expanding their capacity to understand, assist, and work more effectively with others.

8. Interviewers improving the employment selection process and reducing costly turnovers through careful listening.[6]

As the American workforce grows increasingly internationalized and diversified, organizations and their managers must be able to respond to very different workers. As a managerial communication expert notes: "As the year 2000 approaches, managers will witness a movement toward recognizing unique personal qualities in all organizational members. Consequently, the ability to effectively communicate with individuals who have different values, backgrounds, needs, and roles will become more critical. . . ."[7]

The coveted Malcolm Baldrige Awards that are presented each year by the U.S. Department of Commerce to corporations that meet rigid criteria of quality reinforce the value of listening to achieve corporate excellence. One of the 1994 Baldrige Awards went to Wainwright Industries, a family-owned manufacturing company in Missouri, because it values listening. "Listening—and responding—to suggestions from employees and customers was the key to winning. . . ."[8] The CEO and president of General Motors reflects the appreciation for listening that many corporations have discovered: "We listened to what our customers wanted and acted on what they said. Good things happen when you pay attention. . . ."[9] Indeed, many good things can happen, as one management consultant has observed: ". . . when listening increases, morale, safety, quality, sales, and productivity increase also, while unnecessary turnover and absenteeism decrease."[10]

THE ORGANIZATIONAL LISTENING ENVIRONMENT

The **listening environment,** where listening takes place and a listening atmosphere is established, is an important aspect of listening in any organization. A management expert stresses that managers must "create an environment where listening is cherished—and opportunities for structured and unstructured listening are rife. Listening means managers listening to their people, of course. And it means teammates listening to each other."[11]

Building a listening environment in an organization is not a simple task. Research shows that listening in the work environment is a highly complex activity. Factors that can interfere with a well-established listening environment include time pressures, interruptions, ongoing relationships, previous encounters, message sending, and perceptions.[12]

Perceptions of effective listening are crucial to creating a supportive climate in an organization and to overcoming some of the organizational problems associated with poor listening. These problems can include such difficulties as interpersonal conflict, low morale, and poor attitudes. One management consultant suggests that "individuals who listen to their fellow workers create a supportive organizational climate characterized by information-sharing and trust."[13] In a study on worker perceptions of communication competence on the job, listening was found to be the major factor by which people judge the effectiveness of others' communication.[14]

An organization can provide a solid listening environment by (1) providing a forum for listening; (2) creating a physical location for listening; (3) encouraging feedback and reinforcement; (4) providing listening training; (5) giving employees frequent opportunities for listening; and (6) adopting the positive attitude that listening is valuable.[15] Some corporations are serious about developing a listening environment, particularly when it comes to listening to their customers. Apple Computer, Campbell Soup, Control Data, Ford Motor Co., and Stew Leonard's Supermarket in Norwalk, Connecticut, are examples of companies that have realized increases in productivity and quality after strong and supportive listening environments were put in place.[16]

LISTENING AND BUSINESS SUCCESS

Good listening abilities and habits are often the basis for promotions, sales, and the respect of superiors and peers. A good business communicator is both a good speaker *and* a good listener.[17] A corporate CEO highlighted how much listening makes the difference when he said, "You have to be able to listen well if you're going to motivate the people who work for you. Right there, that's the difference between a mediocre company and a great company. The most fulfilling thing for me as a manager is to watch someone the system has labeled as just average or mediocre really come into his own, all because someone listened to his problems and helped him solve them."[18]

The organization that listens truly exemplifies the bottom-up approach to communication. The SBT Corporation of Sausalito, California, is an example of a listening company. To provide employees with a voice in decision making and ensure that all levels of the organization were represented, the president set up weekly group meetings of the line managers and two volunteer employees. SBT's experience has convinced them that quality listening requires commitment and a willingness to listen on the part of everyone in the organization. As the president stated, "Forming groups and changing your management style means little unless you really 'hear' what your employees are saying and unless they are willing to risk telling you what they really think."[19]

With this understanding of the importance of listening in the world of business, let's now examine what listening is.

Profile: Sean Greenwood, director of Internal Communications, Ben and Jerry's, Waterbury, Vermont, ice cream manufacturer.

What is the role of listening in your organization?

Listening plays a very important role at Ben and Jerry's. Since we're such a highly visible publicly held company, it is important that we keep our employees and customers informed and that, in turn, we listen to their needs and concerns. We work to build a healthy relationship based on trust between management and employees, and our corporate culture fosters the expectation that employees can and do have a say in company decisions. Our employees feel comfortable speaking up and know that they will get a response. The lines of communication are open; for example, our CEO is available to receive e-mail suggestions directly from anyone in the company. We recognize the critical role that listening plays, and we work to respond to what our employees and our customers tell us.

How does your company use the different types of listening?

As an ice cream manufacturer, we rely extensively on *discriminative* listening. Our production people depend on their visual and auditory discrimination skills to keep track of our machines. They have to listen to the pusher bar on the shrink wrap machine, for instance. And our research and development people have learned to listen to the verbal *and* nonverbal reactions that people in our focus groups have to new flavors. A person might say "This is good," but react with a "yuck" expression! We also listen *comprehensively*, of course, especially in training new employees to run our production equipment. And we use the input from employees and customers to *critically* assess what they tell us in order to make informed decisions about products and processes. Our efforts to move our corporate headquarters, for example, are based on a careful survey of all our headquarters employees to determine what impact a move will have on each individual. Our management commitment to good listening is *therapeutic* in that we believe strongly in helping others through listening to them. And this commitment extends to *appreciative* listening as well. As part of our corporate culture, we offer incentives to work groups that can bring more joy to the workplace. Our first award was to a production group to install a stereo system so that they could listen at a qualitative level to good music.

The Listening Process

Listening is an active process in which individuals receive, attend to, interpret, and respond to verbal and nonverbal messages. To be effective, the listener must be actively involved in the process, not passively letting the speaker do all the work. The segments of this complex process may occur quite simultaneously in the communication transaction.

MOTIVATION

At the outset, the listener must have the motivation or the desire to listen. Because humans do not have an innate drive for effective listening, it becomes necessary to generate self-motivation to listen. Good listeners find it helpful to emphasize to themselves the importance of listening in a particular situation, to know what they are doing as listeners, and to establish their own objectives (as correlated to the speaker's purpose) for the listening experience. Listening at work often can challenge an individual's motivation, especially if the workday is filled with meetings, briefings, telephone calls, and appointments.

RECEIVING

The motivated listener must then receive the message. The auditory reception of the message requires the listener to attend to the speaker's vocal/verbal message. And the listener also must attend to the speaker's visual stimuli—facial expression, posture, and movement. Indeed, it has been estimated that as much as 93 percent of the total meaning of a message can result from the nonverbal visual cues.[20] Tuning in to nonverbal cues can enable the listener to understand and to interpret the speaker's intended meaning more precisely. A supervisor who reads a "While You Were Out" phone message while talking with you communicates a negative message about your importance at that moment, even if the verbal message seems to be concentrated on your question.

The development of a good listening environment in the workplace must accommodate ready reception of messages. Employees who are crowded together on "open space" office floors may be distracted by telephone calls and conversations at colleagues' desks. Loud printers and other equipment create noise pollution in the office. Poor lighting and the lack of sound control can interfere with careful, consistent receiving. Some ways to minimize such problems is to encourage management to use sound absorbing materials (such as curtains and carpeting), put up partial wall partitions, and supply full-spectrum desk lamps, which duplicate the brightness of the sun.

ATTENTION

After the message has been received through the auditory and visual channels, it must be attended to through the memory system by which the information is stored. The listener must focus on the auditory and visual messages and work to concentrate. There is little agreement as to how the memory system physiologically operates, but it clearly influences the **attention span**, the length of time a person can maintain focus on any given stimulus. The attention span is quite limited. Psychologists suggest that this focus may be no more than sixty seconds, because attention always fluctuates.

"It's entirely possible that our capacity for sustained attention and deliberate thought is being altered by television viewing."[21] People raised in the television generation have come to expect a seven- to ten-minute program format with time out for a commercial break. The fifteen-second commercial and fifteen-second "sound bite" have become the standard by which we process television messages. Thus, this shortened attention span affects the listener's capacity to attend to briefings, to participate in meetings, and to engage in conversations for any length of time. It is a challenge for a listener to control attention in order to get the message.

PERCEPTION

Attention to the message is affected by the listener's memory system and by the perceptual filter. The **perceptual filter** is the extent to which the listener's predispositions alter the message and screen the stimulus. The listener's background, experiences, roles, and mental and physical states influence perception. The influence of perception in the listening process is best understood by the old adage "We see and hear what we want to see and hear." Law enforcement officials recognize this influence when witnesses offer very different descriptions of the same traffic accident at a busy intersection.

INTEREST

Another factor that affects the listener's attention span is one's interest or willingness to receive the message. You may not be interested in the message if the topic doesn't seem relevant to you, if the presentation is dull, or if the speaker lacks humor. Studies suggest that "the louder, the more relevant, the more novel the stimuli, the more likely they are to be perceived by the listener."[22] Armed with that knowledge, the salesperson, to make a sale, must find out what message will engage the customer and then must maintain that interest and attention.

INTERPRETATION

Once the message has been received by the listener through the auditory, visual, and attention processors, the message is interpreted. Interpretation involves fitting the verbal and nonverbal messages into the proper linguistic categories that have been stored in the brain and then analyzing the messages for their meanings. This decoding system varies according to a person's perceptual filters and the category system, so the original intent of a speaker's message may become distorted, misinterpreted, and changed as the listener's meaning is assigned to it. A salesperson, for example, may find that if she attempts to sell a photocopy machine made in Japan to a person who is strongly in favor of "buy American," she will not be successful. The intended purchaser could well distort the message and close off the listening process.

RESPONDING

After a message has been interpreted, the listener responds with internal storage of the information in the long-term memory and with external reactions (feedback) to the speaker.

STORAGE

The receiver may put the information in storage by placing the ideas into the long-term memory for future recall. Although we are not exactly sure how the memory works, the ability to remember is facilitated by visualizing through mental images, by associating the idea to something already in the memory store, by triggering other facts in store, and by mentally summarizing the information. We all depend on job instructions, for example, and it is critical to be able to recall that information in order to perform the task or complete the project. Finding memory strategies that can assist your ability to recall messages is an important part of listening effectively.

FEEDBACK

The listener's internal response may couple with his or her external feedback response to the speaker. Feedback takes many forms: requests for further information or clarification ("Can you give me an example of that?"); positive support for the speaker's message ("That's a good idea"); disagreement with the information ("I'm not sure your figures are accurate"); or encouragement to continue ("I'd like to hear more about that"). Good feedback should be supportive, timely, easily perceived, and designed to further the goals of the communication. Feedback skills are critical to good management, for it is the way that supervisors praise workers' abilities and identify what needs to be improved. And all employees need to be sensitive to the effect that responses, positive and negative, can have on communication relationships with others.

A study on organizational listening found that most employees perceive listening to be responsiveness—to complaints, to suggestions, to questions, and to extra efforts.[23] Everyone in the organization has to work at good feedback. A Forum Group survey of more than 3,200 employees at fourteen large U.S. and Canadian companies revealed that front-line workers as well as managers and supervisors need feedback skills. Those employees who deal directly with customers must be responsive and empathetic in their feedback to get new customers and, as important, to keep customers.[24]

The Goals of Listening

Listening is a complex process that involves concentration and retention of the message throughout the stages of the communication. This complex process occurs on various levels, which depend in large part on the intended purpose of the communication. We listen for different reasons. These listening goals are to discriminate, to comprehend, to provide a therapeutic response, to critically evaluate, or to appreciate a message.

LISTENING FOR DISCRIMINATION

A person may listen at the **discriminative listening level** for the purpose of distinguishing auditory or visual differences. An industrial worker or electronic repair person often has to listen discriminatively to the sound of the machin-

---

What Everyone Wants to Hear

Whether you're trying to build a better relationship with a customer or coworker or ask someone out for a date, you might want to learn to establish empathy. One good way is to listen carefully to people and respond with sentences that begin with:

- *"I can appreciate . . ."*
- *"I can identify with . . ."*
- *"I can understand . . ."*
- *"I see that you . . ."*

When you do this, you signal to the other people that you actually care about what they say and that you're able to understand them.

It sounds like common sense but very few people use this approach. People cry out for affirmation, and there's no better way to make that happen than to communicate that you understand them.

Empathy lets speakers know you're willing to see things from their points of view and that you're concerned about understanding them.

What you're doing is appealing to a person's need to feel special—and everybody has that need.

Source: The Art of Winning Conversation, by Morey Stettner. Prentice Hall, 113 Sylvan Ave., Englewood Cliffs, NJ 07632.

ery in order to know if it is functioning properly. Persons trained as business security officers quickly learn techniques of visual discrimination to identify suspicious individuals through such visual cues as walk, stance, eye shifts, and gestures.

LISTENING FOR COMPREHENSION

Much of the listening we do is at the **comprehensive listening level.** The listener's objective is to understand the material—typically in order to recall and to use the material in some way. This purpose requires that you listen objectively to the entire message for understanding, not for the evaluation of what is communicated. When you listen for comprehension, you discriminate in order to determine through the speaker's vocal and visual cues what is important to remember, what is needed to clarify, or what is irrelevant. Then you have to work to retain and recall the information through whatever memory strategies can facilitate that process for you. Listening to briefings, conference reports, training instructions, or directions all require focused, concentrated comprehensive listening in a business environment.

LISTENING FOR THERAPEUTIC VALUE

You may find yourself, as a coworker or as a supervisor, listening at the **therapeutic listening level.** The therapeutic listener provides a sounding board for a person to talk a problem through to a solution. To be an empathic listener— "seek first to understand, then to be understood"—is the key to effective interpersonal communication.[25] By being a supportive therapeutic listener, a good manager may be able to understand an employee's problems.

Everyone needs therapeutic listeners to gain perspective on problems. Unfortunately, many people can't find such listening sounding boards in their professional lives. If the problem is of sufficient magnitude that it requires a professional mental health practitioner, you should encourage the person to seek such help. Unless you are a trained mental health counselor, do not try to play amateur psychologist. It can often do more harm than good, in spite of your good intentions.

LISTENING FOR CRITICAL EVALUATION

The **critical listening level** centers on understanding the message and then evaluating it. To determine whether to accept or to reject a message, a listener needs to have standards of judgment upon which to conduct a careful analysis of the strengths and weaknesses of a position or decision. These standards

The critical listener needs to analyze the arguments, appeals, and motives of the speaker.

evolve from an understanding of the persuasive process of influence. It is helpful to know how persuasive messages are put together to demonstrate a speaker's trust and expertise, psychological appeals to engage the listener, and reasoned arguments as the foundation. The key to critical listening is to test any persuasive proposition by asking if the recommendation is reasonable and expected. The critical listener needs to analyze the arguments, appeals, and motives of the speaker. Although it is difficult, setting aside preconceived ideas or biased attitudes can help you listen more objectively to the ideas being presented.

You may have to listen critically in order to evaluate a briefing that advocates a new policy or procedure, to weigh the relative merits of solutions proposed in a staff meeting, or to assess whether or not to purchase a particular new computer system for the office. On a daily basis, we are bombarded with persuasive messages designed to get us to buy, do, give, care, vote, and believe. It can be a challenge to remain objective and careful in critically assessing all of these appeals.

LISTENING FOR APPRECIATION

A person may listen at the **appreciative listening level** to gain pleasure or a sensory impression from the material. Noontime concerts in the employee cafeteria, brown-bag training sessions on lighter topics, or after-dinner speeches are just some of the occasions where a person might listen apprecia-tively in the business setting. Listeners often observe how much they can ap-preciate pleasant conversations or even the calming silence of an office after hours. Each listener will have different appreciative responses, which arise from one's background and experiences in life.

Obstacles to Effective Listening

While we can understand what is involved in good listening, the unfortunate reality in many organizations is that many people are not very effective listen-ers. It is estimated that we miss approximately three-quarters of what we listen to.[26] Inefficient, ineffective listening results from many obstacles, which stem from physiology, motivation, self-concept, lack of understanding, and lack of preparation.

PHYSIOLOGICAL INTERFERENCE

We can listen and think three to four times faster than the average person can speak.[27] Studies suggest that with no great difficulty, an individual can receive information at about 500 words per minute. In rapid conversation, people speak about 200 to 250 words per minute, while the normal public speaker, newscaster, or lecturer speaks between 100 to 200 words per minute.[28] Be-cause speakers are presenting material at a much slower rate than the listener can receive and process, our minds have time to wander—to tune in and to tune out.

We tune in and tune out because our attention fluctuates. As we have seen, it is not physiologically possible to maintain focus on any given stimulus for any great length of time—probably no more than sixty seconds at the most. Thus, concentration requires considerable physical energy just to keep the message in focus.

An individual listener also is affected by his or her physical state. For ex-ample, if you have a headache you might have difficulty concentrating on the message. Good listening requires considerable attention energy, and energy requires good health.

LACK OF MOTIVATION

Just as one's physical state is an important factor in listening effectively, so too is one's mental state. As we have seen, the listener's level of motivation is a key to the process. You have to be willing to engage as a listener, to assume responsibility for the outcome of the communication. This motivation can be a challenge if you perceive the material to be irrelevant or uninteresting. The key to motivation is self-control. You need to set aside any negative predispositions and be willing to hear the speaker out. Almost any communication transaction with another human being can be a productive, growing experience for anyone. Since so much of an organization's effectiveness relies on good listening at all levels, effective listeners may find external rewards for good listening in forward-looking companies today.

NEGATIVE SELF-CONCEPT

One's perceptions of oneself as a listener, the self-concept, can have an effect on listening. A positive or negative self-concept undoubtedly influences an individual's listening habits. Many of us tend to be reminded, throughout life, of our poor listening skills. We are seldom reinforced for positive listening behaviors. As a result, people probably are conditioned, at an early age, to view themselves as poor listeners. Messages from parents, teachers, and friends such as "You're not listening"; "Be quiet and listen"; and "Why don't you ever listen to me?" reinforce the belief that we're not very effective at listening. If you assume this negative listening attitude, you can certainly develop the attitude that you really can't listen very well and, therefore, don't need to expend the effort to correct bad habits or improve your listening skills. It's too easy, then, to just give up and leave all the work to the speakers. Executives, managers, supervisors, and employees alike have come to perceive themselves as poor listeners—often because no one ever suggested that they might be otherwise.

LACK OF UNDERSTANDING

Understanding the intended meaning in a message requires an understanding of the verbal and nonverbal symbols being used by the speaker. Sometimes the listener must deal with jargon or "buzzwords," words that may be unfamiliar and interfere with the ability to listen. Each organization and field of specialization, from accounting to zookeeping, has its own internal jargon or terminology for specific functions. It is necessary to learn how to use these words in the proper context.

Further, the listener's processing of the intended meaning can be affected by symbols that create **emotional triggers**—inciting words that sound an internal alarm and evoke an emotional response. "Pink slip" is associated with being "let go," "fired," "riffed," or "terminated," so listeners are often set off with the use of such a phrase.

It also is helpful to separate the factual from the inferential messages as you process what a speaker says. Factual information is based on that which is observable or generally accepted as true, while inferential messages are conclusions or assumptions that a speaker draws. Inferential statements can sound highly factual, and this can obscure the communication. A coworker might tell you that the organization is planning to "downsize," even though no decisions have been reached on the matter—it is just one of the options that the executives are studying. It becomes necessary, then, to determine how much of that message results from assumptions made on the basis of little or no evidence to support the claim.

If you don't understand what the speaker is saying, you need to ask questions. Unfortunately, many people are not very comfortable asking questions and just remain silent. Yet it is only through questions that we can get the information we need to interpret a message with any accuracy whatsoever. Because each person's background and experience are different from each other's, meaning can be found only within the communicators themselves, not in the symbolic words and actions used to convey the messages. To be effective, then, the listener must decode the message as clearly and precisely as possible in order to understand the intended meaning of the speaker.

The challenge to understanding is greater in corporations that are diversified and/or internationalized. As people from different cultures come together in the workplace, misunderstandings are inevitable. Americans tend to speak of people with little regard for their gender, status, or age. However, in some cultures, especially Asian, status, age, and gender are communicated as part of both the verbal and the nonverbal language patterns.

LACK OF PREPARATION

Although listening has been recognized as one of the major keys to achieving productivity and quality in the workplace, many people in business organizations have not been taught principles of listening. For too long, American schools have assumed that people who can hear can listen, so little direct instruction in listening has found its way into the typical language arts curriculum. The U.S. Department of Labor has identified listening as a basic skill required of all employees in the workplace, so listening should receive more attention by educators at all levels.[29]

The two-year advertising campaign by the Sperry Corporation, "We Understand How Important It Is to Listen," generated considerable corporate interest in training employees, managers, and executives in listening behavior.

In 1994 alone, 69 percent of American corporations were found to provide listening training.[30] Research supports that training in listening skills does result in improved listening in corporations.[31]

Thus, it is encouraging that listening preparation is often taught in the corporate environment. Since listening is such a central part of what everyone does in both personal and professional life, it makes sense that listening preparation begin much earlier in the early elementary school years. The International Listening Association and the Speech Communication Association are providing leadership to introduce such instruction in every school.

Improving Listening

Although instruction and training are important to build the foundation for effective listening skills, it is the individual's responsibility to determine the strategies that are effective and use them as the basis for self-improvement. The increased competition in business today requires increased collaboration. The leaders in today's organizations must really listen. It is suggested that "a manager who is committed to seeing people exercise their intelligence will really listen when people talk. But that doesn't happen often because so many managers are more interested in impressing their employees, in trying to appear brighter."[32]

It takes considerable self-discipline, energy, time, and commitment to work at listening and become good at it. But the rewards for doing so can be considerable. Consequently, consider the individual strategies that can provide the basis for self-improvement as a listener (Figure 5.1).[33]

FIGURE 5.1
Strategies for Effective Listening

A good listener is prepared to listen.
A good listener is aware that listening is a two-sided experience.
A good listener allows the entire message to be received.
A good listener suppresses what he or she wants to say until it is his or her turn to speak.
A good listener is conscious of inciting words.
A good listener controls distractions.
A good listener anticipates the subject and the speaker.
A good listener creates a need to listen to important things.
A good listener often paraphrases what has been said.
A good listener monitors the way he/she listens.
A good listener realizes the need to develop a method of remembering.
A good listener works to improve his/her listening behavior.

A good listener is prepared to listen. You cannot hear a turned-off radio or television, so you cannot expect to hear a turned-off speaker. Turning on the speaker is the first step to listening. Be mentally and physically read to participate in the communication. Set an objective, a purpose, a goal for your listening. Raise your energy level, sit up in your chair, and make a conscious effort to listen.

A good listener is aware that listening is a two-sided experience. We often listen only to what we think the message is, rather than taking into consideration who is sending it, the conditions under which the message is being sent, and the purpose behind the message. It is important to engage in and process the total communication experience.

A good listener allows the entire message to be received. How often have you interrupted when you thought that you had the general idea of the message, only to find out that it was not at all what the speaker intended? Have you filled out applications without listening to the directions only to find that you actually did not do it correctly? Listen to the whole; a part might not be enough.

A good listener suppresses what he/she wants to say until it is his/her turn to speak. Individuals who interrupt conversations suffer from what is called egospeak. **Egospeak** is the "art of boosting your own ego, by speaking only about what you want to talk about, and not giving a hoot in hell about what the other person is speaking about."[34] If you attempt to communicate with an egospeaker, you quickly learn that the person really is not interested in what you are saying. You'll hear "You think that's something. Well, I . . ." or "When that happened to me, I . . ." Egospeakers don't listen; they just wait for the other person to take a breath so they can jump in with their story or advice.

A good listener is conscious of inciting words. Some words can set us off, making us react without giving the speaker a chance to be heard because the words carry such explosive meanings. We often have to keep control and listen to the message so as not to lose the context of the idea. If someone uses an obscenity, for instance, do you turn off the entire message? Do words like "credit risk," "downsizing," or "but that's the policy" set you off? Be aware of words that can create listening barriers and work hard not to succumb to their emotional impact.

A good listener controls distractions. Is the person seated next to you talking? Can you hear the speaker? Do you do anything about it? If not, you are just contributing to your listening problem. The effective listener is comfortable asking others to be quiet, closing the windows, or moving closer to the speaker. It is important to adjust so that you can receive the message.

A good listener anticipates the subject and the speaker. The physiological research suggests that listeners have a lot of extra time while engaging in listening. Keep your mind alert and active; anticipate what is coming. A well-organized speaker will offer clues. Listen for such phrases as "And the next major idea is . . ."; "so then we have to . . ."; and "there are three phases to the rollout." Such **verbal markers** tell you what to anticipate so that you can sharpen your concentration skills and get the point.

A good listener creates a need to listen to important things. Are you going to have to make a report to other employees? Must you know the information that the sales manager is presenting? The speaker is boring! So what? You must know the material, so you are going to have to force yourself to break the boring-barrier and listen. Take notes; force yourself to listen. Don't allow yourself to turn off. Because you will have to do so much listening in meetings, conferences, and seminars throughout most workdays, developing your own internal need to listen can help you to identify your goals and raise your attention energy so that you can concentrate even on the most boring speaker or briefing.

A good listener often paraphrases what has been said. By **paraphrasing,** repeating to either yourself or to the speaker what he or she has just said, you are making sure that you understand it. This practice also allows the other individual to adjust or correct any misinterpretations. Paraphrasing forces you to listen intently, as you know that you will have to feed the message back to the source. Paraphrasing also makes the source feel validated and significant, for you are communicating that you are really listening to what he or she is saying.

A good listener monitors the way she or he listens. Did you catch yourself slumping down in the chair? Are you aware that you are counting the holes in the acoustical ceiling tile? Do you know that you have not listened to anything the speaker has been saying? If so, you are monitoring your own listening. Be aware; keep alert. Monitoring your own listening behavior may be difficult and distracting at first. But you will find that you can increase your sensitivity to your own listening responses and, therefore, improve your listening skills.

A good listener realizes the need to develop a method of remembering. Do you often think that you are really listening, but then realize you can't remember what has been said? There are recall strategies that can aid in listening comprehension. Taking notes, for instance, can foster paraphrasing. Paraphrasing leads you to rethink the material as you write it, especially if you put it into your own words rather than write down exactly what the speaker has said. If you can't write down what was said, you probably don't understand it. An excellent device for reinforcing information obtained at a business session or conference is to write a summary memo to yourself immediately following the presentation. This confirms your understanding and allows you to seek out any information you missed. Another device is to associate what is being said to something with which you are already familiar. Make a mental image; visualize it. If the computer technician is teaching you to operate some new software and uses the word "dump," you might visualize the material being thrown into a can for later retrieval. This word picture might latter trigger your memory of how to complete the procedure you've been taught.

A good listener works to improve his/her listening behavior. Individuals who work at listening, taking the time and trouble to identify systematically their listening problems and then consciously striving to overcome those problems, are on their way to improved skills as listeners. Awareness of listening behavior is the first step, but don't stop here. Now work individually with your coworkers, your friends, or your family members to become more efficient, more responsive, and more sensitive as a listener. Put into practice the skills you have learned and carry them into all of your listening experiences.

• • • In Summary • • •

Listening is the active process in which individuals receive, attend to, interpret, and respond to verbal and nonverbal messages. To be effective, the listener must be actively involved in the process, not passively letting the speaker do all the work. The goals of listening are discrimination, comprehension, providing a therapeutic response, critical evaluation, or appreciation. Inefficient, ineffective listening results from obstacles that stem from physiology, motivation, self-concept, lack of understanding, and lack of preparation. Listening is one of the essential skills for organizational success.

═══ Business Communication in Practice ═══

1. Select a period in which you will be functioning as an active listener in a business meeting, a briefing, a class, or a series of telephone conversations. Monitor your own listening patterns. Keep a log of these patterns. Do you egospeak? Are you daydreaming? Are you being distracted?
2. Attend a lecture or a briefing and take notes. After the presentation, compare your notes with those of others in the audience. What were the major points? How did the speaker develop the points? Were your notes accurate? Were they sufficient to trigger recall of the information presented?
3. Make a list of words that incite you. Reflect on how you respond to them and why they have this effect on you.
4. Identify when and where you use the different types of listening: discriminative; comprehensive; therapeutic; critical; and appreciative. Which do you use most frequently? Analyze your listening at these different levels. Which do you do well? Which do you need to improve?

••• Notes •••

1. Vincent S. DiSalvo, "Listening Needs in the Workforce," paper presented at the International Listening Association Summer Conference (July 1984), 2.
2. "Secrets of Being a Better Listener," *U.S. News and World Report* (May 26, 1980): 65.
3. Paul T. Rankin, "Listening Ability: Its Importance, Measurement and Development," *Chicago Schools Journal* 12 (1930): 177–179.
4. E. T. Klemmer and F. W. Snyder, "Measurement of Time Spent Communicating," *Journal of Communication* 22 (June 1972): 142–179. Other research supports Rankin's conclusions about the prominence of listening. See, for example, J. Donald Weinrauch and John R. Swanda, Jr., "Examining the Significance of Listening: An Exploratory Study of Contemporary Management," *Journal of Business Communication* 13 (February 1975): 25–33; and Elyse K. Werner, "A Study of Communication Time," M.A. Thesis, University of Maryland, 1975.
5. Ernest Parker Mills, *Listening: Key to Communication* (New York: Petrocelli Books, 1974). See also John L DiGaetani, "The Business of Listening," *Business Horizons* (October 1980): 40–46.
6. Frank Cancelliere, "Listening: Key to Productivity," *Connections* (November 1983): 43.
7. Judi Brownell, "Relational Listening: Fostering Effective Communication Practices in Diverse Organizational Environments," *Hospitality and Tourism Educator* 6 (Fall 1994): 11.
8. Shelly Reese, "Wainwright Snags Award by Listening," *USA Today* (October 19, 1994), B4.
9. John F. Smith, Jr., "To Our GM Stockholders and Friends:" *General Motors 1994 Annual Report* (Detroit, MI: General Motors): 5.
10. Robert C. Kausen, "A Culture of Listening," *Executive Excellence* (February 1993): 5.
11. Tom Peters, *Thriving on Chaos* (New York: Knopf, 1988), p. 305.
12. Marilyn H. Lewis and N. L. Reinsch, Jr., "Listening in Organizational Environments," *Journal of Business Communication* 25 (Summer 1988): 63.
13. Judi Brownell, "Perceptions of Effective Listeners: A Management Study," *Journal of Business Communication* 27, 401–415.
14. John W. Haas and Christa L. Arnold, "An Examination of the Role of Listening in Judgments of Communication Competence in coworkers," *Journal of Business Communication* 32 (April 1995): 123–139.
15. Peters, 306–307.
16. Ibid.
17. Vincent DiSalvo, D. C. Larsen, and W. R. Seiler, "Communication Skills Needed by Persons in Business Organizations," *Communication Education* 25 (November 1976): 270–275.
18. Lee Iacocca with William Novak, *Iacocca* (Toronto: Bantam Books, 1986), p. 58.
19. Robert Davies, "Managing by Listening," *Nation's Business* (September 1992): 6.
20. Albert Mehrabian, *Silent Messages* (Belmont, CA: Wadsworth, 1971), p. 43.
21. Dorothy Singer and Jerome Singer, "Is Human Imagination Going Down the Tube?" *Chronicle of Higher Education* (April 29, 1979): 65.
22. Larry Barker, *Listening Behavior* (Englewood Cliffs, NJ: Prentice Hall, 1971), p. 31.

23. James A. Gilchrist and Shirley A. Van Hoeven, "Organizations That Don't Listen (and Some That Do): Listening as an Organizational Construct," paper presented at the International Listening Association Convention, Memphis, TN (March 1993).
24. Brian Murphy, "Firms Paying More Attention to Consumers," *The Washington Post* (March 29, 1988), E8.
25. Stephen R. Covey, *The 7 Habits of Highly Effective People* (New York: Fireside, 1989), p. 237.
26. Ralph G. Nichols and Leonard A. Stevens, *Are You Listening?* (New York: McGraw-Hill, 1957), p. 107.
27. *The Power of Listening,* a video, CRM McGraw-Hill Films, LaGrange, IL 60525.
28. Charles T. Brown and Paul W. Keller, *Monologue to Dialogue* (Englewood Cliffs, NJ: Prentice Hall, 1979): pp. 63–64. See also Norbert Wiener, *Cybernetics* (Cambridge, MA: MIT Press, 1961).
29. *What Work Requires of Schools* (Washington, DC: U.S. Department of Labor, 1991), p. 15.
30. "Who's Learning What?" 1994 Industry Report, *Training* (October 1994), p. 49.
31. See Andrew D. Wolvin and Carolyn Gwynn Coakley, "A Survey of the Status of Listening Training in Some Fortune 500 Corporations," *Communication Education* 40 (April 1991): 152–164.
32. Robert McGarvey, "Power to the People," *Entrepreneur* (June 1995): 138.
33. See Andrew D. Wolvin and Carolyn Gwynn Coakley, *Listening* (Dubuque, IA: Brown/Benchmark, 1996), and Roy M. Berko, Andrew D. Wolvin, and Darlyn R. Wolvin, *Communicating* (Boston: Houghton Mifflin, 1995).
34. Edward Addeo and Robert Burger, *Egospeak* (New York: Bantam Books, 1974), p. xiv.

Managing Self-Communication

EXPECTED OUTCOMES

After completing this chapter, you should be able to:

- Define and illustrate self-communication.
- Recognize how your self-communication comprises psychological, physiological, cognitive, and affective components.
- Know how your communicator self is the foundation for communicating with others.
- Be willing to communicate through positive self-talk and a clear self-communication plan.

left the manager's office in a daze. I had an armful . . . the proposal, quarterly reports, profiles, a stack of recent press clippings from the public relations department, and a legal pad full of notes from the two-hour planning session. I had been assigned to lead a project team for the first time. I had to figure out how to manage the boss's perceptions, influence peers, and manage multiple deadlines. How could I do it? Every failure of my life flashed before my eyes. By the time I got back to my office I was filled with self-doubt. I was sure I was going to fail. I wish I had more self-confidence. I wish I thought of myself as a winner instead of a loser.

Y ou are sitting at your desk; you have a problem to solve. You consider your background as it relates to the problem. You think about how you have handled similar problems in the past. You are processing information within yourself—at the intrapersonal level. This processing of messages internally is **intrapersonal communication**—communication within the self. Communication at the intrapersonal level provides an individual with a way to get in touch with his or her world and to verify (or disconfirm) perceptions of the world.[1]

Intrapersonal communication essentially provides the foundation for all of the communicating that we do in our professional and private settings. Because it is the foundation for the busy executive and the hardworking employee, an understanding of how to use self-communication can be helpful in establishing the knowledge and skills necessary for building effectiveness in the business world. To build this foundation, it is important to understand your intrapersonal communication, to know your communication self, and to develop a willingness to communicate.

The Dimensions of Intrapersonal Communication

One's intrapersonal communication is made up of four dimensions: psychological, physiological, cognitive, and affective.

PSYCHOLOGICAL DIMENSION OF INTRAPERSONAL COMMUNICATION

The psychological dimension of intrapersonal communication results from the impact of a communicator's perceptual filter. Psychologically, all of an individual's background, life experiences, and interactions with others forms the **perceptual filter,** the psychological screen through which all messages are encoded and decoded. This psychological screen results from a process of filtering messages through perceptions.

Perception

"**Perception** is the process of becoming aware of objects and events from the senses."[2] Perceptions do not necessarily provide an accurate record of events; they are no more than hypotheses used to make predictions. In taking action, you must be aware that you are acting on your perceptions and not necessarily on all of the information available. This leaves enormous room for error. The perception process occurs in three stages: selection, organization, and interpretation.

Selection

When something occurs, you first select the data to which you are going to pay attention, to maintain focus. This selection may occur on a conscious or an unconscious level. The broad array of possible bits of information for you to grasp depends on varying factors that may catch or center your attention. These selection factors include who is presenting the material; how it is being presented; its physical size, shape, or color; the surroundings; and the medium by which it is presented. If you like the person who is speaking or if you agree with his or her ideas, you are likely to buy into the idea of the message. If a flashy presentation attracts your attention, you might attend to a message that you would miss under other circumstances. Whatever the reason, a person selects certain things to attend to and other things to disregard.

Organization

Once you collect and select the information from the environment, you arrange the data in some sort of order or classification—**organization.** You might group the data by the order in which events occurred, for example, explaining a work accident by relating the incidents that led up to it. Or you might classify things by their kind, such as computer hardware and software.

Interpretation

After you select and organize, the third step in the act of perception is interpretation. Interpretation plays a critical role in every communicative act. In interpreting, you draw from past experiences, from the biases and prejudices you hold, and from your assumptions, expectations, knowledge, and interpersonal motives. If you have had unreliable results with a particular brand of copy machine, you will probably conclude that a replacement of the same brand name will be unreliable also.

Our perceptual interpretations are influenced by certain underlying factors.

1. *First impressions.* Upon seeing or hearing someone for the first time, most people come to some quick decisions about that individual or topic. It is quite difficult to later alter first impressions.
2. *Assuming that everyone is like you.* Almost all of us fall into the trap of thinking that all people act or should act like we do. As a result of this as-

sumption, perceptions may not account for differences in cultures and environments in which people have very different languages and communication styles.

3. *Accepting the positive and assuming the negative.* American culture seems to perpetuate the negative. As a result, we take for granted positive performances and reinforcements and focus on negative messages and behaviors.

Perceptions hold an important place in the business environment. Research in managerial decision making, for instance, indicates that perceptions not only affect the choice of what to do but also the way in which choices are implemented.[3] In addition, the very nature of the business structure makes decision making an important aspect of any organization. In business, when you are attempting to attract customers to buy products, please supervisors in order to get promotions, and work in harmony with other employees, you may find yourself coming up against individuals whose values, attitudes, and beliefs are quite different from yours. These perceptual differences will affect their decision making and have a direct effect on you. You may find yourself in conflict with others because you have a different view of the world. You may find that, in order to maintain a relationship, you have to put aside or modify your views, or you may decide to stick to your perceptions and pay the consequences.

PHYSIOLOGICAL DIMENSION OF INTRAPERSONAL COMMUNICATION

In addition to the psychological dimension of one's perceptual filter, communicators have physiological responses to messages, responses that are closely tied to the psychological responses. It is important for communicators to understand how these physiological factors affect communication.

Stress

The North American culture operates as a competitive society of winners and losers. As a result, we can be victims of threats to security, job retention, or even our basic value system. Modern technology has increased our pace of work and of living. Newfound freedoms bring newfound responsibilities, which can result in confusion and frustration. Competition, threats, and changes create **stress,** a physical response to environmental demands that result in tension.

On the one hand, stress is a necessary and positive characteristic of human existence. It is the impetus for growth, change, and adaptation. In adjusting to the demands of our physical and symbolic environment, there are opportunities for interpersonal and social creativity and discovery. On the other hand, mounting evidence suggests that chronic stress can have devastating physical and emotional consequences. Research suggests that "stress lowers our resistance to illness and can play a contributory role in diseases of the kidney; heart and blood vessels (including high blood pressure); migraine and tension headaches; gastrointestinal problems such as ulcers; asthma and allergies; respiratory disease; arthritis; and even cancer."[4]

Stress is a biological response. The process centers on self-talk (intrapersonal communication), which leads physical hormones to secrete, which can result in alarm. Self-talk interprets the alarm as "Something's wrong"; "I'm afraid"; or "I don't like what's going on."

These physiological responses trigger psychological coping mechanisms that attempt to protect the body. As the body tightens up to protect itself, psychological manifestations are revealed in one's communication. Such signaling devices as stuttering, heightened vocal pitch, increased or decreased volume, grammatical or pronunciation errors, rapid rate, recall lapses, vocalized pauses, pounding heartbeat, shaking, or sweating can result.[5]

Because stress has become such a major issue in the workplace, many businesses have instituted stress reduction workshops and activities, such as exercise programs, to help employees deal with their work pressures.

Are You Coping with Stress?

by Frank Grazian

Job stress is becoming a worldwide epidemic.

That's the gist of an Associated Press story about a report by the International Labor Organization.

The report, titled "Job Stress: The 20th Century Disease," says that stress-related injury claims on the job "have climbed from 5 percent of all occupational disease claims in 1980 to 15 percent a decade later."

The ILO, an arm of the United Nations, estimates "the cost of job stress in the U.S. alone at $200 billion annually."

According to the report, the cost stems from "compensation claims, reduced productivity, absenteeism, added health insurance costs and direct medical expenses for related diseases such as ulcers, high blood pressure and heart attacks."

One cause of stress is the constant monitoring of employees from "how quickly they perform a task to the frequency and length of breaks."

Unfortunately, companies are contributing to stress but doing little to help employees cope with it, notes the report.

Here are some ways management might help to reduce employee stress:

- *Understand that employee helplessness and uncertainty are two major causes of stress. Empower employees to make decisions in the areas they know best, trust them to do their job correctly, and let them know where they stand.*

- *Increase employee self-esteem. One way: Let people know they are valued.*

Here are some ways employees can cope with workplace stress:

- *Realize that stress is based on your perception of something that you feel threatens you—and that you have the power to change that perception. Step back and and ask yourself what about the situation threatens you—and how you can see it differently. One suggestion: Find something in the situation you can control—and do so.*

- *Develop a commitment toward your job. Determine what it is about your job that makes a difference—and see it as a mission. In this way, you'll react to your own pressures.*

- *Develop additional job skills. Take courses, read books, etc. The more competent you feel, the more you'll feel in control of your career.*

- *Gain control of as many aspects of your life as you can. If the job situation seems out of hand, concentrate on those things in your private life that you can direct and regulate.*

- *Avoid trying to be a perfectionist. Just strive to do the best you can under the circumstances.*

- *Learn relaxation techniques. Examples: biofeedback, meditation, deep breathing.*

It is significant to realize that most stressors to which we adapt result from symbolic rather than physical threats. " [A] heated argument with a colleague, the prospect of failure on an important task, the tension of a long wait, or the pressure of an approaching deadline for an uncompleted project can be potent stressors for humans. These symbolic threats are capable of triggering the same hormonal, muscular, and neural reactions that, for other animals, are associated with physical threats to their physical well-being."[6]

According to the National Centers for Disease Control and Prevention, stress, boredom, and frustration at work lead to substantial health problems. In fact, a major report by the Centers reveals that "mental stress accounted for more than one in every ten occupational disease and injury claims" in the workplace.[7] The Centers' research indicates that "contributing to a worker's dissatisfaction with his (her) job are conditions such as work overload, lack of control over the job, nonsupportive bosses and colleagues, limited job opportunities, undefined tasks, rotating shifts, and operating at a machine-set pace."[8]

Because stress has become such a major issue in the workplace, many businesses have instituted stress reduction workshops and programs for employees to help them deal with their work pressures.

There are countless strategies for dealing with stress. For short-term stress reduction, a clinical psychologist recommends some physical techniques:

1. Clench your fists tightly and count to ten. Release them and let your whole body go completely limp.
2. Take a deep breath and hold it while counting to ten. When you exhale, let your breath all out at once and let your body go completely loose and limp.
3. Breathing normally, let go more and more as you let out each breath while counting slowly from ten to zero, one number per breath.
4. Imagine yourself basking in the warm sun on a beach or soaking in a hot tub until you can actually feel the warmth.[9]

In addition to short-term physiological responses to stress, stress reduction experts offer advice for long-term control of stress on the job. Communicators have found these patterns to be helpful:

1. *Do one thing at a time.* Focus on what you do. Don't look back or ahead while you are working on a particular task.
2. *Do the best you can and don't worry about the outcome as you're processing the task.*
3. *Don't worry about things over which you have no control* (which may well be a large part of the operations in a workplace).
4. *When a crisis occurs, face it.* Take constructive action and organize a response. Be flexible.[10]

Ask Yourself Four Questions

Every once in a while, get off the merry-go-round and ask yourself these questions:

• *What are we doing?*
• *What should we be doing?*
• *What should we be doing next?*
• *What should we not be doing?*

Source: Bill New, CEO, Natus Medical, writing in *from 36,000 feet*. . . . 6436 City West Parkway, Ste. 440, Minneapolis, MN 55344.

5. *Say "no" when the request is about a low priority item.* Not all matters have to be dealt with, and even if they do, they may not need immediate attention.
6. *Delegate tasks to others.* Do not assume that you are the only person who can accomplish a goal. Divide major tasks into segments and give various sections to others to accomplish.
7. *Instead of eating lunch, go to the company gym or take a walk.* Exercise is an excellent way to relieve stress. In addition, many people find that while riding a bike, or running, they come up with solutions to problems and plans of action.
8. *Accept the fact that not everything is going to get done immediately.*
9. *Accept that there is no such thing as "perfect."* Do the very best you can.
10. *Don't procrastinate.* Set priorities and a time schedule and follow it. Don't believe the theory of some procrastinators that they work best under pressure.

Communication Anxiety

Communication anxiety is the real or anticipated fear of communicating with others. Communication anxiety affects a great number of people, causing them to believe that they have more to lose than to gain from communicating. Anxious people fear rejection and criticism. The fear can then become a self-fulfilling prophecy. The apprehensive persons will expect to have difficulty communicating, so they will.

A person fearful of communicating with others often attempts to avoid interacting with people, avoiding situations where he or she will be expected to share with others in work groups or in making oral presentations to colleagues. Apprehensive people may fail to speak up, leaving others with indifferent or negative impressions of their work and their contributions to the organization.

Communication anxiety is a problem for individuals in an organization. Its effect on job-related activities impacts on the organization as well. Not only employees but also supervisors must be aware of communication anxiety and realize that individuals may have such problems. Once the condition is identified, a good supervisor should have the resources of referrals for dealing with the problem.

Because communication apprehension results from a lifetime of being uncomfortable with oneself as a communicator, there are no ready-made strategies for an instantaneous "cure." Rather, an individual with communication anxiety needs guidance to find ways to gain acceptance of himself/herself as a communicator, to learn communication skills, and to reach an acceptable level of comfort when communicating with others.

To reach that level of comfort, specialists in communication anxiety have identified various means for dealing with the apprehension. One of these is **systematic desensitization,** a process by which one learns to relax. Systematic desensitization usually centers on deep muscle relaxation. It can sometimes be achieved by listening to tape recordings that have been developed for this purpose or by learning self-hypnosis or through self-hypnosis techniques.[11]

Another strategy for coping with communication anxiety is the process of **cognitive modification.** This method teaches a person to modify the negative self-talk. Many anxious people have been found to give themselves messages like "I can't talk to people"; "I hate to give speeches"; "I'll never get through this briefing." Cognitive modification normally requires the services of a specialist to help one "de-program" the negative messages and replace them with positive, reinforcing statements that shape the communication expectations.

At the self-help level, the communicator who experiences a low level of communication apprehension can help himself/herself. The first step is to accept that you will feel anxious. Everyone experiences anxiety in certain types of communication situations. Great orators throughout history have observed that they have felt nervous before starting to present a speech. Professional speakers and performers frequently testify as to how nervous they feel before

---

Coping with Perfectionism

Striving for perfection can do more harm than good. Taking the time to get everything "just right" only adds to your stress.

Here are some ways to cope with perfectionism:

- *Ask yourself, "Am I doing this to be perfect or do I have a specific goal in mind?" If you're trying to be perfect, stop what you're doing and refocus.*

- *Rate your work on a scale of 1(not important) to 10 (extremely important) if you're afraid it's not perfect. Don't worry about anything below a 9. Live with the anxiety, if necessary.*

- *Try something new or challenging. Because you're working on something different, your focus will be pursuing the task—not on completing it perfectly.*

- *Motivate employees and yourself by praising accomplishments—not by punishing mistakes.*

Note: If you're a perfectionist, the first step may be to realize that trying to be perfect is your way of managing anxiety. To check your perfectionist tendencies, you have to come up with ways to tolerate the anxiety that will result.

What to do: Use stress-reducing techniques—exercise, relaxation tapes, yoga, etc.—to get you through the withdrawal period.

Source: *Sacred Bull: The Inner Obstacles That Hold You Back at Work and How to Overcome Them,* by Albert J. Bernstein and Sydney Craft Rozen, John Wiley & Sons Inc., 605 3rd Ave., New York, NY 10158.

facing their audience. It should be recognized that such anxiety can be productive. It produces the physiological response of increasing your adrenaline and getting you "pumped up" with energy to give the communication your all, your best. The key is to control your nervous energy rather than letting it take control over you.

Set a useful, reachable communication goal. Then prepare to meet that goal: research the firm before going in for the interview; analyze the issues before participating in the meeting; outline and rehearse your briefing several times before you present it. Finally, in presenting yourself in the communication situation, try to become totally involved in the communication itself so that you lose your concentration on yourself and your anxiety.

COGNITIVE DIMENSION OF INTRAPERSONAL COMMUNICATION

Just as our psychological and physiological makeup shapes how we communicate through the internal channels, so, too, does the way we cognitively process messages influence intrapersonal communication. The cognitive process results from what psychologists refer to as schemata that we carry in our cortex.[12] These **schemata** represent the way we mentally organize information in our brains.

Schemata are made up of the mental and linguistic categories of all the information that we have stored away throughout all of our life experiences. An individual's culture, background, family, education, and experience all serve as the framework for creating the schemata that enable us to deal with incoming information. This schematic framework results from how we learn and subsequently use information in processing both verbal and nonverbal messages.

The communicator's **cognitive processing** is influenced by a number of factors that affect how the schema will be used to attend to messages, to interpret messages, and even to store messages in the long-term memory. The **perceptual filter** is a major factor in shaping the cognitive schemata—and vice versa. For it is through the perceptual filter that all incoming messages are screened before being "fit" into one schema or another.

The cognitive process also results from the way one cognitively structures the information. Communicators who are products of Western society generally send and receive messages either **inductively** (using a series of specifics to draw a general conclusion) or **deductively** (using general premises to build a specific conclusion). Communicators who offer deductive arguments work from commonly shared premises through what is known as the enthymeme. When using the **enthymeme,** the common premise does not have to be spelled out, because speaker and listener both share this base for building on the argument.

Communicators build inductive arguments by using a series of specifics as the basis for drawing the conclusion. It is critical that the specifics support the general conclusion; otherwise, the communicator runs the risk of a generalization in which the conclusion is not warranted by the specifics cited.

While North Americans are comfortable with inductive and deductive structures, structures that form the base for the arguments we present, it must be recognized that other societies often function at a more intuitive level. An anthropologist has identified cultures that are more high context and cultures that are more low context.[13] In **low context cultures** such as the United States, communicators must elaborate and spell out their arguments, because communicators do not necessarily share the frame of reference. In **high context cultures** such as Japan, communicators do not have to be so explicit, because communicators often intuitively share the frame of reference. This knowledge of the varying reasoning structures in cultures is imperative for business people to know and be sensitive to in the present multicultural business environment.

In addition to cognitive structure, communication is influenced by the human need for cognitive consistency. Each of us holds certain beliefs, attitudes, and values. **Values** are those ideas or things that we perceive to be of worth. **Attitudes** are our predispositions, positive and negative. **Beliefs** are our convictions, true or false. Most communicators tend to need to keep these values, attitudes, and beliefs in balance, a state known as **cognitive consistency.** If any part of the system is thrown out of balance, **cognitive dissonance** can result and the person becomes confused. To avoid or eliminate cognitive dissonance and create a rational schemata, we try to keep the values, attitudes, and beliefs in balance.

Some communication researchers also have considered the effect of cognitive complexity on a person's communication system. **Cognitive complexity** results from an individual's general level of intelligence. The more intellectually complex one is, the more he or she can deal with higher orders of abstractions and with various levels of information.

The way we cognitively process information has a profound effect on our intrapersonal communication. It frames the way we decode messages through the schemata we have developed from our mental categories. And our information processing serves as the foundation for the way we encode messages that we shape to send to other people.

AFFECTIVE DIMENSION OF INTRAPERSONAL COMMUNICATION

In addition to the cognitive dimensions of intrapersonal communication, there are important affective—emotional—dimensions that play a role in any communicator's processing of messages. One of the key emotions is **fear.** Much of communication apprehension results from the fear of the unknown. No matter how carefully prepared you are for any particular communication with others, you never know exactly what their response will be to you and your message. Thus, there often are anxious moments as you get started and begin to feel comfortable in any communication situation.

Another significant emotion that influences communication is **anger.** Anger is a reaction to frustration. The frustration may be internal and personal, as when you get upset with yourself for not being able to accomplish a task. Or the cause of frustration may be external. For example, in a team project if two subordinates don't finish their part of a project, causing the entire process to be detained, you may feel frustrated because the situation reflects negatively on your leadership. Even though the action that precipitated the feelings are external, the anger feelings are internal, personal. Anger can often be described by examining who has done what. The formula is, *I (specific statement of want/belief/need), but (name of person, including yourself) (other person's action/wants/belief/needs). This makes me feel angry.* For example, *I wanted Deanna and Garrett to finish the cost analysis on time, but Deanna and Garrett didn't complete the analysis on time. This makes me feel angry.*

Since feelings are a natural part of our makeup, our anger is justifiable. It is how we act on that anger that can create either a positive or destructive reaction. Recent research on emotions indicates that in human evolution the first brain was the emotional brain, the second the logical brain. We tend, therefore, to react first on an emotional level, then on the logical level. It is why your first reaction to your subordinate's lack of timely completion of the report may be an angry outburst. When you have had time to think about it, you might react by asking why the job wasn't promptly submitted. It might be that Deanna and Garrett had finished the report on time, but a computer breakdown had caused it to be printed late. If you had reacted by attacking your coworkers for slacking off or being irresponsible, you might find yourself embarrassed when the real cause is revealed.

In the workplace, anger can be a very destructive force, if it becomes excessive. An industrial psychologist, who specializes in helping people deal with anger, observes that "there is a plethora of empirical research indicating that individuals who do manage their anger at work are much more successful than those who don't."[14] It is important to realize that his use of the word "manage" does not mean that a person should work to eliminate her or his feelings, but that there are constructive and destructive ways to deal with anger. Constructively, a person acknowledges the emotion and deals with it by attacking the issue, and not the other person. For example, anger specialists recommend that interpersonally, an individual should:

1. *Validate and acknowledge your anger.*
2. *Calm down and compose yourself.*

How to Keep Your Composure

Your boss or coworker says something that irritates you—and you want to lash back. But you don't want to lose your cool at work. How can you keep your composure without experiencing a lot of stress?
  Some suggestions:

- *Step away and do what's called "a perception check." Ask yourself what you're really upset about. Does the situation revive something that happened to you as a child?*

- *Try to understand why the person behaved that way. You might realize that the intent was not vindictive.*

- *Let your feelings out on paper. Don't edit or censor a thing. Then look over what you've written and destroy the piece of paper. You'll feel better.*

- *Talk with coworkers you can trust. You'll release some emotions—and you might also get an objective assessment in the situation.*

- *Try to determine if you're overreacting. Ask yourself: "If this happened to my best friend, would I think that she or he was no good?" Your answer should help keep things in perspective.*

- *Before you decide to confront the offender, ask yourself these questions:*
  –"What will I gain by taking this action?"
  –"Will I achieve my goals with this particular person?"

Source: Nancy Monson, writing in *New Woman*, 215 Lexington Ave., New York, NY 10016.

---

3. *Identify the provocation.*
4. *Empower yourself; recognize that you* don't *have to accept it.*
5. *Choose an appropriate response.*[15]

The Communicator Self

In addition to knowing your psychological, physiological, cognitive, and affective channels, intrapersonal communication can take you to an understanding of your self-concept, the roles you must play, and your communication style. "Throughout your future business and professional life, your **self-image**—your definition of who and what you are, your assets and liabilities—will continually be challenged, by you or by those you come in contact with. For some people, keeping a self-image intact is not a difficult chore; for others, it presents an ongoing problem."[16] For others, there is a need to alter the self-image, if it is negative and stops you from reaching your potential due to fears, doubts, and feelings about your talents and abilities.

SELF-CONCEPT

"**Self-concept** represents your psychological self—all the experiences, beliefs, attitudes, and values that make up the self; it includes how you perceive the world, how the world perceives you, and how you perceive yourself."[17] A manager who has a positive self-concept projects an image of assurance and appears to be in command of information and situations. Others may perceive this image as favorable and often react positively to such a person.

People evaluate themselves based on their physical attributes, emotional attributes, mental attributes, and relationships with others. The more positively an individual regards these attributes, the more likely the individual will not have to fight off interpersonal negative feelings that block meaningful actions. A person who projects self-confidence, assurance, and interpersonal magnetism is usually one who enjoys a positive self-concept.

Individuals tend to act consistently with the feelings they hold about themselves. Therefore, people who have a negative self-concept may run the risk of seeing themselves as failures and not allowing themselves to be successful. If you expect not to accomplish something, you are likely, then, not to accomplish it. This phenomenon is known as the **self-fulfilling prophecy.** If you do not accept yourself, others will likely have a difficult time accepting you.

A person's self-concept influences the way that individual deals with others. A person with a positive self-image is likely to act in ways that are perceived as positive traits: having a good sense of humor, being optimistic, dealing with people in a direct and understanding manner, not feeling that she or he has to prove superiority, and being reasonably relaxed in the company of others. On the other hand, those who have a negative self-concept are likely to feel pressure to make others like them. Or they may panic at making mistakes, thus alienating others or communicating a lack of confidence in their actions. Such responses can certainly have an impact not only on the individual but also on coworkers and customers alike.

The self is composed of four components. The **spiritual self** relates to the way you think and feel. Your value system, attitudes, and beliefs are part of this spiritual self. The **material self** consists of what you possess—clothing, jewelry, house, automobile—and what these possessions communicate about you. The **social self** is defined through your relationships with others. This part of your self is concerned with how you manage those relationships and how you feel about your kinships with others. The **physical self** relates to how you look and how you feel about how you look. Weight, facial appearance, hairstyle, and body build are all elements that contribute to the physical self.

The more positive your perception of your spiritual, material, social, and physical self, the closer you are to a positive self-concept. Persons who have positive self-concepts about their communication abilities usually are effective, evidencing minimal apprehension and demonstrating self-assurance. A

Business Professionals Share Their Views

Profile: Linda Eaton, senior consultant, Franklin Quest Company, Salt Lake City, consultant to many of the Fortune 1000 companies.

How does a person develop a strong self-concept?

A great self-concept is acquirable. Martin Seligman's *Learned Optimism* is a great guide for businesspersons to use to assist them in the development. It basically stresses that positive people (a) take credit for their actions, (b) take responsibility, (c) identify negative experiences as learning opportunities, not things that happen to them (a la "victim") but rather things they had a hand in shaping.

Is there a correlation between positive self-confidence and leadership?

Leaders have positive self-concepts, a vision, and the confidence to develop and share that vision. Leadership builds on the belief in the self and a positive self-concept.

How does a person's self-concept affect businesspeople in the changing work environment, especially as it relates to downsizing and mergers?

As George Bernard Shaw once said, "Luck is the marriage of opportunity and preparation." A downsizing, a merger, or an acquisition is not necessarily a good or a bad thing. Those with strong self-concepts view their jobs as a vehicle for self-development, and therefore are less negatively emotionally impacted by change.

person with a negative self-concept often communicates a lack of self-confidence.

There are ways to alter a negative self-concept. This process starts when the person gains an understanding that having the negative self-image is not in her or his best interest and is causing interpersonal and interactive difficulties. In other words, your negative self-concept is a problem for you. If you desire to change, the first step is to recognize the problem, then to develop a strategy to alter that aspect of your self-image. Sometimes you can make the change on your own, and sometimes you need assistance, such as a personal trainer to help change body shape, a beauty consultant to aid changing your hairstyle and makeup, or a mental health professional to aid in developing a more positive self-concept.

SELF-IDENTITIES

Many different selves can result from the many different roles that one must play. These are self-identities. It is revealing to make a list of the roles that you assume, even on a daily basis: employer, manager, employee, friend, team leader. Each role may call for a different kind of communication response.

Thus, the successful communicator is one who is able to adapt to the different roles that he or she plays and adopt communication strategies that enable the person to be successful at playing the role.

In organizations, understanding how to assume different roles is a critical skill. A person may be a manager, for instance, responsible for the results of a group of people charged with a particular task. At the same time, that individual must be part of the work group of managers who report to the executive at the next higher level in the organization. This establishes what is known as the **linking pin,** the reality that the manager must be effective not only in leading his own work group, but also in linking that group to the organization at the next level in the structure. Not all individuals are successful at making this link, often because they do not recognize the need to adapt to the different roles and expectations of them at the executive level.

SELF-TALK

Intrapersonal communication specialists have come to realize that communication with the self is the foundation for all that we accomplish as communicators.[18] As a result, in an effort to achieve the qualities identified in this chapter, the communicator must begin to monitor and, as necessary, modify his or her own **self-talk,** verbal and nonverbal inner speech.

If your self-talk is negative ("I could never do that." "My boss doesn't like me."), then it is possible to reprogram yourself in a more positive frame and thus be a more willing and effective communicator.[19] To have an effect, though, positive self-talk ("That's going to be an interesting challenge." "Yes, I'll have to talk with her.") has to reach your subconscious level so that it is assimilated as part of *your* intrapersonal communication repertoire. To reframe your intrapersonal communication, you must recognize that early efforts to do this will seem unnatural and that only repetition over time will have an effect. You must also recognize that, realistically, making changes in your self-talk is a very difficult task. It is easy to understand the theory, and say you are going to change; but it is difficult to change years of self-doubt. "Stop feeding yourself negative words and start building yourself up with positive ones."[20]

Improving Intrapersonal Communication

One's interpersonal and professional success requires a strong sense of knowing oneself and committing oneself to continuous investigation of the possible need for improvement. No one in the workplace can rest solely on past per-

How to Reengineer Yourself

Respond to these statements with a "yes" or a "no":

- *I believe I have the means to resolve my problems and change the things I want to change.*
- *I am not afraid of taking reasonable risks.*
- *I am not embarrassed to ask for help when I need it.*
- *I can laugh at the funny side of life and myself.*

According to a new book, Reengineering Yourself: A Blueprint for Personal Success in the New Corporate Culture, *you should answer "yes" to most of these statements. If you do, "you compare favorably with productive, successful, and high-energy businesspeople."*

This quiz covers one of five major areas a manager must improve—productivity, communication, leadership, creativity, and team building.

The book is essentially a manual to help managers reengineer themselves in each of these categories.

The main topic is change. As the authors note:

"Change or die. Everything that you thought was finished, understood, clear, is no more. What you were familiar with is gone. The world has changed and continues to change in surprisingly, even shockingly, unexpected ways."

They offer these "axioms":

- *"Change is the essence of everything. Nothing exists without constant change."*
- *"Change is never completed; there is always more to change."*

Score −2 (almost never), −1 (occasionally), 0 (frequently), +1 (most of the time), and +2 (almost always) in the following sample. Praise yourself on all scores of 0 and above.

- *"Individuality. Independent of senseless cultural restrictions and bias. Avoids national and ethnic distortions. Fresh regard for each different situation and person."*
- *"Wonder. Discovers newness in old, familiar things. Finds beauty in most things. Sense of awe. Not bored. Enjoys inner self and focuses on the positives."*
- *"Creativity. Enjoys trying/learning new things, looking for new possibilities. Keeps an open mind and a child's view of the world in everyday activities."*

Source: Reengineering Yourself: A Blueprint for Personal Success in the New Corporate Culture, by Dr. Daniel L. Araoz & Dr. William S. Sutton, Bob Adams Inc. Publishers, 260 Center St., Holbrook, MA 02343.

formance or reputation: "Every single employee should assume responsibility for upgrading his or her job performance . . . and your skills should be in a state of constant renewal."[21] The result of all of this is communication self-management. You can assume responsibility for your own communication responses and attempt to shape them to create the greatest possible benefits in your interactions with yourself, with your boss, with your customers, and with your coworkers alike. This self-management requires that you empower yourself through self-assessment; self-approval; self-commitment; and self-fulfillment.[22]

It has been suggested that this communication self-management can take the form of an intrapersonal **communication plan.** The plan requires that you work through phases to reach your desired communication goals:

1. Assess your current level of effectiveness.
2. State your goals for change.
3. Identify the knowledge and skills required to reach your goals.
4. Analyze the benefits of achieving your goals.
5. Determine the appropriate situation for new communication behavior.
6. Identify the obstacles to achieving your communication goals and how you can overcome those obstacles.
7. Monitor and evaluate your own progress.[23]

Knowing yourself as a communicator is the first step in achieving the necessary level of competence as a communicator in interactions with other people, as "You are the message."[24]

● ● ● **In Summary** ● ● ●

Intrapersonal communication is communication within the self. Communication at the personal level is a means to get in touch with your perceptions of the world and to confirm or disconfirm those perceptions. Intrapersonal communication provides the foundation for all of the communicating that people do in professional and private settings. Your intrapersonal communication is made up of four dimensions: psychological, physiological, cognitive, and affective. An important aspect of intrapersonal communication is self-image. Throughout business and professional life, your self-image, your definition of who and what you are—your assets and liabilities—will continually be challenged, if not by you then by those you come in contact with.

=== **Business Communication in Practice** ===

1. On a sheet of paper, complete the following statements.
   a. Write down whatever first comes to your mind in response to each item:
      I am . . .
      I would like to be . . .
      I believe others see me as . . .
      I am a . . .
      I perceive myself as . . .
      I don't like to . . .
      When I get angry, I . . .
   b. Imagine a person whom you consider to be your "best" friend. Answer these questions as if you were that person writing about you:
      Three words I'd use to describe _____ are _____, _____, and _____.

      _____ would like to change _____ about himself/herself.
         Now write a two-sentence summary of what you have just expressed. Analyze your summary based on the concept that the verb *to be* shapes how we are what we are (the conjugations of *to be* are "I was," "I am," and "I will be"). Determine how this applies to your responses and your summary of yourself.
2. Design a mosaic or collage composite of pictures, drawings, and magazine or newspaper clippings that illustrates your attitudes, beliefs, and values. What effect can your images of yourself have on you as a businessperson?
3. Perceptions test.[25]
   Answer each of these questions T (true) or F (false):
   a. It is unlikely that others will work to see things as I do to try to understand me. On the other hand, they will expect me to do so.
   b. People normally perceive their own behavior as being both consistent and logical.
   c. A high correlation exists between how accurately we perceive ourselves and our ability to perceive others accurately.
   d. People tend to see and hear only what is significant to them.
   e. The more secure and self-fulfilled a person is, the more effective he or she will be in correctly perceiving and accepting reality.
   f. It is unlikely other people will exert themselves to understand new ideas or to see both sides of a difference in opinion when they are personally involved in the disagreement.
      Your instructor can provide you with the "correct" responses to these items.

4. Personal Report of Communication Apprehension (PRCA).[26]

Directions: This instrument is composed of 24 statements concerning your feelings about communicating with other people. Please indicate, in the space provided, the degree to which each statement applies to you by marking the number indicating whether you (1) Strongly Agree, (2) Agree, (3) Are Undecided, (4) Disagree, or (5) Strongly Disagree with each statement. There are no right or wrong answers. Many of the statements are similar to other statements. Do not be concerned about this. Work quickly—just record your first impression. After you have filled out this questionnaire, your instructor will inform you as to how to score it and how to interpret your score.

_____ 1. I dislike participating in group discussions.

_____ 2. Generally, I am comfortable while participating in group discussions.

_____ 3. I am tense and nervous while participating in group discussions.

_____ 4. I like to get involved in group discussions.

_____ 5. Engaging in a group discussion with new people makes me tense and nervous.

_____ 6. I am calm and relaxed while participating in group discussions.

_____ 7. Generally, I am nervous when I have to participate in a meeting.

_____ 8. Usually, I am calm and relaxed while participating in meetings.

_____ 9. I am very calm and relaxed when I am called upon to express an opinion at a meeting.

_____ 10. I am afraid to express myself at meetings.

_____ 11. Communicating at meetings usually makes me uncomfortable.

_____ 12. I am very relaxed when I answer questions at a meeting.

_____ 13. While participating in a conversation with a new acquaintance, I feel very nervous.

_____ 14. I have no fear of speaking up in conversations.

_____ 15. Ordinarily, I am very tense and nervous in conversations.

_____ 16. Ordinarily, I am very calm and relaxed in conversations.

_____ 17. While conversing with a new acquaintance, I feel very relaxed.

_____ 18. I'm afraid to speak up in conversations.

_____ 19. I have no fear of giving a speech.

_____ 20. Certain parts of my body feel very tense and rigid while giving a speech.

_____ 21. I feel relaxed while giving a speech.
_____ 22. My thoughts become confused and jumbled when I am giving a speech.
_____ 23. I face the prospect of giving a speech with confidence.
_____ 24. While giving a speech, I get so nervous that I forget the facts I really know.

● ● ● Notes ● ● ●

1. James W. Hikins, "Intrapersonal Discourse and Its Relationship to Human Communication: Rhetorical Dimensions of Self-Talk," in Charles V. Roberts and Kittie W. Watson (eds.), *Intrapersonal Communication Processes* (New Orleans: Spectra, 1989), p. 53.
2. Joseph DeVito, *The Communication Handbook: A Dictionary* (New York: Harper and Row, 1986), p. 224.
3. E. Frank Harrison, *The Managerial Decision-Making Process* (Boston: Houghton Mifflin, 1975), p. 168.
4. Brent Ruben, "Stress, Interpersonal Communication, and Assertiveness: Marshmallows, Machine-guns, and Target Shooters," paper presented at the Eastern Communication Association Convention, Pittsburgh, PA (1981), p. 2.
5. Joyce Lain Kennedy, "Here Is How to Cope with Stress on the Job," *Cleveland Plain Dealer* (August 14, 1988), 25.
6. Ruben, 2.
7. "Job-Stress Illness Up," National Centers for Disease Control, Atlanta GA, n.d.
8. Robert Byrd, "Job Stress Illness Up," *The Washington Post* (October 3, 1986), F2.
9. Dr. Alfred Barrios.
10. Elizabeth Price, "Keeping Your Cool in Vexing Situations," *Cleveland Plain Dealer* (November 1, 1981), C1.
11. Tapes include "Deep Muscular Relaxation" by James McCroskey, West Virginia University, and "Speech Anxiety Reduction" by Joanna Pucel, St. Cloud State University.
12. See Renee Edwards and Janet L. McDonald, "Schema Theory and Listening," in Andrew D. Wolvin and Carolyn Gwynn Coakley (eds.), *Perspectives on Listening* (Norwood, NJ: Ablex, 1993), pp. 60–77.
13. Edward T. Hall and Mildred Lee Hall, *Understanding Cultural Differences* (Yarmouth, ME: Intercultural Press, 1990), pp. 6–10.
14. Hendrie Weisinger, *Anger at Work* (New York: Morrow, 1995), p. 1.
15. Ibid. 144–149.
16. Abner M. Eisenberg, *Understanding Communication in Business and the Professions* (New York: Macmillan, 1978), p. 15.
17. Roy Berko, Andrew Wolvin, and Darlyn Wolvin, *Communicating: A Social and Career Focus,* 6th ed. (Boston: Houghton Mifflin, 1995).
18. Donna R. Vocate, "Self-Talk and Inner Speech: Understanding the Uniquely Human Aspects of Intrapersonal Communication," in Donna R. Vocate (ed.), *Intrapersonal Communication: Different Voices, Different Minds* (Hillsdale, NJ: Erlbaum, 1994).

19. See Shad Helmstetter, *The Self-Talk Solution* (New York: Pocket Books, 1987).
20. Susan Jeffers, "Building Your Self-Esteem," *Success* (October 1987): 72.
21. Price Pritchett, *New Work Habits for a Radically Changing World* (Dallas: Pritchett and Associates, 1995), p. 43.
22. Robert McGarvey, "Les Brown: Staying Motivated," *Entrepreneur* (August 1995): 103.
23. Sandra E. O'Connell, *The Manager as Communicator* (San Francisco: Harper and Row, 1979), p. 142.
24. Roger Ailes, *You Are the Message* (New York: Doubleday, 1988), p. 25.
25. Dr. Walter John, director of training, Friendly Ice Cream Corporation.
26. PRCA used with permission of Dr. James McCroskey, West Virginia University.

CHAPTER

7

Managing Communication with Others

EXPECTED OUTCOMES

After completing this chapter, you should be able to:

- Define interpersonal communication and explain its importance in the business setting.
- Effectively use interpersonal communication in telephoning, management-employee relationships, directing, job training, conflict, and conflict management.
- Explain and manage sexual harassment in the business environment.

*W*hile working as a manager for a large corporation, I found myself in a most difficult situation. Several of my employees had come to complain that a coworker had a horrible body odor and they were having a very hard time working next to her. I knew the woman was from a culture where deodorants are not commonly used. Checking the woman's employment record, I learned that the previous manager had talked to her about this problem. Now I had to deal with this awkward and difficult situation. I was at a loss about exactly how to handle the necessary face-to-face encounter without being accused of sexual or cultural harassment.

We spend most of our time talking with people on an interpersonal level—individually (one-to-one) or in small groups.[1] This **interpersonal communication** between people involves the exchange of messages and the development of a relationship based on the effect of those messages.

As we attempt to exchange ideas with other people, we have a purpose in mind. The purpose may be an attempt to help them understand some idea or concept, to gain new information, to change their point of view, to get them to understand why we feel as we do, or to influence them to take some type of action. The success of our interpersonal communication determines whether or not we are successful in achieving our end goal.

During any interpersonal transaction, the communication is multichanneled. We use both verbal and nonverbal channels in message sending and receiving.

As we communicate with the individuals, our mutual feelings about and toward each other—our relationship—has an effect. Our communication is affected by relationship-based factors, such as whether we like or dislike the other person, or whether we are in a power or control position (boss, supervisor) or a subordinate position (employee) with the other individual. In many instances, the hierarchy of power in interpersonal relationships may determine not only the message but also the effect of the message. Experts tend to agree that most problems in communication occur in the relationship dimension rather than in the content dimension—in the way we feel about or toward each other rather than in what is said.[2] As we exchange ideas, we normally do so by the use of symbols, words, which are letter combinations that a particular society has agreed represent certain ideas. We also use images, the ideas or concrete objects that the symbols represent. Another factor affecting our communicating is values, a judgment about what is important, what counts.[3]

During any interpersonal transaction, the communication is multi-channeled. We use both verbal and nonverbal channels in message sending and receiving. Sensitivity to these channels is important, so we don't miss much of the content and purpose of a message.

What is effective interpersonal communication and how can you be an effective interpersonal communicator in the business environment?

Self-disclosure

The values we hold determine much of what we say and do in interpersonal communication. Our verbalizations and actions reflect our values, and our values can be inferred from our verbalizations and actions. Sometimes we decide to reveal what we think or feel; at other times, we decide that the ideas, beliefs, and information may be too private for others to know.

Self-disclosure, the communication of one person's private world to another, is truly an important part of behavior. Another person can get to know you only by what you reveal verbally or by what the person perceives about you from your nonverbal behavior. In making the decision whether or not to self-disclose, a person must remember, "You can know me truly only if I let you, only if I want you to know me."[4]

Be aware that self-disclosure involves a risk. Once someone knows something about you, that information can no longer be private. The conscious act of sharing yourself entails a decision as to whether or not you want others to get to know you. If you decide not to share yourself, then others may think you are shy, arrogant, distant; or they may become suspicious of what you are hiding. On the other hand, if you prefer not to share certain information, then that is your privilege.

You select the information that you give on a job resume, in an employment interview, to your boss, or to your fellow workers, to allow people to know you better. This information also has some implications for promotion and retention.

The hard-work ethic is based on the premise that the boss will promote the best employee, the one who is most successful in job performance. Unless employees personally communicate their achievements, the boss will never know about them. The rule of getting ahead is, "Communicate your contributions and accomplishments to your employer."[5] Many employees fail to follow this "eleventh commandment" and also fail to take steps forward in their careers.

Many of us have been taught not to "toot your own horn," or, in other words, not to brag about our accomplishments. Unfortunately, sometimes the system is set up so that if you do not let others know about your accomplishments, they will go unrecognized. You are your own best public relations director. You must determine what is in your best interest and work to achieve that. Usually this endeavor entails making sure that managers and superiors are aware of your accomplishments without being a constant braggart. Remember, if promotions and advancements are based on accomplishments and your accomplishments go unrecognized, then the advancement will go to others. "People forget, at peril of their career advancement, that the decision not to communicate—keep their mouths shut and their noses to the grindstone—is a negative decision that opens the way to all kinds of misunderstandings. Hard work alone is not magic—the results of that effort have to be communicated if it is to advance your career."[6]

Interpersonal Relationships in the Organization

Individuals form relationships and maintain those relationships so long as the persons involved derive something from the experience. This phenomenon is evidenced by the variety of relationships that develop within any organization—between employees, between bosses and workers, between management peers. To be effective, however, the communicators must be able to meet each other's interpersonal needs and maintain a level of trust in the relationship.

Just like social relationships, interpersonal relationships within the organi-

Here's How You Can Say "No"

The more you take on, the greater the chance that you'll lose effectiveness. And although it's sometimes hard to say "no," you can make it easier if you use these strategies:

• Set clear goals and focus your energy on things that will move you toward them. Being purposeful about how you manage your time will make it easier to say "no" to new activities that seem less important. Don't be rigid and inflexible if a new assignment or opportunity comes along, but let your goals become your reality check.

• State clearly the consequences of doing one more thing. Examples: "If I do this, I won't be able to get to do the other things that I've committed to" or "With what I've got going on right now, I feel certain that I won't do as good a job as I'd like and we'll both be disappointed."

• Suggest someone else who you feel could perform the task better or who may be available sooner. Note: If the request comes from your manager, suggest a project or priority that you're doing that you could drop, delay or give to someone else. Or ask the manager to do the same.

Source: Ken Blanchard, The Blanchard Management Report, 125 State Place, Escondido, CA 92029

zation for which you work may depend on need-satisfaction—the satisfaction of your and others' interpersonal and intrapersonal needs. In other words, each person subconsciously asks, Does the time and effort that I am spending pay off in some way to satisfy my needs?

Our similarity or lack of similarity of interpersonal needs, status, occupations, backgrounds, and education all can have an impact on our willingness and even our ability to communicate with other persons in interpersonal relationships. A manager who has a need to impress his superior, for instance, will be operating at that need level rather than being responsive to the needs of subordinates. Similarly, a person who feels that you are a rival for a job might respond to you in a different way than a noncompetitor will. If you are in a power position, such as a manager or supervisor, you may find that those working below you on the organizational chart will not be willing to share personal information or permit a friendship to develop for fear that the relationship will be used against them. On the other hand, some people may try to manipulate a relationship in order to ask for favors. The very nature of the hierarchical structure of the typical organization, which causes certain individuals to have control over the promotions, hirings, firings, and evaluations of others, makes for complicated patterns of interpersonal communication.

Interpersonal Skills in the Business Environment

Interpersonal communication is at the heart of most business dealings. It is useful to consider some of these interpersonal activities—what they are, and how you might be better able to develop the skills for dealing with them as businesspersons. We will examine telephone use, management-employee relationships, directing, job training, conflict and conflict management, sexual harassment, and employee assertion.

USING THE TELEPHONE

The telephone is often called the lifeblood of an organization. Many of the communicative situations constantly facing businesspeople evolve around the use of the telephone. Businesspeople use telephones to "keep in touch, solve problems, deal with emergencies, and to carry out many kinds of transactions."[7] Many individuals find, however, that messages they have left are not received, follow-ups are not made as requested, phone numbers are incorrectly taken and given, misunderstandings take place, and people are offended because of the manner in which the phone call is made or received. In addition, many people get very upset by voice mail systems, despite their convenience. A variety of telephone techniques and suggested phrases can help businesspeople use the phone in a more communicatively productive manner.[8]

Techniques for Receiving Messages

Whether you are an administrative assistant or an administrator, the telephone can be a boon or a bust. Some specific patterns of communicative action can improve successful telephone use.

- *Answer the phone promptly.* Individuals become upset when they have to listen to numerous phone rings when they know the business is open and someone should be answering.
- *Answer calls with a standard greeting.* For a telephone operator an appropriate greeting might be, "XYZ Corporation." For a person answering her or his own phone it could be, "This is Bill Warren. How may I help you?" Avoid saying, "Hello." It conveys no actual information other than that the phone has been answered and then obligates the caller to ask for information that should have been included by the answer in the first place.
- *Acknowledge requests.* Give a specific answer to questions or requests

rather than saying, "Uh huh," "Nope," "What?" or "Yeah." If covering the telephone for someone, respond with, "I'll try to locate Mr. Urban; he's away from his desk at the moment."

- *Identify yourself when you answer the phone.* This response allows the caller to know to whom he or she is talking, and is a point of reference. It also encourages the caller to copy your example and identify herself or himself. Sound positive and interested. A negative attitude on the phone projects a negative image for the organization.
- *Take notes.* Record pertinent information as it is given. Repeat major ideas to make sure you have the correct information. Repeat numbers, spelling of names and places, and any material you are to convey to another or will need for follow-up or to return the call.
- *Hold or transfer calls promptly and properly.* A customer or client who is cut off often becomes extremely distraught—especially if the call is long distance. If you are transferring a call, indicate what the caller will hear (music, a dial tone, or dead air) and how he/she will know that the call has been successfully transferred. If you know the phone system in the organization sometimes cuts off calls, give the caller the extension number to which he or she is going to be transferred, so that if there is a problem the caller will be able easily to contact the correct number.
- *Use a suitable closing remark.* Indicate what the expected follow-up will be and that the call has come to an end (e.g., "Thank you for calling, James. I will tell Lee to check the report and fax it back with comments").

Many organizations and individuals have regulations concerning who will speak to whom and under what conditions. Correct screening answers would be, "Yes, he is in. May I tell him who is calling?" or "Ms. Randall is in a meeting. When would be a good time for her to return your call?" or "I'm sorry, she is in a meeting. She'll be back in her office at . . ." Other suggestions include:

- *If you must leave the phone, tell the caller what is going to happen.* Be specific. For example, "I will have to leave my desk to get that file. It should take me about two minutes. May I put you on hold or would you prefer that I call you back?"
- *Don't leave a caller on hold more than sixty seconds.* The caller does not know where you have gone or when you will return. Short periods of time seem like eternities when you are on hold.
- *Follow through.* Take action immediately to ensure that the message is carried out. Prompt responses and follow-ups for requested services bring positive reactions from customers.
- *Return all telephone calls within twenty-four hours. Unless there are mitigating circumstances, follow up or delegate someone else to handle the*

matter promptly. A major complaint about business dealings is the lack of promptness in handling requests and complaints. A company can quickly get a negative reputation if it becomes known for its laxity in handling customer requests.

Techniques for Placing Calls

The responsibility for making telephone calls successful centers not only on the answerer but on the caller as well. As the caller, make sure that you are making yourself clear and leave accurate messages.

- *Ask the receiver to repeat the information you have given.* As the caller, if you think the person to whom you are speaking does not or may not have the correct information, request that he/she repeat it. In order not to make it sound like you don't trust the person to whom you are speaking, put the burden on yourself by saying, "Just to be sure I gave you the right information, could you repeat the number I gave you?" Or say, "I'll be expecting Ms. Messersmith to be calling me back at 555-4519 by three o'clock, Eastern Standard Time, this afternoon."
- *Speak at a rate that can be understood.* When you give numbers and other information that need to be written down, make sure your pace is slow enough for the receiver to transcribe the information.
- *Talk in terms the other person can understand.* Avoid using jargon and initials unless the caller is familiar with them.
- *Don't assume knowledge on the part of the receiver.* Give the specifics of why you are calling and what you want. If you wish to have the call returned, say so. If you are going to be in and out of the office, indicate specifically when you want the call returned.
- *Make a checklist of the exact ideas you want to convey.* Don't rely on your memory: you might forget an important item or idea.
- *Have all information you need at your fingertips.* If you need statistics or examples, your appointment calendar, your credit card, or forms to fill out, have them ready and available. Making the person wait while you get these items not only is discourteous but shows a lack of preparation.

USING VOICE MAIL SYSTEMS

The advent of voice mail or answering machines has added a convenience to the process of leaving messages. More and more, rather than the pink "While You Were Out" slips, businesses have turned to voice mail systems. The advantages are numerous. It is no longer necessary to call and recall when someone is not present; specific messages can be left with no interpretation necessary by the receptionist; responses that require research can be left so that the person being called can find out the answers before returning the call; a personal relationship can be conveyed in that the caller's own voice is leaving the message.

Despite these conveniences, many people don't like to leave messages on machines; in fact, some people are so phobic they will hang up the telephone when they hear a recorded message. One of the major complaints about some voice mail systems is that the process is frustrating and confusing as directions are given for selections to be made from a long list of options, and then more options. Frustration builds when it is impossible to speak to anyone directly, but only recorded messages.

In developing a voice mail system, make sure that the convenience to the company does not overshadow the service given to the customer. In general, if at all possible, the first choice offered should be a clear and simple way to access a "real human being."

In leaving a message on your personal voice mail system, make sure that you get all of the information you will need to return the call. A study indicates that you can better serve the caller if you know in advance what the person wants. It is suggested that this message will get the desired results:

> "Hello, you've reached the voice mail of _____. If you need immediate assistance press _____ to speak to _____. Otherwise, please leave the time of your call, your name, number, and a brief message explaining your reason for contacting me. I'll return your call as soon as possible. Thank you."[9]

The reason for including the phrase "a brief message explaining your reason for contracting me" is to allow you to do the necessary research or obtain the materials necessary to deal with the inquiry before you return the call.

Management-Employee Relationships

"The manager who gets results is the effective communicator."[10] One aspect of effective management communication centers on clarity, or the lack of interference. The supervisor must be sure that the employee clearly understands what is to be done, how it is to be done, what to do if there are difficulties, and what the possible consequences are for not successfully carrying out the responsibility. Often, employees need to see clearly how they will benefit from an activity. The lack of clarity may result in interference and thus lead to communicative barriers.

"Workers judge their supervisors by what they THINK his or her motives are."[11] The supervisor who is known to keep promises, report facts honestly, and listen sincerely does not have to fall back on threats, manipulation, and phony good-fellowship in order to achieve job success. He or she creates little or no psychological interference. Supervisors who isolate themselves from employees often are subject to suspicion. Communication becomes difficult when individuals are seldom seen or spoken to. Once a lack of trust develops, achieving a positive relationship in which to foster open communication becomes difficult. It must be noted, however, that building trust with workers can be quite difficult in any organization. There is a tendency for workers to exercise caution in what they self-disclose to their bosses—an understandable reaction to the supervisor-subordinate roles in any bureaucracy. Many employees believe that if they told their supervisors what they really thought about the organization, tension with their bosses would develop. They believe that if they want promotions and raises they should not openly disagree with their supervisors.[12] Do you think they are right?

Certain management characteristics lead to the establishment of effective interpersonal relationships between employees and the manager. The successful manager (1) praises subordinates; (2) understands a subordinate's job; (3) can be trusted; (4) is warm and friendly; (5) is honest; and (6) is a person with whom subordinates are free to disagree.[13]

Management personnel would be wise to remember that "what counts, in the final analysis, is not what people are told but what they accept."[14] You more readily accept an individual who is forthright and honest, even if you do not agree with that person, than one who is constantly open to suspected motives and who practices manipulative activities.

A communicative approach to management that has been extremely successful is called the One-Minute Manager theory. The **One-Minute Manager theory** assumes that almost everybody wants to be working in a meaningful way. Employees want to know they are appreciated. If they feel appreciated, they will put forth maximum effort for you.[15] At the same time, a manager has so many responsibilities that he or she must control the time allotted to any interactions.

According to the One-Minute Manager theory, the effective manager:

1. *Establishes and explains goals thoroughly.* The goals are briefly written out (no more than 250 words) and agreed upon by boss and subordinates.
2. *Practices one-minute praise:*
   Tells people up front that he or she is going to let them know how they are doing.
   Praises people immediately.
   Tells them specifically what they did right.
   Tells them how good he or she feels about what they did right, and how it helps the organization and others who work there.

Stops for a moment of silence to let them know how good he or she feels. Encourages them to do more of the same.
3. If necessary, *take an employee aside for a one-minute reprimand.*[16]

CRITICIZING

One interpersonal task that often confronts managers is the necessity to criticize or reprimand employees. When you offer criticism, you must attempt to make your point without being accusatory, threatening, or judgmental. If possible, do so without hurting the other person's feelings or putting him/her down. Here are some ways you can reduce the risk of offending the other person:

1. *Do not overlook the person's good points.*
2. *Use "I" messages rather than "you" messages.* An "I" statement would be "I'm confused. We've talked previously about your not meeting deadlines, and you promised to alter your work habits. The problem still exists." A "you" statement is, "You're taking advantage of my being understanding and you're wrong. . . ." People are likely to get very defensive when they are given "you" statements. Though this seems idealistic—because most of us have not been taught to phrase "I" messages—the use of I-phrasing is an excellent device for defusing counterattacks and getting people to listen in a nondefensive manner.
3. *Focus on the behavior, not the personality.* Giving fact statements that deal specifically with accounts of the behavior pattern, rather than accusing a person, often will soften the negative message. It is more constructive to say, "This is the third time a report has been late" rather than "You are a procrastinator, your work is always late." It is hard to refute the facts in the first statement; the second opens the possibility of debate over whether the person has the personality flaw "procrastinator."
4. *Diffuse anger, if at all possible.* Let the other person say what he/she has to say in his/her own defense. It may be necessary to continue the reprimand at a later time if the person is unable to listen constructively because of strong emotional feelings.[17]
5. *Whenever possible, criticize in private, giving the person an opportunity to respond and process in privacy.* Attacking someone in public is embarrassing to the person and sets a precedent for future actions against others. There is even some debate concerning the appropriateness of praising in public. On one hand, the praised may feel proud to be lauded in front of others; however, hard feelings may result if others are not praised, or the person is considered to be the "boss's favorite" after receiving public recognition.

How to Give and Take Criticism

To succeed in the workplace, you have to learn how to give—and take—criticism. Suggestions:

- *See the positive side. It may be negative and unpleasant. But done right, criticism can strengthen relationships, motivate and improve performance.*

- *Seize control. Most people feel discomfort when they criticize. You may not want to do it. But when someone criticizes you, you have the power to ease the criticizer's discomfort. Use phrases such as: "Thank you for your interest," "I appreciate your concern" and "I'll think about that."*

- *Pick the right time. Don't criticize another when the person can't act on your comments. Also, hold off if the other person seems over-stressed or pressured.*

- *Send a clear message when it's called for. Sometimes a blunt "You need to improve" may be your best bet.*

- *Remain calm when you give—or receive—criticism. Losing your cool will overheat the situation.*

- *Don't always follow the accepted practice of ending and beginning on a positive note. You may not get your message across and neither person will benefit from the exchange.*

- *Steel yourself to listen no matter how crude a criticizer's approach. Chances are good you'll hear a message in there somewhere. And that message may help you perform better.*

Source: The Take-Charge Assistant. 135 W. 50th St., New York, NY 10020.

HANDLING GRIEVANCES

Another type of interpersonal communication that takes place between supervisors and employees centers on grievances. There are many kind of grievances, which normally take the form of employee complaints. The easiest complaints for the good supervisor to handle are those in which the employee has analyzed the problem, found the cause of the trouble, and presents a straightforward request for the supervisor's help in correcting it.[18] The supervisor then must determine whether the grievance is valid and if the proposed solution is in the best interest of the employee and the organization.

The supervisor will find that his or her tasks, regarding grievances, center on:

- *Diagnosing.* The manager determines what is wrong and defines the nature of the grievance or disturbance.
- *Adjusting.* The supervisor must try to bridge the gap between the employee's demands and the satisfactions that he or she gets.

- *Prevention.* The manager attempts to conduct the organization's business in harmony with the human demands of employees, and to assist the employees in adapting their demands to the conditions of the business. If this can be done, grievances can be minimized.

  Any grievance can be understood by paying attention to:
- The complaint itself or other expressions of the grievance. What is the person really complaining about?
- The concrete conditions with which the employee is dissatisfied or upon which she or he projects dissatisfaction. It is impossible to deal with non-specific matters or general gripes with no examples, as there is nothing specifically that can be corrected.
- The employee's demands for job security, fair pay, advancement, and social recognition. Are there matters that you can deal with or are these part of negotiations or union agreements?
- The employee's position in the company and his or her informal relations with the working group and supervisors. Is the person representing an isolated attitude or is the opinion representative of a significant group?
- The employee's personal situation—individual and social. Some employees can be classified as difficult personalities. If so, the employee may have to be dealt with via non-traditional methods.[19]

DEALING WITH DIFFICULT PERSONALITIES

During your career, you probably will have to deal with people who have difficult personalities, who, through interpersonal means, cause stress for themselves and others. They tend to be unable to accept feedback, corrective suggestions, or job evaluations, and they don't perceive themselves as being difficult. Certain patterns characterize the behavior of difficult personalities:

- *Victimization.* They believe that others are out to get them. They commonly use phrases like "I am being taking advantage of . . ." or "Everybody around here gets away with murder except me."
- *Nonaccountability.* They often fail to submit records, want to work independently although the job does not require working alone, or don't submit reports accounting for their time or action. A common statement may be "I must be free to do my job my way." or "I'm perfectly capable of doing the work, I don't need a babysitter to watch me." They will tolerate no criticism and yet demand to be told how good they are.[20]

　　Three approaches may be used for dealing with difficult personalities: direct intervention, indirect coping, and reactive coping.

Dealing with a Know-It-All

When dealing with a know-it-all, don't attempt to be a know-it-all in return.

When you disagree with know-it-alls, they will immediately freeze their plans and won't budge. Then you've created a standoff.

What to do: Instead of telling the know-it-all why the idea won't work, ask questions about the idea. Remember that know-it-alls love to answer questions.

As they look for answers, they might just discover that some ideas you present might be useful. In fact, they'll probably blend some of your ideas with theirs and think that they came up with all of them.

But remember that well-known communicator Dale Carnegie said that you're doing well if you can make people think that what you've said is their idea.

Source: Ken Nations, human resources development specialist, writing in *Methodist Leadership*. 5615 Kirby Drive, Ste. 800, Houston, TX 77005.

Direct Intervention

In **direct intervention,** the manager actively attempts to change the person's pattern. This approach includes a multistep process: (1) collecting data on what the person has done or has failed to do, (2) ascertaining how the behavior affects the worker as well as others, (3) meeting with the person and asking for his or her perceptions, (4) presenting the complaint or observation, (5) agreeing with the person on a course of action based on the company's and the person's need system, (6) agreeing on an assessment date, and following up. If the problem is solved, the issue is dropped. If not, a separating action (firing or reassignment) may be taken, or an action plan developed based on the necessity for further changes. Steps in the process that can aid in change is for the person to get additional training; work with a mental health professional; or be assigned a mentor who works with the person on specific tasks in which the mentor is an expert so that the person in trouble may learn to imitate successful actions. The types of help usually suggested are retraining, counseling, change of job, or self-help.[21]

Indirect Coping

A manager who arranges to work around the person is practicing **indirect coping.** If a person is difficult to work with in a group, then he or she is not assigned to group activities. If the person does not work well with a particular employee, then each is given responsibilities that eliminate any contact between the two. The difficulty of the indirect approach is that it very seldom solves the problem; instead, the effort may serve to hide it. Because the problem is still present, it could, and usually does, resurface.

Reactive Coping

The manager who engages in **reactive coping** refuses to become involved with either the problem or the person. Instead, the leader allows the person to continue to operate in his or her own way and accepts the conflicts that result. This approach rarely solves the problem. This course of action is usually taken when the employee is so good at a specific task that more negative consequences would come from firing him or her or giving him or her another job than from putting up with the stress created.

In dealing with difficult personalities, it must be remembered that many such people are extremely successful. They may get what they want because they are difficult, and no one wants to buck them. They also may be extremely talented but cannot work well with others.

DIRECTING

Much of the interpersonal interaction in organizations centers on **directing:** the giving of orders and the giving of directions. Whether on the supervisory or production levels, businesspeople often must explain new procedures, instruct employees in the operation of equipment, and clarify policies.

Order Giving

An important responsibility of individuals involved in management or supervisory roles is order giving. A recommended process for order giving is composed of seven distinct steps.[22] By following this process, organizational interference may be eliminated:

- *Step 1: Planning.* The order giver must have a plan. Important considerations in constructing the plan are: What action is needed to get certain results? What is the time available? What are the allowable costs? Who should carry out the order? What kind of order is best suited to get the task done?
- *Step 2: Preparing the person who will receive the order.* Get the attention of the person to whom you are going to give the order. Call a meeting to inform the person that the directions or order will be given. When an order is given, it should be accompanied by a briefing session at which time the objective is pointed out and the method discussed. If prior information is going to be needed, hand it out before the actual presenting session.
- *Step 3: Presenting the order.* The tone and manner in which the orders are expressed are often as important as the words chosen. Even words that are innocuous in themselves can arouse resentment if they are used in an offensive way, thus creating psychological interference. The directions should be clear and precise—the fewer words the better—but take care to clarify any complicated ideas or unclear terms, to avoid semantic interference. Make sure you follow a step-by-step procedure in order to avoid organizational interference.
- *Step 4: Verification.* Watch for feedback or search it out. Make sure the receiver understands what action is expected and how to carry it out.
- *Step 5: Action.* The receiver should now understand the order and then act on it.
- *Step 6: Follow-up.* Unfortunately, most supervisors stop at Step 5, which stops short of knowing whether the action is being carried out effectively. Checkups and follow-ups are critical in any order-giving cycle because, even if the order receiver is doing the right thing, he or she may run into some unforeseen difficulty that interferes with carrying out the order, such as material failure or tool shortage.

- *Step 7: Appraisal.* If the order is carried out as planned, then the order giver has learned a valuable lesson that should be repeated. If not, then corrections must be made. "Almost always when an order has somehow gone wrong and the expected results have not been achieved, faulty order giving is to blame."[23] If the follow-up proves that something is wrong, the order giver should ask these questions: Did I prepare the person? Did I present the right order? Did I verify a reaction? Did I follow up the order?

Direction Giving

One of the common communicative activities that businesspersons are engaged in is giving directions. Directions describe such things as how to do a task, how to achieve a desired end effect, how to reach a goal, or how to geographically get someplace. Some general principles of effective direction giving include: be specific, include the necessary details, organize the ideas, use understandable terms, encourage feedback, break the task into parts, and follow up.

When you give directions, make sure to choose words that indicate exactly what should be done and how to do it. For example, in explaining how a

---

Ways to Give Instructions

Here are some ways to help you communicate better when assigning tasks:

- *Explain the purpose of the assignment. Employees are more likely to give their best when they feel they're being brought into the big picture.*

- *Give employees the real deadline. Even if an employee has a reputation for being chronically late, you'll earn more respect with your honesty than by lying about an early deadline.*

- *Tell them who else is involved in the task. Your explanation may forestall deadline problems. Explain, too, whom the employee can ask for help if you're not available.*

- *Explain why you chose them. This will make employees want to do a good job for you, because you've singled them out for positive attention.*

- *Don't allow sloppy work to sneak by you. And don't make a habit of "redoing" the drafts sent to you. If you do, the employees will start saying to themselves, "Oh well, if there is anything wrong, the boss will catch it."*

- *Summarize what you told them. Then, instead of asking if they have any questions, ask them a question or two.*

Source: The Personnel News, 4701 Patrick Henry Drive, Ste. 1301, Santa Clara, CA 95054.

piece of machinery works, refer to the specific dials, knobs, or instruments that are important to know.

Make sure that you illustrate, either by doing the procedure or giving all the steps in a logical order, exactly what should be done at each step. Phrases like "you know," "stuff like that," and "push that whatchamacallit" are of little value. Indicate if something must be done with the right or left hand, the specific tool that must be available to carry out the operation, the exact names of chemicals or substances that must be combined, and in what order. Don't just say, "type the letter." Specify the margins and spacing you want, if it should be on a letterhead, if you want to proofread it before it is sent out, or any variations from the usual procedure that might be necessary. Some good direction-giving ideas include writing a list of the sequential order that should be followed, providing a drawing of the machinery, or creating a model of what the end product should look like.

Remember that someone new to the job, or who doesn't have your background and experience, may be unfamiliar with the terminology of the job, the names of the streets, or the meanings of the initials and jargon that you commonly use to describe something. Define terms that the person may not easily understand. The phrase "HRD plan" may be clear to you, but someone not familiar with the Human Resource Development methods of business will be lost. Use all the words, indicate that the term is usually referred to as "HRD," and briefly explain what it is, if this information will help the person.

Some new employees, or communicatively apprehensive (shy) ones, may fear that they will be perceived as dense or will be punished for asking questions. Try to encourage questions from the person to whom you are giving directions. You also may aid them by asking them questions as you go along to make sure you are getting the feedback necessary to ascertain whether or not the direction receiver is understanding the message.

Make sure that you don't overload the receiver. If there are many steps in a process, or if the directions are very complicated, it might be wise to break the explanation into parts or give the person a reference tool, such as a diagram, or a list of the steps to follow.

Be certain that you follow up the order giving, if at all possible. Have the person demonstrate how to operate the machine. Request that the person repeat your directions.

Much time and money is wasted yearly by having to repeat directions, retrain employees, and shred improperly written memos, letters, and reports. Tempers become frayed and people become frustrated when they don't understand and can't fulfill their job needs. By being specific, giving the necessary details, organizing the ideas, using understandable terms, encouraging feedback, and following up, the odds of effective direction giving increase. If employees don't understand, you will have to repeat the entire message over, so why not save time and do it right the first time?

JOB TRAINING

Many people in training positions (foremen, supervisors) claim that they do not have time to train their subordinates because they are too busy correcting mistakes. These mistakes might never have been made if the workers had been properly trained in the first place. Step-by-step procedures and the effective use of interpersonal skills provide the basis for proper training.[24] Four steps in training are:

- *Step 1: Prepare the learner.* A worker who knows what is going to be done and why it is going to be done is more likely to be able to carry out the assignment. Knowledge of the importance, benefits, and rewards of doing the job aid an individual in having a positive attitude toward doing it.
- *Step 2: Present the operation.* Organize the ideas in a step-by-step procedure that can be followed exactly by the learner (see the section on Organizational Interference earlier in this chapter). Be organized. Be sure you know the procedure and carry it out. Encourage questions. Avoid information overload. Do not give the receiver more information than can be handled in one session. Divide the training into several sessions if the process is complicated.
- *Step 3: Request that the learner perform the operation.* Stay with the learner until the operation has been performed to make sure that it can be done successfully. Pay compliments, praise success. Ask what the learner is doing at various steps and why. Encourage questions about the operation. If the process is not being done correctly, evaluate whether the procedure, in the way in which you presented it, was the best explanation possible. If so, repeat the procedure; if not, adjust the message—define terms in order to control semantic interference, demonstrate what you had explained previously, or break the operation down into smaller units. A different approach might be necessary for this one employee. Not all people learn the same way and alternate methods may be needed for certain people.
- *Step 4: Follow up with the newly trained worker.* Even after the person has learned the procedure, things can go wrong. Keep an eye on the learner's progress and keep the channels open for communication.

Conflict and Conflict Resolution

A major area of interpersonal concern in the business arena is that of conflict. **Conflict** is the emotional state you experience when the behavior of another person interferes with your behavior. Conflict usually centers on a struggle between incompatible interests, often resulting in psychological interference. Conflict can be a major cause of personal difficulty in the work environment.

CONFLICT IN THE WORK ENVIRONMENT

Working conditions, changes in procedures, salaries, rights and responsibilities, or philosophies of operation are possible sources of conflict in businesses and industries. The issues that arouse conflict may be real or perceived.

Research has identified six specific sources of conflict in the business environment:

- *The role of power.* In a communicative situation, people who are powerful or powerless tend to act in certain ways. The powerful person may demand, control, or threaten. The powerless person may feel put upon, insecure, and unappreciated. A fight for emotional survival may be constantly waged between the powerful and the powerless.
- *The structure of the organization.* Some organizational charts align people against each other. The modes of operation might encourage a fight for power and position because of the line of command where officer must compete against officer, supervisor against supervisor, and worker against worker, rather than working together in a cooperative structure. In addition, union and management may perceive each other as adversaries, resulting in a power struggle for control.
- *Fear (real or perceived).* The possibility of reward or punishment creates an underlying conflict potential. In some organizations the constant threat of disciplinary action, which may include temporary layoffs, demotion, or even firing, can create a conflict environment. Individuals who feel watched and not trusted, who are disciplined and never praised, often feel stressed and are apt to act in ways that create conflict.
- *Personality differences.* The work environment may place people together who have strong philosophical and ethical differences. These differences can be the seeds from which conflict grows.
- *Hidden agenda.* Because of the need to satisfy certain job or personal requirements, some people act in a way that best serves their interests. A sales manager may oppose a new sales plan that eliminates salaries and puts all the salespeople on commissions. Even though the new plan may be in the best interest of the company, the sales manager may come up with many reasons for not putting the plan into action. The hidden agenda, the real motivating but unstated reason, may well be that he perceives a loss in personal revenue if the action is taken.
- *Change.* Whenever change is proposed, a possibility for conflict arises. Attempting numerous changes increases the likelihood of resistance. This is especially true if the proposed changes alter the lifestyle of the individuals involved (e.g., job loss, decreased responsibility, changed working conditions, need to relocate). The acceptance of change takes time and depends on the individual's desire to change.

Some Ideas When Negotiating

Whether you haggle over money, deadlines or vacation schedules, skillful negotiation can influence your boss or colleague to approve your raise, extend your timetable or give you that week off.

Try these tips to improve your negotiating ability:

- *Avoid arguing. Always open with a positive remark.*

- *Telegraph your communication. Say, "I would like to make a point" or "May I ask a question?" The listener is then prepared for your move and might drop his or her guard.*

- *Control the conversation by questioning. Asking questions helps control the content and direction of the negotiation.*

- *Cut out counterproposals. Don't go high after the other person goes low. Suggest shortcomings with the proposal and work to improve it.*

- *Stick to your strong points. Don't say "Yes" to something that will cause future conflict. Ask the party, "Now if we are going to have problems with this agreement, what do you think they will be?" You'll build trust.*

- *Don't be bullied. Walk away from an unfair, difficult negotiator.*

Source: Jack W. Kaine, J.W. Kaine Ltd., cited in *Association Management*, 1575 Eye St. N.W., Washington, DC 20005.

CONFLICT RESOLUTION

Conflict resolution is an attempt to reconcile differences in order to accept, reduce, or eliminate the conflict. Conflict resolution is based on accepting two basic principles of conflict.

First, conflict does not have to be hidden or disposed of. Reasonable people can disagree and don't have to be either right or wrong. Or they can recognize that, due to the nature of the conflict, the participants may be powerless to bring about change. Sometimes, the best way to deal with conflict is to acknowledge that it exists and that, due to certain conditions or requirements, there is little or nothing that can be done about it. For example, a manager may purchase computers that are less than the "state-of-the-art" because they were "a steal," and several programmers know that the slower response time will mean their coding will be more time consuming. Because the employees have no control over the purchasing of equipment, the conflict over which system to purchase is for naught.

Second, conflict can't be dealt with as an intellectual issue unless the individuals involved are really interested in solving the dilemma. Logically explaining something to another person will do little good unless that person is open to active listening. Because of the very nature of the way in which most people perceive conflict, most arguing does not solve problems. People usually think that the way to deal with conflict is to change the other person. Rather than being directed at the resolution of some specified issue, conflict tends to be unfocused, destructive, or indirectly aggressive, where attacking the people involved often holds higher priority than addressing the issue. Conflict can be resolved only if the participants accept the concept of peacemaking. Peacemaking centers on understanding the concept that behaviors, not personalities, and issues, not people, are involved.

Options for Conflict Resolution

Three options are possible for resolving conflict: win-lose, lose-lose, or win-win. A **win-lose approach to conflict resolution** centers on one person or company winning and another person or organization losing. For example, assume that your company has merged with another. This action necessitates selecting which company logo will be retained. If you have proposed that your firm's logo be used because you believe it has higher recognition value and someone else has proposed theirs, then a natural competition emerges because only one logo can be chosen. There will be a winner and there will be a loser as long as no other alternatives are possible.

The **lose-lose approach to conflict resolution** takes place when one person believes so strongly that the other person is wrong, or so desires the other person defeated, that he or she is willing to lose in order to defeat the other person. Let's say that you and two others propose brand new logos for the newly merged organization. If you are competitor A and you dislike competitor B, and there is a chance that your suggestion won't be chosen and that hers will, you might side with competitor C to make sure that your "enemy" doesn't win. Thus, you lose and your enemy also loses.

A **win-win approach to conflict resolution** results when people are willing to work together through peacemaking in order for both to feel that they have accomplished their goal. Using our example, if it appears that opinion is split between two proposed new logos, one win-win option would be for you to work with your competitor to design an insignia that both of you could take credit for and of which you would be proud.[25]

Styles of Conflict Resolution

Each person has a unique style for handling conflicts. The usual styles of conflict resolution are avoidance, accommodation, smoothing over, compromising, competition, and integration.[26]

Avoidance Some people choose to avoid dealing with the issue and settle for the status quo. This avoidance usually takes the form of attempting to withdraw from contact with the other person, or avoiding the issue of conflict when the possibility for taking some action is present. If, for example, someone has been asking for help with work, the avoider may leave his or her desk if the person requesting help comes toward the avoider's desk. Or, if asked about doing extra work, the avoider may answer "Yes," when really wanting to say "No." This avoiding method is rarely successful because the conflict does not go away by itself, even though the avoider wishes it would. Avoidance can be effective only if the conflict is short-lived or minor.

Accommodation In **conflict accommodation,** one person puts other people's needs above his or her own. During conflict, an accommodating individual gives in and lets the other person have his or her way, thinking that the other person's needs are more important. If someone asks for a favor, the accommodating person will give in, even though he or she may not want to do so.

This style of resolution rarely solves the problem, for one person wins while the other loses. The winner feels great; the loser often feels used. It does, however, give the accommodator peace and quiet—at all costs. If peace and quiet is the most important consideration, then accommodation is a positive method.

Smoothing Over The end goal of **conflict smoothing over** is to give the impression that everything is all right. The person who smoothes over conflict usually lets the other person know what he/she wants, but not in a forceful enough way to get the other person to take the required action. The major purpose of smoothing over is to maintain the relationship. If a fellow employee asks you to help with a report, you could smooth over by saying, "Well, OK, but I've really got a lot of work of my own to do." You hope that the person will take the hint and withdraw the request. Usually, that is not the case. The desired assistance is available, so why should the requester be concerned?

If the relationship with the person is important, and the other person appears willing to end it if you don't act on his request, then smoothing over may be appropriate.

Compromise In **conflict compromise,** concerns are identified and addressed. The advantage of this method over avoidance, accommodation, or smoothing over is that the issue is discussed and often resolved.

In its best form, compromise allows each person to understand the views and needs of the other. Each can then propose solutions to the problem and trade back and forth until an agreeable settlement is reached. Unfortunately, this style often results in both participants being dissatisfied, as neither gets exactly what he/she wants.

Competition Power is at the center of **conflict competition;** the name of the game is winning. Someone must win and someone must lose. I get my way or you get yours. Whoever is stronger, more powerful, and more cunning will be the winner. Threats, abuse, and even blackmail are the tools of the competitor.

The competitive style gets the issue out into the open. And, one way or another, someone gets his/her way. If you win, you will probably feel good about the victory. Unfortunately, you also may be a loser. Competitive conflict resolution usually results in hurt feelings, frustrations, and destructive working relationships and friendships. In spite of the negative aspects of this method, an aggressive methodology is often applied regularly by some businesspeople.

Integration The ideal method of conflict resolution is **conflict integration** in which communicators confront the problem directly and work toward a solution that all parties can agree upon. This method takes time and a commitment that focuses on preserving the relationship and the dignity of all involved. Integration centers on the concept that the most critical issue at stake in conflict resolution is the self-esteem of the people involved. Integration uses these principles to preserve human dignity and control psychological interference:

- *One or both parties refuse to put the conflict into a win-lose form.* No one has to be victorious; no one has to be defeated. The objective of the confrontation is to resolve the problem and achieve a workable solution, not to win a war.
- *At least one of the participants verbalizes the need to preserve the relationship.* You can disagree with someone without hating or destroying that person. One or both parties give evidence that each understands the other person's feeling, even though one may find the other person's actions unacceptable. Participants restrain themselves from interrupting each other even if the effort is painful. An honest exchange of ideas takes place when there are listeners as well as speakers.
- *Honesty is an indispensable ingredient in integration.* Tell it like it is, why you feel as you do, what can and cannot be done, and why.
- *Both parties refrain from critiquing the other person's behavior and from blaming the other for causing the conflict.* No one can make you mad. You commit yourself to the act of anger. By blaming the other person, little can or will be accomplished.

Working Through a Conflict

In working through a conflict with a coworker or a supervisor, some individuals choose to ignore the conflict, hoping that it will disappear. Indeed, a minor conflict might dissolve in this way and both parties essentially will forget about the incident. Forgetting about the stress may not be so easy, however. Consequently, it may be more appropriate for the communicators to attempt to diffuse the hostility.

Diffusion of a conflict usually can be made more manageable by delaying confrontation. If a person has a conflict with a coworker, for instance, both parties might benefit from not discussing the situation until tempers cool off and the conflict is put into its proper perspective. Achieving a diffusion, however, may be difficult because both parties may be ego-involved in the incident and find it necessary to save face in the relationship.

Direct confrontation of a conflict may be the most open, effective communication strategy to employ in resolving conflicts, particularly if both parties to the conflict are able and willing to handle the confrontation. Some people tend to avoid confrontation because the risk is great: relationships can end and communication can stop as a consequence of dealing head-on with an issue. But in the long run, most people who work with each other on a daily basis often appreciate the chance to "clear the air" and get on with their business. A continuing conflict can disrupt the communication climate and lead to distress and unhappiness on the part of all individuals involved in the situation. Holding grudges and unexpressed grievances takes effort and interferes with progress.

It should be recognized that direct confrontation within any organization is probably more realistic for individuals who have a peer relationship. Direct confrontation with one's own superior may well bring untold risks if the superior is unable to put the confrontation in the proper perspective. People have been fired from their jobs, demoted, and otherwise mistreated for openly challenging a superior, especially one who is unwilling to "lose face" and deal with the communication in a constructive fashion.

One of the most popular and destructive conflicts found in many organizations is the natural tendency to blame the boss for everything that is wrong with an organization. Workers who have direct dealings with an immediate supervisor and little contact with those at higher levels may come to lay all their problems on the head of the manager. The manager then has the task of explaining his or her responses and actions, bringing workers to the understanding of the institutional constraints and procedures that may realistically define the manager's role in working with the employees.

Steps in Conflict Resolution

Unfortunately, no guaranteed solutions or surefire approaches will settle all disputes. In fact, not all conflicts can be resolved. Some steps, however, are useful in attempting conflict resolution.

1. Define the conflict.
2. View the conflict as a joint problem.

3. State the problem.
4. Check your perceptions.
5. Generate possible solutions.
6. Reach a mutually acceptable solution.
7. Implement and evaluate the situation.[27]

For example, a discussion of the major points of a conflict that involved a sales manager having been called by a client who complained about a shipping error that had been reported to the manager could be:

1. "I was embarrassed when the client told me about the shipping error and I knew nothing about it."
2. "For the sake of the organization, we need to keep each other informed."
3. "I need to know about mistakes before someone outside the organization does."
4. "Do you agree that I need to be informed of problems like this?"
5. "In the future, I would like to be informed of problems as soon as they happen."
6. "Can we agree that in the future I will be informed as soon as the problem occurs?"
7. "I'll assume, then, that I will be informed. Two weeks from today we'll have another meeting to determine whether this issue is still a problem."

Assertiveness Avoidance, accommodation, and smoothing over are non-assertive methods of conflict resolution. Nonassertive means of communication do not directly attempt to resolve the problem. Competition is aggressive because it does not take the other person into consideration. When well used, compromise is an assertive act. Integration is always assertive. **Assertive communication** takes place when the individual accomplishes his or her task while taking into consideration the feelings and needs of others.

Assertiveness training is a popular and necessary workshop topic in organizations, as individuals have come to recognize that an assertive communication style can be an asset to upward mobility in career paths. This type of training is often necessary for certain individuals because of their cultural upbringing. For example, women in the North American culture tend to be less assertive than men. Some Asians and South Americans—more commonly women than men—have also been taught to be less assertive.

The assertive individual, who is neither aggressive nor retiring, usually can accomplish his or her objectives within the workforce. The **assertive person** is one who exhibits high-level energy; has courage and flexibility; has strong self-respect and the ability to deal with challenging situations; can handle confrontations; exhibits self-confidence; often establishes influence in group meetings; is allowed the most talking time in meetings; and is able to command all the attention he or she wants or needs. Assertive persons stand out in group meetings because "their contributions receive more consideration than others' and the most significant points and remarks are usually addressed to them."[28]

In asserting, describe your perspective. Statements of "I believe" and "It makes me think . . ." will get more positive results than "You are . . ." and "You make me . . ." An effectively assertive person is polite but firm; open to suggestions but not namby-pamby; cooperative but not gutless.

Being assertive really means understanding yourself and being comfortable with who and what you are. It does not mean that you are impolite, irascible, uncouth, or defensive. It does not mean using abusive language, or daring someone to knock the chip off your shoulder.[29] The assertive individual considers his or her needs and decides if the consequences of asserting will be greater than those of not asserting. In most cases the answer will be to take a stand, get at the problem, and solve it. The major question in deciding whether or not to assert is, "What is the worst thing that can happen?" Ultimately, you will usually conclude that you no longer believe you are being victimized or manipulated by others. No one but you is deciding what you will do, and when you will do it; no one is insisting that you take actions you don't want to take.

The assertiveness code is this: Is it hurting anyone? Is it harming you? Do you enjoy it? If so, it's okay.[30]

To be assertive:

- *Clarify the situation and focus on the issue.* (What is the goal? What do I want to accomplish?)
- *Determine how the assertive behavior will help you accomplish your goal.* (Will explaining your needs or stating what you want resolve the problem and get the desired action?)
- *Determine what you usually do to avoid asserting yourself in this situation.* (In the past, what did I do in similar situations? Did it accomplish my goal? Did it solve the problem?)
- *Why do you want to forgo past behavior and assert yourself instead?* (Was I unsuccessful with my usual style of conflict resolution? If so, then a new methodology is in order. Is this issue important enough to risk the hurt or rejection, or loss of a friend or a job that I might suffer if I assert myself?) What might be stopping you from asserting yourself? (Do I have irrational beliefs? Am I afraid to change the past? Is the person victimizing me to the degree that I am afraid to act?)
- *Do you have the information you need to go ahead and act?* (Do I know what must be solved? Am I sure of my facts in the case?)
- *Can you let the other person know that you hear and understand him/her, let him/her know how you feel, tell him/her what you want?* (Do I have the skills to assert myself effectively?)

Here are some basic principles that may help you be effectively assertive:

1. *Give a decisive "no" when expressing refusal.* Explain why you are refusing but don't be unduly apologetic. Where applicable, offer the other person an alternative course of action.
2. *Request an explanation when asked to do something unreasonable.*
3. *Look in the eye the person with whom you're talking.*
4. *When expressing annoyance or criticism, comment on the person's behavior, rather than attacking him/her.* ("I feel taken advantage of when you ask me to help you check the final spreadsheet numbers for your status report and you go on a break," versus "You're not fair! You make me do your work and you go on a break.") An attack will usually start a conflict, while the "I" statement is less likely to elicit a defensive response.
5. *Remember that no one knows what is going on in your head unless you tell people what you are thinking and feeling.* Hoping doesn't bring about action or change; doing does.[31]

Effective assertion involves making statements concerning the situation, problem, or desired change. Assertive statements require thought and skill.

Types of Assertive Messages There are three types of assertive messages: simple assertive statements, empathic statements or responses, and confronting responses. A **simple assertive statement** is a statement of fact. An **empathic assertive statement/response** recognizes the other person's position but is stated in a way that expresses your own needs. It may follow a simple assertion, or be the first step in the assertive process. A **confronting assertive response** usually follows a simple assertion or an empathetic response. It describes the person's behavior and then states your position.

The type of assertion to use depends on the situation and the message you want to convey. Assume that you are waiting at the copy machine and someone from another department pushes in front of you.

- *Simple assertion:* "I have been here waiting for the copy machine." (This is said directly to the person, in a matter-of-fact way—not loudly or accusingly. The hope is that the person will move or wait until you are done, thus solving the problem.)
- *Empathic statement/response:* "I know you're probably in a hurry, but I have been waiting for the copier for some time." (This can be said as a follow-up to the simple assertion you just made, or it can be the opening statement. The intention is to recognize that the person may have a reason for doing what was done, but that you are not going to allow it to happen.)
- *Confronting response:* "I have been waiting here long before you arrived. I would like you to wait until after I have finished." (The intent is to allow the person to know what is wrong and how he or she can correct it.)

Sometimes development of an in-depth message is necessary for dealing with a major problem. As good public speakers have demonstrated: develop the message, rehearse it, and present it.

DESC Scripting A method for planning an assertive message has been described as DESC Scripting.[32] **DESC Scripting** entails describing, expressing, specifying, and stating possible consequences, as illustrated in the following:

- *Describe:* Describe as specifically and objectively as possible the behavior that is bothersome to you. (Example: "I was told during my last review that I would receive a 10 percent raise. There is only a 5 percent raise in my current paycheck.")
- *Express:* Say how you feel and think about this behavior. (Example: "I am confused because I have not received the amount that we agreed upon.")
- *Specify:* Ask for a different, specific behavior. (Example: "I would like my paycheck to reflect the amount we agreed upon.")
- *Consequences:* Spell out concretely and simply what the reward or consequences will be for changing the behavior. (Example: "If this is corrected I will take on the Spencer Industries Account as we discussed as part of the increased responsibility that would accompany the increase in pay" or "Should we discuss this with Janet in Human Resources?")

Remember that in DESC Scripting you may stop at any time during the process when you receive satisfaction. If, following the description step, the supervisor shows you a copy of the order and indicates that she sent in the request, but that the payroll department may not yet have received it, then you need go no further.

If you go as far as the consequence step, be certain that you are willing to carry out your promise or threat. If you are not willing to quit, don't threaten to do so. If you aren't willing to sue, then don't propose that solution. If the Human Resources Department or the union (if you are in a unionized industry) will not handle the matter, then threatening to complain to them is an idle bluff.

Sexual Harassment

Why do we need to discuss sexual harassment in today's corporate business environment? First, it is a serious and growing problem, as evidenced by the rise in the number of cases brought to the Equal Employment Opportunity Commission, the federal agency charged to address charges of sexual harassment. Second, many corporations have undertaken a commitment to a respectful workplace with a zero-tolerance policy on the issue. It is also a business issue. Firms are determined to eliminate reduced productivity among its employees, loss of talent due to turnover, negative publicity in the media, and the costs of litigation. The cost to corporate America is staggering; millions of dollars are awarded in damages but untold millions are lost as executives scramble to prepare for depositions and litigation, careers are damaged, reputations are ruined, and personal fortunes are lost in defense costs.

SEXUAL HARASSMENT DEFINED

What is **sexual harassment?** Sexual harassment is a newly evolving area of the law, and its definition is open to subjectivity; however, some aspects are clear. Let's look at the EEOC Guidelines on Sexual Harassment.

Harassment on the basis of sex is a violation of Title VII of the 1964 Civil Rights Act of 1964 as amended in 1991. Unwelcome sexual advances, requests for sexual favors, and other verbal or physical conduct of a sexual nature constitutes sexual harassment when:

1. Submission to such conduct is made either explicitly or implicitly a term or condition of employment;
2. Submission to or rejection of such conduct by an individual is used as a basis for employment decisions affecting the individual; and
3. Such conduct has the purpose or effect of unreasonably interfering with an individual's work performance or creating an intimidating, hostile, or offensive work environment.

Corporations, employees, and their business associates can be found liable for offensive behavior as described by the EEOC. Generally speaking, behavior or commentary that is unwelcome and of a sexual nature, especially that which is "repetitive, pervasive, severe," can be found to meet the legal definition of sexual harassment. The courts will decide whether or not a person has grounds for a claim by using the reasonable person (or in some states the reasonable woman) standard. The courts view the impact of the behavior or commentary, not the intent of the sender of those messages.

Most importantly, from the standpoint of communication, sexual harassment is an interpersonal communication act. It is one person aggressing against another. Often the decision of whether sexual harassment has taken place is determined by the communication components. The major questions considered are: Who are the participants? What is the setting? and What is the purpose?

What forms can sexual harassment take? They can be physical, verbal, or visual in nature and can take the form of written or published materials. Anyone can be the recipient and anyone can be the initiator. Although statistics show a greater instance of one gender as the recipient, sexual harassment can happen to anyone regardless of gender, corporate position, age, affectional preference, or socioeconomic background. Common forms of "hostile environment" sexual harassment include verbal abuse, offensive touch, physical exposure, and retaliation for complaints.

What factors can contribute to subtle sexual harassment situations? Certainly, different communication styles and world views can account for some of the difference. It is often helpful to look at the different communication styles of men and women to see how messages we send can be misinterpreted by someone with a different frame of reference. This is not to suggest that the very blatant behaviors are excusable citing communication differences, but rather to suggest that we may find ourselves in situations that shock us because we would never have intended our messages to be interpreted in certain ways.

COMMUNICATING ABOUT SEXUAL HARASSMENT

One of the questions often asked regarding sexual harassment is, "What should I do if I am a recipient of unwelcome behavior?" In general, if you question a person's actions as being inappropriate:

- *Trust your instincts.*
- *Don't blame yourself.* You are the victim, not the perpetrator. A common ploy by harassers is to intimate that the victim encouraged the unwanted actions/advances by wearing a certain type of clothing or behaving a certain way. In almost all instances, this is a ploy to turn the innocent person into the guilty party. Those people with weak self-concepts often fall for this ploy.
- *Get emotional support.* Turn to a mental health professional, an expert in harassment, or a support telephone service/line that deals with harassment.
- *Say no clearly and early to the individual whose behavior and/or comments make you uncomfortable.* Don't allow the person to continue with the harassing actions or verbalizations. Call a halt to it immediately by saying emphatically, "I will not (allow you to speak that way to me), or (put up with that type of talk), or (do not touch me)."
- *Document every incident in detail.* Keep a record. Write down everything that happened, including exactly what was said or done, with dates and times, and any other supporting evidence. Share the information with another person in order to verify the acts having taken place. If possible, get a witness to attest to the action(s).
- *Find a way to speak out.* Make a statement to someone in the personnel or human resources department of your organization or alert your supervisor.

- *Seek out supportive individuals within the firm.* More and more businesses are designing safe zones. A **sexual harassment safe zone** is a person or department responsible for providing resources for persons who perceive they have been harassed.
- *Seek out company and union channels and use them.*
- *File a charge with a local, state, or federal antidiscrimination agency if necessary.* As with any legal action, it will be your responsibility to prove the harassing actions or verbalizations. Be sure you can document the accusations.

If a friend shares that he or she has been or is being harassed, you should

- *Listen without judging.*
- *Validate that sexual harassment is wrong and affirm that whatever feelings are being expressed are his/her right to have.* Victims sometimes are confused and don't trust their own judgment. They need affirmation as to their rights and responsibilities.
- *Offer to help explore resources and support the recipient's efforts to seek help.* Offer to be of assistance in whatever way you can, but be aware that you are not the person that was harassed.
- *Be prepared for displaced anger as the recipient may not be able to channel it appropriately.* In some instances, when a person is feeling stressed, she or he will attack the nearest source. So, don't be surprised if the victim turns her or his wrath on you, even if you are trying to be helpful. The person is not really attacking you, just acting out of frustration.
- *Do not take matters into your own hands, but rather help the individual find the appropriate channels either inside or outside of the company.* Unless you are a lawyer or a mental health professional, be aware of your limitations.

Sexual harassment is a complex issue. It can be the result of a number of social, economic, cultural, and power issues. However, as more and more individuals enter the workplace with strong communication skills and an enhanced awareness of the kinds of behaviors that should be left outside of today's work environment, we may move closer to the elimination of sexual harassment.

• • • In Summary • • •

Interpersonal communication between people involves the exchange of messages and the development of a relationship based on the effect of those messages. Our communication is affected by relationship-based factors, such as whether we like or dislike the other person, or whether we are in a power or control position (boss, supervisor) or a subordinate position (employee) with the other individual. In many instances, the hierarchy of power in interpersonal relationships may determine not only the message but also the effect of the message. One of the most important aspects of interpersonal communication is self-disclosure, your communication of your private world to others.

Interpersonal communication is at the heart of most business dealings. Specific forms of interpersonal communication in the business environment are telephone use, management-employee relationships, directing others, job training, conflict and conflict management, understanding and dealing with sexual harassment, and the role of employee assertion.

▬▬ Business Communication in Practice ▬▬

1. Select an object or a series of objects that have to be assembled (a necktie; a shoe with shoelaces; a camera and film; a screw, screwdriver, and a piece of wood). Plan the directions you will be giving to a member of the class. Your classmate will carry out the task by following your directions exactly as given. If he or she is not successful, redo the directions and try again. Keep adjusting until the task can be accomplished using your directions.
2. Think back to a strong verbal exchange (either a positive or a negative incident) you have had with someone you consider very close (best friend, parent, brother, or sister). What were the emotions of the interaction? Describe how the relationship had an effect on what happened. Base your discussion on the chapter's comments about relationships and their effects on communication.
3. Think back to a situation in which you made a telephone call to a business and you experienced frustration. What happened? How could the business or their personnel have corrected the problem?
4. Think back to the last time you were involved in a conflict. Were you arguing issues or personalities? Did you resolve the conflict? If so, how? If not, why not?
5. Bring to class a bag or box that has five items in it that represent some value, belief, attitude, or personal attribute you have. The class members will show each of their objects and explain why they brought it. After the presentations, discuss the following:
   a. Was it difficult to talk about yourself in public? If so, why?
   b. Are there other items you could have brought that would have given some different insights into your belief/value/attitude system? Why did you choose not to present those things?
   c. If you had to share your thoughts only with your best friend, rather than with the class, would you have presented different items or given different information?

Diversity Simulation

Directions: Read the following scenarios. In a small group, determine what might be the viewpoint of the individual in each simulation and how he or she would be likely to respond. What would be the goal of each individual? What would be the barriers to effective communication? What can be done to resolve this situation? What moral obligations exist? Optional assignment: Research the laws on sexual harassment. Do any of these scenarios fall within the legal restriction of the Equal Employment Opportunity Commission's guidelines on sexual harassment?

1. James is the department manager for a Fortune 100 consumer products firm and has been with the company for eleven years. He is well liked and someone who genuinely cares about the people who work for him. He takes pride in the low turnover in his department, the family atmosphere, the quality award the department won last year, and the willingness of workers to do what is necessary to meet deadlines and honor client commitments. Two days before the launch of a campaign for a new line of baby-care products, James gets an e-mail message marked "urgent" from one of his district representatives, Lynn, who tells him that she has to see him in the office this afternoon. When she arrives, James turns his attention to her urgent problem, a matter she "had to discuss in person." Lynn has been a media consultant for the last five years and has single-handedly built the "Next Generation" market with hip advertising and promotions. James has high regard for her talent and her professionalism. When Lynn comes into his office, James hears her tell this story: The senior media buyer, Gerald, with whom Lynn has worked on this campaign has intimated that Lynn's success with this new campaign hinges on his media placements and that if Lynn is "nice" to him, he will "move heaven and earth" to get the best coverage and reach. Lynn tell James that at first she tried to laugh it off and "keep it light." But now, she says, his insistence (and the impending launch deadline) mean that she runs the real risk of damage not only to this campaign but also to her career. Lynn asks for James's help in defusing the situation. James tells her that he will see what he can do; after all, he doesn't want his employees to be unhappy. After Lynn leaves, James sits in his office and thinks through what he should do.

2. Robert is an editor with a major financial publication. He takes great pride in his work and spends a great deal of time in the office not only working on his own projects but also helping the younger people develop good work habits as well as their own sense of style. He is a friendly and caring individual, but he views the workplace as a workplace and believes that he comes there "to work." Robert's work area is adjacent to an open workspace where several of the administrative assistants sit, making corrections and handling office duties. Many times, the largely female

group congregate at the coffee maker outside Robert's office. Occasionally, their conversation topics turn to their sexual exploits and recent conquests. Their laughter and commentary is often overheard by those around them but they do not seem to notice or care. They seem to take no notice of Robert at all, working away in his office. Robert does care, because he finds that his concentration is interrupted and that he cannot block out the "really juicy" commentary. He wonders if he should, or could, say anything to them. If he did, what would they think of him?

3. In one of the region's most successful law firms, eight recent law school grads from prestigious programs were hired. Long hours, tedious work, high pressure, and close quarters produced a tight-knit group, bound by their common indenture and common aspirations. Often, they ate together, pulled all-nighters together, and pitched in for one another. After the second year, the only female associate, Dana, and her husband decided to start a family. Determined to continue her career, Dana asked for the same tough work schedule, continued to keep her same workload, and kept the same long hours. In her seventh month of pregnancy, Dana was surprised to see six of the guys walk toward her and was shocked to see one of them, Paul, pull out a water cannon and shoot it at her stomach so that her "water broke." As the six of them burst into laughter and "high fived" each other, Dana ran to the ladies room. The remaining associate, Dave, who had not been part of the group, stepped forward and said to the group, "If anything happens to that baby, I will offer Dana my deposition about this juvenile behavior. In fact, I'll represent her in a discrimination suit." The other guys in the group walked away mumbling comments about his not being a "regular guy" and a "wet blanket." Dave sat there staring at the group wondering how they could do this to Dana.

Diversity Simulation

Directions: Divide the class into triads. Two people will play the assigned roles, and the third person will act as an observer. The observer is to look for conflict resolution strategies, language choices, nonverbal communication cues. Each simulation should last no more than ten minutes. Each observer should then give feedback to the participants. Optional assignment: A simulation is presented before the whole class, with all the class members acting as observers. Following the first simulation a discussion takes place and suggestions are made to dealing with the situation. The process continues as time allows.

1. (Manager and first-year Accountant) The auditing workpapers are missing from the prior year's audit in preparation for a client's second-year audit. The manager on the project accuses the young accountant, to whom the

file was given, of misplacing them and being sloppy. The accountant has not yet begun to work on the project and believes that the files are in the work cubicle and tries to calm the manager's anger.

2. (Managing Director and Analyst) A manager tells a first-year analyst at an investment banking firm that vacation plans must be canceled as the firm has an opportunity to bid on a municipal bond offering due in five days. The analyst has made plans to attend her parent's twenty-fifth wedding anniversary party that weekend and asks the manager to be excused.

3. (Administrative Assistant and Salesperson) Several of the members of the department like to joke and banter in an open work area as a way of relieving stress in a demanding sales environment. One of the administrative assistants is unable to concentrate and, as a result, is unable to meet deadlines. Finally, after a poor performance review, the administrative assistant decides to speak to one of the people often involved in the banter.

4. (Manager and Employee) During a performance appraisal, a manager delivers seven pages of criticism and suggestions to a first-year employee. Stunned and unable to react at the time, the employee returns to the manager's office three days later and seeks clarification and guidance.

5. (Administrative Assistant and Employee) An administrative assistant reveals an employee's performance appraisal results and salary information to other staff members. The employee decides to confront the administrative assistant.

6. (District Rep and Salesperson) A salesperson froze up in the middle of a presentation to an important client and the sale was lost. When the district supervisor heard about it, the salesperson was severely criticized. The salesperson decides to try to see the client once again to make the presentation and make the sale.

7. (Coworkers) Over pizza with your workplace friend, you discuss your great idea about streamlining the invoicing procedures. Three days later, your boss announces the new procedure at the department meeting and credits your "friend" with the idea. You decide to confront the friend before going to the boss.

8. (Coworkers) As part of a team, you work long and hard on a high-profile project. When the presentation is ready, another member of your team is selected to give the presentation to senior management and does not credit the team with the work. You decide to confront the presenter.

9. (Customer and Employee) You are the district rep for a line of cleaning products. One of your customers calls and blasts you about the damage the cleaning product did to a couch, threatening to sue for damages. You attempt to handle this complaint.

••• Notes •••

1. E. T. Klemmer and F. W. Snyder, "Measurement of Time Spent Communicating," *Journal of Communication* 22 (June 1972): 142–158.

2. For an excellent discussion of relationships and power as a communication affecter, see Charles T. Brown and Paul W. Keller, *Monologue to Dialogue,* 2d ed. (Englewood Cliffs, NJ: Prentice Hall, 1979).

3. Ibid., 96.

4. Sidney Jourard, *The Transparent Self* (New York: Van Nostrand Reinhold, 1964), pp. 5–6.

5. Carl J. Armbruster, "Communication Aids Getting Ahead," *Elyria (Ohio) Chronicle-Telegram* (July 30,1978), D3.

6. Ibid.

7. Howard Muson, "Getting the Phone's Number," *Psychology Today* (April 1982): 42.

8. Based, in part, on a series of handouts distributed by the Community Education Division, Lorain County Community College, April 1982.

9. Bob Lucas, Bob Lucas and Associates as presented in *Communication Briefings,* Alexandria, VA, April 1995.

10. Richard C. Anderson, *Communication: The Vital Artery* (Watsonville, CA: Correlan Publications, 1973), p. 2.

11. *Effective Communication on the Job* (New York: American Manufacturing Association, 1963), p. 115.

12. A. Vogel, "Why Don't Employees Speak Up?" *Personnel Administration* 30 (May–June 1967): 21.

13. Gerald M. Goldhaber, *Organizational Communication* (Dubuque, IA: Wm. C. Brown, 1986), p. 205.

14. *Effective Communication on the Job* , 115.

15. James T. Yenckel, "Careers: Praise the Worker and Pass the Profits," *The Washington Post* (September 27, 1982), C5; based on interviews with Kenneth Blanchard and Spencer Johnson, authors of *The One Minute Manager* (New York: Morrow, 1982).

16. Ibid.

17. Eileen Mazer, "How to Really Say What's on Your Mind," *Prevention* (September 1981).

18. *Effective Communication on the Job, A Guide for Supervisors and Executives,* rev. ed. (New York: American Management Association, 1963), p. 223.

19. Ibid., 231.

20. John Hollwitz, "Difficult Personalities," an unpublished paper presented at the Speech Communication Association Convention, Chicago, November 1, 1984.

21. Ron Walker and Daniel Barnes, "Communicating with the Difficult Personality: Problems in an Academic Setting," an unpublished paper presented at the Speech Communication Association Convention, Chicago, November 1, 1984.

22. *Effective Communication on the Job,* 207–209.

23. Ibid., 209.

24. Ibid., 169.

25. Lawrence Rosenfeld, "Conflict's NOT a Four-Letter Word," unpublished work-

shop manual, 1982, 5, as adapted from Deborah Weider-Hatfield, "A Unit in Conflict Management Communication Skills," *Communication Education* 30 (July 1981): 265–273.

26. For a complete discussion of conflict and resolution, see Roy Berko, Lawrence Rosenfeld, and Larry Samovar, *Connecting: A Culture-Sensitive Approach to Interpersonal Communication Competency*, 2d ed. (Ft. Worth, TX: Harcourt Brace, 1997), Chapter 11.

27. The procedure presented was conceived by Richard Weaver, in *Understanding Interpersonal Communication* (Glenview, IL: Scott, Foresman, 1978). It is a variation of the Dewey problem-solving method as presented in John Dewey, *How We Think* (Lexington, MA: D. C. Heath, 1910).

28. Eugene Raudsepp and Joseph Yeager, "Office Power," *Passages* (April 1981): 8–10, 12.

29. Leah Curtin, "A Profile of Assertive Behavior," *Supervisor Nurse* (May 1979): 7.

30. Based on L. Z. Bloom, et al., *The New Assertive Woman* (New York: Dell Paperback Books, 1976).

31. Ibid.

32. Based on Sharon Bower and Gordon Bower, *Asserting Yourself* (Reading, MA: Addison-Wesley, 1976).

Interviewing

EXPECTED OUTCOMES

After completing this chapter, you should be able to:

- Understand the important role that interviewing plays in organizational decision making.
- Know how to structure an effective interview with an opening, body, and closing.
- Recognize and adapt to various types of informative, persuasive, personnel, and public interviews.
- Understand the interviewer's and interviewee's responsibilities for effective communication in interviews.

When I learned my resume had hit the mark and landed a spot on the campus recruiter's schedule, I was overjoyed. The company was my first choice. I had an excellent record of achievement in the academic, work, and social/volunteer arenas. I studied the company's annual report, downloaded recent press coverage about their actions, visited the corporate home page, and learned a great deal about their specialty—marketing trends in the world of consumer products. Now, sitting outside the recruiter's cubicle in my blue interview suit and power tie, next to others waiting in their blue interview suits and power ties, I wondered if it would all come down to likability, having that "something extra." But how to convey that? How to take a twenty-minute interview and turn it into an irresistible personal infomercial?

As people make decisions at all levels within the organization, they are aided in the process by one-to-one interpersonal communication. Indeed, throughout any typical workday most communication within an organization occurs in face-to-face interactions. Often, on the basis of interpersonal communication, employees decide issues, such as who to hire, how to accomplish a task, what tasks to accomplish, what the organization's goals are, who to fire, and who to train or retrain.

The face-to-face decision making frequently takes the form of formal or informal interviewing. An **interview** is person-to-person communication (usually between two persons, but sometimes three or four persons may be involved) with a basic decision-making purpose. In the interview, one person assumes the role of initiator or questioner (the **interviewer**), while another person serves as the respondent (the **interviewee**). "The interview is the most common form of purposeful, planned communication."[1]

Many people associate the word *interview* only with the employment interview. There are many other types of interviews, however. Some are formal and some are informal. Often, people participate in interviews without even recognizing that they are actually taking part in one. Such transactions might be more productive and satisfying, however, if the interviewer uses principles of effective interviewing in order to accomplish the communicators' goals. For example, it is helpful to give the interview, even the informal interview, a structure.

Structuring the Interview

Careful organization can ensure that all essential points are covered in the interview. Most interviews take the basic form of opening, body, and closing.

THE OPENING OF AN INTERVIEW

The **interview opening** should accomplish two objectives: (1) to establish **rapport**—a communication bond—between the communicators and (2) to establish the overall purpose or objective of the interview.

Establishing rapport is a crucial step at the beginning of many interviews. The interviewer and the interviewee normally need a comfortable communication climate in which to respond openly and honestly. Ideally, the two people should create some type of common bond. An interview should not be regarded as a debate confrontation in which there are winners and losers.

Certain key host functions should be performed by the interviewer—offering to take the interviewee's coat and offering a cup of coffee or a place to sit are part of this initial step. It can also be helpful to discuss any personal

THE IDEAL INTERVIEW

Objective: Survive "cut," manage impression of self, relate answers to job description, project energy and enthusiasm, and maintain poise.

Prepare: Questions, Industry, Firm, Position

**Participate in the Interview
Greetings, Introductions, Rapport, Forecast**

| Provide specific descriptions of past behaviors | **Answer Questions:
Educational Background
Work-Related Experience
Career Goals
Personal Qualities** |

Link responses to job description and "successful" behaviors

Ask 2–3 questions about the company

INTERVIEWER EVALUATES CANDIDATE

| If **"Yes,"** they sell Firm and Opportunity | If **"No,"** they sell Firm but not Opportunity |

Indicate interest in position, offer final "sound bite"
Record Observations, Send Letter, Strategize Next Step

elements that might be appropriate. You might share an interest in sports or in gardening, or you might have attended the same college.

For those who consult with marketing and sales representatives selling products or services to institutions, it is surprising how frequently these sales-people neglect to start out by building rapport. Instead they often attempt to deal with the customer as "the institution" rather than as a person. Establishing rapport can help cut through the stereotypes of "Here comes XYZ Corporation" or "Today I have to sell books." Ignoring this first step often turns off potential buyers or clients. It does not take long to develop a comfortable communication climate. Once the rapport is established, you can move on to defining the purpose of the interview.

The purpose of the interview usually is predetermined. Both the interviewer and the interviewee have understood this purpose when they set the original appointment. It is helpful, however, to reiterate that purpose at the onset to make sure that both parties understand the objectives of the interview. The purpose sets the stage for the type of interview conducted, so it is important to spell out the objective.

THE BODY OF AN INTERVIEW

Following the opening—establishing rapport and setting the purpose—the participants move to the body of the interview. The interview **body** is the heart of the discussion in which interviewer and interviewee handle the questions and responses to those questions.

Types of Interview Questions

If you are the interviewer, there are five basic types of questions that can help you structure the content of the interview: open, closed, mirror, probe, and leading questions.

The **open question** provides for a wide range of responses and gives the interviewee room to elaborate a response. "How do you feel about the new Management By Objectives system?" and "How would you characterize your management style?" are open questions.

The **closed question** narrows and structures the responses that you will receive. Use closed questions when you need a direct to-the-point answer. "Did you take an advanced calculus course?" and "Was there time to fully implement the new program?" are examples of closed questions.

The **mirror question** reflects the content of what the respondent has just said. At times it may be useful to reflect on the emotion being communicated as well as the content. "You say you disagree with that particular operation?" and "You feel strongly about this, don't you?" are examples of mirror questions.

The **probe question** is designed to get more specific, more detailed information or opinions from the interviewee. It is a good follow-up to open questions. "You have indicated that you prefer zero-based budgeting. Could you tell me why?" and "You believe that the new promotion system can be more effective. Which aspects of it would be more productive?" probe the interviewee for more information.

The **leading question** literally leads the interviewee to a response. A sample of a leading question is "You don't really feel that tax shelters are justified, do you?" Some interviewers use the leading question to ascertain whether the interviewee can easily be lead to a conclusion. Other interviewers use it to test the interviewee's ability to stand up for her or his convictions. Other interviewers use the leading question in order to see whether the interviewee will be an ally concerning issues and actions on which the interviewer has strong convictions and needs a supporter.

The Format of the Interview

It is helpful to arrange the questions in advance to establish a general outline—the **interview schedule.** This schedule might take the form of the funnel or the inverted funnel type of format.

The **interview funnel schedule** structures the questions from the more general to the more specific. Thus, if you want to gain more information about a new system, this format schedule might be suitable.

General: "Could you describe the basic procedures of the new evaluation system?"

More specific: "How does the evaluation system operate? When does it occur?"

Specific: "Why was the system instituted? Do you think it will work? Why?"

On the other hand, it may be necessary to start out with specifics and move to the general—the **interview inverted funnel schedule**—as in a reprimand interview.

Specific: "Are you aware that your productivity has continued to fall off significantly in the last quarter?"

More general: "You realize that we have discussed your productivity before?"

General: "Why does your productivity continue to be a problem?"

An interview schedule is, at best, a general guide for the questions to be covered in the body of the interview. The best interviews are structured yet spontaneous enough so that the two parties can adapt to each other and to what is said. You will want to listen carefully and even allow the interview to go in a different direction if you find that other points are more interesting or more relevant to the purpose. Thus, you don't want to adhere slavishly to your checklist of questions if it is not accomplishing the purpose. On the other hand, your questions can give a general direction to the topics to be included in the body of the interview so that you will accomplish your purpose.

THE CLOSING OF AN INTERVIEW

Once the body of the interview has been completed and you are satisfied that the material has been covered, you should move to the **interview closing.** The closing should tie together what has been covered in a short summary. The summary can reiterate what has been accomplished in the interview, but it is not necessary to rehash every detail that has been discussed.

Further, an effective closing should provide the opportunity for both parties to clear up any last questions, to agree on what has been accomplished, and to agree, if necessary, on the next step. It's wise not to end the interview until the final step is clarified, especially if you want to close a sale, to know when to hear about employment decisions, or to know how to implement a solution. The closing is the time to make a final, lasting impression with the interview partner.

The closing deserves as much care and attention as the rest of the interview process. A problem-solving interview might close with "Then we've agreed that you'll train the new operators before they are allowed to work with the machinery." A persuasive close might be "We'll deliver the calculators on Tuesday. The total price for each, including shipping, will be $550."

Types of Internal Business Interviews

Interviews are conducted within organizations for a variety of decision-making purposes. These purposes characterize the various types of business interviews that may be used: informative, problem solving, persuasive, employment, performance appraisal, counseling, reprimanding, and public. Because the employment interview and the performance appraisal are so important to all workers, an extended discussion of these types of interviews is especially in order.

THE INFORMATIVE INTERVIEW

When we seek information, an **informative interview** structure may serve the purpose. A manager who needs to communicate information about a new personnel procedure, for example, may want to conduct personal interviews with each supervisor so that the information is clearly disseminated throughout the plant.

Communicators in an informative interview should take care to distinguish fact from opinion so that the information transmitted will be as accurate as possible. Developing rapport at the outset of an informative interview is important; an interviewee who feels comfortable with the interviewer is more willing to be open and provide substantial information.

A good informative interview should be structured carefully so that the goals are achieved in a clear, accurate fashion. A sample schedule for an informative interview is:

Purpose: To interview a partner in a successful catering business in order to learn about his background, the evolution of his business, the function of his business, the experiences he has had in the business, and his observations about the business.

I. Opening
  A. Establish rapport
  B. Explain purpose
II. Education
  A. What was your college major?
  B. How has your education benefited you in your field of work?
  C. What classes in your major were helpful to you? What nonmajor classes have been beneficial?
III. Evolution of the business
  A. How did you become interested in owning your own business?
  B. How did you get involved in this particular business?
  C. How long did it take before you knew that your business was successful?
IV. Functions of the business
  A. How many people do you employ?
  B. What is your relationship with your employees?
  C. What type of people do you come in contact with most frequently?
  D. What skills does your position require?
V. Experience
  A. What was your biggest shock when you entered the business world?
  B. Now that you have owned your own business, would you ever consider working for someone else?
  C. What are the biggest pressures you face in owning your own business?
  D. What are the advantages of being your own boss?
VI. Observations
  A. What suggestions would you have for a college student interested in owning a business?
  B. Do you believe that a person needs any special personality traits to own a business?
  C. What do you think has been your greatest asset leading to your position as a successful businessperson?
  D. Do you plan to stay in this business? What else might you do?

VII. Closing
   A. Summary
   B. Interviewee—other questions?
   C. Thanks

The informative interview can be a valuable management tool. For example, the CEO of the Mackay Envelope Corporation schedules a personal, private meeting with each of his company's 400 employees to find out what's working and what isn't. The strategy enables him to project the image that he truly cares about each and every person and that their work and their ideas do make a difference.[2]

THE PROBLEM-SOLVING INTERVIEW

Another type of interview crucial to the decision-making function of any organization is the **problem-solving interview.** If a corporation is faced with a problem (for instance, the possible need for downsizing), it might consider interviewing a variety of employees and customers in order to determine the nature and the source of the problems with an eye to locating solutions. In one problem-solving format, personnel departments are finding the communication audit to be a useful decision-making technique. One stage of the communication audit involves employees being interviewed about their perceptions of communication problems—and their solutions—within the organization.

A good problem-solving interview should be structured so that problems are discussed thoroughly before solutions are suggested. Such a structure can ensure that both the interviewer and the interviewee understand the nature of the problems to be solved. Otherwise, you may find yourself discussing a variety of solutions that do not tackle the real problem.

An example of an interview schedule for a problem-solving interview follows:

Purpose: To determine how the organization can more effectively meet its information processing needs.

   I. Opening
      A. Establish rapport
      B. Explain purpose
  II. Identification of the problem
      A. Amount of information that must be processed
      B. Limitations of the present computer system
 III. Criteria
      A. Information processing goals for year 2005
      B. Standards and requirements of any system for the company: networks; hardware; software

IV. Solutions
   A. Brainstorm various approaches to the present computer problems
   B. Analyze the advantages and disadvantages of each brainstormed solution
V. Selection of the best solution
   A. Which approach would best meet the company needs?
   B. How can the solution be implemented?

THE COUNSELING INTERVIEW

A special type of personnel problem-solving interview is the **counseling interview.** In this type of interview, the interviewer serves as a "sounding board," allowing the interviewee to talk through his or her own problems. For example, if a manager discovers that the employee has some job-related problem that he or she probably could solve if given the opportunity to talk it through, this interview form would be appropriate.

Understanding how to identify and to help resolve human problems in the workplace is a sensitive and complex task. It is not surprising that many supervisors prefer to ignore their subordinates' problems, as if to say "that's not my problem." In fact, any employee problem that affects his or her problem *is* the supervisor's problem. If these problems are left unattended, the economic and emotional results can be painful for the organization, for the other employees, and for the troubled person.[3]

To handle the role of sounding board, the interviewer should use only those verbal and nonverbal responses that can serve to keep the interviewee talking. Nondirective responses such as a nod of the head and verbally reflecting what the interviewee has just said are useful strategies for conducting this type of interview.

It should be recognized that we are not advocating that the supervisor play amateur psychologist. Problems of a serious nature clearly should be referred to professional therapists. Many organizations employee psychologists, counselors, or human resource specialists to assist with difficult situations. It is important, then, for the supervisor to determine early on if the problem can be handled through a counseling interview or if it requires more professional intervention. The counseling interview assumes that the interviewee will *want* to and will *be able* to deal with his or her problem. Sometimes we encounter people in the workplace who really want to make no effort to deal with their problems; they just want to whine about them! Others simply do not have the intellect, emotional stability, or the skills needed to work through their problems.

A good counseling interview can be scheduled in a straightforward fashion, much like a problem-solving interview, as this sample schedule illustrates:

Purpose: To offer assistance to the employee in order to deal with a personal problem that relates to another worker.

I. Opening
   A. Establish rapport
   B. Identify purpose of the interview
II. Body
   A. Encourage the individual to talk about what is wrong
   B. Consider various ways to deal with the problem
   C. Discuss options
   D. Decide what course of action to take
III. Closing
   A. Summary
   B. Next steps to be taken
   C. Motivator to put plan into action

THE PERSUASIVE INTERVIEW

In addition to informative and problem-solving types of interviews, you may need to conduct a **persuasive interview,** in which you desire that some type of action take place as the result of the interview. Selling products on a one-to-one basis represents a typical type of persuasive interview.

It is important to adapt your motivational appeals directly to the interviewee's needs or interests. For example, you appeal to a government procurement officer's interest in saving money in the federal budget by pointing out how converting to a different accounting system can be cost effective.

Overall decision making within the organization can be facilitated by persuasive, problem-solving, and informative interviews. Issues can be tackled and new procedures implemented at all levels through these structured interpersonal communications. Organizations also make use of a variety of personnel interviews in order to accomplish other decision making functions.

THE EMPLOYMENT INTERVIEW

"It's the wish of every job-seeker that the invitation to an (employment) interview will ultimately result in a job offer. The **employment interview** is usually the employer's final step in either selecting or screening out a candidate."[4] It is helpful to know how to prepare for and participate in the employment interview and the role of the interviewer in the process.

Job Search Process

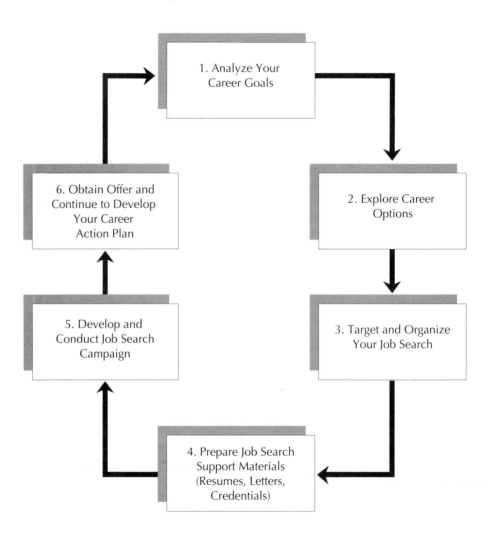

Preparing for the Employment Interview

Surprisingly, only "about two out of 100 job hunters are prepared for the interview. Preparation means doing your homework on the company you're applying to, and, if possible, the people to whom you are going to talk. It's just impossible to wing it."[5]

Some of the most common complaints that interviewers have about interviewees is that they have unrealistic attitudes, vague interests and goals, poor preparation, little information about the job or the organization, ignorance about work life, poor scholastic records, and undesirable personal factors.[6] Likewise, interviewees have been found to possess poor communication skills including difficult in expressing specifics, reticence to speak up, and giving trite answers.[7]

A national study has identified some significant factors that lead to favorable hiring decisions for newly graduated job seekers. In order of importance, interviewees in this study were judged on their:

1. Communication skills
2. Grade point average
3. Work experience
4. Appearance
5. Extracurricular activities
6. Location preference
7. Academic accomplishments[8]

Conducting an Informational Interview Career specialists recommend you first conduct some **informational interviews** with personnel directors or professionals in the field you want to enter. Use these informational interviews to learn about the career field—what it takes to enter the field and to succeed in it. This strategy will help you determine if you even want a career in the field, and it can give you perspective on what it will be like to work in the field. The process also can provide valuable practice in participating in interviews, as well as expand your background information about the field that you can use in future interviews.[9]

Locating Employment Sources In addition to gaining information about the field, it is important to locate employment sources. Before you can interview for a position, you must locate an organization that might be interested in hiring you and for which you are interested in working. An employment agency can be helpful, either for general information about various types of occupations or for specific types of service (e.g., accounting, marketing). College placement bureaus are another good source for locating openings. Many professional organizations also provide such services. Want ads, college advisers, friends, and family members all might serve as sources of information. It often is necessary to use a wide network of people and sources to locate the suitable and possible employment possibilities.

Preparing a Resume Your preparation must also include the development of a professional **resume.** As illustrated in Figure 8.1, your resume should document certain kinds of information:

JAMES SCRUGGS
1210 First Street
College Park, Maryland 20742
(301) 555-1234

EDUCATION
University of Marymount
Bachelor of Arts in Organizational Communication, May 1995
Cumulative grade point average: 3.2 on a 4.0 system.
Prepared to analyze communication problems between/among employees and supervisors;
develop training programs in communication audits; design communication strategies for
implementing change.

EXPERIENCE
Lee Company, Arlington, Virginia
Internship, Personnel Training Office
Fall 1995
Participated in needs analysis and design of communication training program for managers.

Taylor Personnel, Baltimore, Maryland
Internship, Human Resource Office
Summer 1994
Edited training manuals, assisted in development of communication improvement employee
modules

Woodcrest, Ohio Recreation Department
Summer Education Camp Counselor
Summers of 1992 and 1993
Taught elementary and junior high school students computer skills

COCURRICULAR ACTIVITIES
Communication Union Forensics and Debate Club
Debater, 1991-95
President, 1994-95

Student Government Association,
Elected member, 1994-95

Alpha Epsilon Pi Fraternity
Member, 1991-95
Public Relations Chairperson, 1993-95

HONORS/AWARDS
American Debate Society, Marymount Chapter, Debater of the Year, 1995
Lambda Pi Eta, National Speech Communication Honor Society, 1995.

COMPETENCIES
Fluent in French
Computer Skills: Excel, Word, WordPerfect, Access, and dBase

FIGURE 8.1
Sample Resume—Graduating College Student

1. Personal data: name, address, telephone number
2. Education: your formal high school and post-secondary education and training including degrees and certificates, relevant subjects studied, honors, and activities
3. Experience
   a. By function: describe briefly the work you performed.
      OR
   b. By job: list your most recent position and work backward. For each job, list dates of employment, name and address of employer and nature of business, position held, specific job duties and scope of responsibility, and your accomplishments.

Before you can interview for a job, you must locate an organization that would be interested in hiring you and for which you are interested in working.

4. Additional information: knowledge of foreign languages; volunteer or leisure-time activities that might be relevant; special skills such as word processing or computer programming; ability to operate special equipment; membership in professional organizations; publications; patents; inventions; special awards and recognitions.

5. References: Provide the names, positions, and addresses of at least three persons who have direct knowledge of your work competence. Some resume specialists recommend that the job seeker should not list references on the form; rather, identify "References available upon request" on your resume, or omit this section.[10] If you do this, be sure to have a separate sheet listing your references that you can give to the interviewer if he or she requests it during the interview.

Resume specialists[11] offer several tips that can be useful when constructing a resume.

1. There is no set standard length; however, one typed page is usually long enough for recent graduates with little or no work experience.

2. Emphasize the positive by focusing on those parts of your past that stand out favorably.

3. Type the resume accurately. Be sure that all words are spelled correctly, that proper grammar is used, and that the words and phrases are not pretentious.

4. Adapt your resume to the position for which you are applying. A printed, "generic" resume will not get the attention of employment officials.

5. Start your resume with your name at the top. It is not necessary to head it with "resume."

6. Recognize that your resume is not going to impress everyone. Adopt a style and tone with which you are comfortable and which is appropriate to the profession. A resume for work in an artistic field might look more "creative" than that for work in a Wall Street firm.

Among certain companies, there is a movement toward **electronically screened resumes,** in which resumes are scanned into computers and sorted by key words to identify candidates with specific abilities and talents.[12] Unsolicited resumes, even when no job openings exist, are being filed in a computer for possible future reference.[13] The companies that are turning to this type of electronic screening are the large companies, those that receive numerous applications for few jobs. But even some small companies have turned to firms that do electronic screening for them in order to save on the organization's personnel resources.

What's Your Interviewing IQ?

By Rebecca L. Ray, Ph.D., and Armanda C. Squadrilli
(from *Executive Female,* May/June 1989, pp. 31–32)

Picture this scenario: You have an interview for a great job with a major corporation. Your appointment is with the executive who's going to make the final decision. You're pretty confident: After all, you have the skill and experience required for the position; it seems like a perfect fit. Yet, you walk out of the interview with an uneasy feeling. Your intuition is right: You aren't offered the job.

You can land or lose out on a job based on a 60-minute interview. No matter what your credentials are, you must convince a prospective employer that you're the best candidate for the position. Competition for interesting, challenging and well-paid jobs is fierce. Getting your foot in the company door is one thing, keeping it there is another.

You can gain the winning edge that will help you clinch a job offer by sharpening your interviewing skills. To see how you rate during an interview, take the following quiz.

Quiz

In the blank space following each statement, indicate whether you "always," "sometimes" or "never" do this during the interviewing process.

1. When I First Contemplate Changing Jobs, I:

   a. Identify what I don't like about my present job (for instance: no chance to advance; low salary; crunching numbers; etc.). _____

   b. Pinpoint the aspects of my present and past job(s) that make/made me feel most satisfied and productive. _____

   c. Determine my career goals for both the next five and 10 years. _____

   d. Review my skills, experience and accomplishments. _____

   e. Find out the state of the job market for my field. _____

   f. Determine my job-related strengths. _____

   g. Determine my weaknesses and how they can be presented in a more positive light. _____

   h. Identify my admirable character traits and work habits. _____

   i. Identify my least-admirable qualities and how they can be corrected. _____

2. Before Starting to Job Hunt, I:

   a. Decide what type of position I want. _____

   b. Find out which executive search firms deal in my area of interest. _____

   c. Determine how I'll make use of my network of contacts. _____

   d. Set a time frame for finding a job. _____

   e. Decide what my salary requirements are. _____

   f. Determine how flexible I am in terms of commuting. _____

g. Decide whether I would (or could) relocate for the right position. _____

3. During the Entire Job-Hunting Process, I:
   a. Reexamine and reevaluate my goals and objectives. _____
   b. Tailor my résumé and interviewing strategy to suit available openings, even if these jobs weren't part of my original plan. _____
   c. Increase my self-promotional activities during slow spells (for example, by networking, writing to the personnel departments of companies I'd like to work for, etc.). _____
   d. Stay in touch with interviewers, recruiters and referral sources. _____
   e. Keep informed about the status of job openings. _____
   f. Determine my options and the tradeoffs I'm willing to make so I can make a decision when I receive an offer. _____

4. When Updating My Résumé, I:
   a. Include accurate descriptions of both my current and past duties. _____
   b. List relevant skills, degrees, certificates and licenses. _____
   c. Use powerful verbs to describe my achievements and responsibilities, such as "created," "streamlined," "invented," "launched," "supervised" and "controlled." _____
   d. Give concrete examples of my accomplishments—particularly how I cut costs, boosted productivity, saved time and/or increased profits. _____
   e. Check for accuracy, logical order, and typographical errors. _____
   f. Make sure the writing is clear and the layout clean (the information doesn't seem crowded on the page). _____
   g. Use high-quality, white bond paper. _____

5. When I Write a Cover Letter, I Make Sure That:
   a. I use high-quality paper. _____

b. The structure conforms to standard business letters. _____
c. The first paragraph identifies the position I'm seeking and how I learned of the job opening. _____
d. The next two or three paragraphs contain information that underscores the match between my skills and the requirements for the position. _____
e. In the last paragraph, I request an interview and say that I'll call in four or five days to set up an appointment. _____

6. When I Contact an Executive Recruiting Firm, I:
   a. Send or bring additional copies of my résumé. _____
   b. Tell the truth about my current employment status. _____
   c. Inform the recruiter about any companies I have already contacted. _____
   d. Let the recruiter know which companies, if any, I don't want to work for. _____
   e. Keep the recruiter informed about my job-hunting status, and how close I am to accepting an offer. _____
   f. Insist that the recruiter notify me before sending out my résumé. _____
   g. Stay in touch with the recruiter on a regular basis. _____

7. To Prepare for Job Interviews, I:
   a. Research recent developments and trends in my field and read any information about the company, including magazine or newspaper articles, the annual report and company brochures. _____
   b. Find out the responsibilities of the position. _____
   c. Try to learn about the company's corporate culture and office politics, either through the recruiter or by calling colleagues or friends who work there. _____
   d. Practice typical interviewing questions, either by myself or with a friend acting as the interviewer. _____

e. Formulate answers to probable questions, especially why a company should hire me. _____

f. Jot down the skills, qualities and accomplishments I want to highlight during the interview. _____

g. Take workshops to polish my communication and presentation skills. _____

h. Prepare interesting questions to ask the interviewer about the company or job to show that I've done my homework.
_____

8. On the Day of the Interview, I:

a. Dress in conservative business attire.
_____

b. Don't wear excessive makeup, jewelry or perfume. _____

c. Allow adequate time for travelling.
_____

d. Arrive at least 10 minutes before my appointment. _____

e. Leave my coat in the reception area.
_____

f. Control my nervousness by breathing slowly and deeply. _____

9. On the Day of My Interview, I Bring with Me:

a. A conservative attaché case. _____

b. A leather-bound note pad, or a legal pad in a folder. _____

c. A good-quality pen. _____

d. Additional copies of my résumé.
_____

e. Samples of my work (such as articles, ad campaigns, designs, etc.). _____

10. Upon Meeting the Interviewer, I:

a. Smile warmly and firmly shake hands.
_____

b. Address the interviewer by his/her last name unless instructed otherwise.
_____

c. Comment on some aspect of the interviewer's office, such as the color scheme or an attractive object, in order to break the ice and to appear friendly and personable. _____

11. During the Interview, I Try to Look Confident and in Control by:

a. Looking directly at the interviewer when I'm talking. _____

b. Sitting and standing erectly. _____

c. Making sure I control nervous gestures or movements, such as tapping my pen or swinging my leg. _____

12. In Order to Sound as Professional as I Look, I:

a. Use good grammar and a varied vocabulary. _____

b. Strive to sound animated and enthusiastic. _____

c. Adopt an easy conversational style.
_____

d. Avoid saying "ah" and "um." _____

e. Articulate clearly. _____

f. Give concise, logical answers. _____

g. Pause no more than three to five seconds before answering a question. _____

13. During the Interview, I:

a. Decline anything to eat or to drink.
_____

b. Decline an offer to smoke. _____

c. Don't drop names or offer insincere flattery. _____

d. Don't interrupt the interviewer. _____

e. Tailor my answers to reflect the link between my qualifications and the requirements of the job instead of merely reciting my job history. _____

f. Answer tough questions openly and honestly. _____

g. Make sure I weave in the points I want to make. _____

h. Answer illegal questions at my discretion and sidestep grossly illegal ones.
_____

i. Ask questions that uncover the particular problems a prospective employer wants solved, then relate how my skills or experience make me the right person to tackle them. _____

j. Speak positively of former bosses and companies. _____

k. Speak only of my triumphs, if possible, and discuss any failures in terms of the lessons I learned from them. _____

l. Project enthusiasm, confidence, energy and dependability. _____

m. Discuss interesting or unusual aspects of my background to provoke interest or to see if the interviewer and I have a common bond. _____

n. Don't make disparaging remarks, in general, about people, places and things. _____

14. After the Interview, I Ask Myself:

a. What questions did I answer ineffectively? _____

b. What skills/experience did I fail to highlight? _____

c. How did I show interest in the position? _____

d. How did my nonverbal behavior and dress compare with that of the interviewer? _____

e. How well prepared was I for the interview? _____

f. Was there anything I wish I could do over? _____

15. Within Three Days, I Write a Short Follow-up Letter Thanking the Interviewer for His/Her Time and Interest. In the Letter, I:

a. Reiterate my interest in the position. _____

b. Highlight my related skills and experience _____

c. Mention any other skills I didn't bring up in the interview. _____

Scoring and Analysis

Give yourself 2 points for answering ALWAYS, 1 point for answering SOMETIMES and 0 points for answering NEVER. Add up your score for each section and then calculate your overall score. If you scored between:

175 to 194: You're a first-rate interviewee.

150 to 174: You're taking most of the appropriate steps to ace an interview.

125 to 149: You're good at interviewing but you need to polish some of your skills.

0 to 124: You need to refine your interviewing technique. Analyze what you've been doing wrong, then think of ways to improve your performance.

If you scored less than two-thirds of the possible number of points in any given category, examine it thoroughly to determine your weak areas. For example, low scores in sections 3 and 7 indicate that you don't take an active enough role in the job-hunting process, while low scores in sections 4 and 5 reveal that you need to spend more time preparing your résumé and cover letter so you can land an interview. A low score in section 6 indicates that you're not taking advantage of the opportunities available through recruiters. Scoring low in section 14 reveals that you don't evaluate your performance after an interview so you can avoid making the same mistakes. Identify the most easily-resolved problems and formulate a self-improvement plan.

In order to ensure consideration of your application it is wise to follow the electronic format suggestions.[14] These include: "white paper only documents, typed with highly readable spacing, non-serif typefaces (fonts), and such niceties as underlining, bolding, italics, off-white paper, and reverse blocks should not be used. (Some scanners can't deal with these variations.)"[15] For further details on format and content needed for scannable resumes see Figure 8.2.

As in any type of communication, a resume must be adapted to the audience and the purpose. Therefore, in order to assure that the resume fits the specific job and the organization, it is best to prepare a resume for each job application rather than having a generic resume printed in mass quantity. With the general availability of computers and printers, this previously time-consuming task is simplified.

Acquiring Information about Your Prospective Employer Once you secure an interview, prepare for it. Acquire sufficient background on the company that you will interview with. You will need to know the interviewer's full name and how to pronounce it. (You might need to call the personnel office and ask the secretary about these matters before you arrive.) To learn about the company, talk to former or current employees. Read information in the company's annual report and in other specialized publications such as *Standard and Poor's Corporation Records* or the *Dun and Bradstreet Reference Book*. You can order corporate information from Dow Jones via the Internet through *Business Week*. Many companies send organizational information to their interviewees. If not, call the company and ask them to send you materials.

Preparing Questions to Ask during the Interview You should arm yourself with questions that you might wish to ask. It is important that you determine specifically what the job entails; the organization's goals; the benefits the company offers its employees (e.g., insurance packages, retirement plans, coverage of travel expenses, reimbursement for retraining or educational advancement, stock options, and vacation time); the people with whom you would be working; and anything about the company's culture.

Participating in the Employment Interview

Plan to arrive at the designated place at least ten minutes early to ensure that you are in the right place. It is best not to appear at the interviewer's office more than about five minutes before the appointment so that you don't create an awkward situation in which office staff have to deal with you before the interviewer can greet you.

There is no way to anticipate exactly what will transpire during an interview. Several suggestions, however, may assist you. Employment interview specialists generally agree on these communication strategies.[16]

1. Greet the interviewer by name.
2. Take your cues from the interviewer at the start—where to sit, etc.
3. Don't chew gum or smoke.

FORMAT

To maximize the computer's ability to read your resume, provide the cleanest original and use a standard style resume.

The computer can extract skills from many styles of resumes such as chronological (list and describe up to 6 jobs in order by date, achievement (describe achievements rather than job titles), functional (organize by skills rather than job titles), and combinations of resume types.

The most difficult resume for the compute to read is a poor quality copy that has an unusual format such as a newsletter layout, adjusted spacing, large font sizes, graphics or lines, type that is too light, or paper that is too dark.

Tips for Maximizing Scannability

- Use white or light-colored 8 1/2 × 11 paper, printed on one side only.
- Provide a laser printer original if possible. A typewritten original or a high quality photocopy is ok. Avoid dot matrix printouts and low quality copies.
- Do not fold or staple.
- Use standard typefaces such as Helvetica, Futura, Optima, Univers, Times, Palatino, New Century Schoolbook, and Courier.
- Use font sizes of 10 to 14 points. (Avoid Times 10 point.)
- Don't condense spacing between letters.
- Use boldface and/or all capital letters for section headings as long as the letters don't touch each other.
- Avoid fancy treatments such as italics, underline, shadows, and reverses (white letters on black background).
- Avoid vertical and horizontal lines, graphics, and boxes.
- Avoid two-column format or resumes that look like newspapers or newsletters.
- Place your name at the top of the page on its own line. (Your name can also be the first text on pages two and three.)
- Use standard address format below your name.
- List each phone number on its own line.

CONTENT

The computer extracts information from your resume. You can use your current resume; however, once you understand what the computer

FIGURE 8.2
Preparing a Scannable Resume

searches for, you may decide to add a few key words to increase your opportunities for matching requirements or getting "hits."

Recruiters and managers access the resume database in many ways, searching for your resume specifically or searching for applicants with specific experience. When searching for specific experience, they'll search for key words, usually nouns such as writer, BA, marketing collateral, Society of Technical Communication, Spanish (language fluency), San Diego, etc.

So make sure you describe your experience with concrete words rather than vague descriptions. The computer system will extract the words and information from your sentences; you can write your resume as usual.

Tips for Maximizing "Hits"

- Use enough key words to define your skills, experience, education, professional affiliations, etc.
- Describe your experience with concrete words rather than vague descriptions. For example, it's better to use "managed a team of software engineers" than "responsible for managing, training . . ."
- Be concise and truthful.
- Use more than one page if necessary. The computer can easily handle multiple-page resumes, and it uses all of the information it extracts from your resume to determine if your skills match available positions. It allows you to provide more information than you would for a human reader.
- Use jargon and acronyms specific to your industry (spell out the acronyms for human readers).
- Increase your list of key words by including specifics, for example, list the names of software you use such as *Microsoft Word* and *Lotus 1-2-3*.
- If you have extra space, describe your interpersonal traits and attitude. Key words could include *skill in time management, dependable, high energy, leadership, sense of responsibility, good memory*.
- Use common headings such as: *Objective, Experience, Employment, Work History, Positions Held, Appointments, Skills, Summary, Summary of Qualifications, Accomplishments. Strengths, Education, Affiliations, Professional Affiliations, Publications, Papers, Licenses, Certifications, Examinations, Honors*.

Source: Reprinted with permission of RESUMIX, Inc.

FIGURE 8.2
Continued

4. Be ready for any type of question. Be prepared with detailed descriptions or stories about your past experiences that relate to this position. Listen carefully to what the interviewer asks. Most interviewers open with questions such as "What can I do for you?" "Tell me about yourself." or "Why are you interested in this company?"

5. Don't respond with just "yes" or "no." Give examples and clarify your ideas.

6. Be prepared with some questions that he or she might answer for you. Bring up these questions when you are invited to do so or when it fits in the schedule of questions you are being asked.

7. Sit up in your chair; be alert and interested.

8. Maintain direct eye contact. Interviewers look for people who can look them in the eye. (Note that this suggestions depends upon the culture. In some cultures, direct eye contact is not used consistently, as it would make the interviewer uncomfortable.)

9. Make sure that your good points get across to the interviewer. Point them out on your resume and be prepared to describe the important things that might not be on the resume.

10. Most interviews will follow a question-and-answer formula. Be sure to tell the truth. Avoid phrases such as: "I'll take anything," "I want a challenging position," "I like working with people," or "I'm looking for a rewarding experience."

11. Conduct yourself as if you are determined to get the job you are applying for.

12. Know what salary the job is worth and what you will accept. The interviewer is likely to ask what salary you would accept. Be prepared to offer a realistic figure.

13. Most interviews last between twenty and thirty minutes. Try to anticipate that time frame in timing your responses and asking questions.

14. As the interview comes to an end, make sure that you understand what will happen next—whether the interviewer will call you, whether you should contact someone, or if you are to send some additional information. Whatever the next step, repeat it to the interviewer to make sure that you are in agreement.

15. At the end, thank the interviewer for his or her time and consideration.

It is important to act knowledgeable during an interview. Often it is valuable to anticipate the types of questions that will be asked so that you will feel comfortable in responding.

Questions Often Asked during Employment Interviews Researchers have identified a number of questions that are commonly asked during employment interviews. Here are some typical questions and tips for how to respond to them:

1. What are your short-range goals? (Tip: What kind of job are you looking for?)
2. Where do you want to be five years from now? (Tip: Talk about how you would prepare yourself for future jobs in the company.)
3. What special skills do you have? (Tip: Talk about those skills that you would use in this job.)
4. What kind of job are you most interested in? (Tip: Explain how your interests will help you do a good job.)
5. What characteristics do you think are most important for this job? (Tip: Talk about two or three positive characteristics such as leadership and work under pressure that you would use most often in this job.)
6. What is your greatest strength? What do you think you can do in this job better than anyone else? (Tip: Pick one that best fits the job.)
7. What is your major weakness? (Tip: It's all right to admit a weakness, but also talk about how you're going to turn it into a strength.)
8. What were your most important achievements in your last position? (Tip: Review your accomplishments.)
9. Tell me about yourself. (Tip: Don't be afraid to brag a little. You need to sell yourself. Be honest. Let the interviewer know your successes. This is no time to be shy, reticent, or apprehensive about yourself. Don't give a life history, just enough major points to impress.)
10. Why do you want to work for this company? (Tip: Compliment the company and explain how the company can benefit from your abilities.)
11. What kind of recommendation do you think you'll get from your previous employer? (Tip: Excellent, good—tell why. If you know for sure that you'd get a poor recommendation, don't be afraid to tell why, but follow up with a positive comment. Don't bad-mouth a previous employer.)
12. How do you feel about overtime? (Tip: If this question is asked, you know that there probably are overtime requirements. If you can and want to work overtime, answer enthusiastically. Don't respond with "Well, if I have to . . .")
13. How long would you stay with us? (Tip: Be positive. Say something such as, "I look at this opportunity as the beginning of a longtime relationship.")
14. Why should we hire you? (Tip: Give a summary of your most important qualifications and interests as they apply to the position. Be enthusiastic.)
15. Define the following:
    a. Cooperation. (Tip: Harmony, common goal.)
    b. Responsibility. (Tip: Being accountable.)
    c. Challenging. (Tip: Desire to explore new ways.)[17]

Be aware that though these are the types of questions that might be asked, there are regulations concerning what cannot be asked.

Regulations Governing Employment Interviewing The hiring process, at best, is highly subjective. In the past, this subjectivity was enhanced when there were no guidelines on what types of questions could be asked. Without any guidelines, some workers were denied positions because of information that had nothing to do with their qualifications. The process has been made a little less subjective by the Equal Employment Opportunities Commission, which derived its guidelines from the Civil Rights Act of 1964, and its supporting regulations, which specify that employers must hire people for their ability to do the job without regard to race, sex, religion, or national origin—factors unrelated to their potential job performance. All individuals who participate in the employment interview process should be aware that those equal opportunity employment regulations specify that certain questions are not legal. This means that an employment interviewer may not ask certain questions and an employment interviewee is not required to answer questions that have been determined to be unlawful.

Unlawful inquiries include:

1. Asking the applicant if he or she has ever worked under another name.
2. Asking the applicant to identify his or her birthplace.
3. Asking the applicant to submit proof of age by supplying birth certificate or baptismal record.
4. Asking the applicant for his or her religious affiliation, name of church, or religious holidays that he or she observes.
5. Asking the applicant if he or she is a naturalized citizen.
6. Asking the applicant for the date when he or she acquired citizenship.
7. Asking the applicant if he or she has ever been arrested for any crime and where and when.
8. Asking the applicant how he or she acquired ability to read, write, or speak a foreign language.
9. Requesting the applicant to provide names of three relatives other than father, spouse, or minor-age dependent children.
10. Asking the applicant for a maiden name.
11. Asking the maiden name of the applicant's mother.
12. Asking the full names of the applicant's brothers and sisters.
13. Asking the applicant for a list of the clubs, societies, and lodges to which he or she belongs.
14. Asking the applicant to include a photograph with the application.
15. Asking the applicant to supply addresses of cousins, uncles, aunts, nieces, nephews, grandparents, etc., who can be contacted for references.[18]

On the other hand, it *is* legal to ask the applicant if he or she has the legal right to work in the United States. It also is permissible to ask what foreign language the applicant can read, write or speak fluently, but only if there is a bona fide, work-related reason. If an interviewer does ask you a question you believe is illegal, you might choose to answer it if you believe that the answer will not be harmful to your candidacy. Some applicants use humor to deflect illegal questions. Gross violations should be discussed with a campus career placement officer, a recruiter, or a lawyer.

Be aware that not all interviewers are trained well or know the laws. In many small companies the interviewer may be a supervisor whose major responsibilities is to work and train employees, but not to screen them. Knowing this, be sure you know what you would do if an interviewer asked you a question that you are not legally required to answer.

Even if the interview goes well, there are factors you should consider before accepting a position.

Job Acceptance/Rejection Awareness It is important to remember that before and during an employment interview you are screening the employer just as much as the employer is screening you.[19] Be careful not to accept a job too hastily only to regret it later. Yes, a job is a job, but the wrong job can cause emotional trauma.

Before accepting the position, be certain the job is what you really want or that it can aid you in getting where you want to go. Is the job located where you will be happy with the cost of living, the social, religious, and cultural institutions and the climate of the area? Is the salary compatible with your financial needs? Are the working conditions those with which you are comfortable? Are you a good "fit" with the people who work there? Can you adapt to the corporate culture? What is the reputation of the company?

Future Use for Employment Interviewing Techniques

Once a person secures an entry-level position in a company, it is important to continue to perfect the employment interviewing skills. As an individual strives to move up in a company, one has to be able to participate in screening interviews throughout a career.[20] And these skills are essential to move to other companies and even to other career fields. Further, if you wind up in a company that downsizes, you may find yourself out of a job and in need of a

---

Check Your Interviewing Skills

Few managers are trained to conduct job interviews. Yet candidates are often taught how to prepare for interviews and handle questions effectively.

As a result, notes Robert Half, an outplacement expert, candidates often hold an advantage over unprepared managers.

Take this quiz to find out how well prepared you are to interview applicants. The more "yes" answers, the better.

1. Before the meeting, do you carefully review an applicant's résumé and prepare questions on what you've read?

2. Do you allow yourself plenty of time to spend with the applicant? Do you hold phone calls and devote all of your attention to the interview?

3. Do you take notes during the interview to allow yourself to go back and review your written comments about each candidate?

4. Do you let the candidate do most of the talking by asking open-ended questions, such as "Describe a typical day on your last job"?

5. Do you conduct more-thorough reference checks by making calls yourself and speaking with people who are not on your candidate's list of references? Note: You can get these names by asking people you talk to for names of others who have worked with the applicant.

6. Do you introduce top candidates to the people they'll be working with—and then do you ask your staff for reactions?

Source: Robert Half, founder, Robert Half International Inc., 565 5th Ave., New York, NY 10017.

new one. As a result, the skills that you develop in your initial employment interviewing will serve you throughout your work life.

Remember, regardless of the level of job you are seeking, or where you are in your career, that the cardinal rule of job searching and interviewing is, "present yourself in ways that tell the reader/listener what you can do to help them improve their organization's performance. Use specific examples of things that you can do and did for others."[21]

To this point we have looked at the employment interview from the standpoint of the interviewee. Someone also has to do the interviewing. Individuals who major in human resources management or personnel management often are placed in the position of hiring employees. Sometimes the responsibility falls upon managers or job supervisors. As a present or future businessperson, you may find yourself in the interviewer position in the future.

Business Professionals Share Their Views

Profile: Scott Brandt, college international recruiter specialist, Walt Disney World, Orlando, Florida.

What communication skills do you look for in candidates you are interviewing?

Because of the sheer number of interviews that I must conduct on a college campus, the interviews are scheduled in short fifteen-minute segments, usually with two candidates at once. I look for such communication skills as the ability to respond quickly and directly to questions and the ability to establish and maintain direct eye contact. Since our work at Disney World involves service to the public, it is important for candidates to display basic courtesy. All of our employees are required to maintain high standards in grooming and guest service, so I look for people who communicate well both verbally and nonverbally and who will meet all of our guidelines.

As an interviewer, how do you fulfill the job interview functions of both "selling" the company and gaining information about the potential employee?

Walt Disney World is so highly regarded that is it not at all a "hard sell." We offer a wealth of opportunities for networking and work experience in almost every possible kind of job that you would find in any major city. We are inundated with resumes, so we especially look at an individual's degree *and* work experience. The Disney Company is a Fortune 100 company, so we are quite competitive in our recruitment and selection process. Consequently, the person who has had cooperative or work experience with a Fortune 500 company will have a competitive edge in the recruitment process. In the interview, I listen for indications that the candidate does know something about our organization's expectations and culture.

The Employment Interviewer

Attention to communication details is the key to providing a positive employment interview experience for applicants. And a positive interview experience can have a significant effect on an applicant's further interest in pursuing employment in the company.[22]

Guidelines for conducting employment interviews include:[23]

1. Be courteous.
2. Don't give the person the "third degree," as it is highly risky in this litigious age. It cannot be defended in a court of law. However, use questions that help the other person think about the position.
3. Ask questions that require the respondent to go into detail. Ask for examples or explanations in order to discover reasons behind the person's thinking.
4. Avoid irrelevant questions ("Who do you think will win the playoff?") unless you are trying to set an informal tone early in the session.
5. Avoid illegal questions ("What church do you attend?" "Does your spouse work?").
6. Ask "what if" questions ("What would happen if the government withdrew farm price supports?"). This type of question often allows you to probe the interviewee's perceptions and knowledge of the field.
7. Ask the respondent if he or she needs some time to think.
8. Ask the "W" questions: what, why, when, where, and who. These questions will secure the facts and information that you need.
9. Allow time for the interviewee to ask questions too.
10. End the interview by indicating when and if the interviewee will learn the decision. As a follow-up, provide the applicant with a response as soon as possible.
11. Ask questions that elicit evidence or skills actually related to the position.
12. Treat all candidates in a fair, consistent, and respectful manner. Remember a candidate will likely become a client, a colleague, or a competitor.

THE PERFORMANCE APPRAISAL

Once hired, you will be faced with periodic **performance appraisal interviews** in which your work will be evaluated. Federal law mandates that all federal employees must be systematically evaluated in their job performances according to the specifications set out for the job. Many other organizations, under court orders and governmental regulations, also must follow clear, preestablished procedures. Consequently, managers and supervisors must be trained carefully in the handling of performance appraisals. Indeed, this interview form presents major communication challenges to interviewer and interviewee alike; "few communication activities require the range of skill and strategy" needed to conduct one successfully.[24]

Methods of Performance Appraisal

There are three generally accepted methods for conducting performance appraisal interviews: the tell and sell, the tell and listen, and the problem-solving.[25] Regardless of the type used, it is important for the supervisor to actually conduct the interview. Usually, a performance appraisal is accompanied with some sort of written documentation about a person's work performance. Too frequently, unfortunately, this becomes just a checklist that is handed to the employee to look over and sign with little or no opportunity to discuss. A good performance appraisal needs to highlight the positive dimensions of a person's work so that he or she can continue to build constructively on the positives while also tending to whatever needs to be improved. Thus, the performance appraisal should be set up not to pick apart a person's faults but rather to build on one's strengths.

Of the three techniques, the tell and sell, tell and listen, and problem-solving methods, select the one that best fits the participants and the end purpose of appraisal.

Tell and Sell Method In the **tell and sell method of performance appraisal,** the supervisor plays a role similar to that of the prescribing physician. An evaluation is presented, then the supervisor works to convince the employee to accept it. The method requires considerable persuasive skill in order to motivate the employee to accept it. It can be an unpleasant experience if the evaluation is negative. An atmosphere of defensiveness and hostility may develop, and this can interfere with achieving the immediate and long-term objective of the interview.

In the tell and sell method, the supervisor offers both diagnosis and remedy, so the procedure allows little or no upward communication from the subordinate. This method tends to save time, for the presentation is basically one-sided. It is often frustrating for the employee, because he or she is restricted to a fairly passive role. The tell and sell method is very specific, however, regarding what the employee is to do and what is expected in his or her work performance.

Tell and Listen Method In the **tell and listen method of performance appraisal,** the interviewer communicates the evaluation to the employee and then lets the employee respond to it and suggest needed alternatives. The supervisor offers his or her judgment of the person's work performance, but the method does not necessarily require that the supervisor then convince the subordinate to accept the evaluation.

The tell and listen method of performance appraisal allows the supervisor to become a nondirective listener once the performance evaluation has been presented. During this time, the employee is encouraged to talk about her or his work: what is going well and what needs to be improved—and how that improvement can occur. The interviewer, then, should encourage the interviewee to talk, listen actively, and reflect back what the person says in order to keep the employee talking. While this strategy can be quite therapeutic in allowing the employee to "ventilate" frustrations, it should lead back finally to a focused conversation about what and how to improve the work performance.

Problem-Solving Method The **problem-solving method of performance appraisal** enables the supervisor to assume the role of helper, facilitator. The employee is invited to make a job analysis; to review progress that has been made since the last appraisal; and to discuss satisfactions, problems, needs, innovations, and frustrations that have been encountered since the last appraisal. An agreement must be reached as to which aspects of the job are going well and which ones should be changed and how.

Some Staff Evaluation Don'ts

You can get the most out of your staff if you keep these performance-evaluation "don'ts" in mind:

- *Don't fail to evaluate. Staff can think either you don't care about them or you like their work. Also, at some point, problems will force you to act, and you'll have to take draconian measures.*

- *Don't direct, guide. Too much direction discourages people from using their creativity and initiative. They'll wait for your OK, and you'll never get peak performance.*

- *Don't ignore differences. Base what you expect on each person's maturity level, character and competency.*

- *Don't fail to agree on initiative levels. Example: A waiter has or does not have the initiative to "comp" a meal for a dissatisfied customer. Match levels with ability.*

- *Don't reward ill-gotten results. If people perform by trashing relationships, they destroy the ability to repeat those results.*

- *Don't fail to measure results. You need both hard and soft measures. Look at things such as speed and problem solving as well as relationships. And collect information systematically. If you don't, you could get only bottom-line feedback.*

Source: Executive Excellence, 1 E. Center St., Ste. 303, Provo, UT 84606.

Communicating in Appraisal Interviews

Regardless of the method used, effective appraisal interviews depend upon effective communication skills. Some suggestions for making appraisal interviews a positive experience should be considered by supervisors who must conduct them.[26]

1. Discuss the job; make sure agreement is reached on what the worker is supposed to be doing.
2. If the subordinate's self-appraisal is more favorable than your appraisal, invite the person to tell you specifically why. Often in attempting to explain, the subordinate can see that the self-appraisal is not accurate, or you, the supervisor, might see where you have the wrong perception.
3. Evaluate the job, not the person, unless the effectiveness of the work performance is based on identifiable personal habits. Clothing and appearance, for instance, may not be a legitimate issue if the person is not representing the company in any kind of public position.
4. If you are wrong, admit it. Listen to the subordinate, and if you need to change your perceptions or attitudes about the individual's work performance, be willing to do so.
5. If the employee's performance is truly deficient and must be corrected, indicate exactly what must be done to achieve a satisfactory future evaluation. It also is important to set up a procedure to enable the improvement to occur and to clearly indicate the consequences if the performance does not improve.
6. Focus on the positive. Reinforce those aspects of the employee's work that are effective so that they will continue to perform. Too often, performance appraisals are looked upon as just a critique of one's faults.

Just as the interviewer who conducts the performance appraisal should keep an open mind and develop a supportive communication climate for the interview, so, too, should the interviewee approach the appraisal process with a positive attitude. Some communication strategies can assist you in effectively participating in appraisal interviews.[27]

1. Answer all questions as completely as possible.
2. Offer explanations but do not make excuses or place blame.
3. Ask for clarification as appropriate.
4. Ask for specific suggestions for improvement.
5. Ask for help in improving performance.
6. Ask how much time is available to solve a particular performance problem.
7. Set priorities; do not try to improve everything at once.

8. Avoid getting angry or overreacting.
9. Reiterate the problem or solution for clarification and understanding by both parties.
10. Maintain a positive relationship with the interviewer.
11. Correct any false impressions or assumptions that the supervisor may have about your performance.
12. Close the interview on a positive note and with an open mind.

Performance appraisals, if conducted on a regular basis, can be of immeasurable value to the supervisor, the employee, and the organization. Performance appraisals provide the opportunity for workers and managers to deal in-depth with employee work habits, productivity, and human relationships within the organization.

The University Research Corporation developed an appraisal process that illustrates how the plan can be implemented. Employees are first asked to write an initial self-analysis, evaluating their work against their own standards and expectations. Supervisors offer ways that employees might improve their effectiveness, and then subordinates communicate what help they need from their managers in order to do a better job. In the final stages of the plan, workers and managers review employee career objectives. The process increases worker-boss communication by providing a basis for regular discussions of goals and performance strengths and problems.[28]

The schedule for conducting an effective performance appraisal might resemble this sample schedule:

Purpose: To provide the employee with a thorough appraisal of his or her work since the last performance analysis was conducted.

I. Opening
  A. Greet employee
  B. Establish rapport
  C. Explain purpose of the interview
II. Body
  A. Discuss employee's job.
    1. What are all the activities you do on the job?
    2. Which do you think are the most important?
    3. Which take most of your time?
    4. Are there ways in which you think we could use your time and talents more profitably?
  B. Discuss employee's self-perceptions.
    1. What do you think are your greatest strengths?
    2. Where do you believe you are less confident and competent?

      3. Do you think that you are growing more or less competent in your job as time goes by? How? Why?

      4. Is there any way in which you think you could be assisted in making yourself more valuable to the company?

      5. Is there anything or anyone (including me) that makes your work more difficult?

  C. Evaluate the person.

      1. Identify the positive aspects of the work performance.

      2. Discuss what needs to be improved.

        a. Offer specifics on what and how

        b. Offer assistance for improvement

      3. Discuss the employee's perception of his or her strengths and weaknesses.

      4. Establish an action plan for facilitating the change. Include a specific procedure, deadlines, and re-evaluation steps.

III. Close

  A. Summary

  B. Further questions from interviewee

  C. Next meeting

  D. Positive motivator

THE REPRIMANDING INTERVIEW

If, after performance appraisal or a counseling interview, an employee still has problems on the job, a private **reprimanding interview** might be conducted as a last resort. The reprimand assumes a performance problem and begins at the point where it is necessary to come up with a specific solution to that problem. This format should be used *only* after all previous attempts through appraisal and counseling have failed to change the employee's performance behavior.

One key to effective communication in a reprimanding interview is to be aware of the emotional level. It is normally not effective to discipline an employee while either the person or the reprimander are at high emotional states. While the reprimand must be conducted at the appropriate time to have an impact on changing a person's performance behavior, a wise manager will normally take time to "cool off" before initiating any disciplinary communication.

While some persons responsible for reprimanding simply spell out the problem and the way an employee can correct it (much like a parent scolding a child), a generally more constructive approach is to use an adaptation of the counseling format. Once it is clear what the problem is (and that at this point it has been a recurring problem or a problem of a severe nature), the interviewee should be given the opportunity to discuss the awareness of the problem and how it can be resolved. If permitted to discuss problems with someone who can help put them in a constructive way, many people can handle their own difficulties.

The schedule for an effective reprimanding interview can combine elements of the performance appraisal and the counseling interview. An example follows:

Purpose: To correct an employee's persistent work problem.

II. Opening
   A. Explain purpose
II. Body
   A. Discussion of what needs to be corrected and why
   B. Explanation of what will happen if the problem is not corrected
   C. Discussion of why the problem persists
   D. Exploration of what can be done to solve the problem immediately
   E. Solicitation of employee commitment to correcting the problem immediately
III. Closing
   A. Summary
   B. Next step
   C. Motivator

Types of External Business Interviews

The various forms of interviews reviewed thus far all fulfill internal decision-making within an organization. As a means of internal communication, the interviews can lend purpose and structure to the functioning of the business or corporation. Other interviews, however, occur from outside the organization, requiring some spokespersons of the organization to participate as external communicators in public interviewers. These public interviews usually take the form of press conferences, television talk shows, or radio call-in interview shows.

THE PRESS CONFERENCE

The executive **press conference** has become a basic responsibility for most business and corporate CEOs and the public relations directors who represent them, for the reactions of a leader are important news stories in and of themselves. Some have noted that "the press conference is an institution which is still evolving" and that it is not "at all clear just what constitutes a satisfactory press conference."[29]

A press conference typically is characterized by a number of interviewers—reporters—who ask a variety of questions. The interviewee controls the interview in that he or she must time the conference and must be sure to allow a number of the reporters to ask questions. In a **structured press conference,** the person to be interviewed may give a short opening speech to be followed by a question-and-answer session. In some cases, the questioners are restricted to asking questions only about the subject of the speech that has just been presented. A **spontaneous press conference** is not too structured, so questions may move from one topic to the next. In this format, the reporters present are allowed to ask any questions they desire.

When you conduct a press conference, try to anticipate the general line of questioning in advance and even rehearse some responses so that you will be an articulate spokesperson for the organization. It also is useful in this forum to repeat the question aloud before responding, so that you are sure everyone has heard and understood the question being asked.

THE TALK SHOW INTERVIEW

With the growth of the **talk show** format on radio and television, more and more businesspersons are being invited to explain new products, defend their company's policies, and clarify actions being taken by their organizations. Many of the same characteristics of the press conference are contained in the talk show format. The questions usually are asked by one interviewer—the show's host—in a one-on-one setting. Sometimes more than one guest participates so that the show takes more of the form of a group conversation. If there is a studio of a call-in audience, members of the audience may be given the chance to participate with questions of you as well.

A television show host may set up a general line of questions in advance so that you will be able to prepare for the appearance. A good talk show will often function as if it were a relaxed "chat," while operating under the time constraints and subject limitations, which should take some of the pressure off of you. If the talk show host is especially famous, it will be important to keep in perspective that it is his or her show, so do not expect to be a "centerpiece"! It is important to maintain composure and to be responsive at a conversational level while on the air.

A popular radio format is the call-in show where the interviewee, as an expert guest, appears with the show's host to field phone-in questions. Some of these shows do not pre-screen the callers, so you might encounter some irrelevant, unclear, or even hostile questions. A wise business representative has such materials as annual reports and statistical information available for quick reference.

When you participate in a talk show, remember to consider the ramifications of what you say. Try to avoid getting trapped into saying something that can be embarrassing to you or your company. When responding with the corporation's views, identify it as such: "The company's view . . ." or "We believe. . . ." If the ideas are yours, identify them as your opinions: "I think . . .".

Talk shows can provide opportunities to reach a wide audience with your message. It is important to be able to "bridge" from the interviewer's questions into the key points that you want to be sure to present. "Yes, and in addition . . ." and "What's really important here . . ." can be transitions to allow you to emphasize your message.[30]

• • •   In Summary   • • •

An interview is person-to-person communication (usually between two persons, but sometimes three or four persons may be involved) with a basic decision-making purpose. In the interview, one person assumes the role of initiator or questioner (the interviewer), while another person serves as the respondent (the interviewee). The interview is the most common form of purposeful, planned communication.

Interviews are conducted within organizations for a variety of decision-making purposes. These purposes characterize the various types of business interviews that may be used: informative, problem-solving, persuasive, employment, performance appraisal, counseling, reprimanding, stress, and public.

═══ Business Communication in Practice ═══

1. Select an individual who is involved in a specific occupation you may wish to pursue. Make an appointment to interview the person. Prepare a schedule of questions that you will use during the interview. Your goal is to find out as much about the career field as possible, including educational requirements, job descriptions, working conditions, communication needs, etc. Plan to report to the class on the interview, including the questions used, the results of the interview, and your perceptions of how the interview went.
2. Pair with a classmate. Interview your classmate about his or her major field of study and why that major was selected. Use this information to introduce your classmate to the rest of the class.
3. Prepare a schedule of questions that you would use as a guideline for interviewing *yourself* for a position that you are interested in. Determine

how you could most effectively respond to the various questions that you might be asked in an actual employment interview.

4. Make an appointment to interview a career counselor at the career center on your campus. Ask the counselor what specific suggestions he or she can offer for how to be successful in projecting yourself in future employment interviews.

5. Scan the Help Wanted ads in your Sunday newspaper. Notice the number of ads that indicate the need for "effective written and oral communication skills" in order to qualify for the position.

▭▭ Diversity Simulation ▭▭

Directions: The simulations may be performed before the entire class or in groups of three to five participants.

If done before the entire class, two students are selected to play the roles of the participants in each interview. Each role player is given a copy of the role to be played. Role players may not know the contents of their partner's role play description. After the students carry on a five- to ten-minute interview, observers are to comment on their interviewing techniques and give constructive suggestions on ways the participants could have performed more effectively.

If done in small groups, two students are designated as participants and the remainder of the group are to perform as observers. A general class discussion should follow each interview with the observers commenting on the interviewing techniques and suggesting other ways the participants could have performed.

Interview I

Worker You have been working for this company for over three months, and you were told you would certainly get a raise in salary in a relatively short time if you concentrated on "giving it your all." This you have done, putting in lots of overtime. No one seems to have noticed, however, and believing that you are entitled to more pay, you have asked for an appointment with your supervisor to state your case.

Supervisor You begin this interview with the standard statement "Can I help you?" You know very well what the worker wants. You have indeed been watching him or her and plan to grant a raise, but you want the worker to be able to express clearly *why* he or she should have it rather than John, Bob, and Alice—all of whom have been on the job at least three months longer than this worker has. You also want to find out if the worker is willing to continue to accept additional responsibility and overtime.

Interview II

Interviewee You are applying for a job as a human resources assistant in an office. You *really* want the job, and your qualifications are excellent. You have done two human resources internships at major companies and you graduated with a 3.6 point average with a major in Human Resource Management. You are, however, a rather shy person. You have been told all your life not to be a braggart. Explain why you would be best suited for this position and try to make a good impression.

Interviewer This is the fifteenth applicant for the job. So far, no one has impressed you as being able to communicate under stress—an important part of this job, which includes dealing with employee complaints. This applicant doesn't seem too promising either, and you are tired after a long day. Open your interview with the standard question "Why do you think you are particularly qualified to handle this job?" Be sure to find out how she or he operates under stress. If the applicant comes up with satisfying answers to your questions, hire the person.

Interview III

Female Complainer You have what you consider a legitimate gripe about working conditions where you are employed. A male coworker who has been with the company six months less than you, and who has received several work-related reprimands, has been recommended for a promotion. You sincerely believe that you should have been promoted and that the reason you weren't is that you are a woman. You know that your supervisor has chosen men over women for the past three promotions in the department and has been heard to say "a woman's place is in the home."

Male Supervisor You felt forced to employ this woman in order to fulfill the minority requirements although you were certain a man would have been better for the job. You believe that "a woman's place is in the home." However, you are concerned that she will go to the American Civil Liberties Union or one of those "liberal woman's lib" organizations with her grievance. Try to keep her from taking that step and convince her that she *doesn't* deserve a promotion, but the male worker does.

● ● ●　Notes　● ● ●

1. Charles J. Stewart and William B. Cash, Jr., *Interviewing* (Dubuque, IA: Brown and Benchmark, 1994), p. 1.
2. Harvey Mackay, "One-on-One Meetings Send a Message to Employees—and Net Results," *The Denver Post* (August 6, 1995), 4G.

3. John Meyer and Teresa Meyer, "The Supervisor as Counselor—How to Help the Distressed Employee," *Management Review* (April 1982): 44.
4. Carole Carmichael, "Questions to Ask before You Take a Job," *Fort Lauderdale News* (December 14, 1980), C1.
5. James Yenckel, "Careers: Facing the Interview," *The Washington Post* (October 20, 1981), D5.
6. Donna Goodall and H. Lloyd Goodall, Jr., "The Employment Interview," *Communication Quarterly* 30 (September 1982): 116–122.
7. Ibid.
8. Ibid.
9. Richard Nelson Bolles, *What Color Is Your Parachute?* (Berkeley, CA: Ten Speed Press, 1995).
10. Caroline Donnelly, "Writing an Advertisement for Yourself," *Money* (January 1974).
11. Ibid. Also see "How to Write a Resume," 1 (March 1984).
12. Robert E. Steinman, "The Latest Wrinkle in Job Search," *Cincinnati Enquirer* (October 8, 1995), G1.
13. Ibid.
14. Ibid.
15. Ibid.
16. *Merchandising Your Job Talents* (Washington, DC: U.S. Department of Labor—Employment and Training Administration, 1976), and "How Do You Talk to a Job Interviewer?" *The Washington Post* (October 7, 1984), advertising supplement.
17. Adapted from Pat Hartsel Dennison, Private Industry Council of Lehigh Valley, Inc., Allentown, PA.
18. Robert Minter, "Human Rights Laws and Pre-Employment Inquiries," *Personnel Journal* 52 (June 1972): 432.
19. Carmichael.
20. Linda Shrieves, "Older Job Seekers Need a Resume That Makes Waves," *The Washington Post* (August 27, 1995), H5.
21. Steinman.
22. Steven M. Ralston and Robert Brady, "The Relative Influence of Interview Communication Satisfaction on Applicants' Recruitment Interview Decisions," *The Journal of Business Communication* 31 (1994): 61–77. Also see K. Michele Kacmar and Wayne A. Hochwarter, "The Interview as a Communication Event: A Field Examination of Demographic Effects on Interview Outcomes," *The Journal of Business Communication* 32 (July 1995): 207–232.
23. Peggy Scherretz, "If You Ask Me: Nothing Personal," *The Washington Post* (February 15, 1982), B5, and Lawrence G. Muller, Jr., "Straight Talk," *Security Management* (January 1982): 25–26.
24. Judi Brownell, "The Performance Appraisal Interview: A Multi-Purpose Communication Assignment," *The Bulletin* (June 1994): 20.
25. For a review of the literature on communication in performance appraisal interviews, see Deloris McGee Wanguri, "A Review, an Integration, and a Critique of Cross-Disciplinary Research on Performance Appraisals, Evaluations, and Feedback: 1980–1990," *The Journal of Business Communication* 32 (July 1995): 267–293.

26. For a complete description of these points, the reader might be interested in reviewing Robert Hoppock, "Seventeen Principles of Appraisal Interviews," *Effective Communication on the Job* (New York: American Management Association, 1963), pp. 242–245.
27. Stewart and Cash, 203–204.
28. Described in James T. Yenckel, "Careers: The Ratings Game," *The Washington Post* (March 25, 1982), B5.
29. Charles Paul Freund, "Whose Press Conference Is It, Anyway?" *City Paper* (January 29, 1988), 12.
30. Brian Ruberry, "Talk of the Town," *Entrepreneur* (July 1995): 116–121.

Group Communication: Characteristics of Business Groups

EXPECTED OUTCOMES

After completing this chapter, you should be able to:

- Define groups.
- Compare and contrast working as an individual versus working in a group.
- List and define the types of groups used in business environments.
- Analyze the norming, storming, conforming, performing, and adjourning phases of group evolution.
- Describe the role of power in groups.
- Formulate an agenda for a business meeting.
- Conduct a voting process as a part of group decision making.
- Explain the decision-making techniques used by business groups.
- Discuss how culture affects groups.

I was a supervisor of a division at a large manufacturing company. At a meeting of all the supervisors, the Vice President of Operations told us that we needed to develop a plan for switching from a two- to a three-shift work schedule. We spent almost four hours working on a plan, which we then presented for implementation. When I got back to my office I found a printed plan for the switch signed by the Vice President. It was different from the one we had developed. My secretary told me it was delivered while we were still meeting. All of the supervisors were disgusted. The next time we were asked to meet and develop a plan of action, there was little enthusiasm and no ac-

tion was taken. If a group leader wants employees to work together, she or he has to be honest and gain the members' respect. Obviously, this Vice President didn't have our respect after what he did!

Many of the decisions made within businesses and organizations are the products of group actions. "Ninety percent of the Fortune 500 companies use problem-solving and decision-making groups in their daily operations."[1] "Executives typically spend an average of ten hours per week in formal committee meetings."[2] What is a group? And why do groups play such a large role in organizational life?

Groups Defined

A group is not just any collection or aggregate of persons. "Groupness" emerges from the relationships among the people involved.[3] The traditional definition of a **group** is "an assemblage of persons who communicate, face-to-face, in order to fulfill a common purpose and achieve a goal."[4] In addition, a group has been described as "A collection of people who influence one another, derive some satisfaction from maintaining membership in the group, interact for some purpose, assume specialized roles, and are dependent on one another."[5]

Groups are often classified by their size. **Small groups** usually contain three to twelve persons; **large groups** normally have more than a dozen people. Another distinction between the small and large group centers on the characteristics of each. For example, in the small group there is a limited number of people so that each is aware of and has some reaction to the other, each person has a sense of belonging, and members who so desire can have a significant amount of oral interaction.[6] This closeness is usually not possible in a large group. In fact, large groups often formally and informally break up into small groups to provide some of the same intimacy that is present in small groups.

Another factor that separates large and small groups is the rate of participation. Participation rates have been shown to be affected significantly by differences in the size of the group. For example, on six-person juries there is a greater vocal participation than on twelve-person juries during the deliberation process.[7] In addition, small groups inhibit disagreement and dissatisfaction more than do large groups, because each person has a greater opportunity to discuss differences of opinion.[8]

Despite these differences between large and small groups, there are also common characteristics. Both large and small groups develop norms and procedures by which they operate.

Group versus Individual Actions

Groups, by virtue of their collective identity, offer the participants great advantages. However, there are disadvantages to groups as well.

ADVANTAGES OF GROUPS

The group process affords an opportunity for input from many people who have different points of view. A group can also provide the opportunity for a person to participate, particularly those who may feel less threatened in a small group than they do when taking action by themselves.

Groups also offer the advantage of challenging ideas before they are put into action. A group is composed of people with varying backgrounds and interests. Thus, before an idea receives group acceptance, it will probably receive the scrutiny of many, rather than one, evaluation. Since any one person's experiences are limited, the congregate viewpoints should result in a better, more reasoned decision.

In addition, taking part in group action can lead to greater commitment among participants to the decisions reached by the group. Workers involved in discussing new procedures, for instance, may approach their tasks with more enthusiasm, because they directly helped develop those procedures.

Research in group communication has also revealed what is known as the **risky shift phenomenon,** which suggests that decisions reached after discussion by the group are filled with more experimentation, are less conservative, and contain more risk than decisions reached by people working alone before the discussion is held.[9] In other words, there is a tendency for members to increase their individual willingness to assume risks as a result of group activity. A group of managers who have come together to solve a problem of worker morale, for instance, may be more likely to adopt a radical strategy (even confrontation) than any one of the managers acting alone. This holds true because a manager by himself or herself is apt to be more careful and assume less risk in dealing with almost any issue.

DISADVANTAGES OF GROUPS

Although the group process does offer these important advantages, it also has some disadvantages. For example, group discussion takes much longer than individual decision making because it involves many people with diverse points of view. The process also requires participants to give up some individuality for the purpose of compromising with other group members.

Yet another disadvantage of the group process may occur when people blindly commit themselves to group cohesion to the exclusion of careful analy-

---

Is It a Team or a Group?

How can you tell the difference between a group and a team? Consider this definition from Larry Hart, president of Summit Performance Associates in Atlanta:

• A group that shares a common ZIP code is a group. If it shares a common mission, it's a team.

Hart also offers these guidelines to help you decide when a task requires an informal group and when it requires the effort and coordination of a team:

• A group will do if the task is not complex and the group's relevant experience level is high.

• You need a team if the group's experience level is low and the task is complex.

Source: Larry Hart, writing in Atlanta Business Chronicle, 1801 Peachtree St. NE, Atlanta, GA 30309.

sis. This phenomenon is called **groupthink** and is defined as "the mode of thinking that persons engage in when concurrence seeking becomes so dominant in a cohesive in-group that it tends to override realistic appraisal of alternative courses of action."[10] For example, when the board of a corporation decides to take over another corporation, it may well be based on strong recommendations by the organization's CEO, Chief Financial Officer, and a team of merger and acquisition experts. With this powerful group in favor, a commitment on the part of the other board members is ensured. The group goes forward, often without considering alternatives or the consequences of the action.

To prevent groupthink:[11]

1. Recognize that there is such a problem as groupthink, which stems from the pressure to conform to group norms.
2. Seek information that challenges an emerging concurrence.
3. Develop a norm in the group that legitimizes disagreement.
4. Avoid coping with problems of defective decision making/problem solving that is not marked by effective decision-making/problem-solving techniques.
5. Be aware that though cohesion is a normally a positive aspect of group maintenance, "the more cohesive a group is the greater is the danger of groupthink. Two factors which contribute are the illusion of invulnerability and the unquestioned belief in the inherent morality of the group."[12]

Another problem often faced by groups is the **Pollyanna-Nietzsche effect** in which the group's members believe that their solution is indeed the best and will work flawlessly. Since a group has usually taken so much effort to reach its conclusion, once the solution is proposed, it is often just assumed that the action will work. There is almost a Pollyanna—excessive optimism— and a Nietzsche-like belief—an idealized belief—that the group is superhuman and can do no wrong. This assumption results in not monitoring the solution in action and assuming that all is well. In order to avoid this, groups must carefully evaluate the implementation of any solution and constantly be vigilant to adjusting the recommendations if things do not go as assumed.[13] This is a critical process, for example, in many work teams that must be persuasive to management so that their proposals are implemented.

Types of Groups

People in business communicate in various types of groups including the work team, committees, media-conferences, electronic meetings, focus groups, public meetings, and town meetings.

When Team Members Balk

Some people have trouble fitting into a workplace team. Here are some you might encounter with suggestions on how to deal with them:

- **The Geniuses:** They know a lot and master tasks easily. A lack of challenge frustrates them.

    Solutions: Make them team leaders, tap them for special projects and rotate their jobs more often.

- **The Silents:** Basically shy, they work well and get along but won't share ideas or take part in meetings.

    Solutions: Team them with more assertive coworkers or send them to assertiveness training. And give them jobs that will force them into the limelight.

- **The Stewards:** They think they work for the union and must oppose management on principle.

    Solutions: Let the team as a group deal with their complaints on the spot. Let management deal with them on performance issues.

- **The Underemployeds:** The proverbial square pegs, they're overtrained and the job is too easy.

    Solutions: Have them coach others and give them leadership roles. Ask how they would expand their jobs or make them more interesting.

- **The Overemployeds:** They can't do the job, and more training won't help.

    Solutions: Pair them with an underemployed, find work they can do, or consider termination.

Source: Training, 50 S. 9th St., Minneapolis, MN 55402.

WORK TEAMS

In the business setting, there are a number of different kinds of groups. One of the most prevalent in American industry is the **work team.** As organizations work to accomplish their goals they have found, based on the success of Japanese and Swedish industry, that it is important to set up small groups of workers who function as teams to make decisions about the work to be done and then to implement those decisions. The team approach can be highly successful, because the sports metaphor of a "team" is one to which many workers can readily relate. For a work team to achieve its goals, it is necessary for management to "empower" the team, allowing it to be decisive and responsive. There must be considerable management commitment to training the members how to work in groups, to allowing the groups to have sufficient time to function, and to carrying out the decisions made. These work teams, when effective, can develop the "initiative, the sense of responsibility, the creativity, and the problem-solving ability" to run themselves.[14] Organizations such as Honeywell have found that the use of work teams leads to improved employee morale, greater responsiveness to and flexibility in meeting customer needs, and increased quality.[15]

Participants in any group must be aware that although participation in the decision-making process can lead workers to greater commitment to their work or to the decision made, in some cases social loafing may take place. **Social loafing** occurs when group membership leads people to work less than they may individually. "When the individual thinks his or her own contribution to the group cannot be measured his or her output tends to slacken."[16] A slacker in a work group can have a negative effect on the morale of the entire group.

COMMITTEES

Most organizations rely heavily on committees. Because it is often difficult for a large group of people to accomplish much more than voting on policy matters, it may become necessary to send certain tasks to a **committee,** a small group responsible for study, research, and making recommendations about the issue at hand. The committee's actions are usually then brought back to the entire group for final action.

In order to ensure that committees work effectively, a series of management guidelines have been developed:

- have clear objectives
- include a diversity of members from throughout the organization
- be flexible in allowing members to move in and out of the committee
- be sure that everyone is allowed a voice in the deliberations
- balance the needs of the committee with the needs of the rest of the organization
- cooperate
- work as a team
- enjoy the experience
- share the results throughout the organization and
- assume the responsibility for study, review, guidance, direction, and evaluation, but allow the implementation to be handled by management.[17]

MEDIA-CONFERENCES

It is estimated that everyday in the U.S. 20 million meetings are held and 80 percent of all meetings last less than thirty minutes.[18] As technology becomes increasingly sophisticated, organizations do not always have to rely on in-person, face-to-face meetings to conduct their business. Technological advances have led to the popularization of the **media-conference,** which allows a group to conduct meetings via telephones, computers, or television.

Recognized as the fastest-growing segment of the telecommunications indus-try, teleconferencing, the use of interactive television broadcast to various settings, has become a $150-million-a-year business.

Media-conferences bring their own special communication demands, be-cause the electronic channels cut out the visual messages if the telephone is the channel, or intensify one's attention to visual cues if the videophone is used.

Corporations such as Marriott, Bank of America, Microsoft, Aetna Life In-surance, and the United Steel Workers of America make regular use of media-conferences, as do nonprofit and collegiate associations. Many universities and hotels have built media-conferencing centers in their facilities for their own as well as for public use. Recognized as the fastest-growing segment of the telecommunications industry, **teleconferencing,** the use of interactive television, telephone, and video phone, has become a $150-million-a-year business.[19]

Group communication technology is more than telephone/videophone systems. Most organizations have bought into computerized electronic mail systems as well. Groups can now hold **electronic meetings** via e-mail, again offering a means for instant connections without having to bring people together in the same physical presence. The e-mail process is primarily one of writing and reading on the computer screen, of course, but it encourages a more conversational oral style than traditional letters and memos.

Some techniques that should be used for audio and video meetings include:[20]

- Speakers should be close enough to the microphones to be easily heard.
- Participants should control noise of papers, tapping on table, and other distracting habits that the microphones will pick up.
- High-quality graphics must be prepared that fit the television format.
- Materials that are needed must be mailed or faxed in time for reference during the session if audio, or are too complex to be seen on video.
- Participants should be identified continuously during the process.
- Departures and entrances should be announced.
- If you are participating in a video conference, wait until the camera is on you before you speak.
- Limit the agenda to no more than one hour. If longer, a break should be built into the schedule.

FOCUS GROUPS

Motivational research has led many organizations to the use of focus groups. **Focus groups** are designed to test reactions to a particular product, process, or service offered by an organization. A randomly selected group of participants who are representative of the user group or the consumer group are brought together with a professional facilitator to discuss, for example, the proposed new product or to discuss reactions to an advertising campaign. The reactions are carefully recorded and quantified in a report to the agency as input for decision making. While some experts decry focus groups as "unscientific," most organizations that use them find the input to be a valuable addition to more controlled surveys and sales figures.

PUBLIC MEETINGS

In addition to internal group interactions, organizations usually find it necessary to conduct **public meetings** for various purposes. Officers of corporations are required to hold an annual shareholders meeting in order to ensure that the decisions they reach are in the best interests of the stockholders they serve and to fulfill the legal requirements of many states to hold open meetings.

A public group meeting may consist of some expert(s) or witness(es) in a **symposium** format. In this format all the participants give prepared speeches, with no interaction between each other or from the audience. These short presentations are often followed by a forum. A **forum** is an interaction during which questions and answers are fielded by the participants from each other as well as from the audience members.

TOWN MEETINGS

In a **town meeting** the presenter opens with some sort of short, prepared statement, which establishes the framework for the meeting. Individuals in the audience then engage in a forum with the speaker. The ensuing dialogue can be useful for both speaker and audience to explain their positions and to share viewpoints on such issues as proposed zoning ordinances or bond issuance.

Businesses planning to develop shopping centers or build new facilities often need to explain their actions to the citizenry. The results of these meetings may lead the organization either to go ahead with their plans or to withdraw the proposal. In 1994 negative citizen reaction at public meetings was credited with persuading the Disney Corporation to withdraw plans to build a Disney World–type historic theme park in Northern Virginia. On the other hand, positive reaction can encourage development. In several instances, communities have banded together and sought out foreign automobile manufacturers to come into their area to foster economic development. The positive group action included granting tax incentives, offering low-cost property, and setting aside zoning requirements. Toyota and Saturn ads include the names of the communities in their advertisements as a way to say, "Thank you for the local group encouragement," as well as to mitigate "Buy American" sentiment.

Group Operations

Groups are continually evolving. Normally, group operations go through five phases: norming, storming, conforming, performing, and adjourning.[21]

GROUP NORMING

Group norming is the orienting aspect of people coming together and starting to form a group or welcome new people into an existing group. Depending on the nature of the assemblage, an exchange of names and other demographic information usually takes place. In a new group, the discussion is often cautious and doesn't deal immediately with the purpose or goals of the group. The norming process usually proceeds more rapidly when the people in the newly formed group have a history of working together, or know each other personally.

During the norming stage the group establishes **norms,** the rules or standards by which the group will operate. The obligations of the members, what they can and can't do, and the mode of operation are normally established. These norms can be explicit (written and agreed upon, such as in the form of a constitution) or implicit (understood, but not formalized).[22]

The source of the group's norms arise from influences outside of the group. They may be rules preset by others, such as when a corporation president indicates what the purpose of a group is and how it should operate. Norms can be handed down, as when a local franchise of a large company is given rules by the national organization; they can be developed by the group based on their past experiences or through trial-and-error; or they may be influenced by a member or the leader who has experience in the group process or who has strong enough persuasive skills to influence others. Regardless of the means, setting boundaries is a critical group function.

Group procedures that must be decided upon include:[23]

1. Planning an agenda. Group meetings normally follow actions in a step-by-step order. An **agenda** is the list of topics to be discussed or the problems that must be dealt with in the order in which they will be acted upon.
2. Handling routine "housekeeping" details. Taking attendance and the rules of how decisions and announcements will be made are among the procedural details that must be agreed upon.
3. Preparing for the next meeting. If the group is ongoing, it is necessary to decide when it will reconvene. It is sometimes necessary to designate who will be responsible for certain details for the next session.

GROUP STORMING

Groups seldom norm and work toward their goal without some disagreements. Most groups, either in the process of setting rules or in working toward their goal, enter into a period called **group storming,** when a period of conflicts erupt. These conflicts may be caused by a power struggle between persons interested in being the leader; they may be based on strong differences of opinion over the purpose of the group, the rules of operation, or how decisions will be made. Or they may result from personality conflicts between group members. Many group conflicts can be readily resolved if members are willing to listen to each other and be flexible.

Don't assume that there is something wrong if a group you are in doesn't go through storming. Some groups seem to meld together and never find a need to conflict. On the other hand, be alert to the lack of storming as it may mean that the group members are just giving in or going along so that the work can get done quickly and can get on with other tasks. This situation could result in weak group decisions and actions.

Group Social Tension

Underlying group storming are two types of social tensions—primary and secondary. **Primary social tension** refers to the normal jitters and feelings of uneasiness experienced when groups first congregate. Think of an experience in which you entered, such as going to work for the first time on a new job. Group interaction at this point is usually of very low intensity. Often there are long periods of silence, discussion of frivolous topics, tentative statements, over politeness, careful avoidance of conflict. Interruptions evoke profuse apologies. The situation can be compared to boxers sizing each other up.[24] Your strategy as a competent communicator is not to avoid primary tension, but to let it take its natural course. Primary tension tends to be short-lived and cause for little concern, unless it escalates to an unmanageable level. With time, it normally disappears. Besides the initial primary tension, even long-standing groups may experience primary tension at the outset of each meeting. This is especially true if groups meet infrequently. Members will test the water to reaffirm their standing in the group.[25]

Group Secondary Tension

Secondary social tension is the stress and strain that occurs within the group later in its development. The cause of the problem is often the need to make a decision. Disagreements and conflict inevitably emerge when group members struggle to define their status and their roles in the group. Shortage of time to accomplish the task is often a cause. Differences of opinion is another, as is a difficult member. The absence of secondary tension can be good or bad. The positives include the fact that the group has learned to work well with each other or has few ego problems or task problems. The negatives include the possibility that group members are unmotivated, apathetic, or bored. Signs of secondary tension include abrupt departure from the group's routine, a sharp outburst by a group member, a sarcastic barb, or hostile and antagonistic exchanges between members. Extreme secondary tension is unpleasant for the group. If left uncontrolled, it may threaten the group's existence. The group's goal should not be to eliminate the tension, but to use the tension in a positive way. Tension can be energizing, the source of creative thinking, and can bring the group together. The real challenge is to manage the tension within acceptable limits. The bottom line is whether the group can continue to function in the task area and maintain a satisfying social climate.

Some general communication storming strategies that groups have found helpful include:

1. *Allow for a get-acquainted period before the first meeting so that group members get to meet each other informally.*
2. *Schedule an informal chat period before each meeting so that there is nonpressured interaction between participants.*
3. *Remind the group that disagreement can lead to a superior outcome, while reminding them that the purpose of the assemblage is to achieve the group goal, not individual goals.* Tolerate, even encourage, disagreement and deviance, but keep the disagreement and deviance within tolerable limits. Be aware, however, that some people can't tolerate any disagreement. They may have a history of physical or verbal abuse and panic when bickering starts, fearing it will escalate into a full-fledged war. Others may have been brought up to believe that fighting is rude and must be avoided at all costs. Whatever the situation, even though allowing some disagreement can be a positive force in a group, be aware of the possible deep-developed sensitivity of some members.
4. *If appropriate, use humor, joking, and shared laugher to lighten the mood.*
5. *Try to use fair-fighting techniques.* Stick to attacking the issues and not the person who disagrees with your stand. Don't keep repeating the same argument over and over. Don't call the other person or her or his ideas "stupid" or "dumb."
6. *Be an active listener.* Even though you have a clearly defined viewpoint, be aware that the other people believe their viewpoints are as valid as yours. Listen . . . you might discover that another's view has some validity.
7. *Look for possible places to compromise.* Be careful, however, that in reaching a compromise that you don't so dilute the solution that it will not achieve its goal of relieving the problem.

The Role of Power

One of the major areas of storming is the role of power. Competition appears to be unavoidable in human transactions, and one of the major centers of competition is who holds the power. **Power** is the ability to influence anther's attainment of goals. Power normally resides in an individual or a group. Power can center on controlling another person or persons, the power to influence efforts of others, and the power to accomplish a goal.

There is a power structure in all groups. A person may exert power because he or she has information or expertise that will enable the group to reach its goal. For example, a group dealing with a financial crisis often will turn for advice to the person most knowledgeable in economics or accounting. In some cases the power centers on some type of legitimate authority. The person who was appointed chairperson of the committee by the CEO of a company holds the position legitimately, and therefore can act as the leader regardless of the feelings of the group. Sometimes this circumstance also leads to the ability to give rewards or punishments. A supervisor, for example, often has the ability to decide on pay raises, reemployment, and bonuses, thus putting her or him in a control position.

Another power factor centers on personal qualities. Some people have the charisma or likability to become the power source. It is often believed that our most effective leaders are those who get people to willingly follow them, or follow them because of their charisma.

Unresolved Storming

Not all groups survive the storming stage. Some groups find that because of the personalities of the group members, the inability to decide on norms, or the lack of clarity of purpose, they simply cannot work their way through storming. When this occurs, either the group ceases to exist or it continues to operate in a storming fashion until it is dissolved by the person or group who formed it. Unresolved storming often leads to lethargy, in which groups members do little because they believe nothing will come of their efforts.

GROUP CONFORMING

Groups that work their way through the storming stage can then go on to work together. This coming together is called **group conforming.** A group has reached the conforming stage when there is agreement on such things as the norms and the group's purpose, and when it has know-how to handle the role of power. At this point the group is ready to work toward their agreed-upon mission.

GROUP PERFORMING

Group performing is the action phase of group existence. It is during this phase that the members clearly start to work toward goals. They have developed a history, know each other, have worked out their mode of operation, and agreed to move forward to accomplish their task and maintenance roles.

All decision making in a group contains both task and maintenance dimensions. These dimensions are not independent entities that stand in opposition to each other. They are interrelated. The **task dimension of groups** includes decision making, informing, appraising/examining, problem solving, and creating interest in staying on track. Some consider accomplishing the goal the entire purpose of the group and concentrate solely on making sure

---

Work Groups: How to Get Hot

When most of us hear the words "hot group," we think of Casey Kasem and America's Top 40. Not Jean Lipman-Blumen, Ph.D. She thinks of intensely focused work groups whose enthusiasm gives new meaning to the expression "I love my job."

Unlike most work teams, hot groups become so emotionally involved with their task that they actually behave like people in love. "The excitement of the task and the interaction that comes with it can be an enormous turn-on," says Lipman-Blumen, professor of organizational behavior at Claremont Graduate School. As a result, hot groups often set performance records and even volunteer for extra work.

Sounds like every manager's dream—but there's a catch. Such groups are hard to create, and when they do arise they are often short-lived. Their unorthodox work habits and tendency to isolate themselves from the parent organization can incense management, hastening their demise.

But other times they hit the jackpot. Consider Apple Computers, started by a hot group of free-spirited twentysomethings striving to build a computer for the masses rather than large businesses. Taking on corporate goliath IBM spurred them to create the revolutionary Macintosh.

Alas, there's no simple formula for spawning hot groups. Like hothouse flowers, they're exquisitely sensitive to their environment and wilt for no apparent reason. But you can optimize conditions for their growth:

- *Offer workers a thrill.** Crises and intense competition are the most powerful external motivators of hot groups. Any provocative project, however, can excite passion and intensity.*

- *Feed their soul.** Hot groups are inspired by the search for truth and the feeling that they're making a difference. "Their task has to have meaning to people, society and the organization," says Lipman-Blumen. That's why hot groups are particularly common in research institutions.*

- *Provide a connective leader**—an individualist with a team player mentality (and the subject of Lipman-Bluman's book, The Connective Edge). Such leaders are willing to share both the work and the glory.*

- *Banish Bureaucracy.** Freedom is essential for hot groups. Workers quickly lose enthusiasm when entangled in red tape.*

—Alyssa Rappaport

---

that the group "stays on task." However, most groups also need to attend to the **maintenance dimension of groups**—meeting the interpersonal needs of the group members. The main purpose of maintenance is to develop **group cohesiveness,** the interconnectedness of the membership.

As social beings, most people like to be with others, interact with them, have a good time, bond together. In addition, some like to express opinions, be heard, and express feelings. Others gain positive feelings from participating in a job well done, while others want to learn. Ignoring these aspects of group process, and only concentrating on the task functions, can lead to an empty experience for some of the participants.

GROUP ADJOURNING

Some groups find it necessary to adjourn, to disband. In business settings, certain groups are consulted to accomplish a particular task. At the completion of the task, the group disperses. Committees, for example, are often appointed to do a job, such as select a new company logo, plan a program audit, or decide on which computer hardware to purchase. Work groups may be formed to investigate ways in which teams of workers should carry out their tasks. Once the task is accomplished, or the procedure is developed, the group terminates. When groups are appointed for a specific task, the ending is a natural part of the actions of the group, normally not requiring any specific action, other than awareness the task is done.

On the other hand, some groups have no specific end goal, but are ongoing. Sometimes, even these groups may come to an end. Members may lose interest, people may leave the organization thus depleting the membership, or group members may determine that the group no longer has a purpose. In these cases, the ending of the group may be accomplished when group members vote the group out of existence or simply stop holding meetings. It is advisable that group members take an action to formally bring the group to an end. If not, members of the group may feel that they have not reached a true ending and feel incomplete, similar to not completing the process of saying good-bye to someone who suddenly dies.

Making Group Decisions

One of the most prominent functions of the group communication process is that of decision making. There are vast cultural differences in how people think, apply forms of reasoning, and make decisions. It is important to realize, when working in the business setting in decision-making groups, that not everyone follows the same patterns. Likewise, not all persons from any culture act in exactly the same way as every other person in that culture. However, research and observation of experts have confirmed that there appear to be some norms that can be used as guidelines for making generalized assumptions. As with any generalization, care should be taken to consider the exceptions.

Japanese work groups depend heavily on the **consensus-building direction-taking decision-making process,** in which everyone affected by the decision is included in the process. The final decision must represent every member of the group.[26] For the Chinese, however, "decision-making is more authoritative than consensual; decisions are made by higher authorities without the inclusion of subordinates."[27]

"Middle-Easterners—for example, Arabs—tend to use a procedure that can be described as using an **intuitive-affective decision-making approach.** Broad issues that do not appear to be directly related to the issue at hand are brought up; issues are linked together on the basis of whether or not the speaker likes the issues. Personal bias is often exercised."[28] Negotiation teams from Saudi Arabia, for example, do not make decisions on the basis of empirical reasoning. While subordinates are consulted informally, the leader always makes the final decision.[29]

A work group in Mexico tends to use a **centralized decision-making process.** Mexicans often view authority as inherent to the individual, not the individual's position. The delegating of authority is equivalent to surrendering assets. Making trade-offs is common for Mexican negotiators, including adding issues that are not part of the original business at hand.[30]

In the Western cultural view, and that which is the basis for most decision making in most North American business environments, it is generally believed that people can discover truth and, therefore, make sound decisions by applying the **scientific method of decision-making process.** This procedure involves a five-step process: identifying the problem, searching for solutions, testing those solutions, putting the chosen solution into practice, and then following up to see if the solution has solved the problem. Despite this general belief in the scientific method, in Western businesses the solution may often be made by upper management with little or no input from those who will probably have to carry out the solution. Many organizations are changing this practice and are encouraging more bottom-up decision making into their scheme of management.

In North American decision making, the need to develop a process leads a group to consider setting up the **procedures** (rules of operation) to be followed in reaching a decision. Formal organizations usually develop a constitution and bylaws that clearly spell out these procedures. A set of parliamentary guidelines such as *Robert's Rules of Order* is usually adopted as a framework for handling procedural agreements and disagreements.[31] Individuals who chair formal meetings should learn these rules of order. Less formal organizations may allow the leader of the group to determine the operational procedures. Whatever method is used, the group should agree on a method before beginning any formal work.

FORMULATING AN AGENDA

For the members of a group to be aware of the order in which items will be handled, or the format that will be followed for discussing a matter, an agenda should be formulated. An agenda, the order of business for a meeting or for a discussion, allows the group to cover the topic systematically and thus accomplish the task in the most efficient way possible. The agenda should be used like a road map: it should contain just enough detail to allow the group to travel the path to the task but should not be so rigid that it does not allow for any detours.

In a typical business meeting, the agenda has a basic format:

    I. Call the meeting to order
    II. Reading the minutes of the previous meeting
    III. Committee reports
    IV. Discussion of unfinished business
    V. Proposal of new business
    VI. Adjournment of the meeting

In a group discussion, unless it has been done beforehand, the participants usually start by wording a **discussion question,** which is the issue or problem that will be dealt with. For example, if the purpose of the group is to establish an effective and consistent system of performance reviews, the question could be "What should be done to solve the problem of inconsistent performance reviews?"

Some general principles for wording a discussion question are:

1. Be sure the purpose is put in a question form (otherwise, it cannot be discussed).
2. Keep the question short and simple (so that it can be easily understood).
3. Word the question so that it avoids bias (you cannot honestly discuss a question that states the expected conclusion).
4. Word the question so that it goes beyond a "yes" or a "no" answer as you want to ensure the consideration of alternatives.

One way to plan a discussion agenda is for each member to research the subject and prepare his or her own agenda in advance. Then the group can meet for a short time (possibly fifteen minutes) to share individual outlines and draw up a group agenda. No discussion of the issues should take place while the agenda is being put together; this phase only lists possible topics. Of course, the formulation of an agenda varies according to the specific type of discussion being planned.

A frequent task of groups is a **problem-solving discussion,** a situation in which a group of people get together to resolve a problem. Because the problem-solving discussion is a good technique for gaining input from a variety of sources, many organizations prefer this approach. These organizations profess that those who participate in making policy decisions are more productive in the long run because they have a greater commitment to imple-

---

How to Handle the Agenda

A meeting agenda should be used as a device to focus discussions.

Some suggestions:

- *Keep in mind that the key purpose of an agenda is to limit discussion so that the meeting doesn't get out of hand. Anything not on the agenda shouldn't be allowed to come up.*

- *Limit the number of agenda items to allow attendees the time to become more informed about each one.*

- *Don't place the simpler items first on the agenda in attempt to dismiss them before the major items come up. Handle the most difficult ones first while everyone's fresh.*

- *Watch for secret agendas on the part of two or more attendees.*

  What to look for: *A conspirator selects one part of the agenda to address. He or she then steers to the matter the others wish to bring up. This opens the door for another conspirator to ask a question or discuss the secret-agenda subject.*
  How to handle: *Step in and either dismiss the item out of hand or offer to call another meeting to discuss it later. Any other approach will cause the meeting to get out of control.*

- *Don't use the agenda as a fact sheet. Hand out additional data sheets if necessary.*

- *Avoid making position statements in an agenda. Let it serve as a guide.*

Source: Effective Meetings: The Complete Guide, by Clyde W. Burleson, John Wiley & Sons, 605 3rd Ave., New York, NY 10158.

---

menting their own decisions. After all, once people have spent time and effort working on a plan of action, they are more likely to abide by that plan.

In a problem-solving discussion, a question of policy may be worded in several ways. For example, "What should be done to solve the problem of falling sales in the Northeastern Ohio territory?" or "What should be the company's stand on the union's request for increased health benefits?"

Let's assume that you are in a group that will discuss the question, "What can be done to solve this company's problem of computer hardware and software incompatibility?" Your problem-solving agenda might look like this:

I. What is the problem?
   A. What do we need to know in order to deal with the problem?
      1. What computer hardware are we currently using?
      2. What computer software are we currently using?
      3. Are we experiencing computer hardware and software incompatibility?

    B. How does this problem concern us?
       1. As employees?
       2. In relationship to our clients?
       3. As it relates to the organization's profits?
II. What are the causes of the problem?
    A. Is the company's process of selecting hardware and software well defined?
    B. Is the organization being unduly influenced by the corporation's ownership of a software company?
    C. Has the company's policy of purchasing the "best" product, without regard to compatibility, caused problems?
III. What are possible solutions?
    A. Would setting restrictive company guidelines help?
       1. Would a company-wide standards group help?
       2. Would deregulation of the company's policies help?
    B. Would purchasing entirely new software and hardware help?
    C. Should the company hire a computer consulting firm to make recommendations?
IV. What are the possible solutions?
    A. Which of the solutions proposed is workable?
    B. Which of the solutions proposed is desirable?
    C. Which of the solutions proposed is practical?
V. What is (are) the best solution(s)?
VI. How can the best solution(s) be put into effect?

Following such an agenda allows for complete discussion and a well-thought-out solution.

In addition to detailing a system for conducting business and arriving at results, the group is responsible for determining how decisions will be accepted by all members of the organization.

VOTING

A voting process can serve a useful purpose in providing a system for arriving at final decisions. **Voting** takes place when each member is given the opportunity to indicate agreement, disagreement, or no opinion on an idea or candidate. The purpose of voting is to ensure that the members of the group know of the outcome of the discussion and the decision made. There are four common voting methods: consensus, majority, plurality, and part of the whole. It is imperative that the method of voting be agreed on before the group starts working toward the final solution, for any alteration in the method can affect the outcome of the group's action.

Consensus refers to "all."[32] In a consensus decision, every member of the group must agree on a proposal before it can be put into action. This method is often used for decisions in which dire consequences can result from the outcome of the action. For example, most juries operate by consensus. Some believe that "the only true way in which the minority may be protected is using consensus since true consensus requires agreement, commitment, satisfaction and compromise."[33] Those who oppose this concept believe that because getting everyone to agree is almost impossible, a weak decision results as people compromise and compromise until the conclusion reached is overly watered down.

In a **majority** vote the winner or winning idea must receive more than half of the votes, excluding those who do not vote or who abstain (that is, those who do not want to vote).[34] For example, if there are ten people in a group and all vote, it will take six votes for a majority to prevail. If, however, one of the people does not vote, then it will take five votes for passage according to the majority method.

Plurality means "most."[35] Often when there are more than two options available, a group may turn to plurality voting. If, for example, three candidates are running for an office, in plurality voting the one who receives the most votes is declared the winner. In the same way, if five ideas have been proposed as solutions to a problem, the solution selected will be the one receiving the greatest number of votes.

Part-of-the-whole voting occurs when a specific number or a specific percentage of those who are eligible to vote is all that is required to bring about some action. For example, some articles of incorporation or corporate charters (the rules of operation of an organization) can be changed only if 75 percent of those eligible to vote agree to the change. A group has the right to set any number or percentage it wishes for action to take place. Group members are encouraged to decide on these numbers before starting the decision-making process. The number or percentage selected can have a profound effect on the outcome of a proposed action.

DECISON MAKING

In the North American culture there are a number of approaches to structuring the decision-making discussion. They center on two concepts: first, "effective group decision making requires an analysis and understanding of a problem before members search for solutions";[36] and, second, "effective decision-making groups normally engage in creative exploration of unusual, even deviant, ideas during initial discussions."[37] These two steps assure that the group works toward solving an agreed-upon problem, and that all the resources and creativity of the members are utilized. Three methods of decision making are The Six-Step Standard Agenda, 1-3-6, and Nominal Group Technique of Decision Making.

Six-Step Standard Agenda[38]

The **six-step standard agenda** is a direct outgrowth of the traditional reflective-thinking process, which stresses that a problem be identified, analyzed, solutions be sought, a solution be selected and implemented.[39] This method varies from the traditional technique in that it is more complete and in some ways more flexible. The procedure for this method is:

- Step 1: *Problem identification.* A question is worded that states the problem. The query may be a **question of fact** (whether something is true and to what extent); a **question of value** (is something good or bad, right or wrong, and to what extent; or a **question of policy** (whether a specific course of action should be undertaken in order to solve a problem).
- Step 2: *Problem analysis.* Collect the necessary information needed to identify the problem. This includes gathering facts, determining how serious the problem is, determining what harm is associated with the problem, deciding whether the harm is serious and widespread, and determining the cause of the problem.
- Step 3: *Solution criteria.* Before the solutions are addressed, determine what criteria will be used to evaluate the possible solutions. One of the most common set of criteria centers on workability, practicality, and desirability. Workability is whether the solution will solve the problem. Practicality is whether the solution can be put into effect. Desirability is whether harm will be caused by implementing the solution.
- Step 4: *Solution suggestions.* Brainstorm for possible solutions to the problem. **Brainstorming** consists of generating possible solutions without evaluating them at the time they are proposed. Guidelines for brainstorming include:[40]

  1. Don't evaluate ideas while brainstorming.
  2. Don't clarify or seek clarification of an idea during the collection stage.
  3. Encourage zany ideas. Some of the best solutions are those that haven't been tried before or are out of the normal stream of action.
  4. Expand on the ideas of others.
  5. Record all ideas without reference to who contributed the idea.
  6. Encourage participation from all group members.

- Step 5: *Select a solution.* Explore the merits and demerits of all the ideas collected during brainstorming and apply the prior agreed-upon criteria. Another method of selecting the solution is to apply an evaluation technique entitled RISK.[41] The basic steps in applying RISK are:

  1. Members think of any risks, fears, or problems associated with the solution.
  2. Members brainstorm potential negative consequences either individually or as a group.

3. All potential problems are posted on a chart or blackboard for all members to see.
4. Time is given for additions to the list.
5. Each negative is again discussed.
6. The group weighs the risks and consequences against the perceived benefits.
7. A decision is made to implement, delay for further study, modify, or kill the proposal and search for a better alternative(s).

- Step 6: *Solution implementation.* Put the solution into effect and monitor it by follow-up testing and observation to make sure it is working. If it is not working, repeat steps four through six.

1-3-6 Decision-Making Technique[42]

The **1-3-6 decision-making technique** takes place after the specific decision to be made or the problem to be solved is agreed upon by the group, and they are ready to work toward solution. It is named "1-3-6" for its group configurations in which each individual works alone, then is placed in a group of three, and then in a group of six to make decisions.

The steps in this technique are:

- Step 1: All individuals in the group list what they believe should be done to solve the problem or the best possible decisions regarding the issue. This process is a self-brainstorming session. All ideas generated are listed, with no evaluation.
- Step 2: Participants are divided into subgroups of three. Each group combines its members' lists. No items are deleted, but possibilities are combined and solutions or decisions are reworded. There is no discussion of the value of the ideas during this step.
- Step 3: The group is divided so that two subgroups of three people each meet and combine their lists. Again, duplicate ideas are eliminated, and solutions or decisions are reworded. No evaluations are made.
- Step 4: The entire group reassembles. A spokesperson for each subgroup reads aloud the subgroup's list. All items are written on a long sheet of paper or on a chalkboard. (It is important that everyone in the room be able to read the lists, so large writing is imperative.)
- Step 5: The items are numbered.
- Step 6: Each person prioritizes the total list—ranking in order all items with no ties. The most important or best solution or decision should be numbered "1," the next "2," etc. Each person's individual rankings are recorded on a sheet of paper.
- Step 7: The rankings are collected and tallied. The top items are identified. The final number to be used should be in proportion to the number of items

generated from Step 4. If thirty or more items were generated, the top ten would be a reasonable final list. For fewer items, about one-half to one-third of the total is appropriate. (Determine this number in advance to alleviate conflict over how many should be included in the final list.)

- Step 8: Individuals select their top choices and then are randomly divided into subgroups of no more than six persons. If possible, a representative of each of the subgroups from Step 3 should be in each of the newly formed units. (This is not imperative, but if there is a lack of clarity in a statement, the individual from the subgroup that generated the idea may be able to clarify its meaning.)
- Step 9: Each subgroup selects what it considers to be the best solution using the individual selections from Step 8. At this step, evaluations are made. Statements may be reworded, but no new solutions may be introduced.
- Step 10: Spokespersons for each subgroup report on the decision of the subgroup. If all subgroups have selected the same solution, the process is completed. If not, the solutions that received the support of at least one subgroup are retained and the others are eliminated.
- Step 11: Subgroups reassemble and select what they consider the best solution from those remaining on the list.
- Step 12: A spokesperson of each subgroup reports on the selection of his or her subgroup. Steps 11 and 12 are repeated until a single solution is chosen.

The 1-3-6 decision-making technique is illustrated in Figure 9.1.

Some smaller groups adopt an alternative approach, using only Steps 1 through 6, and then have all members meet together to reach a final solution. This approach can be used for groups of less than ten people.

Nominal Group Technique[43]

The **nominal group technique** centers on the concept of brainstorming without direct group interaction. This technique encourages idea generation from all individuals but avoids criticism, destructive conflict, and long-winded speeches. Some believe that the technique is not satisfying because there is little or no interaction among the participants.[44]

The step-by-step procedure is:

- Step 1: Members write down ideas, options, alternatives, or solutions without any open discussion.
- Step 2: Members present to the group, in a round-robin fashion, without discussion, their ideas, which are recorded on large sheets of paper for everyone to see.
- Step 3: Members can ask questions of each other, but no evaluation is done, and counterproposals are presented. Similar proposals are combined.

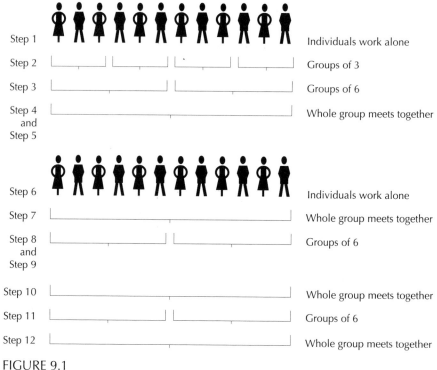

FIGURE 9.1
1-3-6 Decision-Making Technique

- Step 4: Members individually rank the various proposed solutions, and the 25results are tallied to determine the relative support for each solution. An optional approach for Step 4 is for each person to select five favorite ideas and write them down on a card in rank order. The rankings are averaged and the ideas with the highest averages are then allowed to be considered in future steps.
- Step 5: Members individually vote on the higher priority ideas. If a top five priority was used in Step 4, then a top three priority is used in Step 5.
- Step 6: Step 5 is repeated. If a top three priority was used in Step 5 then a single top choice is made.

An alternative to this method is to proceed until Step 5. Following Step 5 an open discussion among all participants is held, with a preset maximum of time allowed for each speaker. Following the presentations, each person is allowed to vote for her or his choice, with the majority prevailing.

The Nominal Group Technique

About fifteen years ago, social scientists Andre Delbecq and Andrew H. Vande Ven developed the Nominal Group Technique as an alternative to conventional problem-solving meetings. It's very rigid, but their research indicates that the technique provides more and better-quality solutions than standard techniques.

- *Have pads and pencils for each person. For small groups, use a U-shaped table with an easel at the opening. Groups larger than fifteen people should be broken down into groups of eight at round tables.*

- *State the problem, but instruct your people not to discuss the problem among themselves. Ask them to write down all aspects of the problem. Then consider these in a group discussion, following which you (the leader) define the problem as they see it.*

- *Give the people five to fifteen minutes to write down all the possible solutions they can think of.*

- *Ask each person (or table) to give one idea and record it on a chart. Keep going around the room until you have written down all ideas. Don't discuss them.*

- *Now anyone can ask the person who thought of a solution to clarify it. There's no evaluation, just explanations.*

- *The group is asked to rank what they consider the five best, five being the highest and one is the lowest. Collect the cards and tally the results. Divide the sum by the number of people. This gives a value to each solution.*

- *Now the group analyzes those ideas with the higher values. At this point encourage critical thinking and analysis.*

- *If an agreement is reached, fine. If not, have the group re-rank the top solutions and then analyze them again.*

The Group Setting

Although often neglected from consideration, the group's setting is an important factor in communication. Where a group meets; the size, shape, color, temperature, and decorations of the room; and where participants sit—all can affect the success of a group. Group meeting spaces represent a "particularly important type of micro-environment which can affect the quality and quantity of communicative interaction, the participants' perceptions of each other, and the task performance of a given group."[45]

Two specific variables that can affect group action are the seating choices and the configuration of the tables.

SEATING CHOICE

Where you sit at a meeting may determine if you are selected as the leader, how much you will participate, and how others perceive you. This is an important concept for you to take into account if you aspire to leadership, or wish to sit quietly and watch the proceedings.

Studies about seating positions have shown that:

- The person who sits at the head of a rectangular table significantly increased his or her chances of being perceived as the leader.[46]
- "At a round conference table, whoever sits at the 12 o'clock position is the most powerful, with power diminishing as it moves around past positions at three o'clock, six o'clock, nine o'clock. The least powerful person sits at the 11 o'clock position."[47]
- Individuals who choose a seat along the sides of a table decrease their chances of being perceived as leaders, and increase the likelihood they will be perceived as individuals with lower status and less self-confidence.[48]
- People seated in a circle will feel more comfortable and interact more than they would if they were in straight rows or seated around a rectangular table.

Some managers have experimented with **no seating meetings** in which all participants stand during the entire session. By standing, it is believed, participants feel an urgency to quickly be productive. Another possible advantage is that if people get tired they may sit on the floor or other seatable surfaces—thus forming an informal group, which some believe leads to a more relaxed and interactive meeting. This technique, of course, is dependent upon the purpose of the meeting and the tolerance levels of the leader and the participants.

TABLE CONFIGURATION

Table configuration or shape is also an important variable in group interaction. The quality and amount of communicative interaction is less with T-shaped or L-shaped seating arrangements than with rectangular arrangements; and it is less at a rectangular table than with a round configuration. The round configuration is the most neutralizing.[49] At rectangular tables, communication usually flows across the table rather than around it.[50] At round tables, if several people sit at one arc of the table, and the others spread themselves around the table, the two seated together tend to be perceived as the leaders, since this place is considered the visual center of the table as the others turn to face the two seated together.[51]

"It seems to be a norm, in the United States at least, that leaders are expected to be found at the head or end of the table."[52] Elected group leaders generally put themselves in the head positions at rectangular tables, and the members place themselves so that they can see the leader. Interestingly enough, in a group consisting of all women, the one at the head of the table is perceived as the leader. However, in a mixed gender group, a woman at the head position is much less likely to be perceived in a leadership role than a man who occupies the end position.[53]

People seem to be aware of the different perceptions related to different seating positions. When people were asked to select seats to convey different impressions, they chose end positions to convey leadership and dominance, positions that furnished the closest distance to convey interpersonal attraction, and seats that afforded the greatest interpersonal distance and least visual accessibility vis-à-vis the end positions to indicate they did not wish to participate.[54]

THE EFFECT OF THE PHYSICAL ENVIRONMENT

The physical environment should be comfortable. A meeting can unravel if the room is too large or too small, if it is too warm or too cold, and if the lighting or the acoustics are not conducive to hearing to seeing each other. Groups function more effectively if coffee and/or sodas and even snacks are provided. Attention to these kinds of communication climate details will likely pay off in members' satisfaction with the group and greater contribution to the group process and product.

Cultural Differences in Groups

Not all societies use groups in the same way. Business groups operate differently in various countries in various cultures. Knowing the conceptual differences of how societies use groups can enhance your effectiveness and make you a more effective group communicator as you work with people from various cultures in group settings.

We are products of the cultures in which we were brought up. We learn the customs and patterns of those cultures, and they carry over into all phases of our lives. Research shows that people from different cultures possess varying attitudes about making independent decisions or being a group participant, about procedures for working in groups, about making decisions, about procedural structure, and about using information. Again, it must be pointed out that not all persons from any culture act in exactly the same way. As with any generalization, care should be taken to consider the exceptions as well as the norms.

CULTURES AND GROUPS

"The United States has the highest individualism index. We [Americans] are, without doubt, the most individualistic culture on earth."[55] This individualism, putting one's self before group loyalty, has a strong historical base. In the North American culture, membership in groups—except those that are mandatory because of a person's work or academic environment—tends to be voluntary.

Because of this attitude, U.S. group members' allegiance often is not a lifelong commitment. This is not the case in other parts of the world. For example, in many East Asian countries Confucianism is the basic philosophy of much of the population. The **Confucian principle of *i*** requires that a person be affiliated and identify with a small and tightly knit group of people over long periods of time. These long-term relationships work because each group member expects the group members to aid and assist each other when there is a need since sooner or later those who assisted will have to depend on those they aided. This mutually implied assistance pact makes for group interdependence.[56]

Not only does the attitude about being in groups vary by culture, but there seems to be a difference in the training needed in certain cultures for group participation. Because many North Americans may seldom participate in groups, they often need to learn about group operational methods when they enter organizations. The same is true of people from other countries with a high level of individualism, such as Australia, Great Britain, Canada, the Netherlands, New Zealand, Italy, Belgium, Denmark, and Sweden.[57] In contrast, people from countries where group adherence is stressed have been involved in groups all of their lives and have clearer understandings of how groups operate. Those countries that are the least individualistic tend to be in Asia and South America and include Venezuela, Colombia, Pakistan, Peru, Taiwan, Thailand, Singapore, Chile, and Hong Kong.[58]

CULTURAL ATTITUDES TOWARD GROUP PROCEDURES

There are also cultural differences in the attitude toward the way a person works in a group. In many East Asian countries, for example, the Confucian principle of *i* leads to a strong distaste for a purely business transaction. This attitude is carried over into meetings, where there is a tendency to mix personal with public relations. For example, business meetings may take place over a long period of time in order for people to establish personal and human relationships. They may include activities like sports, drinking, and travel in the proceedings; foster an understanding of personality and personal situations of the participants; and develop a certain level of trust and a favorable attitude.[59]

A good example of where the business is mixed with the personal relationships is Japan, a nation that stresses group culture and where individualism is submerged and expression is found in hidden ways. This is almost the exact opposite of the way Americans operate. In the United States, people work in groups to get tasks accomplished. In Japan, the individual's sense of identity is the group. This attitude is based on a long history of ruling families, which created a social structure that bound together families, villagers, and strong leaders. In the United States, the stress has been on rugged individualism, with the group of less importance the individual. In Japan the word for describing a group is "we." In the United States, often groups are divided between "us" and "them." For example, management and workers often find themselves on opposite sides at the bargaining table.

A comparison between East Asian and North American communication patterns that affect group action is illustrated in Figure 9.2.

CULTURAL CONTRASTS
IN PROCEDURAL STRUCTURE

Another way in which cultures vary in a group is in the role of procedural structure. "Negotiation outcomes to Americans depend upon events at the negotiation table, not the role of the negotiator or prenegotiation socializing."[60]

FIGURE 9.2
East Asian and North American Communication Patterns

EAST ASIAN PATTERNS	NORTH AMERICAN PATTERNS
1. Process orientation Communication is perceived as a process of infinite interpretation	1. Outcome orientation Communication is perceived as the transference of messages
2. Differentiated linguistic codes Different linguistic codes are used depending upon persons involved and situations	2. Less differentiated linguistic codes Linguistic codes are not as extensively differentiated as in East Asia
3. Indirect communication emphasis The use of indirect communication is prevalent and accepted as normative	3. Direct communication emphasis Direct communication is a norm despite the extensive use of indirect communication
4. Receiver centered Meaning is in the interpretation	4. Sender centered Meaning is in the messages created by the sender
Emphasis is on listening, sensitivity, and removal of preconception	Emphasis is on how to formulate the best messages, how to improve source credibility, and how to improve delivery skills

Source: From *Intercultural Communication: A Reader,* 7/e by Larry Samovar and Richard Porter. Wadsworth Publishing Co., 1994, p. 80. Copyright © 1994. Reprinted by permission of Wadsworth Publishing Co.

The Japanese tend to avoid discussing bargaining tactics. Prenegotiations often move slowly and cautiously. Japanese tend to avoid disagreement during formal negotiations, as disagreement is considered distasteful and embarrassing. On the other hand, prenegotiation is often crucial for successful Middle Eastern negotiations. Only after trust is acquired may the hard negotiations start to take place.[61] For Mexicans, the beginning stage of negotiations is often used for social discourse and gaining trust among participants. Then they proceed to negotiate.[62] Brazilians are so sensitive to the necessity for the exchanging of pleasantries that if they feel the other side is impatient to get down to business, they may actually slow down the entire process until everyone is comfortable.[63]

CULTURAL CONTRAST OF THE ROLE OF INFORMATION

Even the information or ideas used for making the decisions may differ in different cultures. In the Western view, proven facts and the opinion of persons who are experts in the field under discussion tend to be of utmost importance. Westerners, therefore, will attempt to make their points by quoting experts and stating facts. The Eastern view, on the other hand, is best illustrated by Taoist thought, which holds that "truth, not the individual, is the active agent, and ways of knowing take a variety of forms."[64] Therefore, in negotiations, followers of the Eastern philosophies rely on commonly held beliefs and values, quotations of proverbs and wise sayings, and referring to past traditions to develop their arguments.

Even the way in which decisions are approached may contrast. American negotiators tend to compartmentalize issues, focusing on one issue at a time, instead of negotiating many issues together. "They tend to rely on rational thinking and concrete data in their negotiations."[65] In the United States, negotiating toward the final decision usually takes on a form of **proposal-counterproposal negotiating,** in which a plan or solution is presented and then a counteroffer is made. For example, in a group meeting related to salary negotiations the employees will propose a particular salary dollar amount and explain why they think this amount is appropriate. The management would make an offer of a lesser amount and offer counterarguments. This process continues until an amount is agreed upon.

The French, on the other hand, seem to "have no problem with open disagreement—they debate more than they bargain and are less apt than Americans to be flexible for the sake of agreement."[66] "They start with a long-range view of their purpose, as opposed to Americans, who work with more short-range objectives."[67]

Proposal-counterproposal negotiating with the Japanese tends to be ineffective because their teams usually take so long to make decisions. In addition, "Japanese negotiators make decisions on the basis of detailed information rather than persuasive arguments."[68]

Male and Female Roles in Groups

In addition to geographical cultural implications to group action, research shows that gender can also be a factor. Think about groups in which you've participated. Can you remember any instances where references were made to the gender of an individual as it related to her or his being a group participant or a leader? Do you think that being a male or a female has an effect on being a leader or a member of the group? Is gender a factor in group task or group maintenance?[69] Generally, the studies on leadership and group processing indicate that "women tend to be more process-oriented than men. Men are more goal-oriented. For women, the process is as important, or more important, than the product."[70] Other studies indicate that "individuals prefer managers who possess masculine characteristics."[71] This finding carries over into the fact that men are more likely than women to be selected as the foreperson of a jury.[72] Research concerning educational groups indicates that students believe that classes led by women are more discussion-oriented, while classes taught by men are more structured and emphasize content mastery more.[73] Males are perceived to be less supportive and less innovative than females.[74] In addition, some differences may be accounted for by the fact that if the women in the group have a subordinate position, are younger than their male counterparts, or have less experience than some of the men in the group, the differences in communicative behavior may be based on status or experience.

Do you believe that men are more assertive than women or that women are too emotional to make rational decisions? If you answered "yes," research proves you wrong. Several supposed truisms about males and females regarding their participation in group actions have been demonstrated to be *untrue*, including the supposed belief that women are too emotional to make rational decisions; that women have a low commitment to work, compared with men; and that men are inherently more assertive than women.[75] Even though these myths have been uncovered, being a member of a particular gender does seemingly relate to your group participation and perception. For example, "being the only member of one's sex in a mixed-gender group affects the perceptions of other group members and often skews the opportunities to communicate and the feedback one receives."[76] In addition, males are perceived to be more dominant and females more submissive during group communication involving both men and women, whether the communication is verbal or nonverbal.[77] And research shows that males typically offer 40 percent more comments during deliberation than females.[78] Research also shows that "males initiate more interactions than females,"[79] and males tend to dominate talk in task groups.[80]

Yes, it appears there is a difference, or at least perceived differences, between the genders as they participate in groups in the North American culture. Remember, however, that as in all cases of generalizations, there are men and women who defy the research findings and act outside of the norm patterns.

• • •   In Summary   • • •

Groups have traditionally been defined as an assemblage of persons who communicate, face-to-face, in order to fulfill a common purpose and achieve a goal. Groups may be classified as small groups—three to twelve persons—or large groups—more than a dozen people. Groups, by the very nature of their collective identity, offer the participants great advantages. However, there are disadvantages to groups as well. Groups may be classified as a work team, committees, media-conferences, electronic meetings, focus groups, public meetings, and town meetings. Groups are continually evolving and they go through five operational phases: norming, storming, conforming, performing, and adjourning. One of the most prominent functions of the group communication process is that of decision making. Not all societies use groups in the same way; therefore, groups operate differently in various cultures. Many of the decisions made within businesses and organizations, and with clients, are the products of group actions.

▬▬   Business Communication in Practice   ▬▬

1. Some people would rather work alone than in groups. This chapter explains some advantages and disadvantages of group action and decision making. Be prepared to defend or counter this statement: "The advantages of working in a group outweigh the disadvantages." Go beyond the arguments given in the chapter to use personal or hypothetical examples in developing your answer.

2. Consider a group in which you have worked that was not successful in reaching its goal or that had difficulty in reaching its goal because of the leader. What was the problem? How could the problem have been solved?

3. Identify a specific culture (e.g., ethnic group, racial group, women, gay men). Prepare a short paper, which may be given as an oral presentation

in class, that indicates what the research shows about the characteristic patterns of how they operate as group members.

4. Mentally revisit a group you have participated in. Write a short paper, which may be given as an oral presentation, which analyzes its norming, storming, conforming, performing, and adjourning stages.

• • • Notes • • •

1. *Group Problem-Solving and Meeting Dynamics*, a manuscript submitted for blind review (Cincinnati, OH: Southwestern Publishing, 1993), p. 2.
2. Ibid.
3. Ibid., 3.
4. Ernest Borman, *Discussion and Group Methods* (New York: Harper and Row, 1969), p. 304.
5. Stuart Tubbs and Harold Moss, *Human Communication* (New York: Random House, 1987), pp. 251–252.
6. John Brilhart, *Effective Group Discussion*, 2d ed. (Dubuque, IA: William C. Brown, 1974), p. 17.
7. J. Dan Rothwell, *In Mixed Company* (Ft. Worth, TX: Harcourt Brace, 1992), p. 40.
8. Ibid.
9. Charles H. Kepner and Benjamin B. Tregoe, *The Rational Manager: A Systematic Approach to Problem Solving and Decision Making* (New York: McGraw-Hill, 1965).
10. Irving Janis, *Victims of Groupthink* (Boston: Houghton Mifflin, 1972).
11. For an extended discussion of groupthink, see J. Ganis, *Groupthink: Psychological Studies of Policy Decisions and Fiascoes* (Boston: Houghton Mifflin, 1983).
12. Ibid., 141–144.
13. *Group Problem-Solving and Meeting Dynamics*, 7.
14. Charles C. Manz and Henry P. Sims, Jr., *Business without Bosses* (New York: Wiley, 1993), p. 211.
15. Ibid., 2.
16. Bibb Latane, Kipling Williams, and Stephen Harkins, "Social Loafing," *Psychology Today* 13 (October 1979): 104.
17. Gerald L. Wilson and Michael S. Hanna, *Groups in Context* (New York: McGraw-Hill, 1990), 63–65.
18. Kathleen Wagoner and Mary Ruprecht, *Office Automation: A Management Approach* (New York: Wiley, 1984), as quoted in "Group Problem-Solving and Meeting Dynamics," p. 30.
19. Ron Zemke, "The Rediscovery of Videotape Teleconferencing," *Training* (September 1986): 46.
20. *Group Problem-Solving and Meeting Dynamics*, 30–31.
21. A concept proposed in B. W. Tuckman, "Developmental Sequence in Small Groups," *Psychological Bulletin* (1965), pp. 383–399, and discussed in Rothwell, pp. 55–80.
22. Rothwell, 65–66.

23. Matt Helms, "License to Hate," *National College Magazine* (September 1992), p. 61.
24. Ibid., 64.
25. Henry M. Robert III and William J. Evans, *Robert's Rules of Order, Newly Revised.* (Glenview, IL: Scott, Foresman, 1990).
26. Larry Samovar and Richard Porter, *Intercultural Communication: A Reader* (Belmont, CA: Wadsworth, 1994), p. 298.
27. Ibid., 291.
28. Ibid.
29. Ibid.
30. Ibid.
31. Robert and Evans.
32. Ganis, 204.
33. Robert and Evans, 52–53.
34. Ibid., 395–396.
35. Part-of-the-whole voting is sometimes referred to as 2/3 voting. For a discussion, see Robert and Evans, 396–397.
36. Rothwell, 195.
37. Ibid.
38. Ganis, 197.
39. John Dewey, *How to Think* (Boston: D. C. Heath, 1910), pp. 68–78.
40. Ganis, 219.
41. Ganis, 203.
42. Adapted by Roy Berko from Eileen Breckenridge, "Improving School Climate," *Phi Delta Kappan* (December 1976), pp. 314–318.
43. *Group Problem-Solving and Meeting Dynamics*, 27.
44. Rothwell, 221.
45. Dale Leathers, *Successful Nonverbal Communication* (New York: Macmillan, 1992), p. 373.
46. Ibid.
47. Ibid., 374.
48. Ibid., 373.
49. Ibid., 375.
50. Mark Knapp and Judith Hall, *Nonverbal Communication in Human Interaction*, 3d ed. (Ft. Worth, TX: Harcourt Brace, 1992), p. 168.
51. Ibid.
52. Ibid., 167.
53. Ibid., 168.
54. Ibid.
55. George A. Borden, *Cultural Orientation: An Approach to Understanding Intercultural Communication* (Englewood Cliffs, NJ: Prentice Hall, 1991), p. 133.
56. Samovar and Porter, 79.
57. Borden, 105.
58. Ibid.
59. Samovar and Porter, 79.
60. Ibid.
61. Ibid., 292.

62. Ibid.
63. Ibid.
64. Ibid.
65. Ibid., 291.
66. Ibid.
67. Ibid.
68. Ibid.
69. For a discussion of the research on women and men as leaders and group members, see Judy Pearson, *Gender and Communication* (Dubuque, IA: William C. Brown, 1985), p. 339.
70. Janet Fox, "Changing Leadership Styles," *Amtrak Express* (May/June 1993).
71. Pearson, 338.
72. Laurie Arliss and Deborah Borisoff, *Women and Men Communicating* (Ft. Worth, TX: Harcourt Brace, 1993), p. 168.
73. Lea Stewart, Alan Stewart, Sheryl Friedley, and Pam Cooper, *Communication between the Sexes* (Scottsdale, AZ: Gorsuch Scarisbrick, 1990), p. 162.
74. Ibid., 163.
75. Pearson, 338.
76. Barbara Bates, *Communication and the Sexes* (New York: Harper and Row, 1988), p. 155.
77. Arliss and Borisoff.
78. Ibid.
79. Stewart, Stewart, Friedley, and Cooper, 159.
80. Ibid.

Group Communication: Participating in Business Groups

EXPECTED OUTCOMES

After completing this chapter, you should be able to:

- Define and explain the role of the participants, the leaders, and the leadership of groups.
- Compare and contrast the role of disagreement in the group process.
- Acknowledge the role of the hidden agenda in the group process.
- List the types of group communication networks and explain the communicative role of each.
- Define the authoritarian, democratic, and laissez-faire leader types.
- Explain why a person would want to be a group leader, and demonstrate how the person would proceed to acquire the leader/leadership role.
- Discuss the role of gender as a factor in group activities.

We were getting nowhere. I finally said that I thought the group ought to take a break for a few minutes. The brainstorming session relating to the new community outreach strategies had gone well while ideas were being generated, but when it came time to select the top idea to present to the steering committee, things got nasty. Bob believed the only idea worth presenting was his. Deborah announced that Bob's idea had been tried three years ago and had been a dismal failure. That's when Bob and Deborah, along with their respective followers, started a downward spiral into the land of personal *attacks. Jean, who was responsible for facilitating the session, looked at me after everyone had marched out and said, "Where do we go from here? I need help. I had a negative performance review last time and this isn't going to help."*

Groups are made up of people. Those who compose the group assume the roles of leaders, leadership, and participants. As you interact in a group, the role or roles you assume affects what you do and the influence you will have on the outcome of the group's actions. **Participants** are those members of the group who interact to bring about the actions of the group. **Leaders** are those who guide the group. **Leadership** refers to those who influence the group to accomplish its goal. An in-depth understanding of the specific role of each will shed light on the communication dynamics of the group.

The Participant

As a group member you will be performing varied communication activities. Foremost of these will be speaking and listening. In the process of participation you will probably evaluate information, propose concepts, and agree and disagree with the ideas of others.

RESPONSIBILITIES OF GROUP MEMBERS

All participants should remember that the entire group is responsible and accountable for final decisions. Thus, being a member of the **silent majority**—those who say nothing during the decision-making process—does not release you from accountability for the decision. For example, if the group decides on a new logo for the firm, although you may have said nothing during the discussion and even may not have voted on the issue, you are part of that decision. You cannot get off the hook announcing after the decision is made, "I didn't say anything and I didn't vote, so I'm not responsible for any negative reaction."

Group members should be knowledgeable. Though personal beliefs are important, facts and expert opinion will reveal what authorities believe and what tests have proved. In other words, the use of supporting evidence ensures that your conclusions will have more substance and credibility. Good research techniques will enable you to locate and develop adequate support for your positions. When you can apply evidence such as statistics, testimony, and illustrations to your discussions, your participation will be enhanced.

Some groups are plagued by people who insist on dominating the discussion and the decision-making process. Indeed, these people can destroy the entire group, because a person who dominates a discussion group does not allow varying points of view to be presented, and, therefore, the purpose of the discussion and the basis for group action—an interchange of information and ideas—become impossible to achieve. Discussion should not be a solo performance by one group member. And, although it is difficult when you have very strong opinions and believe that you are right and others are wrong, as much as possible each participant should respect the rights of the others. This does not mean that you should not participate if your views differ from others. However, there is a point at which continued bickering can be destructive to the group's mission. After presenting your point of view and your evidence, it may appear that your ideas will not be accepted. Your task, then, is either to work toward reaching a compromise into which you can enfold your ideas, or to accept the fact that you have done everything you could to get your viewpoint presented and accepted, and failed to achieve your goal.

It is important for you not to assume that rejection of your idea means rejection of you, personally. Unfortunately, many people have difficulty making this distinction. They assume that if one of their ideas is rejected, they, too, have been deemed unworthy. Not understanding this concept causes people to "fight to the death" for their beliefs to be accepted. In reality, what they are fighting for is to establish or to retain their own legitimacy. This misunderstanding often causes the self-perceived rejected person to start personally attacking others, rather than sticking to the issues. These personal attacks often do little to get your position accepted, but they can lead to alienation within the group. They often cause people to take sides, not on what *solution* is right or wrong, but on *who* is right or wrong. This process can divide the group, leading to internal rifts and destroying chances of group cohesion and goal accomplishment.

A further responsibility of discussion participants is to respond to each other with pertinent, meaningful comments and questions. Normally, group members should assume an active role in communicating with each other so that the entire group can benefit. Of course, there are times during group interactions when you do not want to participate. You may think that you do not have the necessary information to offer; or you might not have strong enough feelings about the discussion taking place to interject; or you might observe that your beliefs have already been presented by someone else and repeating the same ideas would be a waste of the group's time. Whatever the reason, to knowingly and willingly choose not to participate is your privilege. However, remember that choosing not to participate because you are intimidated by the leader or other participants, or because you are afraid that your ideas don't have much worth, is an act of abdicating your responsibility as a group member.

Participants in a group discussion should try to set aside their own prejudices and beliefs in order to listen and respond to what others say. This ability to suspend judgment is difficult, but it reduces group conflict so that progress can be made toward the group's goals. Try to resolve any conflicts by adopting an openness to compromise and conciliation and by trying to work out differences of opinion. Rather than trying to win arguments, you are wise to recognize and, if possible, adapt to the viewpoints of others—provided you believe their judgments are in the best interest of the group process and you can live with the compromise. Although this advice is theoretically sound, remember that in adopting this approach, generally, compromises, because they can require people to give up their beliefs and move to "watered down" solutions, are often not satisfying to all concerned. Also, do not allow a verbal bully to force you into a compromise or adopt a solution that you believe is not in the best interests of the group.

COMMUNICATING AS A GROUP MEMBER

Group interactions are most effective when the participants are aware of how and why they are communicating—in other words, their role as speakers and listeners. These roles can be described with regard to your attitude toward the group, maintenance roles, task roles, and basic communication skills.

Attitude toward the Group

In general, group participants should treat each other with respect. For most people this is not a problem. Individuals will not always agree, and disagreement can be helpful, as it opens the decision-making process to a variety of viewpoints and allows for differences of opinions to be aired.

Group members are more committed and active when they have positive attitudes about the group. Think back to times when you have been proud of your group—its achievements and activities. Having been on a winning athletic team, having solved a complex problem, having planned an event or an activity and been pleased with the results: all of these accomplishments help build group pride. And members who have pride in the group will show commitment to the group. If this is not the case, one of the tasks of the group is to investigate why there are negative attitudes. Dealing with this issue(s), and being able to solve the problems, may make working in the group more pleasurable, increase the productivity of the membership, and encourage rather than discourage participation.

Taking an active role in the group through volunteering ideas, showing willingness to work on subgroups and committees, and making supportive comments is an important part of a communicator helping the group to work cohesively.

Group interactions are most effective when the participants are aware of how and why they are communicating—their role as speakers and listeners.

Performing Communicative Maintenance Roles

Performing maintenance roles is as important to the group's communication as are the members' attitudes toward the group. Aiding the members to have positive feelings about each other and about their work assists in getting the work done in a positive manner. If you are typical, if you like the people with whom you are working, if you find the environment pleasing, and if there is a supportive attitude in which you are praised and rewarded for your efforts, you probably work better and are more dedicated. Being aware of this dynamic, and assisting in developing positive feelings about the group, are important maintenance functions.

Research shows that individuals who are communicatively supportive to the maintenance functions reinforce other's ideas, participate in the group in a constructive way, separate people from ideas, try to remain flexible, express their feelings, and describe their reactions.[1] In other words, such a participant tries to compliment others; realizes that there will be differences of opinions; avoids attacking the person, but sticks to the issues; is aware of the need to compromise when it is appropriate; makes an effort to listen to other's opinions; and attempts to describe her or his feelings about what is happening. Notice the use of words like "tries," "realizes," "is aware," and "attempts." Realistically, no one can fulfill all of these supportive roles, all of the time. However, being aware of and performing these functions, and making an effort to fulfill these obligations, is a worthy goal for all group participants.

Performing Communicator Task Roles

Ideally, all members of a group remain open-minded, engage in conflict only by dealing with the issue and not attacking the other members of the group, and cooperate in the group interactions. However, it is unrealistic to expect this behavior from all members in all circumstances. The best that can normally be achieved is that members understand that they can be constructive or destructive and then perform constructively. Constructive communicator task roles include initiating ideas, encouraging diverse ideas, using reasoned thought (separating facts from opinions, criticizing weak or unsubstantiated ideas, using good reasoning, offering evidence, integrating ideas), staying open-minded, being aware of hidden agendas, being an encouraging participant, being cognizant of time constraints, and remaining attentive to nonverbal cues.

Initiating Ideas Group actions are based on someone proposing actions. Therefore, the initiation of ideas is imperative. At first, in most groups, people tend to be a little shy about presenting ideas. But, as the group moves from norming to performing, this reluctance to put forth ideas is overcome.

Encouraging Diverse Ideas Another important aspect of task communication is to encourage the offering of diverse ideas. Conservative thinkers stick to the "tried and true." They tend to exclusively recreate past solutions for problems, sticking mainly to the status quo. Creative idea-generators go beyond the norm and search for different solutions. These ideas may seem crazy at first, but many seemingly crazy ideas have satisfied major needs. Historically, space travel, the invention of the computer, even the light bulb, were all "far out" ideas. Perhaps in the near future someone will propose some nonconventional idea to cure AIDS or cancer or to ensure a lasting world peace. Don't be stifled by the "tried and true"; think creatively, even if it risks your being called a dreamer or an idealist. Joining Alexander Graham Bell, Michelangelo, George Washington Carver, Madam Curie, and the other inventors, scientists, and explorers who have made a difference isn't a negative act.[2]

Using Reasoned Thought One of the important roles of task communication is to support sound ideas and to develop well-thought-out concepts. Separating facts from opinions, criticizing weak or unsubstantiated ideas, using logical reasoning, offering evidence, and integrating ideas are important obligations of a constructive task communicator.

Wrapping Up Those Meetings

Ever attend a meeting or run a meeting where you had lots of discussion, but no closure on any ideas?

If so, you might want to consider these suggestions from Harvey Mackay, author of two New York Times No. 1 best-sellers:

● *Recap what you consider to be the key points made. Summarize the pros and cons of each point you've discussed.*

● *Ask for what you want. Example: "I would like your approval to get started on this project by the 15th."*

● *State the benefits of what you're proposing. This shows why they should have the good sense to go along with you.*

If you don't ask for what you want, you won't get it.

Source: Successful Meetings, 355 Park Ave. S., New York, NY 10010.

Staying Open-Minded In general, most of us come to a conclusion, believe it is correct, and defend it staunchly. To be an effective task communicator, however, is to be open to the possibility that someone else's ideas may be as valid as, if not more valid than, ours. There may be things we haven't thought of, approaches we haven't been exposed to, ideas that challenge our beliefs. Being open to the possibility that someone else may have relevant information is a positive attitude for a group member. Don't overlook the possibility of combining ideas to create a blended solution.

Being Aware of Hidden Agendas In fulfilling your communication task role, be aware that some individuals will attempt to accomplish their goals at the expense of others. Some members of a group enter the task process with a **hidden agenda**—an objective or purpose for joining the group that goes beyond the constructive interests of the group as a whole. When individual members work for their own unstated ends rather than for the group's objectives, the result is usually counterproductive. A hidden agenda is apparent, for example, when a department manager discussing budget allocations promises to support any plan that divides the resources equitably but then opposes all the plans that are presented. In this case, the manager has a hidden agenda—he or she wants most of the funds for his or her department and thinks a delay will tire the participants and lead to a decision that favors that department. Thus the manager is trying to manipulate the group toward a personal goal. In your role as an effective task communicator, listen carefully to the proposals and arguments of other members and be alert to the possibilities of hidden agendas.

Attentiveness to Nonverbal Cues In your role of being an encouraging task communicator, be aware of verbal and nonverbal cues. If you observe that a group member is anxious, for instance, you may want to allay his or her fears by such comments as "That idea is really worth thinking about" or "I'm glad you brought that up." If you observe that a participant has not contributed to the discussion and appears nervous, you can say "It's important we get your opinion, because everyone's ideas are relevant." Or you can ask the person directly to react: "Barbara, will you please give us your reactions to the proposal that we give all administrative assistants a 10 percent raise?" Such encouraging comments tend to make reticent communicators less shy and give support to those who need it. This support then invites them to become more active participants.

Being Cognizant of Time Constraints To perform the role of a task communicator, you also need to be sensitive to time factors so as not to dominate a discussion with too many statements or with lengthy comments. You run the risk that everyone will tune you out, or your contributions will be so overpowering that the group process will be lost because of your dominance.

Be wary of the participant who knows that time is short and the meeting is coming to a close, and then suggests a new, untested, or undiscussed solution.

Business Professionals Share Their Views

Profile: Barbara G. Rosenthal, qualitative research consultant

What is the role of groups in your work?

As a qualitative research consultant, I work for companies all over the country in their development of product lines and/or their advertising campaigns. In addition to in-depth interviewing, I make extensive use of focus groups to get reactions of typical consumers to proposed products or ads. The focus groups are an important part of my work, because the dynamics of the group enables me to get to a deeper level of response from the representative participants. I find that the synergy of the group helps the individual participants respond to products or ads both in the thinking and the feeling levels.

What does it take to be a good group facilitator?

Most of my work as a group moderator is to be a good listener so that I can be sure that all of the group members do participate actively and so that I can provide a thorough report of the group's responses to the client. Since a focus group meets for a rather short, prescribed time frame, I have to establish trust with the members, build rapport, and develop cohesion within the first three minutes. It is important to communicate an unconditional positive regard for each member in the group. I have to "work" the group in order to engage all of the members early on in the process so that they will feel committed to the group and its goal. A focus group can't just be a serial interview of each participant; I have to understand how groups function and work to accomplish my group objectives.

What do you look for in group participants?

Many specialists in qualitative research look first for "articulate" people. I don't feel that is the most important quality. It's more important that focus group participants be able to listen so that they can understand the questions and the others' comments as well in order to respond as specifically and meaningfully as possible. A good participant is one who is willing to share his or her thoughts and feelings and is willing to let others share their thought and feelings too. To participate in a group, you need to be sincere, interested, honest, and responsive.

This device is commonly used by group members who know that when time pressures increase, group members may act impulsively. If someone suggests a solution late in the discussion, make sure that it is not acted upon until the group has time to think through the advisability of taking the proposed action.

Encouraging Participants   Being encouraging rather than discouraging can also aid in task accomplishment. Negative messages in a group discussion can easily shut down the communication. Avoid **communication stoppers,** comments such as "That will never work," "We've tried that before," or "That's ridiculous."

The effective group communicator also attends to nonverbal messages. It is important to maintain eye contact with those speaking and to actively engage, physically, in the discussion. Facing toward the person who is speaking normally shows attentiveness and can increase the likelihood of actually receiving the message. The person who looks away or turns her or his body from the speaker can communicate a lack of involvement in or respect for the discussion, or disagreement with the comments being made. Research shows that rapid speech rate, fluid gestures, relaxed posture, verbal fluency (such as avoiding "uhs," and "ohs," and saying "things like that" or "you know") are positive communicators.[3] "To keep a meeting moving along and behaviors under control," suggests one meeting management specialist, "let your own body language be one of your strongest allies."[4]

The effective group communicator, therefore, should be an active participant in the discussion. Active participation means: initiating ideas, encouraging diverse ideas, using reasoned thought (separate facts from opinions, criticize weak or unsubstantiated ideas, use good reasoning, offer evidence, integrate ideas), staying open-minded, being aware of hidden agendas, being an encouraging participant, being cognizant of time constraints, and remaining attentive to nonverbal cues.

ROLES OF GROUP MEMBERS

Participants in small groups function in a variety of roles. It is helpful to recognize these roles and monitor not only your behavior, but that of others. This monitoring often allows you to understand why you and others are doing what you are doing. This awareness opens the possibility of your altering your behavior or alerting others to the roles they are playing if actions being taken are detrimental to the group's progress. It also allows for praising yourself and others as you discover that the role you are playing is productive. Remember that the titles and descriptions are classifications to explain the roles group members may assume in their task and maintenance functions within groups. These designations are by no means all-encompassing, nor are they mutually exclusive. Like any model, they are simply ways to identify certain patterns of role behavior in task and maintenance.[5]

As a participant in a group, you or others may assume roles that are considered positive for group action. These roles include:

- *Initiator-contributor:* presenting new ideas or new perspectives
- *Information seeker:* asking for facts and clarifications
- *Opinion seeker:* asking for opinions to get at some of the values of the group
- *Information giver:* presenting facts and opinions
- *Opinion giver:* presenting values and opinions

- *Elaborator:* providing examples and solutions and building on the contributions of others
- *Coordinator:* identifying relationships among the ideas presented in the discussion
- *Orienter:* clarifying ideas for the group through summaries and identification of the group's direction
- *Evaluator-critic:* analyzing the group's decisions
- *Energizer:* stimulating the group to greater productivity
- *Procedural technician:* handling mechanical tasks such as paper distribution and seating arrangements
- *Recorder:* recording the transactions of the group
- *Encourager:* supplying positive reinforcement to the group members
- *Harmonizer:* mediating various differences among group members
- *Compromiser:* attempting to resolve conflicts within the group
- *Gatekeeper-expediter:* keeping the channels of communication open by encouraging the members
- *Standard setter:* establishing group norms and patterns of behavior
- *Follower:* passively accepting the ideas of others

In addition to performing roles that facilitate the group process, individuals may consciously or unconsciously assume roles that can be counterproductive to the group's efforts. It is wise for participants to be able to recognize these roles and, if possible, to avoid falling into such patterns. It is just as important to make others aware that they are assuming these roles:

- *Aggressor:* attacking the group or the problem under discussion
- *Blocker:* providing negative feedback and opposition
- *Recognition seeker:* attempting to focus attention on oneself
- *Self-confessor:* expressing one's own feelings and perspectives rather than focusing on the group
- *Playboy or playgirl:* playing around with little or no regard for the group process
- *Dominator:* attempting to take over the group
- *Help seeker:* expressing insecurity and self-deprecation to gain sympathy
- *Special-interest pleader:* disregarding group goals and arguing the case of some special, specific group

COMMUNICATION NETWORKS

Groups operate by different formal and informal patterns, which link members together. The patterns are called **group communication networks.** Early research on communication networks indicated five basic forms (see Figure 10.1).

Communication
networks:
a. wheel
b. chain
c. Y
d. circle
e. all-channel

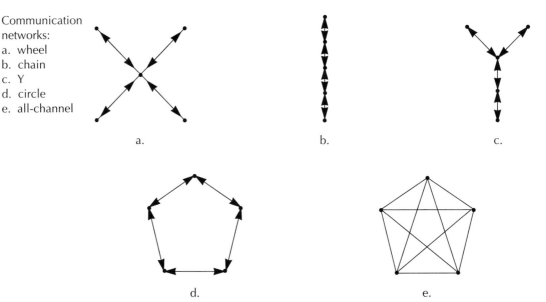

FIGURE 10.1
Group Communication Networks

Each of the dots represents an individual communicator, and the arrows illustrate the way the information flows. The leader, or the person of influence, is at the center of each flow of information. For example, in the wheel, the chain, and the Y, there is a clear leader or power figure. Therefore, this pattern is referred to as a centralized network. In general, the centralized networks such as the chain, the wheel, and the Y are most effective for a group to deal with simple problems. These are the systems that are often dependent upon a strong leadership figure to guide the proceedings. They can work most rapidly as the leadership normally has a great deal of influence and can direct the participation toward accomplishing the task.

In the circle and the all-channel, there is no central focal person; thus, the term "decentralized" is used to describe this pattern. The decentralized networks such as the circle and the all-channel, in which ideas flow freely, are more effective for solving complex problems. The decentralized networks often can result in greater member interaction and satisfaction, as there is more interplay between the participants and less influence by a power figure. In the decentralized network the leader plays less of a director role, and more of a participant role.

Research concerning communication networks indicates that group members have higher morale in a decentralized than in a centralized communication network. Decentralized communication networks are most efficient when groups must solve complex problems, but a centralized network is most efficient when the group must solve simple problems. And centralized communication networks are more likely to result in a work overload for the leader than decentralized communication networks.[6]

DEALING WITH DIFFICULT GROUP MEMBERS

One assumption for understanding how to deal with groups members is: 90 percent of the people who are members of groups are reasonable most of the time. There will be conflicts and differences of opinion, but the people will work for the good of the group and will work things out. About 9 percent of the members will be somewhat difficult to work with. They have hidden agendas, disagreeable personalities, and seem to be marching to the tune of a different drummer much of the time. Then there is the remaining 1 percent. These people were created, but no one is exactly sure why! Their obstructive nature gets in the way of any attempt to cooperatively deal with them.

The explanation of the percentages and the roles of difficult people in groups can serve as the basis for understanding how to deal with this classification of group members. For example, in dealing with the 90 percent, applying the concepts presented in this chapter about effective group communication should be sufficient to work things out and work toward the group goals.

As for the 1 percent—the impossible people—there is very little that you can do to work constructively with them. Reasoning with them, or giving in to their demands, will accomplish little. These individuals simply are out to make life miserable for themselves and for everyone around them. They often are incapable of listening, processing, and working toward group cohesiveness. They tend to be so self-absorbed that there is no way to work things out short of always giving in to them. Giving in seems only to encourage their behavior and, in the future, they will likely escalate their negative actions, knowing that eventually the group will give in to their tantrums and negativism. One coping method sometimes applied is to expel them from the group. Another is to ignore them. A third is to recognize that they must have their say but it is no one's obligation to listen. Unfortunately, if one of these individuals is the group leader—the boss, the professor, or the dominant power figure—the problem is compounded. Even group experts and psychologists have no recommendations for what group participants should do if this is the case. Quitting the job or leaving the group may be the only solution if things get too bad.

That leaves the 9 percent who are often termed as "difficult group members." Difficult people are those who cause continued problems regarding the task and/or maintenance accomplishment of the group. They engage in actions such as continued disruptions, long speeches, irrational requests, insulting behavior toward others, and interruption of participants. Before taking any action, be sure that the actions are actually taking place and that the person is, in fact, difficult. Sometimes we perceive a person to be difficult because their ideas are different from ours. Is the problem yours, or is it really that the person is difficult?

Experts seem to agree that in dealing with these people, six general axioms should be followed:[7]

1. *Don't placate the troublemaker.* Allowing the disrupter to manipulate the group in order to keep the peace rewards the troublemaker for objectionable behavior and encourages similar actions in the future.
2. *Refuse to be goaded into a reciprocal pattern.* Resist the temptation to meet fire with fire.
3. *Don't provide a soapbox for the troublemaker.* Try and defer the confrontation. You cannot ignore disruptive behavior especially when it becomes chronic.
4. *Try to convert disruption into a constructive contribution.* There is a difference between being disruptive and being constructive. Use the person's ideas to ask for other ideas. This technique takes the discussion away from the person and allows others to speak.
5. *Confront the difficult person directly.* If the tirades or actions are disruptive, tell the person. Continued disruptions and other negative actions that stop task and maintenance progress are not in the best interest of the group and need to be addressed. Ideally, the confrontation will be assertive and present the facts, detailing exactly what the person has done. You should not insert your opinion, be aggressive, or attack the person rather than the issue. For example, instead of saying, "You are always making stupid and irrelevant comments," state, "The last two times we have discussed the issue of selecting a new logo for the company, you changed the subject to why you believe the company should expand its product line and why you believe you should be made responsible for selecting the new products. Neither of these statements had to do with the topic being discussed and didn't help us solve the issue at hand."
6. *Separate yourself from the difficult person if all else fails.* Some individuals leave no other option except ostracism by the group. As already stated in the discussion of dealing with impossible people, quitting the job or leaving the group may be your only salvation.

We participate in groups not only as participants but as those who perform the roles of leader or leadership. An understanding of that aspect of group communication can prepare you to assume such a role.

Leaders and Leadership

The strength of a group is found not only in effective participation but also in meaningful leadership. The leader of a group is the person who is recognized as being responsible for guiding the group through its tasks. The leader may be elected, may be appointed by an outside source (by the division manager, for instance), may volunteer, or may emerge by taking control of the proceedings (for example, a senior accountant at a finance meeting). A group may also have more than one leader. For instance, a group may have several chairpersons. Furthermore, in some groups the recognized leader may not be the only one who is guiding the group; other members may share this function either by being appointed or by assuming such responsibility.

The ability to influence others' opinions and actions is known as leadership (see Figure 10.2). It can be demonstrated by one or more people in a group, and the use of the power that derives from leadership can be viewed in two ways. **Leadership power** is enforcing obedience and the ability to influence others to perform.

FIGURE 10.2
Model of the Leader-Leadership Relationship

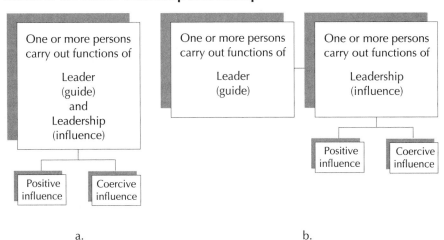

a.

b.

Berko-Wolvin-Wolvin model of the leader/leadership relationship. The leader is the group's guide. Leadership is the ability to influence, which can be used either positively or coercively. Both leader and leadership functions can be carried out by (a) the same person(s), or (b) separate persons.

Source: From Communicating: A Social and Career Focus, by Roy Berko, Andrew Wolvin, Darlyn Wolvin. Copyright © 1992 by Houghton Mifflin Company. Reprinted by permission of the publishers.

First, leadership power can be defined as enforcing obedience through the ability to withhold benefits or to inflict punishment. In this sense, power is coercive. **Coercion** centers on offering a selection of choices, all of which are undesirable. For example, in a meeting of production lineworkers to discuss whether shifts should be rotated, many of the workers may not want this action to be taken. But if the supervisor is in favor of rotating the shifts, then the power of the position may come into play. He or she may say, "It's my responsibility to determine staff assignments, and anyone who cannot accept this idea can request a transfer to another department." Thus, the decision has been made through coercive power because the options offered may not be desirable to the workers.

Second, leadership power can be defined as the ability to influence others to perform or produce results. This kind of power does not use force or coercion. With this type of power, the influence of the person, rather than the authority of the position, is paramount. For example, in a meeting of lineworkers, the foreman may see conflict within the group and may suggest a solution whereby those workers who want to be on a rotating shift may do so and those who do not may select a permanent shift. The foreman presents reasons for this solution and asks the others for suggestions. Eventually, the group accepts the foreman's suggestion with or without changes because it was explained well and because the foreman was willing to accept alterations and had a record of being flexible in such situations. This influence through positive leadership in a group is a productive way to use power for the benefit of the entire group.

The tendency of certain people in leadership positions to act coercively has given rise to an examination of alternate leadership styles. One of these styles is **transformational leadership** in which the person takes on the role of transforming agent. A transforming agent is one who can change both the behavior and the outlook of his or her followers. This person keeps the interest of the group and its goals in mind rather than forcing her or his will on the group. Therefore she or he gives up the command and control model of leadership.[8]

Another style is **superleadership** in which people are led to lead themselves and thereby release the self-leadership energy within each person.[9] Such an approach is especially appropriate to today's down-scaled organizations where all qualified employees will not have the opportunity to move up the corporate ladder into management and/or executive positions. Consequently, each person can and should be encouraged to develop his or her own leadership skills to stay at a productive level within changing organizations.

TYPES OF LEADERS

Regardless of leadership style, some people will use their power to influence the outcome of any group effort. As such, leaders exhibit characteristics by which their style of leadership can be categorized. Three basic types of leaders have been identified.[10]

What It Takes to Be a Leader

Based on surveys of more than 15,000 people, which of these traits do you think was selected as the key to effective leadership:

- Being fair-minded?
- Being cooperative?
- Being honest?
- Being imaginative?

If you guessed "honest," you get a high mark. It scored far above any of the others in a list of 20. In fact, the top four characteristics of admired leaders and the percentage of people who selected them are:

- Being honest—87%
- Being forward-looking—71%
- Being inspirational—68%
- Being competent—58%.

"If these qualities alone were running for office," says the authors of Credibility, "they are the ones that would achieve consensus and victory."

Honest people, say authors James M. Kouzes and Barry Z. Posner, have credibility—and that's what gives leaders the trust and confidence of their people.

High credibility leaders foster such things as greater pride in the organization, a stronger spirit of cooperation and teamwork, and more feelings of ownership and personal responsibility.

What are some of the other characteristics of credible leaders?

- They do what they say they will do. They keep their promises and follow up on their commitments.
- Their actions are consistent with the wishes of the people they lead. They have a clear idea of what others value and what they can do.
- They believe in the inherent self-worth of others. And they learn "how to discover and communicate the shared values and visions that can form a common ground on which all can stand."
- They are capable of making a difference in the lives of others—and liberating the leader in everyone.
- They admit their mistakes. They realize that attempting to hide mistakes is much more damaging and erodes credibility. But when they admit to making a mistake, they do something about it.
- They arouse optimistic feelings and enable their people to hold positive thoughts about the possibilities of success.
- They create a climate for learning characterized by trust and openness.

Source: Credibility: How Leaders Gain and Lose It. Why People Demand It, by James M. Kouzes and Barry Z. Posner. Jossey-Bass Inc., Publishers, 350 Sansome St., San Francisco, CA 94104.

An **authoritarian leader** dominates and directs a group according to personal goals and objectives, regardless of how consistent these goals are with the group members' goals.

A **democratic leader** directs a group according to the goals of its members and allows them to form their own conclusions.

A **laissez-faire leader** lets group members "do their own thing."

"Evidence suggests that neither the directive nor nondirective approach is consistently more effective. Each approach works better under certain conditions."[11] "The key to leadership effectiveness is matching the appropriate style to the group environment."[12] Thus, if group members are very task oriented, they may be productive while working with a laissez-faire leader. The laissez-faire style may be disastrous, however, if group members are unable to function productively on their own. In contrast, a democratic leader will work well with a group that requires minimal supervision. If group members cannot accomplish their tasks because they lack self-discipline, an authoritarian leader may be needed to direct their activities and assign specific responsibilities. Research on leadership style suggests that the power position of the leader, the task at hand, and the needs of the group should determine how and when a leader must adapt his or her style to any given group.[13]

PATTERNS OF LEADER/LEADERSHIP EMERGENCE

If a leader is not appointed for a group, one of the questions that arises is, "How does a person interested in becoming a leader proceed?" Research shows that emergent leaders exhibit a significantly higher rate of participation than do nonleaders.[14] In addition, "leaders become leaders when they exert influence over others on behalf of the group."[15] It is also noted that leaders tend to conform to the group's norms, values, and goals, while displaying the motivation to lead—knowing the rules of order, having charisma, being positive about themselves, encouraging others to communicate, being a supportive listener.

There appear to be a series of actions you should carry out if you *don't* want to be a leader. These, though disputed by some, include:[16]

1. be late or miss important meetings.
2. be uninformed about a problem or issue.
3. manifest apathy and lack of interest.
4. attempt to dominate conversations.
5. be rigid and inflexible when expressing viewpoints.
6. use offensive and abusive language.
7. be quiet.
8. fail to provide solutions to problems.

There also are research findings to indicate that there is gender and ethnic bias in leader emergence. Men seem to have an advantage over women. In addition, there is an ethnic bias. Ethnic minorities, in mixed ethnic groups, have difficulty emerging as leaders.[17] This does not, of course, mean that women and ethnic minority members cannot and should not be leaders. The awareness of the need to understand group process, to be an effective communicator, and to be prepared to work hard to achieve the leader position can aid the person of any background to develop the strategies to achieve her or his goal.

WHY PEOPLE DESIRE TO BE LEADERS

With the understanding that there is a great deal of responsibility placed on leaders, that they often find themselves the target of attacks, and that they are blamed if things don't go right, why would anyone want to be a leader? Ask yourself, would you like to be the chairperson of the board of a large corporation or a bank branch manager? Why do people want to be a Director of Corporate Communication, a CEO, or the Director of Staff Training?

Five basic reasons why people want to be leaders can be mentioned:

1. *Information.* The leader is privy to special information. Many leaders like to be "in the know."
2. *Rewards.* Leaders receive praise, attention, payment, power, and special privileges for being in the position. There is a certain aura that comes with the office, as well as respect and power. Being a corporate executive making several million dollars a year seems to be more satisfying to some than working for a fraction of that amount, in spite of the greater responsibilities, pressure, and time constraints. Some people also like to be in the "public eye." Note that more than one corporate and business leader does advertisements for their companies, whether the organization is a local auto dealership or the product-producing corporation itself.
3. *Expectations.* Certain people have enough faith in themselves to believe that they can accomplish the task or have better solutions than someone else. Listen to politicians running for office. They have platforms that attempt to explain why they are more capable of making things better than their opponents. Their ability to persuade a majority of people that their plan or their abilities are better than the opponents' is one of the reasons they are elected.
4. *Acceptance.* Some people believe that they gain respect by being selected as leader. They equate the title of president, chairperson, or boss with being accepted.

5. *Status.* There is evidence that acquiring status in one group can allow for status in other groups. A record of past leadership often is the basis for selecting someone to another leadership position. Members of the board of directors of hospitals, corporations, and banks are often the same people who hold leadership in other organizations.

RESPONSIBILITIES OF LEADERS

Regardless of style, a group leader has the responsibility for guiding the group toward accomplishing its task and for maintaining it as a functioning unit. For this reason, the leader should be as knowledgeable in the group's particular area of concern as all the group members are, so that the concern is treated thoroughly and objectively. Many groups prefer their leaders to serve primarily as organizing agents who lead the discussion—more as a moderator—rather than as active participants. Such practices stem from a fear that a leader who participates by citing personal views and evidence may dominate a discussion. This does not suggest, however, that a leader cannot or should not participate; it only implies that care should be taken to allow and encourage all members of the group to participate.

A leader also has unique responsibilities in a discussion because he or she opens the discussion, establishes the topic area, and sets the ground rules. The leader also may need to do such tasks as establish the meeting date and place, and arrange the physical facilities. If necessary, the leader should introduce group members. As the discussion proceeds, he or she can provide meaningful transitions from one area of the agenda to the next. A good leader also concludes the discussion with a summary that highlights what the group has accomplished and what the next step will be. Clearly, the leader has many responsibilities for ensuring the successful outcome of any group discussion, and these responsibilities require commitment to the group and its objective.

It is important that the leader try to avoid **groupthink**—a way of thinking that develops when the participants become more interested in group unity than in rigorous decision making. When groupthink prevails, group members may be reluctant to use high-level criteria to override decisions that threaten group unity. In order to avoid groupthink, a leader should be impartial and avoid endorsing any positions until after complete, active discussion takes place; instruct everyone to critically evaluate ideas and express doubts; appoint several members to be "devil's advocates" and be critical evaluators; subdivide the group to separately work on the same question and encourage the airing of differences; and invite outside experts to attend meetings and provide interpretive insights.[18]

A leader has responsibilities prior to, during, and following a meeting. These responsibilities include:[19]

In preparation for the meeting:

- Define the purpose of the meeting
- List specific outcomes that should or must be produced from this meeting
- Establish the starting and ending times of the meeting
- Notify members of the purpose and/or the agenda, their necessary preparations, and time and place of the meeting
- If specific resource persons are needed, advise them and prepare them for the meeting
- Make all necessary physical arrangements
- Bring necessary work items (e.g., pencils, paper, charts, data sheets, reports)

During the meeting:

- Describe the importance and purpose of the meeting
- Make an effort to establish a climate of trust and informality (if appropriate)
- Present information handbooks (if appropriate)
- Stimulate creative thinking (if appropriate)
- Stimulate critical thinking
- Promote teamwork and cooperation
- Equalize opportunities to participate and influence

Follow-up to the meeting:

- Remind members who agreed to do post-meeting work
- If minutes are kept, be sure they are written and distributed
- As necessary, notify others of the group's actions or decisions
- If work is necessary before a future meeting, be sure it is done

THE LEADER AS COMMUNICATOR

There is a fundamental link between human communication and leading. Among today's compelling communicators are influential business and corporate leaders such as: Charlotte Beers (Ogilvy and Mather), Dr. Audrey E. Evans (Children's Hospital of Philadelphia), Mary Kay Place (Mary Kay Cosmetics), Bill Gates (Microsoft), and Madam Walker (Walker Cosmetics). "Leaders use slogans, speeches, threats, promises, rituals, goals, gestures, and a host of other symbols in order to influence others." A communication perspective on leadership emphasizes the group as a product of communication and that the leader is the catalyst for the communication.[20] Leaders not only use words

---

How to Run a Good Meeting

Here are some tips on how to run a meeting:

- *Don't compete with group members. Give their ideas precedence over yours.*

- *Listen to everyone. Paraphrase, but don't judge.*

- *Don't put anyone on the defensive. Assume that everyone's ideas have value.*

- *Control the dominant people without alienating them.*

- *Realize that your interest and alertness are contagious.*

- *Keep all participants informed about where they are and what's expected of them. Keep notes on flip charts or a board that everyone can see.*

- *Check with the person who owns the problem to find out if an idea is worth pursuing or if a proposed solution is satisfactory.*

- *Give others a turn at running the meeting. Those who learn to lead learn how to participate.*

Source: *Financial Times,* 14 E. 60th St., New York, NY 10022.

well but "exhibit significantly more nonverbal cues than do nonleaders in task-oriented and informal small groups."[21]

EFFECTIVE LEADERSHIP QUESTIONING

One of the most important responsibilities of a leader is to monitor the proceedings and interject appropriate questions concerning such matters as stimulating discussion, clarifying ideas, and resolving conflict. Some problems and model questions to ask include:[22]

ISSUE:	To draw out a silent member
QUESTION TO ASK:	"Does anyone who hasn't spoken care to comment? Or, "Alexander, what is your opinion of . . . ?"
ISSUE:	To call attention to points that have not been considered
QUESTION TO ASK:	"Does anyone have any information about _____?" Or, "Lisa, would you care to explore this angle of the topic in more detail?"
ISSUE:	To keep the discussion focused on the subject
QUESTION TO ASK:	"That's interesting, but just how does this point fit in with the issue being considered?" Or, "I must have missed something you said. Will you please explain the connection between your suggestion and the point we were discussing?"
ISSUE:	To use conflict constructively
QUESTION TO ASK:	"Since we do not seem to be able to resolve this difference now, could we move on to the next point?" Or, "What aspects of the opposing views are acceptable to all of us?"
ISSUE:	To suggest the need for more information
QUESTION TO ASK:	"Do we have enough information to decide now?" Or, "Is it agreeable to the group that we ask a sub-committee to investigate and bring back the needed information to our next session?"
ISSUE:	To call attention of the source of information
QUESTION TO ASK:	"Where did this information come from?"
ISSUE:	To focus attention on issues rather than personalities
QUESTION TO ASK:	"Which seems to be more important, the facts in the case or the supporters of the different points of view?"

ISSUE:	To prevent few from monopolizing the discussion
QUESTION TO ASK:	"Excuse me, Nadia. Before you continue, may I ask if anyone has a comment on the point you have just made?" Or, "May we hear from someone who hasn't expressed an opinion?"
ISSUE:	To suggest the need for closing the discussion
QUESTION TO ASK:	"We're scheduled to finish discussion in about five minutes. Is there a final comment?"

• • • In Summary • • •

Groups are made up of people. Participants are those members of the group who interact to bring about the actions of the group. Leaders are those who guide the group. Leadership refers to those who influence the group to accomplish its goal. All group members should remember that the entire group is responsible and accountable for final decisions. Groups operate by different formal and informal patterns that link members together.

═══ Business Communication in Practice ═══

1. a. The following are statements on which you are required to take a stand. You may thoroughly agree (TA), agree (A), disagree (D), or thoroughly disagree (TD). Mark each statement with the relevant code.
   1. Corporations have an obligation to their stockholders to make profits; this obligation supersedes all others.
   2. Every member of an organization should be permitted to present views at a meeting, regardless of how long this may take.
   3. The changing moral structure of the present society has led to confusion and breakdown of business morality.
   4. Advertising is necessary for the continuation of the free enterprise system.
   5. Businesses should grant health care benefits to domestic partners, regardless of gender.
   b. You are assigned to a group when you come to class. For each of the five statements, the group must reach a consensus (total agreement) on one of the four responses (thoroughly agree through thoroughly disagree). Group members may rewrite any of the statements until they come to agreement on one of the items.
   c. After the small-group discussion, the class meets to discuss the following questions:

1. What effect did the differences in the group members' backgrounds have on the group's decision?
2. What was the role of the leader in the group?
3. What inferences about how groups operate can be drawn from this experience?
4. What was the greatest problem the group encountered in reaching its decision? Could this problem have been resolved? How?

2. Your class will be divided into groups.
   a. Each group is to take twenty minutes in which to agree on what a time traveler should take into the future, using the following information for these decisions:[23]

   A time machine travels to the year 5847. The world has been destroyed in a nuclear holocaust, and all that remain are a few men and women living a primitive existence and having no record or memory of the past. The traveler decides to rebuild the future world but can make only one trip back and forth in time. On the trip, which can encompass any year between the dawn of humanity and the present time, the traveler may collect such useful items as living things, printed materials, food, toilet paper, and so forth. The only limitation is one of weight: excluding the weight of the time traveler, no more than two hundred pounds of material may be carried into time. Problem: what specific items should the time traveler take into the future?

   b. After the small-group discussion, the class meets to discuss the following questions:
      1. What effect did the differences in the group members' backgrounds have on the group's decision?
      2. What was the role of the leader in the group?
      3. What inferences about how groups operate can be drawn from this experience?
      4. What was the greatest problem the group encountered in reaching its decision? How could this problem have been resolved?

═══ **Diversity Simulation** ═══

Directions: You are the supervisor of a repair crew for the telephone company. Each member of the crew drives a small service truck to and from his/her various jobs. A new truck has just been allocated to you for distribution. The new truck is a Chevrolet.

Step A: You are to decide on your own who should get the new truck. Use the advice given in this and the previous chapters about how to reach conclusions. Write your decision and criteria and bring them to class.

Step B: The instructor will divide the class into small groups. Each group will meet and decide who should receive the truck. Each group will report back to the class on who was selected and the procedure and criteria used in making the selection.

Step C: A discussion on decision making should follow the group reports.

Facts about the trucks and the people in the crew that report to you:

Tom   17 years with the company, has a 2-year-old Ford truck
Betty   11 years with the company, has a 5-year-old Dodge truck
Jane   10 years with the company, has a 4-year-old Ford truck
Charlie   5 years with the company, has a 3-year-old Ford truck
Hank   3 years with the company, has a 5-year-old Chevrolet truck

Most of the people do all of their driving in the city, but Jane and Charlie cover the jobs in the suburbs and surrounding areas. You ask each person to submit a statement explaining his or her reasons for getting the new truck. Here are their reasons:

Tom: When a new Chevrolet truck becomes available, I think I should get it because I have the most seniority and don't like my present truck. I own a Chevrolet car, and I prefer a Chevrolet truck, which I drove before I got the Ford.

Betty: I feel I deserve a new truck and it certainly is my turn. My present truck is old, and since the more senior person has a fairly new truck, you should give me the new one. I have taken excellent care of my present Dodge and have kept it looking like new. A person deserves to be rewarded if she treats a company truck like her own.

Jane: I have more driving to do than most of the other people because my work is in the suburbs. I have a fairly old truck and feel I should have the new one because I do so much driving.

Charlie: The heater in my present truck is inadequate. Since Hank backed into the door of my truck, it has never been repaired to fit right. The door lets in too much cold air, and I attribute my frequent colds to this. I want to have a warm truck, since I have a good deal of driving to do. As long as it has good tires, brakes, and is comfortable, I don't care about the make.

Hank: I have the poorest truck in the crew. It is 5 years old, and before I got it, it had been in a bad wreck. It has never been good and I've put up with it for three years. It's about time I got a good truck to drive, and it seems only fair that the next one should be mine. I have a good driving record. The only accident I had was when I sprung the door of Charlie's truck when he opened it as I backed out of the garage. I hope the new truck is a Ford, because I prefer to drive one.

● ● ● Notes ● ● ●

1. Julie Ann Wambach, *Group Problem Solving: Through Communication Styles* (Dubuque, IA: Kendall/Hunt, 1992), p. 150.
2. For a discussion of creativity, see Daniel Goleman, *Emotional Intelligence* (New York: Bantam Books, 1995).
3. Based on the work of James E. Sikell, Florida Maxima Corporation.
4. Dorrine Turecamo, "Perfect Timing," *Successful Meetings* (October 1992), 119.
5. Kenneth D. Benne and Paul Sheets, "Functional Roles of Group Members," *Journal of Social Issues* 4 (Spring 1948): 41–49.
6. Dale Leathers, *Successful Nonverbal Communication* (New York: Macmillan, 1992), p. 376.
7. J. Dan Rothwell, *In Mixed Company* (Ft. Worth, TX: Harcourt Brace, 1992), pp. 116–119.
8. James MacGregor Burns, *Leadership* (New York: Harper and Row, 1978). For an analysis of leadership by noted social critics and leadership experts, see the March–April 1987 issue of *Liberal Education* 73. Also see Judy B. Rosener, "Ways Women Lead," *Harvard Business Review* (November–December 1990): 119–125.
9. Charles C. Manz and Henry P. Sims, Jr., *Superleadership* (New York: Prentice Hall, 1989).
10. Ralph White and Ronald Lippitt, "Leader Behavior and Member Reactions in Three Social Climates," in D. Cartwright and A. Zander, eds., *Group Dynamics* (New York: Harper and Row, 1968), pp. 318–335.
11. Fred Fiedler, "When to Lead When to Stand Back," *Psychology Today* (September 1987): 26.
12. Rothwell, 147.
13. For a discussion of leadership style, see Fred Fielder, *A Theory of Leadership Effectiveness* (New York: McGraw-Hill, 1967).
14. Arlene Schubert and George Schubert, "Leadership Emergence Via Nonverbal Communication," an unpublished paper presented at the Central States Speech Association convention, Chicago, April 13, 1978, p. 1.
15. Michael Hackman and Craig Johnson, "Teaching Leadership from a Communication Perspective," an unpublished paper, n.d., p. 6.
16. Rothwell, 136.
17. Ibid., 140.
18. "Group Problem-Solving and Meeting Dynamics" (Cincinnati, OH: Southwestern Publishing, 1993), a blind review manuscript, p. 7.
19. Wambach, 168–169.
20. Hackman and Johnson, 2.
21. Schubert and Schubert, 3.
22. Based on a concept developed by Patricia Hayes, Indiana University–Bradley.
23. Contributed by Isa Engleberg, Prince George's Community College, Largo, Maryland. Used with permission.

Public Speaking:
The Purposes and Types
of Business Speeches

EXPECTED OUTCOMES

After completing this chapter, you should be able to:

- Define public speaking.
- Explain the importance of public business speaking.
- Define and explain informative business speaking.
- Define and explain persuasive speaking.
- Define and explain the speech of introduction, speech of welcome, the award presentation, speech of acceptance, the after-dinner speech, the motivational speech, the sales presentation.
- Conduct a question-and-answer session following a speech.

I *work for an advertising agency. My supervisor asked me to represent the firm by making a presentation to a ninth grade general business class. I prepared a speech about careers in advertising. The kids were very inattentive. When the teacher asked for questions, I expected very few queries. Almost every hand shot up. They started asking about how advertisers decide on what appeals to use in developing ads, and how television commercials are made. Afterwards, the teacher told me that the class had been divided into groups and were developing advertising campaigns for products, including the making of television commercials. If I had only called the teacher in advance and asked what he thought the students would have been interested in learning about, I wouldn't have*

> *wasted their time and mine preparing the speech I gave; I would have talked about campaigns and production. I know about those subjects, and they wanted my help. I really learned a lesson about preparing speeches from this experience.*

Public Speaking Defined

Public speaking involves a transaction between a speaker and an audience. You may think that you do not need to be concerned about public speaking, but this is not the case. In the course of your career—and probably sooner than later—you will likely need to give speeches. Learning the process of how to prepare and present a speech should make the process more effective for both you and your listeners.

You also may think that it is impossible to "become" a public speaker. Despite the old adage "speakers are born, not made," the evidence indicates otherwise. You also may perceive that you always will be highly stressed during a speech—that is probably also wrong. "The goals of a public speaking course [or a course which contains a unit in public speaking] include increasing the quality of presentation performance and simultaneously lowering levels of stress experienced during presentation."[1] Research indicates that individuals who have speech training not only perform at higher levels (quality of speech effectiveness) than non-speech trained subjects, but also have less speaker anxiety, commonly referred to as stage fright.[2]

When a speaker stands up to present material to an audience, there is a purpose—something the speaker wants to accomplish. Traditionally, the purpose of speeches or presentations has been considered as either informative or persuasive. However, some communication experts contend that all speaking is persuasive in that any speech attempts to get the audience to do something. For the purposes of our discussion, we will accept that all communication does contain elements of persuasion. "The audience in the traditional informative speaking format must be persuaded to accept the information presented by the speaker. On the other hand, it is acknowledged that the structure of a message and the types of appeals used in the persuasive format differ in that they extend beyond those used in preparing a traditional informative speech."[3]

Using that perspective, material will be presented on both informative speaking and persuasive speaking so that you will have an understanding of the tools and techniques for both types of presentation.

Informative Speaking in Business

The primary purpose of an informative speech is to enhance the listeners' understanding about some particular topic.

TYPES OF INFORMATIVE SPEECHES

Informative speeches in business may be classified according to specific types including the information speech, the informative briefing, the technical report, and the oral presentation of the professional paper.

Information Speech

In an **information business speech,** either the speaker assumes that the audience has little or no knowledge of the subject, or the speaker aims material at the listeners' level of knowledge and attempts to enhance understanding. The speaker's responsibility is to ensure that, upon completion of the presentation, the information or description or directions have been given in such a way that the listeners now understand something that they previously knew little or nothing about.

Because the listener may be relatively uninformed, the speaker must cover the most basic ideas. Exposition in the form of background ideas, definition of terms, and examples must be used in developing the presentation. In speaking to a college group about management techniques used in business, for instance, it would be necessary to define such terms as management, and management techniques. Restating main points so the listeners can remember them is central to the information speech.

Informative Briefing

The **informative briefing** is presented to an audience that already has knowledge about the subject area. Much communication in government, business, and organizations takes the form of briefings. Quite likely, the audience will be a group of professionals in the same field as the speaker; therefore, the amount of exposition necessary in the presentation is limited. The speaker can assume that because people share expertise in a field, they can handle more detailed information.

Technical Report

Technical reports are the backbone of much decision making in organizations. A **technical report** is a "concise, clear statement explaining a process,

---

When Presenting and Competing

If you have to make a business presentation against competition, begin by finding out just how strong your competition is. What to do:

● If it's strong, try to be the first one to present. If you can set high enough standards, you might make the others suffer by comparison.

● If the competition is weak, consider going last. You might just provide what the decision-makers have been waiting to hear.

The key: *Make your presentation as polished and well-planned as you can, regardless of when you present.*

Source: The McGraw-Hill 36-Hour Course: Business Presentations, by Lani Arredondo, McGraw-Hill Inc., 1221 Avenue of the Americas, New York, NY 10020.

detailing a technique, or discussing new elements either to individuals within a business or industry or to people outside the organization."[4]

Like any other informative speech, a good technical report offers enough background to clarify the proposal before the group. Often it is helpful to supply handouts of any technical drawings or statistics so that each member of the audience will have that information for immediate and for future reference. Audience members tend to appreciate the opportunity to participate in a thorough question-and-answer session following a technical report so that points can be clarified and other possible viewpoints explored.

Professional Paper

A variation of the technical report is the presentation of a professional paper. A **professional paper** is usually a research-based, comprehensive written analysis of a topic in one's professional field. Most business professionals are expected to participate in professional societies, for example, the American Management Association and the American Society for Training and Development. Consequently, individuals are called upon to present their research and findings in professional papers at annual meetings and conventions of such societies and professional organizations.

CHARACTERISTICS OF INFORMATIVE SPEECHES

Certain characteristics typically define an effective speech. It should be audience centered, it should contain supporting details, and it should attract the attention of the listeners.

Audience Centered

As an informative speaker, you must ascertain if the listeners know anything about the topic you intend to address. Are the listeners experts or novices in the field? Do they share your interest in and commitment to the material you intend to cover? These questions can guide you in making decisions about the vocabulary you will use and the development of supporting details to clarify your points.

Supporting Details

A good informative speech should provide sufficient supporting data to enhance the understanding of the listeners. Thus, the selection of statistics, examples, testimony, and analogies should be guided by your perception of what will be informative and interesting.

In developing and presenting a speech, the sender must be aware that the presentation should be audience centered, contain supporting details, and attract the attention of the listeners.

Level of Interest

One of the occupational hazards of informative speakers is the "so what?" or "ho hum" response from listeners. Listeners have been found to be more attentive to speakers who use a variety of familiar, concrete, humorous, novel, and vivid materials.

Persuasive Speaking in Business

A **persuasive speech** is intended to influence the opinion or behavior of an audience. The materials in a persuasive speech are derived from problems about which people hold differing beliefs and opinions, such as controversial matters that call for decisions or action. The persuasive speaker tells listeners what they ought to believe or do.

Within the organization, persuasion generally would involve an employee making a proposal for action, such as a new procedure, a change of policy, a reorganization, or employment of additional staff. Outside of the corporation, the organization's representative might be attempting to get the audience to take an action that directly affects the company or group he or she represents, such as approving a zoning change to permit plant construction, relaxing pollution control standards, or purchasing the company's products.

GOALS OF PERSUASIVE SPEAKING

A persuasive speech or presentation may be directed toward either conviction or actuation.

Conviction

In a **speech of conviction,** the speaker attempts to convince the listener to believe as the speaker does. Topics in this category might include "There is no real danger of nuclear fallout from atomic plants," or "XYZ Corporation has developed a clear set of equal opportunity guidelines."

Actuation

A **speech of actuation** should move the members of the audience to take the desired action that the speaker has proposed: buy the product, sign the petition, go on strike, or adopt the plan presented.

PERSUASIVE STRATEGIES

Historically, the process of persuasion has centered on developing an ethical, logical, and emotional platform. It is believed that listeners are more likely to go along with your plan or arguments if you make them feel that they can trust you because of your credibility, the strength of your arguments, and your appeal to their needs.

Developing Credibility

The persuasive message that you present can be made compelling through the development of your own credibility as a speaker. You can demonstrate your credibility (that you are a believable source of information) by establishing your trustworthiness and competence.[5]

Some speakers demonstrate how their past record should lead the audience to have faith in them. Showing how your persuasive plan is in the best interests of your listeners also can enhance your credibility. Another way to be perceived as credible is by demonstrating that you are well researched on the subject.

Psychological Appeals

As you analyze your audience, try to determine the psychological state of its members and what psychological appeals might be most motivating to them. Remember, "emotions are simply more motivating than facts."[6] This does not eliminate the need for factual, solid support for your position, but requires that you use both facts and emotional materials.

In selecting supporting materials, choose those that contain the desired elements of the appeals within them. Though there are many psychological appeals available, a recent marketing study indicates that the most persuasive are romance/sexuality, guilt, pity, power, worry, embarrassment, and fear.[7]

Building the Arguments

To succeed in your persuasive mission, you must present claims in a way that will get the audience to agree with you. One determination necessary is what type of arguments to use. The two most common methods of developing arguments in the Western culture are the deductive and inductive argument format.

Deductive Arguments If you determine that your listeners already agree with your point of view, you may be able to build your speech deductively—arguing from general to specific points. The **deductive argument,** which is historically the traditional and formal method of viewing persuasion, typically follows a syllogism form:

    Major premise: All speakers who prepare achieve their speaking goals.
    Minor premise: You are a speaker who prepares.
    Conclusion: Therefore, you achieve your speaking goals.

Inductive Arguments Should your analysis suggest that your audience opposes your point of view, it might be wise to structure your ideas as inductive arguments. **Inductive arguments** are developed by listing specific examples that listeners can accept, leading them to reach a general conclusion with which they may finally agree. The theory is that if they accept the examples, and the examples lead to the conclusion, the conclusion will be accepted as well. For example, as a listener you question whether or not you can be an effective speaker. The speaker appeals to your logic by leading you through this inductive argument:

    You are bright and articulate.
    You have something to say.
    You have been trained in speaking skills.
    Therefore, you can be an effective speaker.

    If you accept that you are bright and articulate and that you have some-

---

A Speech Tip

When preparing a speech, begin at the end.
  Write down what you will want the audience to do as a result of having heard your speech.
  Keep this in perspective as you're preparing the rest of the speech.

Source: *Speechwriter's Newsletter,* 212 W. Superior St., Ste. 200, Chicago, IL 60610.

thing to say, and you have been trained in speaking skills, then you should accept the argument that you can be an effective speaker.

Persuasive speakers should also be aware that, in reality, no single reason will be a good reason for all members of the audience. People tend to attach the label "good" to those reasons that are most suitable for them or that make sense to them, whether or not those reasons are actually the most appropriate for all of the people involved.

In order to build effective arguments, consider the concept that explains decision making based on field-related standards, group standards, and individual standards for judgment.

Field-related standards of judgment center on the idea that different types of businesses, and the employees of those businesses, have varying concepts as to what constitutes a good reason. Profit, speed, efficiency, community service, employee welfare, safety, well-being, and job security are specific, field-related good reasons.

The particular gathering to which you are speaking may have **group standards for making decisions.** Ask yourself about the group: Do they consistently accept or reject certain types of ideas? Do they positively or negatively respond to specific things time and time again? When they have made similar decisions in the past, were they consistent in the reasons for reaching these conclusions?

Is there a person who has a great deal of influence in the group's decision making? If so, it may be effective to direct your reasons toward that individual, for if you convince that person, the others might go along, thus putting into effect the concept of **individual standards for judgment.** Is it possible to identify what will influence that person? Is the person more affected by strong, logical appeals or psychological appeals?

Resistance to Change

Persuasive speaking is a difficult process. Regardless of how well you establish your credibility, develop psychological appeals, or structure your arguments, you may not succeed in your mission. Some basic tensions might cause individuals to resist your arguments and appeals and be unwilling to change or adopt your point of view. The research on resistance to change suggests that people will tend to resist being persuaded if any of these applies:[8]

1. They have extreme attitudes on the matter being considered.
2. The source is held in low esteem.
3. The suggestion or idea is contrary to their own experience.
4. The proposed idea opposes their reference group.
5. The suggested change requires altering habits developed in early life.

Profile: Robert Goldberg, executive communications consultant, Decker Communications, a national communications consulting and skills building company.

How would you characterize the importance corporations place on presentation skills?

From personal experience, I know communication training for corporate America is growing. Many of our clients need the training for their employees even more when the competition heats up and they need to master these very skills in order to stay alive. In an age of employee "rightsizing," many of our clients tell us that their remaining employees are the best of the field and they want to make them the best they can be so that they are willing to pay the money to see the results of training: enhanced employee performance.

Is the absence of strong presentation skills a career limiting situation?

Definitely. First, people find they are called upon to speak as members of professions they believed would not demand that of them. For example, the more technical professionals (computer programmers, accountants, and engineers) are called upon to deal with clients as part of the sales force, and they are now no longer able to "hide." Also, there is no longer a clear division between the sales force and the technical expert. The client wants to see the expert, not just the slick salesperson. Second, people are seeing presentation skills as a strong factor in career advancement. When people see colleagues with fewer years of experience or lesser skills (or equal skills and experience) promoted because of better presentation skills, they get the picture.

6. They have gone on public record as favoring or opposing the idea, movement, or process.

Does this resistance to change mean that you shouldn't attempt to persuade? Absolutely not! Many business dealings are persuasive in nature. Knowing, however, that there can be resistance should inspire you to be more diligent in developing your presentations. You need to accept that it may be impossible to persuade everyone but that you may be able to convince enough of the audience, through effective speech development, to accomplish your mission. A politician once gave this advice to a speech writer: "In writing this speech remember that 30 percent of the audience will agree with me no matter what I say. Thirty percent will disagree with me no matter what I say. It's the other 40 percent that I need to persuade." This philosophy is good advice in politics, sales, or in any persuasive situation. You might not be able to get everyone to agree with you, but work toward getting the rest.[9]

Special Occasion Speeches

As a representative of a business, you may be asked to present a speech on a special occasion of some kind. Because they are so specific in nature, they may be informative or persuasive, or have elements of the two. Although there are a great variety of special occasion speeches, those in which you are most likely to participate as a member of the business world are the speech of introduction, the speech of welcome, the speech of presentation, the speech of acceptance, the after-dinner speech, the motivational speech, and the sales presentation. In addition, most speeches conclude with a question-and-answer session.

In giving any special occasion presentation, the speaker should prepare by carefully analyzing the audience and the occasion.

SPEECH OF INTRODUCTION

A **speech of introduction** is one in which a selected individual introduces a speaker to the audience. This type of speech should let the audience know who the speaker is, the subject, the speaker's qualifications to speak about that subject, and other interesting ideas about the speaker or the subject. The speech should be brief (from one to a maximum of five minutes), draw attention to the speaker and not to the introducer, and not embarrass the speaker (unless for some special reason it is appropriate). Make sure you can correctly pronounce the speaker's name. If possible, repeat the speaker's name several times during the speech of introduction so that the audience becomes familiar with it.

Avoid trite phrases like "I'd now like to turn the floor over to" (it's meaningless); "I'm sure you will all enjoy this presentation" (it sets a very difficult task for the speaker); and "It is an honor, privilege, and pleasure to present to you" (it has been so overused it has lost its impact). Instead, start with a story, joke, or a personal reference of your acquaintance with the speaker.

SPEECH OF WELCOME

The **speech of welcome** extends a sincere greeting to a person or to a group. In the business context, this welcome is a common courtesy when a person or a group visits a company or when guests are being honored at a special event. It is usually a short and cordial presentation. The speaker identifies the group being welcomed and the person or organization offering the welcome.

SPEECH OF PRESENTATION

Many organizations publicly observe achievements with presentations of awards, gifts, and memorials. A speech usually culminates in the giving of a tangible token, such as a medal, ribbon, plaque, scholarship, or check. The **speech of presentation** includes mentioning the award, the persons receiving it, the donor, why the presentation is being made, and the qualifications of the winner. Consider when the winner's name will be announced and when the recipient will come forward. In some instances, in order to build suspense, the recipient's name is withheld until the last line of the presentation. In other cases, the name is announced immediately, the winner's credentials are given, and then the presentation of the award is made.

SPEECH OF ACCEPTANCE

When a person receives an honor, an award, or a gift in a public presentation, the recipient is expected to express an appropriate appreciation in a **speech of acceptance.** In some instances, a simple "thank you" is in order, while sometimes recipients feel a need to further express appreciation, pay tribute to the donor, or share the honor with others by referring to their contributions. If appropriate, humor sometimes breaks the tension and is a welcome addition. The acceptance should be presented in a genuine manner. Many speeches of acceptance are too long, mention too many people, and lack sincerity. Do not apologize or belittle yourself for receiving the honor. The individuals who selected you believed you were worthy of the award. By telling them you are not worthy, in an attempt to feign humility, you are questioning their judgment.

AFTER-DINNER SPEECH

The primary goal of most **after-dinner speeches** is to entertain. Entertainment is normally considered to be humor, but it is not always necessary to inspire laughter in order to entertain. A speaker who is interesting or gets an audience to relax can also be called entertaining.

Most after-dinner speeches are composed in one of these formats: (1) a series of anecdotes that are loosely developed about a central theme, (2) a chronological narrative built on the speaker's own experiences or the experiences of the person or organization being honored, or (3) a series of stories built around a theme.

THE MOTIVATIONAL SPEECH

One form of speaking that is prevalent in business and industry is the **motivational speech**—a speech presented to the staff to encourage greater productivity and happiness in their work and in their personal lives.

To have maximum impact, a good motivational speech should be adapted carefully to the needs and interests of the listeners. The speech, designed to inspire or stimulate the meeting attenders, usually develops from the personal experience of the speaker. Often, the speakers will use their experience in rising through the corporate ranks or achieving their life goals as the example for how "you, too, can make it in today's competitive society."

THE SALES SPEECH

One of the important persuasive tasks of many businesses is the sale of products or services. A sales speech is the process of persuading prospective customers to buy a commodity or service, or to act favorably upon an idea that has commercial significance to the seller.[10] The presentation will normally take place at the home site of the customers, be given before a group who will use the product or service and/or the purchasing staff. It differs from one-on-one sales, as you will be dealing with a group, in a formal setting, rather than speaking one-to-one.

Certain techniques are important to a sales speech:[11]

1. Establish a confident and friendly atmosphere. Make the customers know that you are there to be of service.
2. Focus attention on the customers' problem or need.
3. Solve the problem or need by linking product features to customers' benefits.
4. Avoid very technical information unless your analysis indicates that this is the type of customer who must know the specific details.
5. Demonstrate the product if it will help the potential customer understand it better.

QUESTION-AND-ANSWER SESSIONS

Following a speech, whether it is informative or persuasive, many speakers are asked to respond to inquiries in a **question-and-answer session.** This session requires that you have as much back-up information as possible. To help you to develop your answers, try to anticipate questions and be prepared with the necessary facts, examples, and illustrations.

Some useful techniques in handling question-and-answer sessions include:

1. Make sure you understand the question. In order to check your comprehension, paraphrase it for the inquirer.
2. If you don't understand the question, ask for clarification.
3. Repeat the question for the benefit of the other members of the audience. They may not be able to hear the questioner.
4. Don't let the questions take you off the topic.
5. Answer directly. Indicate what you know, why you believe it, or what you believe. If you have no answer, either say so or volunteer to find out the information and send it to the questioner or provide it at the next session.
6. Before answering, you might want to compose yourself and think through the answer. Some speakers jot a quick outline or write down some key words.
7. Look at the questioner as you answer the question, but also present the material to the audience as a whole.
8. If the questioner starts to give a counterspeech, politely interrupt and ask for his or her question.
9. After answering, check with the questioner to determine whether you answered the question to his or her satisfaction.

Special Challenges during the Question-and-Answer Period

These techniques should be reserved for difficult moments with difficult questioners. Use them sparingly and cautiously. Above all, do not engage In a heated argument in front of others. Take the argument "off-line" or bring it to a swift close. Your goal is to maintain control of the session and underscore the good will of the audience.

Do not let the arguer move you off track; keep bringing your remarks back to your main points.

Example: "I wish to emphasize the main idea here . . ."

Disagree about the conclusion or the interpretation but not the person.

Example: "I don't agree with your assertion that . . ."

If the arguer engages in personal attacks and/or snide remarks, take the "higher road."

Example: "It is important to me to have a professional interchange. Let us both agree to discuss the topic and not our personalities."

If you have explained something several times to the group and one person still doesn't "get it," offer to continue the discussion "off-line."

> *Example:* *"I recognize that this is still troubling you but I don't feel that we can take more of the group's time with this issue. Can we continue this during the coffee break?"*

If you are at an impasse, agree with the other person's right to believe/feel/interpret/conclude, as he/she does but disagree that you must believe/feel/interpret/conclude the same.

> *Example:* *"I respect your right to believe as you do but since my life experiences have been different, I believe very differently. I ask you to respect my different, but equally valid, belief."*

If you can, ignore rude comments and personal attacks completely or dismiss them as irrelevant to a professional discussion.

> *Example:* *"That comment seems out of place in a discussion of professional equals."*

If you are labeled with negative comments, respond assertively.

> *Example:* *"I do not appreciate being called materialistic. Surely my years in the Peace Corps gave me an appreciation of what really matters in life."*

When questions are "off-the-wall" and you choose to respond, quickly answer and move on.

> *Example:* *"I'm afraid that's outside of our scope of our discussion today. The issue I want to clearly convey is that . . ."*

Don't try to respond to a vague, critical remark, ask for clarification.

> *Example:* *"Is there a particular area of my remarks that you disagree with?"*

Know which questions not to answer.

> *Example:* *"As this matter is still pending in the courts, legal counsel has advised me not to discuss this matter."*

Know how to reestablish your point or position and move on.

> *Example:* *"No doubt you could give me an example to the contrary. There's always the exception to the rule. But would one example discount the thousands of times when it is the rule?"*

If the situation is really hostile, consider abbreviating your remarks. If you must remain and all other polite remedies have failed, consider asking your host/coordinator for help in removing the heckler or containing the abusive remarks. Suggest that you will continue when the situation has been addressed. Be very careful as to when and how you introduce this.

● ● ● In Summary ● ● ●

Public speaking involves a transaction between a speaker and an audience. Traditionally, the purpose of speeches is either to inform or to persuade. The primary purpose of an informative speech is to enhance the listeners' understanding about some particular topic. Informative speeches in business include the information speech, the informative briefing, the technical report, and the oral presentation of the professional paper. A persuasive speech is intended to influence the opinion or behavior of an audience. A persuasive speech or presentation may have as its end goal either conviction or actuation. As a representative of a business, you may find yourself presenting speeches on special occasions. Those in which you are most likely to participate are the speech of introduction, speech of welcome, speech of presentation, speech of acceptance, the after-dinner speech, the motivational speech, and the sales presentation. In addition, most speeches conclude with a question-and-answer session.

▬▬ Business Communication in Practice ▬▬

1. Research the life of a businessperson or business author such as Lee Iaccoca, Sylvia Porter, Donald Trump, Madam Walker, Liz Claiborne, Calvin Klein, or Tom Peters. Assume that the person was going to speak before your class. Prepare a speech of introduction for a presentation titled "My life, its successes and failures in the world of business."
2. If you have not already done so, read the speech presented in Chapter 2. Word three questions you could ask the speaker in a question-and-answer session.
3. In the frontmatter of this book, there are short biographies of the authors. Assume that one of the authors was to give a speech to members of your class about how this book was written. Write a speech of introduction you could present.
4. Select an informative presentation from the publication *Vital Speeches* or another source that presents the entire text of a speech. Bring a copy of the speech to class and be able to answer these questions:
   a. How did you determine that it was an informative speech?
   b. What type of informative speech was it? Explain how you determined the type.
5. Select a persuasive presentation from the publication *Vital Speeches* or another source that presents the entire text of a speech. Bring a copy of the speech to class and be able to answer these questions:
   a. What was its goal if it was a persuasive speech?

     b. What persuasive strategies were used? List and classify them. Be able to explain your identifications and classifications.

     c. How were the arguments built?

     d. Which resistances to change might the audience display based on the materials presented? Be prepared to explain your answer.

6. Write a speech of welcome that you might present to a group of high school seniors who are visiting your campus.

7. Identify a speech of acceptance, after-dinner speech, motivational speech, or sales speech that you have heard. Be prepared to explain why you think the speaker's material was or was not effective. Assume you were the person's speech-writing coach. What points would you have given that person that would have aided her/him to improve the material presented?

● ● ● Notes ● ● ●

1. Kent Menzel and Lori Carrel, "The Relationship between Preparation and Performance in Public Speaking," *Communication Education* (January 1994): 17.

2. David R. Seibold, Sami Kudsi, and Michael Rude, "Does Communication Training Make a Difference?: Evidence for the Effectiveness of a Presentation Skills Program," *Journal of Applied Communication Research* (May 1993): 111–131.

3. Roy M. Berko, Andrew D. Wolvin, and Darlyn R. Wolvin, *Communicating: A Social and Career Focus,* 6th ed. (Boston: Houghton Mifflin, 1995), p. 464.

4. Lee Lescaze, "And Have You Had a Briefing Today?" *The Washington Post* (January 6, 1982), A21.

5. For an excellent discussion of the dimensions of credibility, see James C. McCroskey and Thomas J. Young, "Ethos and Credibility: The Construct and Its Measurement after Three Decades," *Central States Speech Journal* 32 (Spring 1981): 24–34.

6. Chuck Cilo, "Emotion a Powerful Tool for Advertisers," *Advertising Age* 18 (July 1983): 28.

7. "Marketing Human Feelings," *Connect* (Summer 1995): 9.

8. Ellen Galinsky and Judy David, "Say Goodbye to Guilt," *Family Circle* (September 1988): 106.

9. Comment made by former Representative Donald Pease, Democrat, Ohio 13th Congressional District, to Roy Berko.

10. George Shinn, *Introduction to Professional Selling* (New York: McGraw-Hill, 1982), p. 3.

11. These steps are a compilation of the concepts expressed in Shinn, *Introduction to Professional Selling;* Cummings, *Contemporary Selling;* and Pederson and Wright, *Selling: Principles and Methods,* 6th ed. (Homewood, IL: Richard D. Irwin, 1976).

CHAPTER
12

Public Speaking: Preparing the Business Speech

EXPECTED OUTCOMES

After completing this chapter, you should be able to:

- Explain the need for prior, process, and post-speech analysis in preparing a speech.
- Illustrate the role of audience analysis in developing a business speech.
- Develop and use a personal speaking inventory.
- Conceive and apply a purpose statement as it relates to a business speech.
- Explain how business speeches are structured.
  Develop a business speech using an introduction, central idea, body, and conclusion.

I was making a sales presentation to a group of potential buyers about a new product line that my company had developed. I had been to a briefing about the products, but didn't have time to read all of the specifications before the meeting. During the speech I was feeling very uncomfortable and kept verbally stumbling. In the question-and-answer session I was asked a series of questions about the products. I didn't have answers for most of the inquiries. It was obvious that I didn't know what I was talking about. I really felt like a fool. A speaker has to prepare for a speech.

Good speeches just don't happen. They are thought about, prepared, and then presented. Although there may be occasions in the business setting when you will speak without much preparation, if possible, it is advisable to take the time to think through what you are going to say and structure it in a manner that will allow you to accomplish your task effectively.

The quality of speech performance correlates positively with the total preparation time, time spent preparing a visual aid, number of rehearsals, the time rehearsing out loud, the amount of research done, and the time and effort spent in preparing speaking notes.

Although there is no one best way to prepare a speech, if you follow a format that allows you to have a clear idea of what you want to accomplish, it is likely that your audience will also gain your message. One method is to first decide on a topic and formulate a purpose statement. Next, do any necessary research to collect material that develops the purpose statement. After this preliminary work, construct an introduction that will get the audience's attention and give listeners the necessary background material so they will be ready to hear the details of the subject. When these details have been provided, move on to the statement of the central idea, which tells the audience what the speech is all about. Then formulate the body of the presentation so that the purpose is accomplished. The conclusion summarizes the points and wraps up the presentation.

In order to prepare an effective speech it is wise to know the components of a speech and the stages of speech analysis.

Components of Analysis

Any act of communication is based on three parameters: the participants, the setting, and the purpose of the communication. In public speaking, these three parameters may affect the topic selected, the language used, the types of examples and illustrations chosen, and the supplementary aids needed to support and/or clarify ideas.

The **participants** include the speaker and the members of the audience. The **setting** includes where the speech is being given, what the time limit is, when the presentation is being made, and the emotional climate. The **purpose** centers on the speaker's expected outcomes for the presentation.

To give effective speeches, analyze the parameters. Conduct your investigation in three stages: prior analysis, process analysis, and post-speech analysis. The majority of the work takes place during the **prior analysis,** which occurs before the speech is given. Watching the audience for feedback—the **process analysis**—and paying attention to the reactions following the speech—**post-speech analysis**—are also important.

Speaking to Diverse Groups

Today's business audiences include an increasing percentage of foreign-born people—both employees and foreigners on temporary assignments.

Speaking to these culturally diverse groups requires special preparation and understanding. Some tips from a new book on how to speak to these groups are:

- *Start by finding out how many foreign-born folks will be in the audience. Ask where they are from and how well they handle the English language. Keep in mind that English taught in foreign classrooms won't qualify them to handle "words" such as, "Waddayathink?"*

- *When speaking, slow down and use natural pauses. "Speaking slower . . . with natural pauses . . . will allow everyone . . . a chance to absorb . . . your message."*

- *Avoid causing them the shame of losing face. How?*
  —Don't call on them unless you're sure they'll understand what you'll be asking.
  —Be sure to give the instructions for an activity twice.

- *Use as many visuals as possible.*

- *Be careful about using culturally specific examples, such as "touchdown" or "the Cosby show." Use universal themes, such as the desire for success or the importance of good friendship.*

Source: Power Speaking: How Ordinary People Can Make Extraordinary Presentations, by Dr. Frederick Gilbert, Frederick Gilbert Associates, 1233 Harrison Ave., Redwood City, CA 94062.

PRIOR ANALYSIS

Prior analysis takes place before the speech. The potential speaker examines herself/himself, the audience, and the purpose of the speech in order to select the topic, the language, and the necessary supplementary aids to be used during the speech.

Most trained speakers begin their planning by doing **audience analysis**—a demographic, attitudinal, and belief evaluation of prospective listeners. Try to figure out who they are. What are they interested in? People tend to tune out material that is trite, overused, uninteresting, and not significant to them.

There are three factors to consider about the audience: audience cultural identities, psychographics, and rhetorographics.[1]

Audience cultural identities include such factors as age, gender, religion, cultural/ethnic/uniqueness background, intellectual level, and occupation.

Psychographics are the attitudes and beliefs such as emotionally charged issues, memberships, political affiliations, and conservative or liberal dispositions of the prospective listeners.

Rhetorographics describe the speech setting—the place, time limit, time of day, and emotional climate.

These factors, when combined, allow you to determine what your audience is like. That information helps you determine the approach you will take to getting and retaining their attention so you accomplish your goal.

Topic Selection

It is not often in business speaking situations that you will have to choose a topic without any real guidance. Normally, business speakers are asked to make presentations because of their knowledge, experiences, or their expertise. Or the speaker decides that she or he has something to say and finds an audience that will listen.

While learning how to perfect your public speaking skills, realize that most people do their best job of speaking when they present something they are interested in talking about. If you are given total freedom to choose a topic, examine yourself first. What are you interested in speaking about? What do you know about that would be of interest to others?

In searching for a topic, consider your **personal speaking inventory**—your life experiences and interests. (To determine your business and personal speaking inventory, do Activity 1 of the Business Communication in Practice section at the end of this chapter.)

In addition to topic selection, or topic refinement, the prior analysis should help you determine the language to be used in the presentation.

Language Selection

A crucial factor in effective communication is the adaptation of your vocabulary to the level of your audience. Of course, this does not mean that you have to talk down to the level of your least-informed listener, but you must be aware that the audience may not be able to understand you. In the business environment, people in a common field understand the language of that field, but do not assume that clients or a general audience will be familiar with narrowly focused terminology.

In selecting your terminology, you may ask, "What words didn't I know before I became the 'expert' I am now?" Clarify those terms for the audience.

You also need to determine the purpose of your speech. Generally, the purpose is a result of your determining what you want from an audience.

Purpose Statement

In developing a message, a speaker should know specifically what she or he wants to communicate. Thus before they even start to develop their presentations, many public speakers write a **purpose statement,** a statement that lists the goal, the topic, and the method by which they will develop the speech.

One of the ways to ascertain the purpose statement for a speech is to answer the question, "At the end of the speech the audience should. . . ." What do you want the audience specifically to know, or be able to do, or believe?

Goal of a Speech The **goal** of a speech is expressed in terms of its expected outcome: imparting new information; securing understanding or reinforcing information and understandings that were accumulated in the past; attempting to get the listener to take some action, accept a belief, or change a point of view.

Topic of a Speech The **topic,** the subject of your speech, should be stated as specifically as possible. If you are not specific, you may find yourself mentally wandering around, unable to find and narrow your material.

Make sure you keep your audience analysis in mind when wording the subject. A topic that fits you quite well may not fit the audience at all. The way you approach a subject may determine whether an audience becomes interested. Examine the topic from the audience's standpoint. If you were listening to someone else speak on this topic, what approach would interest you?

Second, decide how you will develop the speech. If the topic requires an in-depth study of one factor, then present a **vertical development,** a single issue in great detail. If, however, the topic requires a complete survey of surface-level ideas, present a **horizontal development.** Either approach can be successful, depending on the subject and purpose. Be careful, however, of using the horizontal approach. Do not spread the ideas so thin that there is little idea development.

Third, analyze your audience and figure out what you can do to have the listeners gain the material or view you are presenting. As in making any decision about a speech, you are wise to ask yourself what phase of your topic the audience will be interested in hearing about and how to get the idea(s) across. Narrow your topic from broad to specific by deciding how to best approach your listeners.

Method of Development When you write out a purpose statement, use key words to indicate the **method of development** you will employ in reaching your goal. The method of development is your determinant as to how the speech will be developed. Samples of key words are:

"By analyzing"	"To defend"
"By demonstrating"	"To offer to"
"By explaining"	"To share"
"By summarizing"	"To participate in"
"By comparing"	"To support"
"By contrasting"	"To agree with"
"By describing"	"To contribute to"

"By discussing"	"To serve"
"By listing"	"To aid in"
"To accept that"	"To vote for"

When combined, the goal of the speech, the statement of the topic, and the method or process result in the purpose statement. Examples of purpose statements are:

"At the end of the speech I want the audience to know why they should accept my advertising program for our new cola product."

"I want the audience to know about the theory that altering the present top-down organizational structure of this organization can lead to en-hanced employee satisfaction. To do this, I will examine four studies that support this viewpoint."

"To persuade the executive committee to accept the concept that offering mental health insurance coverage for the employees can be a positive act, by explaining that the five most common reasons people are not produc-tive in the work environment are psychologically based."

By keeping in mind these three factors—goal, topic, and method—you can avoid some of the major pitfalls of inexperienced speakers. These pitfalls include not finishing the speech in the time limit, not accomplishing the speech's purpose, and not allowing the audience to gain the information.

PROCESS ANALYSIS

In the second stage of analysis, process analysis, you analyze the feedback you are receiving during the speech itself—an important factor in accomplish-ing your speaking goal. Many novice speakers think that once the speech starts, they can do little to alter or change the effectiveness of the presentation. This is not true. Speakers often need to adjust their materials as they present.

Nonverbal cues of attentiveness, boredom, agreement, and hostility can all be conveyed through posture and facial expression. Some speakers and theater performers are sensitive to what they term a "cough meter." If you have lost your audience, you will hear the results as the people clear their throats, cough, and become restless.

There are various ways to adapt to the feedback you receive. For exam-ple, if you think the audience does not understand a point, you can add an il-lustration, clarify your terms, or restate the idea. If you sense that the audience is not attentive, you can change the volume of your voice, use a pause, move forward, ask a direct question, or insert an interesting or humorous anecdote. Another technique is to direct questions to members questions. This is a device frequently used by professors during lectures.

POST-SPEECH ANALYSIS

A post-speech analysis enables you to determine how the speech affected the audience. This information can be useful in preparing and presenting future speeches. One very direct way to conduct a post-speech analysis is to have a question-and-answer session. The questions your listeners ask may reveal just how clear your presentation really was. The tone of the questions may also reflect the general mood of the listeners, telling you how positively or negatively they have received you and your message. Informal conversations with members of the audience after the speech also will reveal a good deal.

Developing the Speech

Listening to a speech can be an exciting, interesting, or uplifting experience. It can also be a frustrating, boring, and confusing event. **Attention** results from focusing on one stimulus over all others in the environment at any given time. Because we can attend to any one stimulus for only a short period of time, a speech must be sufficiently compelling to ensure that listeners will tune back in to the speech during the tuning-in/tuning-out process. To accomplish this, try to choose concrete, specific supporting materials rather than general or abstract ones. Lively descriptions, colorful choice of language, and a vigorous style can all encourage listeners to pay attention to your message.

The difference between positive and negative listening experiences is often based on whether the speaker has done such things as defined terms, offered clarifying examples, explained abstract concepts, presented proving statistics, restated ideas, and illustrated thoughts with supplementary aids.

SOURCES OF INFORMATION

Most of the information we use to develop messages is based on personal experiences, personal observations, or learning acquired through sources such as school, the media, and reading. As we are exposed to information, we retain a certain amount of it. This knowledge forms the core of our communication. We select words and examples from this storehouse, and we use them to organize messages.

Lively descriptions, colorful choice of language, a vigorous style, and the use of such devices as computer-generated graphics can encourage listeners to pay attention.

In addition to personal knowledge, other sources of information are available to communicators who have the time and need to seek out additional material. These sources include books, magazines, newspapers, special journals, indexes, government publications, and the publications of special-interest groups. Additional sources include nonprint materials such as tape recordings, records, films, videotapes, charts, and models as well as interviews, telephone conversations, or correspondence with recognized experts in a particular field.

Normally, a researcher gets information by going to a library and looking in the electronic card catalog or a reader's guide or asking the reference librarian what sources are available. No matter how thorough this method of search is, many references can be missed. Recognizing this, many libraries and educational institutions have developed a way to tap into formerly unavailable sources through computer search systems. Almost daily, through the electronic highway, even more of these services are becoming available. In some cases these can also be accessed from businesses, dorm rooms, or your own home through use of one of the commercial or collegiate computer networks. A charge is normally made for the use of the service.

The computer search is a computer-based retrieval system that allows the researcher to compile a bibliography or a set of facts relevant to a specific topic. Searches may be used for a variety of purposes, including gathering research or references, compiling a reading list, acquiring statistical information, or simply keeping abreast of developments in a field.[2]

In addition to locating information, a speaker must assess its validity. All sources of information reflect certain perceptions and biases. Consequently, it is wise to try to determine the bias of a source and to interpret its information accordingly.[3] Thus, when doing research for a presentation, it is a good idea to find several agreeing authoritative sources so that your supporting details will be credible to your listeners.

SUPPORTING MATERIAL

When gathering material to develop a speech, keep in mind how that material is useful as support for the main points within the body of the speech. **Supporting material** gathered through research should clarify a point or offer proof—that is, it should demonstrate that the point has some probability of being true. Some forms of support are more useful for clarity, whereas others are more useful for proof.

To make a statement and prove it, begin with a **statement of declaration;** give the necessary exposition (stating the major contention), such as clarifying necessary terms; and then develop the idea with illustrations, specific instances, statistics, analogies, and testimony. Without such clarification and development, the audience often will not understand the idea and will have little reason to accept your contentions.

The forms of support you select depend on your purposes, but the most common are illustrations, specific instances, expositions, statistics, analogies, and testimony.

Illustrations

Examples that explain a subject through the use of detailed stories are called **illustrations.** They are intended to clarify a point, not offer proof. They may be hypothetical or factual. If the illustrations are hypothetical, the speaker should make this clear to listeners by saying, for example, "Suppose you were . . ." or "Let us all imagine that. . . ." In contrast, a factual illustration is a real or actual story. It can be introduced by statements such as "When I came to work this morning. . . ." A speaker must select illustrations carefully so they will be relevant to his or her listeners.

Specific Instances

Condensed examples that are used to clarify or prove a point are called **specific instances.** Because they are not developed in depth, you can say a great deal quickly by using them and can provide listeners with evidence they can relate to your point.

Exposition

An **exposition** gives the necessary background information to listeners so they can understand the material being presented. Sometimes, for example, the speaker will want to define specific terms, give historical information, explain the relationship between herself or himself and the topic, or explain the process that will be used during the presentation.

Statistics

Any collection of numerical information arranged to indicate representations, trends, or theories is an example of **statistics.** Statistics are used by communicators to provide a measurement. Before accepting statistics as proof, the wise speaker asks these questions:

1. Who says so?
2. How does he or she know?
3. What is missing?
4. Did somebody change the subject?
5. Does it make sense?[4]

Analogies

A speaker often uses an **analogy** to clarify a concept for listeners—that is, the speaker compares an unfamiliar concept to a familiar one. For example, in *The Road Ahead*, Bill Gates, CEO of Microsoft, effectively uses analogies to explain complex computer processes for those who may have found the subject daunting.

Analogy is effective only if the listeners are familiar with the object, idea, or theory being used as the basis for the analogy. Comparing one unfamiliar idea to another unfamiliar idea does little except further confuse an audience.

Testimony

A direct quotation (an actual statement) or a paraphrase (a reworded idea) from an authority is known as **testimony.** Speakers provide testimony in communication to clarify ideas, back up contentions, and reinforce concepts. One

---

Putting Humor in Its Place

Humor has a place in your presentations and your work with others. Even if you feel you can't tell a joke, you can still make humor work for you.

Humor should be relevant to the message you are giving. Link it to a point you are making, and make it the type of humor that is in good taste.

● *Analogies are one way to use humor. Linking your present situation or problem to something else often provides an opportunity for humor. The link can be either logical or illogical and could even be a personal anecdote.*

● *Another way to use humor—and an easy one for the person who falls into the "cannot-tell-jokes" category—is to use funny quotes. Get a book of humorous quotes.*

Also: Have you seen an amusing cartoon in the paper or in a magazine? Describe it. Show it on a screen.

Some specifics on using humor:

● *When you are telling jokes or quips, don't pre-announce them. Just insert them here and there.*

● *Avoid anything offensive or sarcastic. If in doubt, leave it out.*

● *Remember that sometimes things occur—such as power failures, dead mikes, etc.—during presentations. Have a joke or comment ready for emergencies.*

Source: Dr. Stephenie Slahor, P.O. Box 2615, Palm Springs, CA 92263.

---

of the most common types of testimonies is referring to ideas or research of experts.

An **expert** is a person who through knowledge or skill in a specific field gains respect for his or her opinions or expertise. We turn to lawyers, economists, architects, and business consultants to answer questions and give advice about their areas of expertise. We trust their opinions because their knowledge has been acquired through personal experience, education, training, research, and observation. We also respect people who have academic degrees, are licensed, have received accreditation, or are recognized by peers as leaders in their fields.

In an effort to present precisely the views of experts, a speaker should be careful to quote accurately, indicate the time and circumstances under which the information was presented, and provide the source of the material. In addition, the testimony should be relevant and no longer than necessary. Listeners have difficulty handling lengthy readings of testimony and tend to tune them out rather quickly.

The selected quotations should be true to the source's original intention. Testimony taken out of context is not only misleading and confusing; it is also dishonest. Before you accept testimony as support, assess it by asking some basic questions:

1. Is the material quoted accurately?
2. Is the source biased because of position, employment, or affiliation?
3. Is the information relevant to the issue being discussed?
4. Is the source competent in the field being discussed?
5. Is the information current, if currency is important?

VEHICLES FOR PRESENTING SUPPORTING MATERIAL

Three means of presenting and focusing supporting material are restatement, forecasting, and the use of supplementary aids.

Restatement

Speakers often forget that listeners may not be able to sift through the information as it is presented. Therefore, to avoid confusion, summarize each segment of a presentation by **restatement** before proceeding to the next one. Effective restatement is accomplished by rewording key points so that major ideas stand out for the listeners without becoming boring or repetitious.

Forecasting

To get the audience ready to focus on the next idea to be presented, speakers use forecasts. A **forecast** is a statement that alerts the audience to ideas that are coming. Forecast statements include "Let's now examine the three examples of . . ." or "By understanding the definition of ____, you can gain insight into . . ."

Supplementary Aids

Many speakers find **supplementary aids**—visual, audio, audiovisual, computer assisted—valuable in supplementing the oral segments of their presentations. Nevertheless, a speaker is wise to ask two questions before deciding to use such aids: Is the aid relevant to the presentation? Will listeners better understand the material through the use of an aid? Aids are intended to facilitate listener understanding, not function as decorative touches.

Visual aids appeal to our sense of sight. They can include real objects, models, photographs, pictures, diagrams, and charts.

Audio aids appeal to our sense of hearing. Such devices as records, tape recordings, and duplications of sounds may be the only way to demonstrate particular sensations accurately for listeners.

Transitions

Preliminary Summaries

Today, I will speak about . . .
There are four major points to be covered in . . .
The history of the issue can be divided into two periods . . .

Connectives

In the first instance . . . the second point is . . .
In addition to . . .
If examined from a different angle . . .
Keep in mind these three points as we move to the fourth . . .
What was the result? (or effect?)
Turning now to . . .
Not only . . . but also . . . (parallel)
More important than these is . . . (hierarchical)
In contrast . . . (different)
Otherwise, we could consider . . . (different)
In other methods (countries, firms, systems, etc.) . . . (different)
Either . . . or . . . (different)
Not only . . . but also . . . (different)
On the other hand . . . (different)
However . . . (different)
But . . . (different)
And yet . . . (different)
Still . . . (different)
On the contrary . . . (different)
Similar to this . . . (similar)
Along the same lines . . . (similar)
One must consider X, Y, and Z . . . (coordinated)
From these three points, we move to the fourth . . . (coordinated)
The fourth step in this process is . . . (coordinated)
On the next level is . . . (subordinated)

Final Summaries

I have spoken about the three aspects of . . .
These four major points (restate them) are the . . .
The two periods just covered (restate them) represent the significant . . .
It must be clear then that X is . . .

Audiovisual aids such as films, videotapes, and tape-slide presentations combine the dimensions of sight and sound.

Computer-generated supplementary aids[5] allow for the creation of attention-getting and clarifying graphics while using a combination of computers and projection equipment. In order to develop electronic aids, the business will need a personal computer and presentation software such as *Lotus Freelance Graphics, Microsoft PowerPoint,* or *Harvard Graphics.* During the actual presentation you will need a large monitor or a liquid crystal display (LCD) panel with an overhead projector and screen, depending on the size of the room.

These tips should help you develop your electronic aids:

1. Use a title and end page.
2. Be sure the type size is large enough for everyone in the room to see.
3. Use bullets or numbers and list key concepts rather than sentences and paragraphs.
4. Use graphic images whenever possible, as they attract more attention than lists of words.

Creating Audiovisuals

- *Keep visuals simple and clear with only one main idea on each chart or graphic.*

- *Charts (Text, Bullet, Graph, Flow, Organizational, Pie, Bar Line) should be carefully designed to best display the intended material in the clearest way for viewers.*

- *Color should be used carefully. Dark colors appear closer and light colors recede. Red and green are difficult for the color blind.*

- *Colors have meaning. Using black, red, and green in a financial presentation can conjure images of profit, loss, and growth in unintended ways. Remember that different cultures have strong associations with various colors so a wrong choice can prove embarrassing.*

- *Choose color schemes that are simple as too much variation can detract from the message.*

- *Color can be used to show the organization of your comments as well as to emphasize important sections. Bright colors are best used as accent colors.*

- *Limit the number of colors in a business-related graphic to seven; to five for charts and graphs; and to two for text.*

- *Choose one gradient background template and consistent color scheme throughout whenever possible and use a horizontal format.*

- *Use units of three (examples, terms, concepts) whenever possible.*

- *Use a solid font for text like Times Roman or Helvetica and use capitals sparingly.*

5. Use a consistent design throughout.
6. Use graphs and charts to show statistical information.
7. Use the electronic presentation from beginning to end.
8. Keep the visuals simple.

Structuring the Message

Have you ever listened to a speech and were unable to follow the thought patterns of the speaker? If so, you were experiencing organizational confusion. Listeners have limited attention spans. They are constantly tuning in and tuning out on speakers' messages. Consequently, it is important to present a carefully structured message that facilitates the listener getting back "on track" at the point that he or she tunes back in on the speech. A careful plan for putting together a speech is a major part of the process of preparing presentations and developing effective speeches.[6]

A public communication message is usually divided into four parts: introduction, central idea, body, and conclusion. This structure may be outlined as:[7]

I. *Introduction* (attention-gaining and orienting material)
II. *Central idea* (the purpose of the presentation and a specific statement of its main idea)
III. *Body* (the major points to be expressed in the presentation)
IV. *Conclusion* (a summarizing and a motivating statement)

THE INTRODUCTION

The purpose of the **introduction** is to gain the listeners' attention and orient them to the material that will be presented.

Attention Material

Many types of introductory devices can be used to gain the audience's attention, including personal references, humorous stories, illustrations, references to the occasion or setting, rhetorical questions, action questions, unusual or dramatic devices, quotations related to the theme, and statements of the theme.

- *Personal references:* the personal reasons for presenting a specific topic.
- *Humorous stories:* a funny story or a joke. The humor should fit the audience and the occasion, be relevant to the material that follows, and set the desired tone.

- *Illustrations:* stories, pictures, and computer graphics. Illustrations help make ideas more vivid for listeners because they create a visualization or an image of the topic to be discussed.
- *References to the occasion or setting:* mutual experiences, common beliefs, or mutual needs. Such references make the audience feel a strong bond, an alliance, an empathy, with the speaker or the occasion.
- *Rhetorical questions:* queries for which no outward response is expected. The speaker does not intend to count how many have or have not asked themselves the question. Instead, his or her purpose is to have the audience members ask themselves the question to build their curiosity.
- *Action questions:* a probing question, the answer to which launches the speech. Such questions make the listeners think and respond at the beginning of the message.
- *Unusual or dramatic devices:* elements that get the attention of the audience because of their curiosity or shock value.
- *References to historical events:* connecting the speech occasion to what may have occurred earlier on the same date that has historical relevance to the audience or to your topic.
- *Quotations related to the theme:* stating the words of a famous person or an expert, reading an account of a specific event, reciting a section of a poem or play, or reading a newspaper editorial. Such quotations must be relevant to the subject. But even when they are relevant, quoted ideas become meaningless if they are not presented effectively. Quotations are most effective when read meaningfully, slowly, and loudly enough to be heard.
- *Statements of the theme:* indications to the audience about exactly what the speaker will address. Unfortunately, many untrained speakers start out their presentations by saying, "Today I am going to tell you about. . . ." Obviously, this is not a particularly effective opener because it lacks creativity.

Orienting Material

Orienting material is designed to give the audience the background necessary to understand the basic material of the speech. It ties the material to the central idea, provides necessary information, establishes personal credibility for the speaker, and makes the subject important to the listeners. Orienting material usually includes historical background, definition of terms, personal history and/or a tie to the topic, and the importance to listeners.

- *Historical background:* explaining what led up to present occurrences.
- *Definition of terms:* defining a term or terms that are going to be used during the entire speech or as the basis for the speech. This does not preclude defining other terms later. Only those terms that are universal to the speech have to be included in the orienting segment.

- *Personal history and/or tie to the topic:* a statement of some personal tie or experience that relates to the topic. This documentation establishes the speaker's authority to speak about the subject.
- *Importance to the listeners:* tying the subject to the audience. Listeners pay attention to ideas and issues that are relevant to them, so it is imperative that the speaker make that link at the outset. One good strategy is to show the importance of the topic based on the interests of the audience.

THE CENTRAL IDEA

The purpose statement, which is designed to help the speaker to prepare a speech, can also serve as the basis for developing a **central idea**—the overall point of the speech. This central idea gives the point of the speech explicitly; at the same time it implies what type of response the speaker wants from listeners. The importance of actually stating the central idea in a speech cannot be overemphasized. The audience that is not given the central idea will often be frustrated and may never be sure exactly what the exact point of the speech is. The central idea should be presented as a statement because a speaker who uses a question is not indicating to the listeners what the main point really is. The statement is concise and contains only one overall idea.

THE BODY

The **body** of a message develops the major points of the speech as well as any subpoints that pertain to the speaker's central idea. When a speech lacks this sort of organization, listeners may become so confused they give up trying to understand it. The subpoints of the body of a speech can be organized in a variety of ways. These methods of sequencing are called **issue arrangement.**

Historically, speakers in the Western cultures have used a direct step-by-step process that calls for a statement of contention and then proof of that contention. Not all cultures regard the Western world's Aristotelian mode of structuring to be the best or only way to structure. In some cultures, a **spiral form of explanation** is used. In this mode, a statement is made, a story or analogy is presented that deals with that statement, and it is often left to the listener to apply the parallels and draw outcomes to apply to the original statement. This organization is not poor, just different from what many Westerners are used to hearing.

Since the course you are taking is probably going to subscribe to the Western mode of structure, an in-depth description of that mode is in order. Again, this is not to say that other formats or approaches are inferior and that, if it is appropriate for your speaking setting, they should not be learned or used.

Methods of Issue Arrangement

Traditional issue arrangement normally takes one of six forms: spatial arrangement, chronological or time arrangement, topical arrangement, causal arrangement, comparison-contrast arrangement, or problem-solution arrangement. When using any of the methods of organization, the speaker does not have to organize the subdivisions in the same way as the major headings. For example, one method could be used for the major headings and another for the subdivisions.

Spatial Arrangement When using **spatial arrangement,** a speaker sets a point of reference at some specific location. He or she then proceeds to give directions starting from the established reference point. Thus the organization is based on keeping the places in a set order following a pattern: left to right, north to south, from the center to the outside. For example, one could explain a production line at an auto manufacturing plant according to what each work station does.

Chronological or Time Arrangement Another method of organization is **chronological** or **time arrangement,** which orders information from a beginning point to an ending one, with all the steps developed in numerical or time sequence—for example, informing an audience of the history of an organization from its founding to the present time.

Topical Arrangement Ideas also can be organized on the basis of their similarities. Thus in using a **topical arrangement,** a speaker explains an idea in terms of its component parts. A speaker discusses all aspects of one component before proceeding to the next. An example of this arrangement is informing potential clients of the various products your company produces.

Causal Arrangement **Causal arrangement** shows how two events or objects are connected in such a way that if one occurs, the other will necessarily follow. In other words, if one incident happened, it caused the second incident to happen (cause to effect). An alternative form would be to give the final result first and then list the events leading up to it. The former method is called cause(s) to effect; the latter, effect from cause(s). For example, a speaker might explain how the new filtration system at the company's production facility will result in the elimination of waste materials being expelled into the river on whose banks the plant is located.

Comparison-Contrast Arrangement The **comparison method** of organization takes place when a speaker tells how two or more examples are alike. If, however, you choose to tell the differences between the two, you will use the **con-**

trast method, developing the ideas by giving specific examples of differences between the two types of items. By combining these two methods into the **comparison-contrast arrangement,** you can tell about both the similarities and the differences. You could compare the similarities between your company and another organization; or you could contrast the differences between your company's present computer system with the newly proposed system; or you could tell the similarities and differences between the accounting system at your previous company with your present company.

Problem-Solution Arrangement The **problem-solution arrangement** is commonly used when a person is attempting to identify what is wrong and to determine how to cure it or make a recommendation for its cure. Such an analysis takes place when the problem is clearly identified, which leads to a consideration of various solutions. The key to effective problem-solution arrangement is to deal with solutions that will be workable (those that can solve the problem), desirable (won't cause further problems), and practical (can be put into effect).

An alternative form of the problem-solution method is the **see-blame-cure-cost method.** In this technique, the evil or problem that exists is examined (see), what has caused the problem is determined (blame), solutions are investigated (cure), and the most practical solution is selected (cost).

When you develop a problem-solution message, it is important to clearly state the problem, its cause, the possible solutions, and the selected solution. This allows your listeners to share a complete picture of your reasoning process and to know why the selected solution is best, how it will work to solve the problem, what it will or will not do, what the costs will be, how long it will take to work, and what is needed to implement it. The problem-solution method can be used to decide among treatments or procedures, products to buy, or machines to employ, as the problems of life, business, industry, and government are confronted and solutions found.

THE CONCLUSION

Depending on the purpose of a speech, the **conclusion** can be used to summarize, pull thoughts together, or motivate listeners to take a prescribed action.

Summary

A **summary** should restate the major points of the speech so that the listener can recap what has been covered.

Getting around the 18-Minute Wall

Listeners lose concentration after 18 minutes of a speech, according to a Navy study reported in The Articulate Executive, by Granville N. Toogood. To get around the 18-minute wall:

● Give them the basics in 18 minutes. Then, devote half an hour to Q & A to expand your main points.

● Alternate 18-minute segments with an associate speaking for two minutes to amplify a point in your speech.

● Speak for 18 minutes, show a 10-minute video and then restart your 18-minute clock.

Source: Across the Board, 845 3rd Ave., New York, NY 10022.

The Clincher

Some communication experts believe that all speeches should end with a summary of the major points, followed by a concluding message, which is called a **clincher.** The conclusion section of the speech can thus have two major parts and can be outlined:

IV. Conclusion
   A. Summary (restatement of issues and restatement of the central idea)
   B. Clincher (concluding message)

   The advantage of following this procedure is that it gives the speaker one more chance to reinforce the major ideas she or he has presented and then wraps up the presentation with a clinching message. Because the central idea must remain with listeners after the presentation, the conclusion section is a vital part of the message and must be developed carefully to attain the best possible results. Clincher message techniques include personal references, humorous stories, illustrations, rhetorical questions, action questions, unusual or dramatic devices, or quotations.

Sample Speeches

Now that you have been exposed to the basic concepts for preparing and presenting a speech, examine these presentations. They should enforce the idea to which you have just been exposed.

SAMPLE SPEECH TO INFORM

Purpose: to inform the listeners about the preparation of a résumé.

Introduction	I. Introduction
Attention-Getting Material Engaging listeners through personal reference	A. Let's look into the future. You have graduated from college and you are now going forth to make it in the real world. No matter what your training and qualifications, you could easily be passed over for that job you want if you do not pay careful attention to the way in which you compose your résumé.
Orienting Material Identifying and defining a résumé	B. A résumé is a document that allows a prospective employer to examine your background and preparation for a job in order to determine if you

are the best candidate for the position. As such, a résumé is a means for you to "sell" yourself to a prospective employer.

Central Idea
Central point of the speech

Partitioning Step
Listing the three points in the body

Body
First Main Point
Discussion of point with quote, explanations, examples, visuals

II. Central Idea
    A. Today I'd like to share with you some ideas on planning a résumé.
    B. When we are finished here, you should know something about the types, formats, and uses of résumés.

III. Body
    A. Types of résumés
      1. Purposes of résumés
        Richard Bolles identifies four functions of résumés: "They can be a *self-inventory,* preparing you before the job-hunt to recall all that you've accomplished thus far in your life; they can be an *extended calling card,* whose purpose is to get you invited in for an interview, by the employer(s) to whom you send that 'calling card'; they can be an *agenda for an interview,* affording the interviewer a springboard from which to launch his or her inquiry about you, after you have been invited in: and, finally, résumés can be a *memory jogger* for the employer after the interview, or for a whole committee—if a group is involved in the hiring decision."
      2. Traditional chronological résumé
      3. Functional résumé
      4. Video résumé and portfolio

Transition
Regardless of the type of résumé you choose, you need to establish a format.

Second Main Point
Discussion of substance of a résumé with explanations, examples, suggestions, visuals

    B. Format of a résumé
      1. Your career objectives
      2. Education
        a. Degrees earned (most recent listed first), schools, and dates
        b. Educational honors and awards

                                    3. Qualifications
                                        a. Special skills
                                        b. Special training
                                    4. Experience
                                        a. Begin with most recent experi-
                                           ence
                                        b. Offer job titles, functions,
                                           accomplishments
                                    5. References (if these are readily
                                       available)

Transition   The format of a résumé can assist you in
                               your use of it.

Third Main Point   C. Using the résumé effectively
Discussion of setting up a   1. Style and substance of the résumé
résumé with explanations,   2. Cover letters
examples, visuals   3. Telephone follow-ups
                                    4. Interviews
                                    5. The résumé as part of your "pack-
                                       age"

Conclusion   IV. Conclusion
Summary   A. In preparing a résumé, you need to
                                      determine what type of résumé to
                                      use, format the information, and
                                      then use it effectively.

Clincher   B. Writing a résumé is actually writing
                                      an advertisement for yourself. Ruth
                                      Blau, a publication and public
                                      information consultant, makes the
                                      point: "Let your paperwork say
                                      something about you. Let it reflect
                                      your personality and your ability.
                                      Let it tell prospective employers that
                                      you are the kind of person they are
                                      looking for."

SAMPLE SPEECH TO PERSUADE

Purpose: to persuade the listeners that their organizations should adopt Total
Quality Management (TQM).

Introduction   I. Introduction
Attention-Getting Material   A. American corporations have lost
Engaging the listeners in   their competitive edge.
the problem

Orienting Material
Involving the listeners in
the goal
Central Idea
Central point of the speech

Body
First Main Point
Discussion of history of
TQM with explanations,
examples, other data

Transition

Second Main Point
Discussion of the
dimensions of TQM with
explanations and examples

Transition

Third Main Point
Discussion of advantages
with explanations, examples,
appeals

B. American corporations must regain
their competitive edge.

II. Central Idea
American corporations should adopt
Total Quality Management.

III. Body
A. The historical foundations of Total
Quality Management
1. The 1930s quality control movement
2. Dr. W. Edward Deming's work in
statistical quality control with the
Japanese Union of Scientists and
Engineers
3. General Electric's Dr. Armand
Feigenbaum's focus on quality
control as everyone's responsibility—*total* quality control
4. Today, many organizations are
adopting TQM programs, including Ford, Hewlett-Packard, and
Xerox

Total Quality Management has an interesting history. Today it has emerged as a major
corporate emphasis.
B. Behaviors and processes associated
with total quality control
1. Commit quality as the priority
2. Focus on the customer
3. Ensure that no defective products
or services are produced
4. Use good information as the basis
for making decisions
5. Involve all employees in solving
and preventing problems
6. Build a strong communication
environment

TQM requires commitment by all. And it has
been found to be well worth the commitment.
C. The advantages of Total Quality
Management
1. Competitive edge
2. Customer satisfaction

3. Employee commitment
4. Economic viability

Conclusion   IV. Conclusion
Summary

A. The history, dimensions, and advantages of Total Quality Management point to the need for instituting TQM in your organization.

Clincher
Specific instance and quote

B. A study of Fortune 500 companies shows that, over the long term, quality leads to higher profitability—the bottom line for all of us. Xerox CEO Paul Allaire says it best: "If we do what's right for the customer, our market share and our return on assets will take care of themselves."

● ● ● In Summary ● ● ●

Any act of communication is based on three parameters: the participants, the setting, and the purpose of the communication. In public speaking, these three parameters may affect the topic selected, the language used, the types of examples and illustrations chosen, and the supplementary aids needed to support and/or clarify ideas. These elements must be considered when planning a speech. Speeches just don't happen—they are normally thought about, prepared, and then presented. Although there is no one best way to prepare a speech, if you follow a format that allows you to have a clear idea of what you want to accomplish, it is likely that your audience will understand your message. A speech is usually divided into four parts: introduction, central idea, body, and conclusion and contains such elements as defined terms, clarifying examples, explained abstract concepts, proving statistics, restated ideas, and thoughts illustrated with supplementary aids.

══ Business Communication in Practice ══

1. Personal Speaking Inventory: In the world of business you will normally be given a topic or told what you should speak about, or you will need to identify those business areas of which you are knowledgeable. Fill out "Speaker Inventory—Form A" to ascertain those areas. There will be other times, such as when you are taking a public speaking or business communication course, or are invited to speak to a non-business-related group, when you may be given an optional choice of topics. If that is the

case, it will help you if you have some potential topics. Answer the questions in "Speaker Inventory—Form B" to develop an inventory to use for speeches in which you are given open choice of topics:

"Speaker Inventory—Form A"
a. Talents and abilities I have that relate to my career choice/job
b. Topics that I am knowledgeable about that relate to my career choice/job
c. Computer or technical skills I have
d. Jobs I have had
e. Experiences at work
f. Business-related books I have read and liked
g. Business leaders I admire
h. Places I have traveled and cultural differences I have observed

"Speaker Inventory—Form B"
a. Vocational interests
b. Hobbies and special interests
c. Things I know how to do (sports I can play, skills I have)
d. Jobs I have had
e. Experiences (accidents, special events)
f. Funny things that have happened to me
g. Books I have read and liked
h. Movies and plays I have seen and liked
i. Interesting people I have known
j. People I admire
k. Religious and nationality customs of my family
l. Talents I have (musical instruments played, athletics)
m. Places traveled

2. Each student will select a controversial business subject area (for example, businesses should be responsible for all pollution they create, only real estate brokers who are full-service should be allowed to sell property). The student identifies a person who is an authority on the subject and interviews that person. Prepare a three- to five-minute speech in which you identify the person, why she/he is an authority on the topic, the person's stand concerning the issue, and the reasons for the stand.

3. Interview a person who holds a position similar to one you wish to eventually have (for example, accountant, security analyst, corporate lawyer). Prepare a three- to five-minute speech to the class that educates them about the post. Include the nature of the position, the financial rewards, the communication skills needed for the job, and the working conditions. You may conduct research beyond the interview if necessary.

4. Cut out three advertisements from newspapers or magazines. Identify and

analyze the appeals the advertiser is using to persuade the reader to buy the product.

5. Listen to three different television or radio commercials. What kind of appeals are the advertisers using to persuade the audience to buy the product?

6. Using a topic related to your academic major, develop a purpose statement for a speech to be given to your classmates. Then prepare another purpose statement for the same general topic but for a different audience. Notice how the outcome of the speech varies according to the nature of the purpose statement.

7. Select a topic. Prepare purpose statements for speeches of thirty minutes, fifteen minutes, and five minutes. Go back and analyze each of the purpose statements you wrote. What changes did you make? Why did you alter the statements?

● ● ●   Notes   ● ● ●

1. For an extended discussion of demographics, psychographics, and rhetorographics, see Andrew Wolvin, Roy Berko, and Darlyn Wolvin, *The Public Speaker/The Public Listener* (Boston: Houghton Mifflin, 1993).

2. *Research on Digital Libraries* (Arlington, VA: National Science Foundation, 1993), p. 1.

3. Robert Newman and Dale Newman, *Evidence* (Boston: Houghton Mifflin, 1969), presents an insight into the types of bias present in many different sources of information.

4. Darrell Huff, *How to Lie with Statistics* (New York: Norton, 1954), pp. 123–142.

5. Based on Michelle Simpson, "Using Electronic Presentations as Visual Aids," an unpublished paper provided to the authors, June 26, 1995.

6. Charles Petrie, "Informative Speaking: A Summary and Bibliography of Related Research," *Speech Monographs* 30 (June 1963): 79–91.

7. For an extensive discussion on the four-part speech structure, see Wolvin, Berko, and Wolvin, Chapter 8.

CHAPTER

13

Public Speaking: Presenting the Business Speech

EXPECTED OUTCOMES

After completing this chapter, you should be able to:

- Define and explain the advantages and disadvantages of impromptu, extemporaneous, manuscript, and memorized speech formats.
- Explain the concepts of how to use effective physical and vocal elements in a business speech.
- Explain and work toward controlling public speech anxiety during a presentation.

I am an advertising account executive. I was presenting a proposal for a campaign to a potential client. I had my secretary put the slides in the order that showed the print ads that were to be used in the campaign. I got to the part of the speech where I was to use the slides. I turned on the machine and showed the first slide. It was upside down! I adjusted it, and then went on to the next visual. It was the wrong one. It turned out that all the slides were out of order. If only I had gone through the visuals before I left the office, I would have avoided the embarrassment, and may have signed the client.

The speaker has analyzed the audience, chosen the general topic, narrowed the topic to a purpose statement, completed the necessary research, selected a method of issue arrangement, constructed the body of the speech using the necessary major headings, selected the method of development, and prepared an attention-getting introduction, a clear statement of the central idea, and a summarizing conclusion. What's next? Presenting the speech!

Modes of Presentation

Four modes of presentation are commonly used when giving speeches: impromptu, extemporaneous, manuscript, and memorized.

IMPROMPTU PRESENTATION

The **impromptu mode of speech delivery,** sometimes referred to as ad lib, takes place when a speech is presented with little or no preparation. When you decide, on the spur of the moment, to stand up and give a response to an idea presented by someone else, or at a staff meeting make a proposal about which you had not thought about previously, you are giving an impromptu speech. Usually, requests for impromptu comments are made because a person has already done research, is currently working on the topic, or is perceived as a credible source on the topic.

If you find yourself in a situation where you are to ad-lib, use the principles for developing a speech explained earlier. Depending on the situation, recall your point of view, or the major ideas you want to stress, or those concepts that will address the question asked or the problem to be solved. Next, if time is available, make a quick list of the major ideas you will include and arrange them according to one of the issue arrangement types (for example, chronological or spatial). Consider how you will begin your remarks. Again, think back quickly to the types of introductions discussed in this text. The easiest one to come up with quickly is the rhetorical question. Then try to figure out how you will end the presentation. Most ad-libbers choose to end by restating the major points. Now, orally present the material: give the introduction; state the central idea; develop the body of major ideas with explanations, illustrations, exposition, and the other methods of support; and then conclude.

If you lack the time to write the ideas down, quickly search through the same process, or as you speak, keep the structure of the speech in mind and continue to think in a sequential order.

EXTEMPORANEOUS PRESENTATION

The speaker who prepares a speech in advance and uses notes or an outline when addressing an audience is using an **extemporaneous mode of speech delivery.** The extemporaneous mode is the preferred presentation of most effective speakers. It encourages the speaker to have natural gestures, speak in a normal voice, and have consistent eye contact with the audience.

In order to ensure that you are comfortable with the outline or notes, practice aloud with them. The general rule for how much written material to use during the speech itself is that there should be enough for you to feel confident that you will not get lost, but not so much that you will read to the audience.

MANUSCRIPT PRESENTATION

In the **manuscript mode of speech delivery,** the material is written out and delivered word-for-word. The advantages of this method are that you have all the words in front of you, the speech can be timed almost exactly, and, if you are going to be quoted, there is no chance of turning the words around. However, a "flat" presentation can result if you have a poor oral reading style or lack the gestures, eye contact, and dynamics necessary to make an audience want to listen.

In manuscript speaking, the presenter must be familiar enough with the text to maintain consistent eye contact while speaking to the audience. Rehearse with the script and know the material so you can visually grab a group of words on a line and then look up to convey the content of the entire line.

MEMORIZED PRESENTATION

A **memorized mode of speech delivery** is a manuscript speech committed to memory. Although knowing exactly what you are going to say may be comforting, the disadvantages far outweigh the advantages. Speakers presenting memorized material tend to use little or no vocal variation. Moreover, a common difficulty with the memorized speech is the risk of forgetting.

The Physical Elements of a Speech

Presenting a speech involves physical and vocal elements. The physical elements of a speech include gestures, physical movements, posture, eye contact, and control of the aids you are using during the speech.

When Speaking

If you need notes to refer to during a presentation, retain eye contact with your audience by using "hidden notes."

Place your brief notes in the frame of a transparency or below your main headings on the flip chart. A quick glance will prompt you to get to the next key point.

Source: Norman B. Sigband, 3109 Dona Susana Drive, Studio City, CA 91604.

PHYSICAL PRESENTATION

Physical presentation—such factors as the use of hands, body movements, and facial expressions—is important in holding an audience's attention. Research has shown that speakers who use hand movements when they talk appear freer, more open, and more honest to an audience than do those who do not demonstrate animation.[1] Consider these suggestions to help your physical presentation:

1. *Arrange your papers on the lectern so that you won't have to play with them.* If you have two pages, place them next to each other rather than on top of each other. This will eliminate the need to handle the papers during the speech.

Physical presentation—such factors as the use of hands, body movements, and facial expressions—is important in holding an audience's attention.

2. *Address the first line of the speech to the audience, not the lectern.* Listeners rapidly determine whether or not to pay attention. If they think you are going to read to them, they are likely to tune you out.
3. *Plant your feet on the ground several inches apart, with one foot slightly in front of the other.* This posture will stop you from swaying and also make it nearly impossible to lean on the podium.
4. *Do not grasp the lectern; let your hands lightly rest on the edges.* That way, if you want to gesture, you can do so easily.
5. *Look at the members of your audience as you speak.* Watch their faces. Eye contact makes the audience members feel like you are speaking to them, and they are much more likely to pay attention to you.
6. *Be familiar with the materials so that you look at the audience rather than at the pages as you go from one sheet to the next.*
7. *It is not always necessary to stand behind the lectern.* If you want to create an informal mood, stand next to or in front of the podium. Some speakers like to sit casually on the corner of a desk or table. Although this position is not recommended for formal presentations, it may work well before a small, informal group.
8. *If you are going to leave the lectern and move to flip charts or to audiovisual or computer aids, determine if you are going to need your cards or notes.* If so, you may want to have that part of your speech outlined or written on cards and take them along with you.

ORAL PRESENTATION

A speech is most interesting for a listener if the speaker is animated and uses a variety of vocal pitch, volume, rate, and pause. Here are some hints regarding vocal delivery:

1. *Speak loud enough to be heard in all parts of the room.*
2. *Talk rather than read.* Readers tend to fall into a flat vocal monotone (no change of volume and pitch).
3. *Stress important words.*
4. *Adjust your pitch and rate to the mood of the material.* If it is exciting, then your rate should increase. If it is dramatic, the rate will slow down.
5. *Group words together so that they make sense.* Do not read or speak words; read or speak ideas.
6. *Try to fit the rate to the complexity of the material.* Complex ideas need a slow rate. Ideas that the audience is already familiar with probably could be presented more rapidly.
7. *Speakers who use manuscripts sometimes <u>underline words to be stressed</u> and make slash marks // to indicate where they want to pause.*
8. *Pause before and after major ideas to stress their importance.*

Some Ways to Use Visuals

If you're not convinced that creative visual displays help communicate a message, these ideas from Jonathan Karas, director of Science House, might change your mind:

● *If you're suggesting that something be cut by 20 percent, take a $100 bill mockup of the real thing and cut 20 percent off it.*

● *To show an increase in the annual wheat crop, show a regular loaf of bread to illustrate last year's production. Use a larger loaf to show the increase.*

● *If real estate costs increase, show a modern house and cut off part of the garage to demonstrate the reality of budget limitations.*

The key: Avoid jargon, lengthy explanations and ancient bar graphs that people are tired of.

Challenge yourself and your colleagues to come up with innovative ways to demonstrate a change. Words alone won't have the same impact.

Source: PR reporter, P.O. Box 600, Exeter, NH 03833.

Using the Flip Chart

- Check the sturdiness of the flip chart stand.
- Limit each chart to one simple idea.
- Lines should have five or six words each with five to seven lines per chart.
- Line the page lightly with pencil to guide your lettering.
- Make sure color selections are not "invisible" and are used as signposts.
- Use large, block letters and have several different color markers available.
- Jot notes in pencil lightly on the sides of the page.
- Keep blank sheets between charts so as not to reveal information before you reach that point in your presentation.
- Put tabs at the bottom of the page to make the page turn easier.
- Check clarity of charts from the back of the room.
- Turn briefly to the chart to refer to it but face the audience as much as possible.
- Consider using two charts so that your prepared charts are on one and your written spontaneous comments can be put on the other.

Handling a Hostile Audience

Consider these techniques to keep cool when your listeners turn up the heat:

- A heckler or adversary interrupts you. Solution: Get audience support by reminding listeners of why you're speaking. Example: "I can discuss that shortly, but let's first finish tackling the critical issues that affect all of us."

- An angry listener stands and refuses to sit down. Solution: Ally yourself with the group. Say something such as: "If you'll please sit down so others can see, the audience would appreciate it."

- A coworker tries to score points with the boss by throwing you a loaded question or contradicting you. Solution: Say you want to stick to the agenda and cover what people came to hear. That subtly suggests that the opponent is keeping them from getting needed information.

- Someone shouts an emotion-laden question such as, "Why did the company have to fire such a loyal group of employees?" Solution: Respond in a soft-spoken tone and restate the question before you try to answer it. Example: "Why did the company, in a fight for survival, have to resort to layoffs?"

Source: Morey Stettner, writing in Investor's Business Daily, 12655 Beatrice St., Los Angeles, CA 90066.

9. *Emphasize the transition from one idea to another.* Key words for this purpose are *moreover, but, nevertheless,* and *however,* as they usually signal transitions to other ideas.

Public Speaking Anxiety

Public speaking anxiety refers to the fears speakers feel before and during speaking. Almost everyone suffers from some form of speech anxiety. Forty-five percent of the United States population (54 percent of women and 34 percent of men) list speaking before groups as the major fear.[2] Another study indicates that "One of the top executives' greatest fears is public speaking."[3] People who say they are afraid to give a speech are not really afraid of giving the speech, per se, but are afraid instead of the negative reaction they will get, both from themselves and from others.

There is a difference between normal anxiety and extreme or disabling anxiety. With normal anxiety, the speaker can remain calm and function. The person with extreme fear becomes befuddled, goes off in all directions at once, and panics to the degree of dysfunction.

It would be reassuring to think that by reading the next several paragraphs you will overcome the fear, if you have it, of getting up and speaking before a group. Unfortunately, this is not exactly the case. However, there are some ways to approach overcoming or dealing with the anxiety. One of the best ways to avoid excessive nervousness is preparation. If you feel comfortable with your topic and your material, and have practiced sufficiently, the normal nervousness that you feel should not cause any major problems as you speak.

Success visualization works for some. Sit or lie quietly and picture yourself going through the speech. In your mind, visualize yourself as you get up from your chair, go forward, put your papers on the lectern, look up at the audience members; see them look back pleasantly, and then give your first sentence. Go through the entire speech, noting the appreciative smiles and agreement of the audience, give the conclusion, hear the audience's applause, and walk back to your chair and sit down. During the entire process, do not see or feel any negative images or emotions. Keep running this positive image tape over and over in your mind. The more you expect positive results, the more likely you will receive them.

As you speak, concentrate on the head-nodders.[4] You will find that in speaking to those people, you get the feeling that someone really is listening to you. The knowledge that someone is listening will be reassuring.

Some speakers find that before they come forward to speak, it helps to take several deep breaths, totally expelling the air with each breath. Others like to shake their hands at the wrists in order to "shake out the nervousness."

The Magic V

Let's say there are 500 people in your audience. It's very difficult to make actual eye contact with 500 people. However, there's a trick to help called the Magic V. When you look at someone, everyone in a V behind that person thinks you are looking at them. Divide the room up into a tic-tac-toe board. Look at one of the "squares" and use the V and the mind touch to lift that section. Once you have them, move to another square.

When the crowd is large, use the Magic V. Draw a "tic-tac-toe" in your mind over the crowd. As you look at each square, you are actually looking at all the people, in a "V" behind the person you are really looking at.

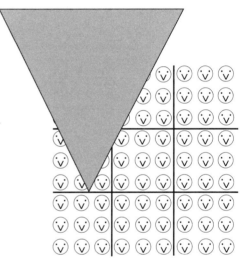

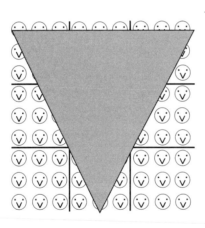

After you have made contact with that group emotionally, switch to another square. Make sure you work the squares at random.

Some people favor grabbing the seat of the chair with both hands, pushing downward and holding the position for about five seconds, then repeating this movement about five times. This exercise tightens and then loosens the muscles, which causes a decrease in bodily tension for some people.

When you are giving the speech, don't put your feet parallel to each other. This stance will cause you to lock your knees and will make your body rigid. As a result, you may experience difficulties in breathing, physical shaking, a dry mouth, and vocal quivering. Instead, place your feet in the triangle stance. To achieve the triangle stance (see Figure 13.1), place one foot—foot A—at a

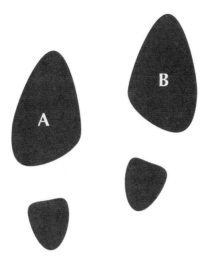

FIGURE 13.1
Foot Placement to Aid in the Relief of Speaker Anxiety

slight angle, and place foot B at about a forty-five-degree angle, as if it were coming out of the arch of foot A. Your feet should be about six inches apart. Shuffle your feet slightly until you feel comfortable and balanced. Place your weight on foot A. You'll feel the leg of foot B relax. You also may find that it helps if you slightly extend the hip of the foot-A side of your body. This process allows you to breathe and gesture easier. As you proceed through the speech, you can alter the stance by the positions of foot A and foot B, always keeping in mind to put your body weight on the foot that is further back. This may sound like an unusual approach, but biologically in this position your body will not lock up and make you tense. You will breath from your diaphragm, your arms and hands will be loose, and you will not lock your knees. What do you have to lose? Try it!

● ● ● **In Summary** ● ● ●

Following preparation of the speech, the speaker must format it and present it. There are four formatting modes that are commonly used when giving speeches. These modes are the impromptu, extemporaneous, manuscript, and memorized. Presenting a speech encompasses physical and vocal elements. The physical elements of a speech include gestures, physical movements, posture, eye contact, and control of the aids you are using during the speech. The vocal elements are animation and the use of variety of vocal pitch, volume, rate, and pause. When effectively used, these elements make a speech interesting. A speaker who is well prepared and knows some relaxation techniques may avoid public speaking anxiety—a fear many speakers experience before and during speaking.

═══ Business Communication in Practice ═══

1. Use the information collected from the interview in Chapter 12 Activity 2 (p. 331). Do research on the same topic. Give a speech comparing the results of the interview with the results of the research. Time limit: a maximum of five minutes.

2. In Chapter 12 Activity 3 (p. 331) you interviewed a person who holds a position similar to one you wish to eventually have (for example, accountant, security analyst, corporate lawyer). Develop a purpose statement about some aspect of the career. Develop and present a three- to five-minute speech.

3. Each student will make a presentation to the class in which a supplementary aid is absolutely necessary for the audience's comprehension of the message. The speech is to be approximately three minutes long.

4. A speaker informs the class about an unusual topic—something the audience has no knowledge of. Sample topics are the derivation of the term "penny stock," the father-son team who headed IBM during most of its history, the role of Norbert Weiner in developing the theory of cybernetics. Be sure the speech has a clear structure and lasts no more than five minutes.

5. Prepare a speech of no more than five minutes informing the class about a controversial business theory. Explain the theory and the various arguments concerning the theory. Do not include your views in the presentation. Be sure the speech is clearly structured. The speech is to be followed by a question-and-answer session.

6. Select an issue confronting businesses. Topics could include safety regulations, employee health care, unionization, air or water pollution, white-collar crime, Japanese competition, or ethical responsibilities of businesses. Give a three- to five-minute speech that explains the nature of the problem and various approaches being taken by organizations to deal with or eliminate the issue. Do not present your views. Do not take a stand on whether businesses are right or wrong. Simply inform the audience about the issue.

7. Select a business-related subject about which you have a strong opinion, or a business-oriented problem for which you have a solution. Present a speech to the class in which you state the problem, the possible solutions or sides to the controversy, your stand on solution, and the reasons for your stand or solution. The speech should be followed by a question-and-answer session in which the class will challenge your solution.

8. You, or a group of students in the class, will select a mission that necessitates persuasive action (for example, getting a college policy changed, convincing a local company to change an operation, persuading a store to remove an unsuitable product). You should attempt to accomplish the perceived goal. Once you've determined the results of the action, present an oral report to the class describing what was attempted, the procedures used, and the results.

9. Submit to your instructor a list of three topics you think you can speak about for a minimum of three minutes. Pick topics that you have experienced, have experiences in, or have learned about in some way: hobbies, special talents, academic interests, travel experiences. Your instructor will pick one of these topics as the basis for an ad-lib speech. The first speaker in the class will be given three minutes to get ready, the second speaker will get his or her topic as the first speaker starts to speak. As soon as the first speaker is finished, the second speaker will begin, and the third speaker will get his or her topic, and so forth.

10. Your instructor will prepare a list of controversial business issues. The subjects will be placed in an envelope. Following the procedure described in assignment 9, you will select a topic and give an ad-lib speech on the subject. Topics may include such subjects as:
    a. A business's first obligation is to its stockholders.
    b. Advertising's major purpose is to sell products, and whatever means the advertiser uses are justified, as long as they are not illegal.
    c. No corporation should be allowed to gain a monopoly position.

11. Read an article relating to some field of business in which you think the class will be interested. Prepare a speech, approximately five minutes in length, summarizing the article, that includes at least three long quotations from the article (twenty words or more).

12. For the next round of classroom speeches, each person will be introduced by a member of the class. Your instructor will indicate who you will introduce. Plan and present the introduction speech.

• • • Notes • • •

1. M. L. Clark, E. A. Erway, and L. Beltzer, *The Learning Encounter* (New York: Random House, 1971), pp. 52–65.
2. "America's Number 1 Fear: Public Speaking," Bruskin/Goldring Research Report (February 1993), p. 4.
3. Ralph Prordian, "One Challenge Many Executives Fear: A Speech," *Wall Street Journal* (September 28, 1981).
4. This concept was agreed upon by the panelists of "Stage Fright, Reticence, Communication Apprehension, Shyness and Social Anxiety: Competing or Compatible Constructs?" (Panel discussion, Speech Communication Association Convention, Chicago, November 3, 1985.)

Written Business Communication

EXPECTED OUTCOMES

After completing this chapter, you should be able to:

- Understand the importance of message, purpose, and reader analysis in preparing effective written communication.
- Understand how elements of style and conventional writing guidelines can enhance the document.
- Understand the importance of organization and design in written documents.
- Understand the standard format of common business documents.

After two months on the task force, I was relieved as I walked into the last group meeting. Not that I didn't genuinely like my colleagues—I did. It was not that the project, a comparative analysis of what 401K pension plans provide, hadn't been interesting. However, the complexity of the task and the seriousness of the mission had made it an exhausting eight weeks. I actually looked forward to going back to my regular workload. At the meeting, I was given the "honor" of preparing the task force report with recommendations, which was due the Monday following that Friday session. I was stunned, but as a junior ranking person on the team, I knew that there was no way out. I asked myself, "How do I take eight weeks' worth of work, boil it down to the specifics, make sure the document speaks to the reader who wants details, and also satisfies the reader who just wants the 'big picture'? As I envisioned the "all weekender," I cursed the fact that I hadn't paid more attention and learned more in the writing and communication classes I took.

The Importance of Effective Business Writing

Some people argue that we are quickly becoming a completely oral society and that formal, written skills are a thing of the past. Not so fast, say others. They counterargue that there is more written material generated today than ever before and that with the advent of electronic mail in the workplace and messages sent throughout the global Internet as well as increasingly common

Virtually all business professionals are called upon not only to create effective written communication, but to edit their documents and those written by others.

facsimile machines and pagers, information comes to you faster and more often than ever before. It therefore becomes increasingly more critical to write in a way that cuts through the barrage of information and reaches your readers.

Virtually every business professional today is called upon to create effective written communication. Regardless of the type of writing or the medium through which it is delivered, the elements of audience and purpose remain important factors when composing clear, concise communication just as they are critical factors in oral communication.

In addition, each industry and each firm will have standards for various types of written documents. Many firms will dictate a structure within which the author is to operate; many will provide software templates for each of the types of writing, offering a standard image to both internal and external readers. For each writer, there are additional demands of good writing: grammatical competency, vocabulary, and style. As there are numerous undergraduate courses, textbooks, and popular press books that address these issues, attention will be devoted here to the specific concerns of the business writer and the types of documents she or he will most likely be called upon to write. Because the written document reflects its author, the writer needs to be attentive to the professional impression a document makes. It is not an exaggeration that one's career advancement can be attributed, in part, to the positive impression created by internal memoranda, letters to clients and customers, "thank you" notes to colleagues, and formal documents to senior management. Finally, written communication can be more precise than oral communication and can reduce uncertainties.

The Writing Process

You may believe that effective writing is not one of your many skills. You may have in your mind an image of the struggling writer, sitting alone in a garret as the winter wind almost extinguishes the last candle warming the impoverished abode as the last finishing touches are made to a sequel to *Les Miserables*. That may be the case for creative writing challenges, but you are much more likely to face a writing task sitting in front of a computer terminal in a cubicle in the midst of pandemonium with your boss screaming that the document you labor over has to be in the overnight pouch in twenty minutes. Usually, this scenario is enhanced by a computer network that goes down and a noisy retirement party in the next office. Take heart—there are ways to approach the challenge that will help you become a good writer, capable of reaching your intended audience, and making an impact.

Effective writing is a learned skill. There are standard ways to approach the situation, which can help you complete documents that will be positively

**Rank Ordering of Writing Competencies as Perceived
by Business Professionals**

COMPETENCY	RANK
Writes well—clearly, concisely, correctly, completely	1
Maintains appropriate level of confidentiality	2
Organizes information into effective sentences and paragraphs	3
Edits and revises documents conscientiously	4
Writes naturally and on the reader's level	5
Writes persuasively	6
Writes routine letters—order acknowledgment, inquiry, etc.	7
Uses proper placement and format for letters and reports	8
Provides effective transition between ideas	9
Uses effective techniques in writing reports	10
Uses psychological factors in writing—positive words, "you" concept, service attitude, goodwill	11
Selects an indirect or direct approach based on the situation	12
Composes at the keyboard	13
Writes special types of letters—sales, claims, etc.	14
Uses subordination and emphasis techniques	15
Outlines material before composing document	16
Uses jargon in appropriate situations	17
Creates bibliographies or finds references	18
Uses longhand to create draft of document	19

Source: Karen K. Waner, "Business Communication Competencies Needed by Employees as Perceived by Business Faculty and Business Professionals," *Business Communication Quarterly* 58:4 (December 1995): 5.

received. Over time practice will result in enhanced performance, giving you increased confidence in this arena.

All documents start with an idea. You will need to formulate a clear understanding of your topic and your purpose. Consider all the many ways you might approach disseminating this information. Don't make judgments about your creative ideas or shut down your exploratory process. Just make a list and let the ideas flow.

Business Professionals Share Their Views

Profile: Penni E. Fromm, PEF Associates, designs and delivers training for Fortune 100 clients around the world. Her corporate clients include Philip Morris, Allied Signal, and AT&T.

How would you characterize the general level of writing ability in today's workplace?

Generally speaking, it is much lower than it should be. I do not think that workers have the same command of writing that they did years ago. I think part of it comes from an education system that does not foster strong writing skills and that is compounded by the inability of managers to edit in a way that the writers are learning from the editing process. Writers don't get any better as a result of the "editing." They can become better writers through coordinating their efforts with managers who share the same ideas about what constitutes clear, effective business writing. Managers should not change a written document for style and personal idiosyncrasies but rather only when there is a serious problem in understanding the intentions of the writer. That would empower the writer and engender more pride in the work.

How can someone learn to be a better writer?

Learn to anticipate the reader's expectations. If your writing is easy to follow, the reader doesn't have to work hard to figure out how the pieces fit. Also, take your ego out of the writing process and recognize that no one is impressed with the vocabulary. Write more naturally.

What one suggestion would you have for someone looking to improve his or her writing skills?

Walk away for a few minutes and come back later and read your document as though you were the reader, without a pen in your hand, and make sure that there are no inconsistencies.

To learn how to communicate in a business area, ask yourself these questions:
- Who is your business reader?
- What is the reader's purpose in reading the document?
- How do you, as the writer, structure your writing to meet the reader's needs?

You may be using techniques for generating ideas: brainstorming, "idea fishing," brainwriting (also known as mind-mapping), or creative visualization. In addition to these, you must spend time evaluating the writing challenge you face by considering four things: the message, the purpose, the audience, and the research or documentation. Then you will turn your attention to the document's image, organization, and layout based on the sample document format you select.

Begin to write the document following the organizational pattern you have chosen. Let your thoughts flow, and do not interrupt your thought process to look up facts or words. Reread the sections, looking for a logical progression from section to section. Then go back to make effective language choices in order to have the greatest impact on the reader. Upon completing the first full draft, let a little time pass. When you return to the document, read it as though it were not yours: find a quiet place, read a paper copy (not on the computer screen), and look for the easy transition of section to section and point to point. Revise with input from other readers as well as your own reactions and comments. That's the "big picture"; now let's look at the various components.

PREPARING TO WRITE THE DOCUMENT

Most writers spend too much time laboring over the exact word or the margin configurations for the Table of Contents and too little time answering basic questions of the document: To whom is this message directed? For what purpose? How do I make the message have the desired effect? This initial analysis can mean the difference between a "brain dump" and a thoughtful document that changes the reader's views and motivates action.

Analyze the Message

What exactly do you want the reader to take away from reading your document? What choices did you make to insure that the message is clearly stated and supported throughout? With the avalanche of information coming to each reader, what makes this message important enough to be worthy of attention and compelling enough not only to maintain interest but also to generate the desired response?

Analyze the Purpose

If a reader does not learn the purpose of the document fairly quickly, time is wasted, as the reader rereads and reframes the information, perhaps finally discarding the document in hopes of finding something of use in another document. All documents should have a clear, defining purpose: to inform, to persuade, or to motivate to act. Everything in the document should support that one, clear purpose. When writers do not communicate that purpose clearly, readers have great difficulty understanding the communication, much less responding in ways intended by the writer. Start by writing down your purpose, then adapting it for the reader.

Analyze the Audience

Most writers (and speakers for that matter) seldom ask themselves the two most important questions: Who is my audience? Why should they care about this? If you cannot answer these questions, it does not matter what else you do. Readers will stop reading your document at the point at which they decide it has no value for them. Also ask yourself these questions:

- What information/attitudes/beliefs do they already hold?
- What are their expectations?
- What is likely to be their interest level?
- What part(s) of the document are they likely to read?
- What do the readers think about the writer?
- How much detail should be offered?

Analyze the Research and Documentation

The great advantage of information access is that the latest facts, figures, and developments can be accessed with a few keystrokes. The downside is that since most everyone can do the same thing, what are you going to do with that information and what do you bring to the document that the reader doesn't already know? Because information is more readily accessible, there is no excuse for outdated research, incomplete analyses, or poor documentation. As a responsible communicator, you will be expected to have completed a thorough search of the available on-line services, the internal resources which may be available to you, as well as current popular press titles and periodicals. How embarrassing to have a reader finish reading your document and then call to ask why you did not reference the major overview of the subject in the *New York Times* just days before you submitted your "comprehensive" report!

WRITING "DO'S" AND "DON'TS"

Follow these suggestions to help make yourself a more effective writer.

The Inverted Pyramid Structure

For years, public relations specialists have used the **inverted pyramid structure** to get information about their clients in front of journalists who sort through literally hundreds of such missives each day. The most important, newsworthy item is listed right up front and is followed by successively less important information or detail as you move down the pyramid. Public Relations professionals know that, in many cases, the release they write will simply be dropped into copy and that when space is tight, the editor will cut from the bottom, leaving room for only the most important information in the first few paragraphs of the release. Think of your document as an inverted pyramid with the most important announcement, information, or development first and then supporting information throughout your document.

The First and Last Positions

We know that the most powerful parts of any presentation, whether oral or written, are the first and the last. Readers (and listeners) expect the writer to get to the point and close with a bang. In fact, readers usually scan a document to see if it is worth reading in its entirety so they look at the opening and closing paragraphs. If the writer is lucky, readers may skim through the body of the text for something that catches their attention. Needless to say, the writer that spends four or five paragraphs warming up to a shocking announcement is likely to lose many readers. Use this knowledge about placement to your advantage and structure your document accordingly.

Parallel Structure

Parallel writing structure is the convention of expressing ideas of equal importance using similar construction. For example, ideas or arguments of equal rank would need connectives such as *and, but, or,* and *nor.* Correlative constructions, used to distinguish between ideas, include *both . . . and, either . . . or, neither . . . nor,* and *not only . . . but also.* Using parallel structure not only helps the reader follow the organization of your document but also gives the reader a clear understanding of how each new piece of information is related to the earlier components. This technique reduces the time needed to read the document and reduces frustration.

Transitions

A good writer not only anticipates the reader's expectations but also helps guide the reader so that those expectations are managed. This is done with the use of **transitional phrases,** which help the reader make the transition from one discussion point to another and eliminates a jarring, rollercoaster ride through the theme park of your document.

Organizational Patterns for Common Documents

Each of the specific formats described here is a generally accepted structure for your guidance. However, each will be further tailored by your company to meet the exact requirements each has with regard to the use of the corporate logo, page layout, and text placement. Many professions will require you to use specific language and a precise format reflecting either corporate philosophy or compliance issues. Adhere to the conventions of letter format regardless of the type of letter. Keep in mind that in most cases, you will want to leave margins of one inch at each side and the bottom and two inches at the top. When left to your own devices, however, you may find these sample outlines helpful.

THE INTERNAL MEMORANDUM

In the upper right-hand corner of an internal memorandum there is generally a space for you to fill in the requested information—name of recipient, department, your name, department, telephone number, date, and subject. After leaving a space of two or three lines, begin typing your paragraphs flush left. Generally, the paragraphs are not indented but rather a space is left between each successive paragraph. When finished with the body of the text, leave four to five spaces before your name (if your company's policy is not to simply initial your name in the upper right-hand corner). Be sure to indicate any enclosed materials as well as any copies sent to other parties. Memos are usually no more than one page in length (Figure 14.1).

THE EXTERNAL LETTER

Any correspondence that leaves your office should reflect well on you, your department, and your company. The customer or client you address sees not the entire firm but you as the embodiment of that firm. A block style layout with margins that are flush left and space between the paragraphs is common. (See Figure 14.2.)

THE PROJECT STATUS REPORT

In the Project Status Report, follow the conventions described and consider this structure: the Project Objective, in which you outline the scope of the project; the Background Information, which gives the reader an understanding of the challenges; the Procedure, which clarifies the steps taken and their interrelatedness; the Key Findings or the outcome of the project; and Next Steps, in which you indicate how past accomplishments lay the foundation for what needs to be done next. Your manager may or may not suggest a summary, which would briefly recap the document and concentrate on the findings and next steps sections. An Appendix of Reference Materials or Exhibit Book should accompany your document so that the detailed materials will be available for the reader who wishes to delve more deeply into your report.

Communic-aid

INDIVIDUAL/GROUP TRAINING, CONSULTING
AND SEMINARS IN:
  ORGANIZATIONAL AND
    CORPORATION COMMUNICATION
  SPEECH PREPARATION
  GROUP DYNAMICS
  TEACHING METHODOLOGIES

To: Margaret Hepler
At: Human Resources, Payroll
From: David Pearson
At: Operations Support
Tel: X4378
Date: October 15, 1996
Subject: YEAR-END REPORT DATA REQUEST

Margaret
    I'm preparing year-end reports for our divi-
sion, and would appreciate the following information:

    1. Present number of exempt and nonexempt em-
       ployees
    2. Number of both categories at the beginning
       of the year
    3. Total present staff payroll
    4. Total vacation days carried over from last
       year for salaried employees only
    5. Personal and sick days for exempt and non-
       exempt

I need this information by December 1, 1996.

Thanks,
Dave

FIGURE 14.1
Interoffice Memo

Farmer's Cooperative Outreach
262 Henry Drive
Elyria, Ohio 44035

September 12, 1995

Ms. Deborah E. Wilson
Manager, Human Resources
Ohio Dairy Association
43 East Windsor Drive
Elyria, Ohio 44035

Dear Ms. Wilson:

I write this letter on behalf of Alexander Lee, a senior at Ohio State University who is currently a candidate for an entry-level position in the public relations department of your firm. I could not be more pleased to do so.

For the past four summers, Alexander has been an intern with us here at the Farmer's Cooperative Outreach. During that time, I have come to know him well and can speak of his many accomplishments. He has always impressed members of my department with his "can do" attitude, his willingness to tackle any task, and his ability to interact with virtually anyone who came in contact with our extensive outreach program. He has the amazing ability to carry on a conversation with anyone and to make each one feel special. Once, I listened in as he helped an elderly, retired farmer wade through the mountain of paperwork to expedite his benefits with the State. I was impressed with his compassion and his sensitivity. Quite simply, he is a young man with a maturity level beyond that of his peers.

I imagine that the position he seeks requires good writing skills. I have taken the liberty of enclosing a proposal he wrote advocating the adoption of a community awareness campaign for an inoculation and health maintenance program for those who live outside the range of traditional medical services. I think you will find it a thorough, considered approach and one worthy of serious consideration. It is currently under advisement here in the department.

Please know that I shall be happy to provide additional information or speak with you directly regarding his candidacy. I recommend him without reservation as I believe that he will be for you, as he was for us, an outstanding member of the department.

Sincerely,

Joan L. Grannier

Joan L. Grannier
Director, Community Relations Board

FIGURE 14.2
Sample Business Letter (Block Style)

THE EXECUTIVE SUMMARY

The Executive Summary differs little from the Project Status Report except in its length (it is shorter) and in its level of detail (it is less detailed). The same structure is appropriate. Keep in mind that all readers are concerned with time. The higher one is on the corporate ladder, the less time is available for reading documents. Senior management will want to scan a document of only a few pages, forgo detail, and be concerned with the bottom line.

THE SALES PROPOSAL

Whenever you present a proposal for the sale of products or services, you need to remember that most people do not embrace change willingly. They will buy your product or service when you can convince them not only of your and your firm's trustworthiness but also of the superior quality and value of your product or service. This can be done in a brochure, an annual report, a client list, or comments from satisfied customers included with the materials you submit. Or you can use this format to organize your proposal. First, begin with the need to consider this new product or service. You may want to speak of a customer's competition or the changing nature of the marketplace. Next, demonstrate your understanding of the customer's business and the challenges faced and discuss the customer's needs. Then link the benefits of your product or service directly to each of the customer needs you identified. Address the issue of cost, and demonstrate that the cost is offset by increased revenue or reduced operating expenses. Reiterate your strengths and the strengths of your company. Summarize the key benefits of your product or service, and then close with the next step that you want your prospective customer to take. An additional section with detailed reference material may be appropriate.

THE RESUME AND COVER LETTER

On the one hand, there is no substitute for the positive impression your cover letter and resume can make on the individual who receives them. On the other hand, there is little you can do to recover from a negative first impression. The first person who receives your resume—usually someone in Human Resources who screens out candidates—is looking for a good reason to eliminate your resume. Bad grammar, sloppy layout, mistakes, or other "red flags" make that decision easy for them. You may be thinking, "my resume is less important than the great stuff I've done." You may well be able to make a good case in the actual interview, but you will seldom get to that stage if the resume fails to stand out for positive reasons. Competition is simply too great in today's market to second-guess why someone had a poorly written resume. In the words of one managing director at a top investment banking firm, "The

THANK YOU FOR AN INTERVIEW

Street Address
City, State, Zip
Date of writing

Name
Title
Street Address
City, State, Zip

Dear Mr./Ms.:

It was a pleasure to visit you and to meet the members of your staff. I was pleased with the opportunity to get a closer look at (name of organization) and to hear of the many ventures being undertaken.

2nd paragraph—(See suggestions below for possible applicable paragraphs.)

I was most impressed with your organization, especially in the area of quality control. As I understand, you will contact me within a month regarding further consideration. I look forward to hearing from you soon. Thank you again for the interview.

Sincerely,
(Handwritten sig.)

Your name, typed

2. Paragraph to cover information unsatisfactorily presented in the interview: In reviewing the interview, I feel that I did not accurately answer your question about travel, schedule requirements, etc. I may have conveyed hesitancy about travel, or extra working hours or other special considerations. Your subsequent explanations and descriptions of the job helped me realize that I would find the situations mentioned to be acceptable.

ACCEPTANCE OF OFFER

Street Address
City, State, Zip
Date of writing

Name/Title
Company
Street Address
City, State, Zip

Dear Mr./Ms.:

I am pleased to accept your invitation to become an engineer for the Arthur Manufacturing Company at the monthly salary of $_____. I am certain that the duties that will be assigned to me will be interesting and challenging.

Thank you for your offer of assistance in finding housing in Pittsburgh. This help will make my relocation much easier.

I look forward to my future association with Arthur Manufacturing. As advised in your letter, I will report to your office at 8:30 a.m. on (date).

Sincerely,
(Handwritten sig.)

Your name, typed

OUTLINE: STANDARD APPLICATION LETTER
(Indented Block Style)

Street Address
City, State, Zip
Date of writing

Name
Title
Company
Street Address
City, State, Zip

Dear Mr./Ms.:

1st paragraph—Tell why your are writing: name the position, field, or general vocation about which you are asking. Tell how you heard of the opening or organization.

2nd paragraph—Tell why you are particularly interested in the company, location, or type of work. If you have had related experience or specialized training, be sure to point it out. Be as specific as you can about your qualifications. Tell where, when, and how they were developed. Communicate to the employer that you understand the position, the organization, and how you would fit into both. Refer the employer to an enclosed resume and/or application form.

3rd paragraph—Close by suggesting specific additional contact and providing details on how and when you can be reached. If your request is for further information concerning the opening, it would be polite to enclose a self-addressed, stamped envelope. Make sure your closing is specific and evokes an action from the employer.

Sincerely,
(Handwritten sig.)

Your name, typed

Enclosures

resume is the flyer for the product—if it doesn't make me want to buy, I don't go shopping." (Review the sample formats for the resume in Chapter 8, *Interviewing,* pp. 202–204, and 210–211.)

THE MINUTES OF A MEETING

The minutes of a meeting may stand alone or be distributed with an internal memorandum. In any case, the general areas that must be covered include date, purpose or topic, attenders, discussion items, action items, tabled items, actions to be undertaken by individuals as agreed upon at the meeting, and an announcement of the next scheduled meeting. Most of these sections will contain information in a "bullet" format with enough detail to accurately reflect the decision or concerns of the group.

The ABC's of Language

Action Most experts agree that the active, rather than the passive, voice is most effective for business correspondence. Using the active voice enhances the document by adding emphasis to deliver the message. If the subject of the sentence acts, then the writer is using the active voice. If the subject of the sentence is acted upon, then the writer is using the passive voice. Generally, using the active voice means clarity, a quicker pace, less confusion, and a greater impact. Consider these examples:

    (active)   Robert prepared the budget for the next fiscal year.
    (passive)   The budget for the next fiscal year was prepared by Robert.

Notice that in the active voice example the reader has a clear idea at the beginning where the action is. Also note the sentence is shorter, which leads to the next topic, brevity.

Brevity Shakespeare wrote that brevity was the soul of wit. Brevity also means the difference between a document used as a doorstop and one that is approachable because it appears to be concise. You can cut the overall length of the document by eliminating word or phrase repetition, awkward phrases, and pompous word choices. Notice this in these streamlined examples below:

    in the event of . . . *becomes* . . . if
    in a timely manner . . . *becomes* . . . soon
    subsequent to . . . *becomes* . . . after
    conduct an in-depth analysis of . . . *becomes* . . . research
    true facts . . . *becomes* . . . facts.

Guidelines for Business Correspondence

The Interior Address for Business Correspondence

Flush against the left margin, the interior address should have a space between it and the date line. The following items should be listed in this order:

Name of the person to whom the letter is addressed including courtesy or professional title (for example, Ms., Mr., Dr., Professor)
Business title if any (e.g., Vice President, General Manager)
Division or branch if any
Company name
Address

Source: Rosemary T. Fruehling and N. B. Oldham. *Write to the Point!* (New York: McGraw-Hill, 1988), pp. 91–92.

The Salutation for Business Correspondence

The safest bet: Dear (Ms,. Mr., or Dr.)(first and last name):
For a senior executive: Dear Ms. Williams: (do not use the first name alone)
For two individuals: Dear Ms. McGarry and Dr. Weaver:
For persons unknown: To whom it may concern:

Avoid informal, personal choices when not completely sure, and never place the person's title on the same line as the salutation.

Source: Rosemary T. Fruehling and N. B. Oldham. *Write to the Point!* (New York: McGraw-Hill, 1988), pp. 93–100.

The Complimentary Close for Business Correspondence

Formal Traditional Closes

Very truly yours,	Very respectfully yours,
Very sincerely yours,	Respectfully yours,
Very cordially yours,	Respectfully,

Informal Traditional Closes

Sincerely,	Sincerely yours,
Cordially,	Cordially yours,
Yours truly,	

Informal Personalized Closes

Best wishes,	Regards,
Warmest regards,	Warmly,
Best regards,	All the best,
With all good wishes,	Thank you,

Source: Rosemary T. Fruehling and N. B. Oldham. *Write to the Point!* (New York: McGraw-Hill, 1988), pp. 102–103.

If you need a great deal of the reader's time to clearly explain a complicated or lengthy business initiative or development, don't shortchange the document. By the same token, if you have information that does not need a huge buildup, go directly to the point. In the words of the Nike commercial, "Just Do It."

Clarity Here are some suggestions to enhance clarity of the document as well as reader receptivity:

- write as you speak, as it creates a relaxed, conversational tone;
- select words for their specificity and accuracy, not for their pomposity;
- use contractions, acronyms, and hyphens sparingly;
- check the overall document to see if your sentences reflect the business average of twenty words per sentence;
- spell out numbers nine and under, write numbers above nine as figures (seven, 517);
- observe rules and guidelines for grammar and punctuation (consult one of the authoritative English handbooks);
- vary the use of simple, compound, and complex sentences as shown:
    simple—single thought
        Capital expenditures were down more than 12 percent.
    compound—two or more independent thoughts
        Capital expenditures were down and revenues were up.
    complex—one independent thought and one or more dependent thoughts
        If capital expenditures were down at the same rate as the past five years, then the planned capital improvement initiative must be revised.
- vary the length of your sentences to increase variety;
- be sure that paragraphs contain only one central idea and its supporting material;
- check to see that the shorter the document, the shorter the paragraphs;
- avoid jargon and buzzwords, which tend to alienate readers because they do not share a common frame of reference with the reader; and
- avoid sexist or other inappropriate language.

Enhancing the Document's Image

The stationery, layout, and format can enhance or detract from the image of written messages. Knowing about these factors can help you when you are preparing documents.

How to Write for the Ear

Keep these points in mind when you write a script for an audio, a video, or a speech:

- *Write short sentences. Simple declarative sentences work best. Sentences cluttered with unneeded adjectives and adverbs may not be clear. Make them memorable: "You need room to negotiate," "Brand names will lose their appeal."*

- *Use short words. Think about why people remember proverbs such as, "A bird in the hand is worth two in the bush" and "A stitch in time saves nine."*

- *Avoid rows of sibilant sounds such as, "Some supervisors seem stifled." They're hard to say.*

- *Try to end sentences with a one-syllable word. It's like having punctuation written in. Listeners can't see periods.*

- *Avoid words listeners might not understand. Use "although," not "albeit"; "polite," not "affable"; "secret," not "arcane."*

Source: Frank Seltzer, 6034 Palo Pinto, Dallas, TX 75206.

STATIONERY

Once the thrill of seeing your name on the letterhead passes, you will need to pay attention to the choice of stationery and the messages it sends to the reader. Corporate letterheads should never be used for personal business or matters outside the scope of your business responsibilities. Any external document you write should reflect your own professionalism as well as the reputation of the company. *The Complete Guide to Executive Manners*[1] offers a wealth of advice regarding not only the proper use of stationery but also the appropriate format for letters and notes of all kinds, both formal and informal.

LAYOUT AND FORMAT

Select enhancements to the document that make sense and conform to company policy. In a longer document, use consistent headings and footers, and use the same layout for major and minor section titles. When selecting type fonts, use no more than two in the body of the text. Use one for the headings and titles and another for the body of the text. Select a font that is businesslike, not the latest trendy style you happen to have on that new graphics package. Stick to one similar to Times New Roman or Helvetica. Generally, a ten or twelve point size is preferable.

When making graphics choices, remember that less is more. Avoid cartoons, silly borders, and embroidery. This is a business document, not a creative arts class. Be sure to leave enough white space around graphics and text when you want to emphasize the material or when you want to break the material into sections.

Use bullets sparingly, as their overuse can appear to be clipped and harsh. They can be a wonderful way to get through a great deal of information in a shorter document and can help the eye of the reader move quickly and easily through the text.

Electronic Mail at the Workplace

Businesses are increasingly turning to electronic mail, or e-mail, as a system for sending and receiving messages. Effective business communicators must be aware of the advantages and disadvantages of using this mode, and also of special writing techniques to use when corresponding electronically.

SPEED VERSUS ACCURACY

Although the e-mail system affords greater speed, it is not an excuse to drop all conventions of proper grammar and written etiquette. If your e-mail system offers a spell or grammar check, take a few moments to scan your document. After you push the "send" button, it's too late to discover the misspelled word or critical figure that changes your entire message.

PRIVACY CONCERNS

Know that your e-mail messages might have a much larger audience and a much longer lifetime than you think. Although your missive is not sent out on a physical sheet of paper, it can be retrieved, copied, duplicated, forwarded or used against you in a court of law. Cybersleuth Joan Feldman, owner of Seattle-based Computer Forensics, Inc., says, "I don't think a lot of people understand that the contents of their computer is fair game (during an investigation)."[2] Whether the FBI wants to conduct a sting operation for child pornography on an online service or a company wants to search the contents of your computer's hard drive to settle a dispute, the technology is there to retrieve even those files you think you deleted. In addition to concern for your own privacy, also be concerned about making statements or accusations over the fairly informal "bulletin board." A recent lawsuit involved a member of an online service who made accusations about a corporation only to find that the corporation tracked down the author of the statement and went to court. Tread lightly.

ETIQUETTE

If you use e-mail with the same level of gravity you would use for other written communication, you likely will encounter no problems. There are, however, a few things to be aware of. Highly sensitive or personal information should never be delivered via an e-mail system, as this form of delivery can seem exceptionally impersonal and cold to some individuals. You should not read or forward someone else's e-mail without their permission. Be as brief as possible; trivial messages can be as costly for the recipient to retrieve as an important message. Use the "Subject" line so that if the recipient is pressed for time, he or she can see whether or not the message is urgent. Use the "urgent" designation selectively and only when it is justified.

Abbreviations can be helpful when used correctly (see Figure 14.3). Be careful when you use e-mail symbols (often called "smileys" or "emoticons") so that you do not inadvertently send the wrong message (see Figure 14.4). Use capital letters sparingly as they are perceived as "shouting." Remember

Big Brother Keeps Busy Reading E-mail

The sleuths who root out damaging e-mail from computer memories also advise companies on how to reduce their own vulnerability. Some tips on e-mail etiquette from Computer Forensics Inc. of Seattle:

• Ask yourself: Would I want a jury to read this e-mail?

• Be polite. Make sure short messages don't come across as brusque or curt.

• Don't send offensive jokes or frivolous messages.

• Don't write anything you wouldn't want repeated. E-mail can be forwarded to hundreds of people, in and out of a company.

• Work out problems face to face, not on e-mail.

• Protect your password, and always log off when not using the system.

ALPHABET SOUP

As you explore the world of online communication, you'll discover a whole new language. E-mail users have developed a vocabulary, which includes acronyms for commonly used phrases, to save time and money. These abbreviations can be confusing if you don't know what they stand for, but once you learn them, they make e-mail easier. Here is a partial list:

AAMOF	As A Matter of Fact	OIC	Oh, I See!
BAK	Back At Keyboard	OTOH	On The Other Hand
BBFN	Bye Bye For Now	PNCAH	Please No Cussing Allowed
BRB	Be Right Back		Here
BTW	By The Way	PTMM	Please, Tell Me More
CMIIW	Correct Me If I'm Wrong	TIA	Thanks In Advance
CUL	See You Later	TIC	Tongue In Cheek
F2F	Face-To-Face	TNTL	Trying Not To Laugh
FITB	Fill In The Blank	TNX	Thanks
FYA	For Your Amusement	TTKSF	Trying To Keep Straight
FYI	For Your Information		Face
HHOK	Ha Ha Only Kidding	TYVM	Thank You Very Much
HOUEW	Hanging On Your Every	WRT	With Respect To
	Word	WTGP?	Want To Go Private?
IAC	In Any Case	YIU	Yes, I Understand
IKWUM	I Know What You Mean	YIWGP	Yes, I Will Go Private
IMHO	In My Humble Opinion	<G>	Grinning
IOW	In Other Words	<J>	Joking
KWIM	Know What I Mean?	<L>	Laughing
LOL	Laughing Out Loud	<S>	Smiling

There are many more; you'll discover them as you explore the world of online communication. Additional listings may be found on online services, wherever users post lists they have come across or come up with on their own. On American Online, you can find these by performing a file search for files containing the word "acronym." As you become more proficient at e-mail communication, you'll probably come up with a few of your own to add to the mix.

FIGURE 14.3
Alphabet Soup

that sending inflammatory or offensive remarks (called "flaming") can be a career limiting move.[3] Finally, be aware that if you leave your terminal while it is logged on, any messages that are sent will appear to come from you—a situation that opens the door for all kinds of problems. Think of it as an open microphone that you need to guard carefully.

FUNNY FACES

One of the biggest challenges of electronic communication is trying to convey emotions. E-mail users have invented symbols to convey things that would be conveyed by tone of voice over the phone or facial expressions in person. These symbols are called "smileys" or "emoticons" and are mostly small faces composed of several keyboard characters. (You have to tilt your head to the left to view them.) Here are some of the most common examples:

:-)	Happy/Smiling	|-O	Yawning/Snoring
;-)	Winking	:-P	Sticking Tongue Out
:-(	Frowning/Sad	:'-(	Crying
:-&	Tongue-tied	:'-)	Crying For Joy
:-S	Incoherent	:->	Sarcastic
:-D	Laughing	<:->	Devilish
:-@	Screaming	O:-)	Angelic

A few smileys are not faces; here are several of the most popular:

{}	A hug (usually in multiples	—<—@	A rose
	—{{{{}}}}}	12x—<—@	A dozen roses
{initials}	To hug a specific person		

Some of these smileys have more than one meaning depending upon the user, but in general the definitions are very similar. You can find more complete listings online; users often post their own lists of smileys. On American Online, select Keyword: File Search, then enter emoticons. As you become an e-mail expert, you may come up with some smileys of your own to add to these lists.

FIGURE 14.4
Funny Faces

Analyzing the Written Document

One of the tasks writers face is the need to edit—not only their documents but also those written by others. When reviewing the effectiveness of a written document, consider the following questions related to message, purpose, audience adaptation, research/documentation, organization, image, and language:

The Message
   Does the document reflect my best efforts?
   Is the message clear, concise, and consistent?

When Editing Your Own Copy

Whenever you write something, you should know how to edit and polish your own copy. Here are some guidelines to follow when editing for:

● **Brevity.** *Cut every word that adds nothing to meaning. Examples: Change "during the course of" to "during" and "few in number" to "few."*

● **Clarity.** *Don't use vague adjectives when specific ones are called for. Don't write, "We received numerous inquiries." Instead write, "We received 145 inquiries."*

● **Tone and style.** *Make sure your words sound as if they come from a human being—and not an institution. Example: Instead of writing, "Further notification will follow," write, "I'll keep you informed."*

● **Variety.** *Avoid starting each sentence with the same part of speech, such as a noun or pronoun. Caution: Don't try to start each sentence with a different part of speech. Just strive for some variety.*

● **Content.** *Make your purpose immediately clear. Don't force your reader to wade through several paragraphs before understanding why you wrote the piece.*

● **Paragraph strength.** *See to it that each paragraph deals with only one topic. Including too many will make your reader work too hard.*

The Purpose
 Have I clearly indicated a purpose to inform, persuade or motivate to action?
 What did I do to enhance the effectiveness of my rationale?
 Did I clearly communicate my purpose in writing?
 Have I chosen the best way to present the message?
The Audience
 Have I clearly targeted the intended readers?
 Did I adapt the message for the information/attitudes/beliefs they already hold?
 Did I allow for their expectations?
 Did I appeal to their interest levels?
 What have I done to ensure that the readers will read the document the way I want them to?
 What have I done to ensure that the readers will respond to the document the way I want them to?
The Research/Documentation
 Is the documentation recent, reliable, and relevant?
 Does the documentation reflect my best efforts to provide enough information for the readers?
 Is there a consistent style of reference for all information?

The Document's Organization
  Does the document follow a standard format?
  Does there seem to be a natural progression from section to section?
The Document's Image
  Is the structure of the format clear?
  Are headings and footers consistent?
  Are type fonts used consistently and unobtrusively?
  Are graphics used to enhance the written text?
  Are bullets used effectively?
  Is there adequate white space around the text?
The Document's Language
  Is it active, concise, and clear?
  Are words chosen for their specificity?
  Are standards of good grammar used?
  Are standards of correct punctuation used?
  Are rules of capitalization used?
  Is the construction parallel?
  Are the transitions smooth?
  Is jargon avoided?
  Is noninclusive language of all types eliminated?
  Is the tone appropriate?

Clear, concise, effective written communication is one of the cornerstones of the successful businessperson. This chapter was designed not to substitute for a course in business writing but to make you aware of the challenges that you will face and to alert you to the variety of your communication encounters, both written and oral, as opportunities for you to enhance your professional status.

● ● ● In Summary ● ● ●

Virtually every business professional today is called upon to create effective written communication. To develop an effective document ask yourself, "What exactly do I want the reader to take away from reading this document?" All documents should have a clear, defining purpose: to inform or to persuade. Everything in the document should support that one, clear purpose. Ask yourself, "Who is my audience and why would they care about this?" To generate materials to develop your ideas and arguments, complete a thorough search of the available online services, the available internal resources, as well as current popular press titles and periodicals.

Begin to write the document following the organizational pattern you have chosen. Let your thoughts related to that component flow, and do not interrupt your thought process to look up facts or words. Reread the sections, looking for a logical progression from section to section. Then go back and make effective language choices in order to have the greatest impact on the reader. Upon completing the first full draft, let time pass. When you return to the document, read it as though it were not yours: find a quiet place, read a paper copy (not via the screen), and look for the easy transition of section to section and point to point. Revise with input from other readers as well as your own reactions and comments.

Written business documents you may need to prepare include the internal memorandum, external letter , project status report, executive summary, sales proposal, resume and cover letter, minutes of a meeting, and electronic mail. Be aware that the stationery, layout, and format can enhance or detract from the image of written messages.

▬▬ Business Communication in Practice ▬▬

1. Write a status report detailing the cost of your education, the value of the money spent, your performance, the prospects for jobs, and the competition you face for those jobs. Support your findings with current research and detailed facts and figures.
2. Review term papers and reports you wrote in high school or during your first months in college. Do they seem less effective than the documents you now write? Why? What choices have you made in recent documents that are missing in the earlier ones?
3. Each person in the class will write his or her own cover letter and resume. Then, in groups of four, each person will share the documents with the others, who will offer feedback and suggestions, noting especially when items are not clearly written. Request feedback from others as well, including your instructor, career counselors, and other campus-related professionals.
4. Review letters written to you by various corporations. Which ones seemed to be the most professional? Why? What differences do you notice among them?
5. Select a prominent company in your hometown. Write a sales proposal for a new product or service that you believe would be of value to them.

●●● Notes ●●●

1. For advice on letters refer to Letitia Baldrige, *Complete Guide to Executive Manners* (New York: Rawson Associates, 1985).
2. Mike Snider, "E-Mail Isn't as Private as You May Think," *USA Today* (October 10, 1995), 6D.
3. Diana K. McLean, "E-Mail Etiquette," *PC Novice* (September 1995): 42–44.

Glossary

After-dinner speeches Presentations normally intended to entertain, though they may center on a serious theme. In the business environment they take place after banquets or at conferences.

Agenda The outline of topics to be discussed at a meeting or the procedure that will be used to discuss how to solve a problem. It enables the group to cover the issues systematically and thus accomplish the task in the most efficient way possible.

Analogy Comparison of an unfamiliar concept to a familiar one in a way that clarifies a concept for listeners.

Anger A reaction to frustration. The frustration may be personal (when you are upset with yourself for not being able to accomplish a task) or external.

Appreciative listening level Listening that takes place as the receiver gains pleasure or a sensory impression from the material being received.

Artifacts The clothing that a person wears, also makeup, eyeglasses, and beauty aids—all of which convey messages.

Assertive people Individuals with strong self-respect and the ability to deal with challenging situations, handle confrontations, and establish influences in group meetings. They are allowed the most talking time in meetings and are able to command attention.

Attention Focusing on one stimulus over all others in the environment at any given time.

Attitudes Positive and negative predispositions.

Audience analysis The process of making demographic, attitudinal, and belief evaluations of prospective listeners.

Audience cultural identities Factors such as audience members' age, gender, religion, cultural/ethnic uniqueness, background, intellectual level, and occupation.

Audio aids Devices that appeal to the sense of hearing, such as records, tape recordings, and duplications of sounds that may be the only way to demonstrate particular sensations accurately for listeners.

Audiovisual aids Devices such as films, videotapes, and tape-slide presentations that combine the dimensions of sight and sound.

Authoritarian leaders Leaders who dominate and direct a group according to personal goals and objectives regardless of how consistent these goals are with the group members' goals.

Avoidance The attempt to withdraw from contact with another person, or staying away from the issue of conflict when the possibility for taking action is present.

Behavioral Kinesiology (BK) A scientific field of study that purports that every major muscle of the body relates to an organ. All the organs in our body are affected by the music and other aesthetics that we are exposed to daily.

Beliefs True or false convictions held by an individual.

Body of an interview The heart of the discussion, in which the speaker handles the questions and responses to those questions.

Body of a speech The central part of a speech, in which the speaker develops the major points of the presentation as well as any subpoints that pertain to the central idea.

Bottom-up communication system System that empowers workers to make decisions and provide imput in the management and decision-making process. This communication approach is based on the concept that change and initiative within an organization should come from those closest to the problem.

Brainstorming Communication process that consists of generating possible solutions to solve a problem without evaluating them at the time they are proposed.

Causal arrangement Pattern of arrangement that shows how two events or objects are connected in such a way that if one occurs, the other will necessarily follow.

Central idea of a speech The overall point of a speech.

Centralized decision-making process Process based on the concept that authority is inherent within the individual, not the individual's position. This system makes trade-offs a common device for negotiators.

Chronemics The study of the use of time.

Chronological or **time method of arrangement** Pattern of arrangement in which the speaker organizes the body of a speech from a beginning point to an ending one, with all the steps developed in numerical or time sequence.

Closed question An interview question that narrows and structures the responses that the interviewee will give. It is a good technique to use when a direct to-the-point answer is desired.

Closing of an interview The end of the interview when the parts of the session are summarized.

Climate The general atmosphere of supportiveness or defensiveness that people feel within a group.

Clincher to a speech Technique for concluding a presentation. Clincher techniques include personal references, humorous stories, illustrations, rhetorical questions, action questions, unusual or dramatic devices, or quotations.

Clusters Groups of gestures.

Coercion A technique that offers a selection of choices, all of which are undesirable, so that the receiver perceives that he or she has no choice.

Cognitive complexity A person's ability to deal with higher orders of abstractions and complex levels of information.

Cognitive consistency The balance of an individual's values, attitudes, and beliefs.

Cognitive dissonance The confusion that results when a person cannot keep values, attitudes, and beliefs in balance.

Cognitive modification A method for teaching a person to modify her or his negative self-talk.

Cognitive processing The scheme used to attend, interpret, and store messages in the long-term memory.

Committee A small group responsible for studying, researching, and making recommendations about an issue.

Communication anxiety Real or anticipated fear of communicating with others, caused by the belief that there is more to lose than to gain from communicating.

Communication plan A step-by-step format for reaching a desired communication goal.

Communication stoppers Negative phrases such as "That will never work," "We've tried that before," or "That's ridiculous," which can shut down the communication.

Communication technology Another name for the electronic media, which includes devices such as television, computers, and teleconferencing tools.

Comparison-contrast method of arrangement Pattern of arrangement in which a speaker organizes the body of a speech by telling both the similarities and the differences of several concepts.

Comparison method of arrangement Pattern of arrangement in which a speaker organizes the body of a speech by telling how two or more examples are alike.

Competition Dynamic based on the concept that in working toward the solution to a problem, someone must win and someone must lose. Power is at the center of the process.

Comprehensive listening level Listening that occurs when the listener wants to understand the material being presented so that it can be recalled and used.

Compromise The basis for negotiating a solution in which all parties give up something they desire in order to get something that all can agree to as an acceptable solution.

Computer-generated supplementary aids Presentation aids that use a combination of computers and projection equipment to create attention-getting and clarifying graphics.

Conclusion to a speech The final part of a presentation that summarizes, pulls thoughts together, or motivates the listeners to take a prescribed action.

Concreteness Quality of being specific rather than abstract by being real rather than artificial and by using concrete language to describe specific experiences and behaviors.

Conflict The emotional state a person experiences when the behavior of one person interferes with another's behavior. Conflict usually centers on a struggle between incompatible interests, often resulting in psychological interference, as well as the appearance of incompatible interests.

Conflict resolution An attempt to reconcile differences in order to accept, reduce, or eliminate the conflict.

Confronting assertive response Response that often follows a simple assertion or an empathetic response. It describes the person's behavior and then states the asserter's position.

Confucian principle of *i* Part of a belief system that requires that a person be affiliated and identify with a small and tightly knit group of people over long periods of time—a situation that results in group members' aiding and assisting each other when there is a need.

Congruency Technique used in nonverbal communication analysis by which past patterns are compared to present actions in order to observe user consistency and, therefore, understand the meaning of certain actions.

Connotation The feeling or emotional aspects of a subjective word's meaning. These words all need clarifications and examples to understand the user's intent.

Consensus A voting technique that means "all." In a consensus decision, every member of the group must agree on a proposal before it can be put into action.

Consensus-building direction-taking decision-making process Process in which everyone affected by the decision is included in the process.

Context (also referred to as **setting**) The situation in which the communication takes place, including the people and the emotional attitude.

Contrast method of organization Method of organizing the body of a speech by indicating the differences between the two ideas or things.

Corporate communication department The coordinating unit of a business that manages the internal and external communication functions of the organization.

Corporate culture A company's traditions, rituals, values, history, interactions, and norms. The culture is what makes the organization unique and gives it a personality of its own.

Counseling interviews Interviews in which the interviewer serves as a "sounding board" allowing the interviewee to talk through problems.

Critical listening level Listening that occurs when the receiver understands and then evaluates a message based on a careful analysis of the strengths and weaknesses of a position or decision presented.

Cross-functional work teams Teams composed of people from several departments brought together to communicate with each other, to solve problems, create new products, or to participate in new marketing initiatives.

Decode The process used to clarify received messages.

Deductive arguments Arguments that follow a syllogistic form of idea development in which general premises are used to build a specific conclusion. Historically, these are the traditional and formal method of viewing persuasion.

Democratic leaders Leaders who direct a group according to the goals of its members and allow them to form their own conclusions.

Denotation Referential word meaning, based on the concept that certain terms have specific meanings.

DESC scripting An assertive system in which the asserter develops a sequential series of statements that describes what is wrong, expresses how this makes the asserter feel, specifies what course of action should be taken, and then states possible consequences if that action is not undertaken.

Dialect A social or regional variation of the words and pronunciation of a language.

Direct intervention The active attempt of one person to change another person's pattern of behavior.

Directing The giving of orders and directions for the purpose of explaining new procedures, instructing employees in the operation of equipment, or clarifying policies.

Discriminative listening The listening level used to distinguish auditory and/or visual differences.

Discussion questions Questions used in group discussions and interviews to identify the issue or problem that will be dealt with.

Ebonics, Black English or **African American Vernacular English (AAVE)** A language system that has highly consistent grammar, pronunciation, lexicon, and stylistic features. It is the first language variety learned by many African Americans in their home settings and used with family and friends.

Egospeak The art of boosting your own ego by speaking only about what you want to talk about, and not caring about what the other person is speaking about. Egospeaking techniques include interrupting, dominating a conversation, and discounting the ideas of the conversation partner(s).

Electronic meetings Meetings conducted via e-mail that offer a means for making instant connections without having to bring people together in the same physical presence.

Electronic resume screening A technique in which resumes are scanned into computers and sorted by key words to identify candidates with specific abilities and talents.

Emblems Nonverbal gestures that have a direct verbal translation or dictionary definition within a specific societal group.

Emotional triggers Inciting words that sound an internal alarm and evoke an emotional response.

Empathic assertive statements/responses Communication that recognizes the other person's position and expresses understanding but does not evaluate or give advice.

Employment interviews Interviews that represent the employer's final step in either selecting or screening potential employees.

Encoding The process of a receiver decoding a message that has been received.

English Only movement A campaign to make English the official language of the United States.

Enthymeme A deductive method of reasoning in which the common premise does not have to be spelled out, because speaker and listener both share this base for building on the argument.

Ethical principle of utilitarianism Belief that an action is right or good if it contributes to the well-being of society in general.

Ethics A systematic attempt, through the use of reason, to make sense of individual and social moral experiences in such a way as to determine the rules that govern human conduct and the values worth pursuing in life. Ethics is not just something practiced by individuals: it is a value shared by society as a whole. The word ethics comes from the Greek word ethos, meaning custom and character.

Executive press conference A session in which members of the media ask questions of a representative of a company centering on the organization's policies, products, services, ethics, or social commitments.

Experts People who through knowledge or skill in a specific field gain respect for their opinions or expertise.

Exposition The part of a public speech that gives the necessary background information to listeners so they can understand the material being presented. Common forms of exposition are definition of terms, subject matter related to historical information, and explaining the relationship between the speaker and the topic.

Extemporaneous mode of speech delivery Method of speech delivery in which the speaker prepares a speech in advance and uses notes or an outline when going before an audience.

External communication An organization's means of communicating with its customers, stockholders, regulatory agencies, and other publics.

Fact That which has been proven, usually through empirical investigation, or has been deemed true because of long-term acceptance.

Factual statement   A declaration of fact.

Fear   A reaction to the feelings of insecurity based on something which is endangering or which is unknown that conjures up insecurity.

Feedback   The process of sending information about the effect of a message. It may be used by the original encoder to adjust her or his message if the feedback indicates that there has been a problem in the receiver gaining the intent of the message sent.

Field-related standards of judgment   Explains why individuals reach conclusions based on what constitutes what they consider to be good reason.

Focus groups   Gatherings of people brought together to test reactions to a particular product, process, or service offered by an organization.

Forecasts   Statements that alert the audience to ideas that are to be presented. Forecast statements include "Let's now examine the three principles of . . ." or, "By understanding the definition of ___, you can gain insight into . . ."

Forum   A type of public group discussion during which participants field questions and answers from each other as well as from the audience members.

Funnel schedules   Structure for addressing questions by a group or in a public speech from the general to the specific.

Goal   The purpose of a speech expressed in terms of the presentation's expected outcome, including: imparting new information; securing understanding or reinforcing information and understandings that were accumulated in the past; attempting to get the listener to take some action, accept a belief, or change a point of view.

Grapevines   Informal channels by which gossip and news spreads from person to person.

Grievances   Employee complaints.

Group   An assemblage of persons who communicate, face-to-face, in order to fulfill a common purpose and achieve a goal.

Group cohesiveness   The interconnectedness of the members of the group.

Group communication networks   Formal and informal communication patterns that link group members together. The forms of the communication networks are the wheel, the chain, the Y, the circle, and the all-channel.

Group conforming   The stage of group action when the members come to agreement on such factors as the norms, consensus on the group's purpose, and how to handle the role of power.

Group norming   Period in the group process when the members of a group come together and start to form the group or welcome new people into an existing group.

Group performing   The action phase of a group when the members work toward the organization's goals.

Group standards for making decisions The factors that group members use to consistently accept or reject certain types of ideas. They usually develop over the group's history and are a learned technique for reaching agreement.

Group storming The period in the group process when conflicts erupt.

Groupthink The mode of thinking that persons engage in when concurrence seeking becomes so dominant in a group that it overrides realistic appraisal of alternative courses of action.

Hidden agenda An objective or purpose for the way a person acts in a group by which she or he puts personal interests above the good of the group as a whole. The real reason for the person's action are not revealed.

High context cultures Cultures in which communicators intuitively share a common frame of reference. (Japan is a high context culture.)

Horizontal organizational structure Organizational structure for the body of a speech that presents a complete survey of a topic, rather than an in-depth investigation of a single aspect of the topic.

Hyperkinetic Description of people whose bodies are always in action. They operate on fast time.

Hypokinetic Description of people who seem to take forever in making decisions and taking action. They operate on slow time.

Illustrations Examples that explain a subject through the use of detailed stories.

Illustrators Gestures that accompany speech and help enhance the words being spoken.

Impromptu mode of speech delivery (sometimes referred to as ad lib) Method of delivery that takes place when a speaker makes a presentation with little or no preparation.

Indirect coping Technique for dealing with a difficult group member in which the manager does not assign the person group responsibilities. The difficulty of the indirect approach is that it very seldom solves the problem; instead, the effort may serve to hide it.

Individual standards for judgment Situation that occurs when realizing that certain people in a group influence the group's actions and, therefore, in order to get the group to take a desired action, the leader must identify what will influence that person.

Inductive arguments Arguments developed by listing a series of specifics from which are drawn a general conclusion.

Inference The passing from one judgment to another, or from a belief or cognition to a judgment.

Inferential statement A statement that can be made by anyone, is not limited to the observed or the factual, and can be made at any time and about any time (past, present, or future).

Informal communication channels Communication that originates spontaneously outside the formal channels of businesses and is the natural response to the need for social interaction and information.

Information business speech A presentation given in such a way that the listener now understands something that he or she previously knew little or nothing about.

Informative briefing A speech presented to an audience that already has knowledge about the subject area with the intention of broadening that knowledge.

Informative interviews Interviews that seek information.

Integration A conflict resolution style in which a communicator confronts a problem directly and works toward a solution so that the issue is resolved and the relationship and the dignity of all involved are maintained.

Interactive process model of communication A format for communication that goes beyond one-directional communication by adding the elements of feedback and adaptation.

Interdepartmental communication Communication between departments in a business that usually centers on such matters as policy changes or common projects.

Internal channels of communication Methods of transmitting messages as a function of an or-ganization's internal communication.

Internal communication The flow of messages within a network of individuals and groups inside a company.

Interviewing Person-to-person communication, usually between two persons, but sometimes three or four persons, with a basic decision-making purpose. In the interview, the interviewer assumes the role of initiator or questioner and the interviewee serves as the respondent. It is the most common form of purposeful, planned communication in organizations.

Interview schedules Arrangements of the questions that the interviewer(s) will use during an interview.

Interviewee The person being interviewed.

Interviewer The person who assumes the role of initiator or questioner during an interview.

Intimate zone The distance between communicators that extends from direct physical contact to a distance of eighteen inches.

Intradepartmental communication Communication between department members of the same organization.

Intrapersonal communication Communication within the self.

Introduction to a speech The beginning of a presentation, intended to gain the listeners' attention and orient them to the material that will be presented. Forms include personal refer-

ences, humorous stories, illustrations, references to the occasion
or setting, rhetorical questions,
action questions, unusual or dramatic devices, quotations related
to the theme, and statements of
the theme.

Intuitive-affective decision-making approach An approach to decision making in which a speaker
uses intuition to develop a persuasive message by discussing issues that do not appear to be directly related to the topic at hand.

Inverted funnel schedule The interview format which starts with
specific ideas and moves to the
general.

Inverted pyramid structure A
technique used by writers who
sort through numerous missives.
The most important, newsworthy
item is listed first and is followed
by successively less important information or details as the writer
moves down to the base of the
pyramid.

Kinesics The physical actions used
by a communicator.

Laissez-faire leader Leader who
allows group members to do their
own thing while he or she observes.

Language The structure system of
symbols that catalogs the objects,
events, and relations in the world
and structures the form by syntax
(grammar rules) and semantics
(meanings) to make sense of what
is said, heard, written, or read.

Language switchers Individuals
who are fluent in more than one
language or dialect and can select

the appropriate dialect or language to use in various situations.

Large groups Assemblages of more
than a dozen participants brought
together to accomplish a goal.

Leader An individual who guides
a group.

Leadership The ability to influence a group to accomplish its
goal.

Leadership power The control
given or taken by the person(s) in
charge of a group to influence the
members' performance.

Leading question Form of inquiry
used by an interviewer that leads
the interviewee into giving a desired response.

**Linear process model of communi-
cation model** Illustration of communication that suggests message
flow in one direction, from a
sender to a receiver.

Linking pin A theory that explains
that a manager must be effective
not only in leading a work group
but also in linking that group to
the management at the next level
of the organization's structure.

Listening An active process in
which individuals receive, attend
to, interpret, and respond to verbal and nonverbal messages.

Listening environment The environment in which the listening
takes place as well as the atmosphere in that environment.

**Lose-lose approach to conflict reso-
lution** Approach to resolving
conflict in which one person feels
so strongly that the other person
is wrong, or so desires the other
person be defeated, that he or she

is willing to be defeated in order to defeat the other person.

Low context cultures Cultures in which communicators elaborate and spell out their arguments, because it is believed that the other communicators do not necessarily share the same frame of reference. The United States is a low context culture.

Maintenance dimension of groups The effort to meet the interpersonal needs of the group members in order to develop group cohesiveness, the interconnectedness of the membership.

Majority A method of deciding the winner or winning idea by requiring that the winner receive more than half of the votes, excluding those who do not vote or do not want to vote.

Manuscript mode of speech delivery Speech delivery method in which the speaker writes out the speech and delivers it word-for-word.

Material self What a person possesses and what that communicates about the person. Included are such things as clothing, jewelry, house, and automobile.

Media-conferencing Conferencing method in which a group conducts meetings via telephones, computers, and/or television.

Memorized mode of speech delivery The presentation of a manuscript speech which has been committed to memory.

Messages The information that a sender encodes to send a potential decoder. To be effective, the message should be purposeful and appropriately coded.

Method of development The method by which the body of a speech is organized.

Mirror questions Questions that reflect the content of what the respondent has just said. They are useful for reflecting not only the emotion of a message, but the content.

Motivational speeches Presentations to encourage greater productivity and happiness by staff members in their work and personal lives.

Neurolinguistic programming The notion that people acquire their nonverbal communication patterns from hereditary and environmental influences.

No seating meetings Sessions in which all participants stand during the entire session. By standing, it is believed, participants feel an urgency to be productive in a short time frame.

Nominal group technique for decision making Technique that centers on brainstorming, the probing for ideas without a discussion of the ideas, in order to collect the data for later action.

Nonassertive means of communication Communication that does not directly attempt to resolve the problem.

Nonverbal communication All message sending and receiving not manifested by words, spoken or written. It involves the messages sent by such factors as clothing, jewelry, facial expressions, the movements, touch, eye contact, vocal behaviors, the use of time, space, and silence.

Norms The rules or standards by which a specific group will operate.

1-3-6 nominal group technique A decision making technique named "1-3-6" for its group configurations in which each individual works alone, then is placed in a group of three, and then in a group of six to make decisions.

Open question A technique used by an interviewer which provides a list of alternative responses and gives the interviewee room to elaborate on a particular response.

Opening of an interview The beginning of an interview, which should create a communication bond between the communicators and establish the overall objective for the interview.

Orienting material Communication material designed to give the audience the background information necessary to understand a speech by explaining such factors as the historical background of the topics, definition of terms, personal history of the speaker and/or his or her tie to the topic, and the importance of the information to the listeners.

Paralanguage (vocalics) All the vocal sounds except the words themselves.

Parallelism writing structure The convention of expressing ideas of equal importance using similar construction. This structure not only helps the reader follow the organization of a document but gives the reader a clear understanding of how each new piece of information is related to the earlier components.

Paraphrasing The repetition—either to yourself or to the person who has sent the message—of what has been said in order to establish understanding.

Part-of-the-whole A method of deciding the winner or winning idea in a vote by requiring that the winner receive a preset number or preset percentage of votes from those who are eligible to vote.

Participants The people involved in a communicative event, including the speaker and the message receiver(s) and/or those members of a group who interact to bring about the actions of a group.

Perception The process of becoming aware of objects and events through the senses. The perceptual filter establishes an individual's screen for selecting, organizing, and interpreting all incoming data.

Perceptual filter The psychological screen through which all messages are encoded and decoded. The listener's background, experiences, roles, mental and physical states that influence perception.

Performance appraisal interviews Interviews to systematically evaluate an employee's job performance.

Personal speaking inventory A listing of an individual's life experiences and interests which can be used as the basis for selecting a topic for a speech.

Personal zone A physical space within which a person feels comfortable. In the North American culture, most people feel comfortable with about three feet of space around them when they are with individuals whom they know, but with whom they do not have intimate relationships.

Persuasive interviewing An interaction in which the interviewer desires that an action take place as the result of the interview.

Persuasive speaking A presentation intended to influence the opinion or behavior of an audience.

Physical characteristics Personal qualities such as physique, general attractiveness, body and breath odors, height, weight, and hair and skin color, that communicate information about an individual.

Physical self How a person looks and feels about his or her looks, including weight, facial appearance, hairstyle, and body build.

Plurality A method of deciding the winner or winning idea by requiring that the winner receive the most among the candidates or ideas that are being considered for selection.

Pollyanna-Nietzsche effect An attitude by group's members who believe that their solution is the best and will work flawlessly.

Post speech analysis The speaker's effort to ascertain the effect of a speech by paying attention to the reactions following the presentation, including verbal feedback and written evaluation.

Power The ability of one person to influence another's attainment of goals.

Primary social tension The normal jitters and feelings of uneasiness experienced when groups first congregate.

Prior analysis The information that a speaker collects before the speech is given in order to ascertain audience demographics, attitudes and readiness to receive the speaker's message.

Probe question A question designed to get specific detailed information or opinions from the interviewee. It is normally used as a follow-up to an open question.

Problem-solution arrangement A method for organizing the body of a speech in which the speaker identifies what is wrong and how to cure it.

Problem-solving discussions Discussions that take place when a group of people get together to resolve a problem.

Problem-solving interviews Interviews conducted in order to discuss problems and ascertain solutions.

Problem-solving method of performance appraisal A job evaluation discussion in which a supervisor and employee review the worker's job performance and discuss satisfactions, problems, needs, innovations, and frustrations that have been encountered.

Procedures A group's agreed-upon rules of operation which will be followed by the assemblage in reaching decisions.

Process analysis The speaker's effort during a speech to watch the audience for feedback and adjust the speech to achieve the goal of the presentation.

Professional papers A research-based, comprehensive written analysis of a topic in one's professional field.

Proposal-counterproposal negotiating A negotiating technique in which a plan or solution is presented in an attempt to solve a dispute, or negotiate a price for a service or product, then a counter-offer is made. The process continues until either a solution is reached, or one of the participants decides to withdraw from the process.

Protocols The cultural customs regarding how certain actions or activities should take place. A handshake when meeting someone is a protocol of many Western cultures, while bowing performs the same function in some Asian cultures.

Proxemics The study of the dimensions of space and environment and how a culture uses them.

Psychographics The study of the attitudes and beliefs of the prospective listeners, such as emotionally charged issues, memberships, political affiliations, and conservative or liberal dispositions.

Public speaking A speech transaction between a speaker and an audience.

Public speaking anxiety The fears

speakers feel before, during, and after presenting a speech.

Public zone The space distance of more than twelve feet between communicators.

Pupilometrics A theory that suggests people can't control the response of their eyes; therefore, it is possible to detect whether or not a person is lying through a sophisticated examination of eye movements.

Purpose The objective or goal of a communicative act, including a public speech, interview, conversation, or group meeting.

Purpose statement A declaration a speaker prepares and uses when developing a speech, listing the goal, the topic, and the method by which the speech will be developed.

Quality circles Groups of workers who do similar tasks and meet on a regular basis to identify and analyze work-related problems and recommend solutions to management.

Quality management An approach adopted by many Japanese firms after World War II and now used by some Northern American businesses. Its purpose is to empower employees to make decisions and deal with problems as they arise.

Questions of fact Inquiries as to whether something is true.

Questions of policy Inquiries as to whether a specific course of action should be undertaken in order to solve a problem.

Questions of value Inquiries to determine whether something is good or bad, right or wrong, and to what extent.

Question-and-answer session An interaction, usually at the end of a speech, when a speaker is asked to respond to inquiries posed by members of the audience.

Rapport A bond created between communicators.

Reactive coping Response of a business person, usually an employer or manager, who refuses to become involved with another person's problems, but instead allows the person with the problem to operate in his or her own way.

Receivers Persons who obtain and decode a message.

Regulators Nonverbal acts that maintain and control the back-and-forth speaking and listening between individuals. Regulators include head nods, body shifts, and eye movements.

Reprimanding interviews Interviews intended to discipline an employee because of a performance problem.

Restatement Rewording or summary of each segment of a speech before proceeding to the next point so that major ideas stand out for the listeners.

Resumes Written documents prepared by job seekers, and submitted to prospective employers, listing the person's qualifications including education, job experiences, and skills.

Rhetorographics Analysis of the setting in which a speech will take place, including the place, time limit, time of day, and emotional climate.

Risky shift phenomenon The notion that decisions reached after discussion by groups are filled with more experimentation, are less conservative, and contain more risk than decisions reached by people working alone.

Sales speeches Presentations intended to persuade prospective customers to buy a commodity or service or to act favorably upon an idea that has commercial significance to the seller.

Schema The mental and linguistic categories of all the information that a person has stored through life experiences which enables him or her to deal with incoming information.

Scientific method of decision-making process A format by which a problem is identified, a search is conducted for solutions, testing is done of those solutions, the best solution is selected, the solution is put into practice, and a follow-up is done to see if the solution has solved the problem.

Secondary social tension The stress and strain that occurs within a group after it has been operating for a period of time.

See-blame-cure-cost method Problem solving technique in which the evil or problem that exists is examined (see), what has caused the problem is determined (blame), solutions are investigated (cure), and the most practical solution is selected (cost).

Self-concept How a person perceives the world, how the world perceives the person, and how the person perceives himself or herself.

Self-disclosure The process of a person revealing personal information about herself or himself to others.

Self-fulfilling prophecy The belief that individuals tend to act consistently with the feelings they hold about themselves; therefore, people who have a negative self-concept may see themselves as failures and not allow themselves to be successful, while positive-thinking individuals are likely to anticipate experiencing success.

Self-image A person's definition of who and what he or she is, including assets and liabilities.

Self talk Communication that takes place when a person tunes in to her or his own verbal and/or nonverbal inner speech.

Sender The person who devises a message.

Setting The environment in which a communication act takes place, including where and when.

Sexual harassment Unwelcome sexual advances, requests for sexual favors, and other verbal or physical conduct of a sexual nature in the workplace.

Silent majority Those meeting attenders who do not take an active role during the decision-making process.

Simple assertive statements Statements of fact.

Six-step standard agenda for decision making Problem-solving sequence in which a problem is identified, analyzed, solutions sought, a solution selected and implemented.

Small groups Groups of from three to twelve persons.

Smoothing over A nonassertive communication technique which centers on the concept that maintaining the relationship is the most important issue. The person who smooths over lets the other person know what they want, but not in a forceful enough way to get the other person to take the required action.

Social loafing Behavior that takes place when group membership leads participants to work less than they may individually.

Social self The part of the self that is concerned with how we feel about our kinships with others.

Social zone A space of four to twelve feet that is reserved for strangers or those with whom you don't have an intimate or personal relationship.

Spanglish A blending of Spanish and English that is spoken by some Hispanic-Americans.

Spatial arrangement A way of organizing the body of a speech in which the speaker sets a point of reference at some specific location, then proceeds to give directions starting from the established reference point.

Specific instances Condensed examples that are used to clarify or prove a point.

Speech of acceptance Presentation given by the recipient of an honor, an award, or a gift.

Speech of actuation Presentation intended to move the members of the audience to take the desired action that the speaker has proposed, such as buy a product, sign a petition, go on strike, or adopt the plan presented.

Speech of conviction Presentation intended to convince the listener to believe as the speaker does.

Spiral form of explanation Explanation in a message in which a speaker makes a statement; tells a story or presents an analogy which deals with that statement; then lets the listener apply the parallels and draw outcomes that apply to the original statement.

Spiritual self The way a person's value system, attitudes, and beliefs define who the person is.

Spontaneous press conference Press conference that takes place when the reporters present are allowed to ask any questions they desire with no attention to a preset or restrictive structure.

Standard American English (SAE) Dialect of English spoken in the United States by professionals and generally accepted as the most desirable and the most credible in the world of business.

Statement of declaration A speaker's statement of the major contention, followed by the development of the idea with illustrations, specific instances, statistics, analogies, and testimony, intended to get the audience to accept the contention(s).

Statistics Collection of numerical information arranged to indicate representations, trends, or theories.

Stress A physical response to environmental demands that create tension.

Structured press conference Press conference in which a number of reporters ask questions following a short opening speech. The questions must relate to the subject of the speech.

Success visualization A process of confidence building in which a positive image is repeated over and over in a person's mind in order to set up an accomplishment based on positive expectations.

Summary The final part of a speech in which the speaker restates the major points of the speech so that the listener can recap what has been covered.

Superleadership style Approach to leadership based on people's ability to lead themselves and thereby release the self-leadership potential and energy within each person.

Supplementary aids Communication aids that supplement the oral segments of speeches, including visual, audio, audiovisual, and computer assisted materials.

Supporting material Material gathered through research to use in a speech to clarify a point or offer proof.

Symposium A type of group discussion format in which all the participants give prepared speeches, with no interaction between each other or from the audience. These short presentations are often followed by questions and answers presented by the speakers as well as from the audience members.

Systematic desensitization A method of dealing with communication anxiety that centers on applying deep muscle relaxation techniques.

Talk show Radio and television programs, as they relate to the business community, that center on a host and a business representative(s) explaining new products, defending their company's policies, and/or clarifying actions being taken by their organizations.

Task dimension of groups Group responsibilities, including decision-making, informing, appraising/examining, problem solving, and creating interest in staying on track.

Technical reports Concise, clear statements that explain a process, detail a technique, or discuss new elements either to individuals within a business or industry or to people outside the organization.

Telecommuters Individuals who are employed by a company and do all or part of their work at home.

Teleconferencing The use of interactive television, telephone, and video phone to conduct a meeting.

Tell and listen method of performance appraisals Approach to employee evaluation in which the

supervisor informs the employee of the supervisor's evaluation of the employee's job performance, followed by the employee responding to the evaluation and suggesting needed alternatives.

Tell and sell method of performance appraisals Approach to employee evaluation in which the supervisor works to convince the employee to accept the evaluation and work toward constructive change.

Testimony A quotation or paraphrase from an authority known as an expert, used to clarify ideas, back up contentions, and reinforce concepts.

Therapeutic listening Listening that provides a sounding board for a person to talk a problem through to a solution with a speaker who displays empathy, rather than advice.

Top-down process A business communication flow-structure in which individuals who have been given the upper-level decision making responsibilities determine the policies and procedures and inform those on the next level of these decisions and strategies for carrying out the decisions.

Topic The subject of a speech or business report.

Topical arrangement A way of organizing the body of a speech in which the speaker explains an idea in terms of its component parts. A speaker discusses all aspects of one component before proceeding to the next.

Touch A form of intimate behavior that is an aspect of nonverbal communication and includes holding and caressing.

Town meetings Group meetings that provide an opportunity for the audience to engage in a discussion in which each person's views can be voiced.

Transactional process model of communication An understanding of communication that centers on two or more people simultaneously sending and receiving messages.

Transformational leadership Leadership in which the person responsible for leading a group keeps in mind the interest of the group and its goals, rather than forcing her or his will on the group.

Transitional phrases Written or spoken statements that help the message's receiver move from one discussion point to another.

Values Factors which a person perceives to be of worth.

Verbal markers Statements made by a speaker or writer which tell a receiver what to anticipate so that the person can sharpen her or his concentration in order to gain the point being presented.

Vertical development A method of organizing a speech in which a single issue is discussed in great detail.

Visual aids Devices used to supplement a speaker's oral presentation which appeal to the receiver's sense of sight. They can include real objects, models, photographs, pictures, diagrams, and charts.

Vocalics All the vocal sounds except the words themselves.

Voting Procedure in which each member is given the opportunity to indicate agreement, disagreement, or having no opinion on an idea or candidate.

Win-lose approach to conflict resolution Effort to resolve conflict in which one person or company wins and another person or organization loses, based on the decision agreed upon or enforced.

Win-win approach to conflict resolution Effort to resolve conflict in which people are willing to work together toward reaching a decision through peacemaking in order for all to feel that they have accomplished their goal.

Work teams Small groups of workers who function as teams to make decisions about the work to be done and then to implement those decisions.

Yiddish As an American dialect, a blending of English and a German-based dialect traditionally spoken by many Jewish people in Western European countries.

Index

Action chains, 99
Adaptation, 9
Advertising, 15
After-dinner speech, 301
Aesthetics, 96–99
African American Vernacular English
    (AAVE), 58
Anger, 142–143
Artifacts, 93–96
  casual Friday, 94
  defined, 93
Assertiveness, 177–180
  assertive person, 177
  definition of, 177
  DESC scripting, 180
Audience cultural identities, 309
Audiovisual aids. *See* Supplementary
  aids

Behavioral kinesiology, 96
Black English, 58
Bottom-up process
    of communication, 16
Brainstorming, 251
Business communication
  appropriate, 22–24
  clothing, role of in, 93–95
  criticizing, 163
  changing world of, 2–6
  directing, 167–169
  direction giving, 168–169
  ethics in, 31–53
  ethics use in, 43–44
  external, 6
  groups, role of in, 231–290
  handling grievances, 164–165
  improving of, 19–26
  internal, 6
  job training, 170

  management-employee relationships,
    161–170
  need for effective, 6–7
  nonverbal, 79
  nonverbal, role of culture in,
    100–105
  order giving, 167–168
  organizational culture, 12
  planning of, 19–20
  preparing of, 20–21
  protocols in, 23
  space, role of in, 91–92
  written, 344–366

Channel, 8
Chronemics, 99
  action chain, 99
  hyperkinetic, role of, in, 99
  hypokinetic, role of, in, 99
Cognitive modification, 139
Communication anxiety, 138–140
  cognitive modification and, 139
  communication apprehension, 138
  systematic desensitization and, 139
Communication ethics, 31–53
  business, defined, 34
  business and, 32
  corporate responsibility and, 36–39
  defined, 33
  ethical dilemma as part of,
    32
Communication system
  components of, 8–12
  models of, 8–12
Communication technology, 21
Computer-generated supplementary
    aids, 320–321
  creating, 320
Conflict/conflict resolution, 170–178
  accommodation, 174

Conflict/conflict resolution (cont.)
    assertiveness, 177–180
    avoidance, 174
    competition, 175
    compromise, 174
    defined, 172
    integration, 175
    lose-lose approach to, 173
    power, role of in, 171
    steps in, 176–177
    styles of, 173–176
    win-lose approach to, 173
    win-win approach to, 173
Confucian principle of I, 258
Connotation, 63
Context, 8
Corporate communication departments, 24
Corporate communication flow
    model of, 25
Cross-functional work teams, 14
Cultures
    groups in, 257–261
    high context, 141
    low context, 141
Cybernetics, 78

Decision making
    centralized process, 246
    consensus-building process, 245–246
    intuitive-affective process, 246
    nominal group technique, 253–255
    1–3–6 decision-making technique,
        252–253, 25
    problem-solving discussion, 247–248
    proposal-counterproposal
        negotiating, 260–261
    scientific method of, 246
    six-step standard agenda, 251–252
Decoding, 8
Deductive arguments
    defined, 297
    development of, 297
Denotation, 63
DESC scripting, 180

Dialects, 56–60
    African American Vernacular English,
        58
    Black English, 58
    connotation, as factor in, 63
    defined, 56
    denotation, as factor in, 63
    Ebonics, 58
    language switchers, 59
    nonstandard, 58
    Standard American English, 57–58
Difficult people, dealing with, 165–166
    direct intervention, 166
    groups, in, 277–278
    indirect coping, 166
    reactive coping, 166

Ebonics, 58
Egospeak, 126
Electronic mail (e-mail), 360–363
    emotions in, 363
    etiquette, 361
    privacy concerns, 361
    vocabulary for, 362
Employment interview, 199–218
    interviewer, role of in, 218
    most often asked question in,
        212–213
    participating in, 209–212
    preparing for, 200–201, 209
    questions to ask during, 209
    regulations governing, 214–215
    resume, 201–204, 210–211
Encoding, 8
Enthymeme, 140–141
Ethics
    business, defined, 34
    capitalism and, 36
    changes in, 36
    code of, 42
    corporate responsibility and, 36–39
    defined, 33
    use of, 39–43
Expert, 317–318
    defined, 317
Extemporaneous speech, 335

Fact
    fact versus inference, 64–65
    factual statements, defined, 64
Feedback, 9
Female-male language. *See* Gender

Gender
    female-male language, 66–71
    roles in groups, 261–262
    sexism of Standard American English,
        66–67
Group communication, 231–290
    advantages of, 233
    agenda for, 246–247, 248, 251
    brainstorming during, 251
    committees, 236
    communication network in, 275–277
    cultural differences in, 257–261
    decision making in, 245–246,
        250–255
    difficult people in, 277–278
    disadvantages of, 233–234
    electronic meetings, 237–238
    focus groups, 238
    group adjourning, 245
    group conforming, 243
    group norming, 239–240
    group operations, 239–245
    group performing, 243–244
    group storming, 240–242
    groups, defined, 232
    hot groups, 244
    large groups, defined, 232
    leader/leadership, 267, 279–287
    male and female roles in, 261–262
    media-conferences, 236–238
    nominal group technique, 253–255
    1–3–6 decision-making technique,
        252–253, 254
    participants, role of in, 267–275
    power, role of in, 242
    problem-solving discussion, 247–248
    proposal-counterproposal
        negotiating, 260–261
    public meetings, 238–239
    setting of, 255–257
        silent majority, 267
        six-step standard agenda, 251–252
        small groups, defined, 232
        symposiums, 238–239
        teleconferencing, 237
        town meetings, 239
        types of, 234–239
        voting as part of a, 249–250
        work teams, 235–236
Group communication networks,
    275–277
Group think, 284

Hyperkinetic, 99
Hypokinetic, 99

Impromptu speech, 334
Inductive arguments
    defined, 297–298
    development of, 297–298
Inference, 64–65
    inferential statements, 64
Informative public speaking, 293–295
    characteristics of, 294
    informative briefing, 293
    professional paper, 294
    technical report, 293–294
Interactive process model of
    communication, 9–10
International Association of Business
    Communicators, 42
    code of ethics of, 42
Interpersonal communication, 153–189
    criticizing, 163
    defined, 154
    difficult personalities, dealing with,
        165–166
    directing, 167–169
    direction giving, 168–169
    handling grievances, 164–165
    management-employee relationships,
        161–170
    order giving, 167–168
    organization, role of in, 156–157
    self-disclosure, role of in, 155–156

Interviewing, 190–230
   body of, 193–194
   closed question, 193
   closing of, 194
   counseling interview, 198
   defined, 191
   employment interview, 199–218
   format of, 194
   funnel interview schedule, 194
   ideal model of, 192
   informative interview, 195–197
   interview schedule, 194
   interviewee, defined, 191
   interviewer, defined, 191
   inverted interview schedule, 194
   leading question, 194
   mirror question, 193
   press conference, 224–225
   open question, 193
   opening of, 191
   performance appraisal, 219–223
   persuasive interview, 199
   probe question, 194
   problem-solving interview, 197
   purpose of, 191
   rapport, establishing in, 191
   reprimanding interview, 223–224
   structure of, 191–193
   talk show interview, 225–226
   types of, 195–226
Intrapersonal communication, 131–152
   affective dimension of, 141–143
   anger, role of in, 142–143
   attitudes, role of in, 141
   beliefs, role of in, 141
   cognitive complexity, role of in, 141
   cognitive consistency, role of in, 141
   cognition dimension of, 140–141
   cognitive dissonance, role of in, 141
   cognitive processing, as factor in, 140
   communication anxiety, as factor in,
      138–140
   defined, 132
   dimensions of, 132–143
   enthymeme, role of in, 140–141
   improving of, 146–148
   interpretation, as factor in, 133–134

   intrapersonal communication plan,
      148
   organization, as factor in, 133
   perception, as factor in, 132–133
   perceptual filter, role of in, 140
   physiological dimension of, 134–140
   psychological dimension of, 132–134
   schemata, as factor in, 140
   selection, as factor in, 133
   self-concept, role of in, 144–145
   self-identities, role of in, 145–146
   self-image, role of in, 143–146
   stress, as factor in, 134–138
   values, role of in, 141
Inverted pyramid structure, 350

Kinesics, 82–88
   defined, 82
   reading of, 87

Language
   assumption, as part of, 61–62
   clarity, as part of, 62–63
   concreteness, as part of, 63
   defined, 55–56
   dialects, as part of, 56–60
   difference between spoken and
      written, 65–66
   fact versus inference, as part of,
      64–65
   intercultural implications of use of,
      71–73
   male and female, 66–71
   meaning in, 60–61
   problems in use of, 61–65
   use in business, 73
Language switchers, 59
Leader/leadership, 267, 279–287
   desire to be, 283–284
   leader, defined, 267, 279
   leadership, defined, 267, 279
   model of, 279
   patterns of, 282–283
   responsibilities of, 284–285
   superleadership, 280
   transformational leadership, 280
   types of, 280–282

Linear process model of
    communication, 8–9
Listening, 111–130
    appreciation level of, 122
    attention, role of in, 116
    business listening, 112
    business success and, 114
    comprehension level of, 120
    critical level of, 120–121
    defined, 115
    discriminative level of, 119
    egospeak, role of in, 126
    feedback, role of in, 118–119
    goals of, 119–122
    improving of, 125–128
    interest, role of in, 117
    interpretation, role of in, 117–118
    levels of organizational, 112–113
    listening environment in
        organizations, 113
    motivation, role of in, 116, 123
    negative self-concept, role of in, 123
    obstacles to effective, 122–128
    paraphrasing, role of in, 127
    perception, role of in, 117
    physiological interference, role of in,
        122
    preparation, role of in, 124–125
    process of, 115–119
    receiving, role of in, 116
    responding, role of in, 118
    storage, role of in, 118
    therapeutic level of, 120
    understand, role of in, 123–124
    verbal markers, role of in, 127

Manuscript speech, 335
Memorized speech, 335
Message, 8
Methods of issue arrangement, 323,
        324–325
    causal arrangement, 324
    chronological/time arrangement, 324
    comparison-contrast arrangement,
        324–325
    defined, 323

problem-solution arrangement, 325
    see-blame-cure-cost arrangement,
        325
    spatial arrangement, 324
    spiral form of explanation, 323
    topical arrangement, 324
Motivational speech, 302

Neurolinguistic programming, 78–79
Nominal group technique, 253–255
Nonverbal communication, 76–110
    aesthetics, 96–99
    affect displays, 84
    artifacts, 93–96
    behavioral kinesiology, 96
    categories of, 81–105
    chronemics, 99
    color, as a factor of, 97–98
    culture and, 100–105
    dealing with, 105–106
    defined, 77
    emblems, 82
    eye behavior, 84–85
    facial expression, 85–86
    illustrators, 84
    importance of, in business, 79
    kinesics, 82–88
    light, as a factor of, 97
    music, as a factor of, 96–97
    neurolinguistic programming, as part
        of, 78–79
    paralanguage, 88
    physical characteristics, as factor of,
        92–93
    proxemics, 89–92
    pupilometrics, 84
    reading of, 81
    regulators, 84
    sources of, 78–79
    space, 89–92
    touch, 86
    verbal-nonverbal relationship, 80–81
    vocalics, 88

One-minute manager theory, 162–163
    defined, 162

1-3-6 decision-making technique,
    252–253, 254
Organizational networks, 16
Organizations
    climate in, 12–13
    cultures of, 12
    ethics in, 31–53
    external channels in, 13
    grapevine in, 13, 14
    horizontal organizational structure,
        16
    informal communication channels,
        14
    interdepartmental communication in,
        13
    internal channels in, 13
    interpersonal communication in, 158
    intradepartmental communication in,
        14
    major sources of information in, 15
    management-employee relationships,
        161–170
    nonverbal communication,
        importance of, 79

Paralanguage, 88
Paraphrasing, 127
Perception, 132–133
    defined, 132
Perceptual filter, 140
Persuasive speaking, 295–299
    defined, 295
    goals of, 296
    persuasive strategies, 296–299
    speech of actuation, 296
    speech of conviction, 296
Press conference, 224–225
*Principles for Managing in a Time of
    Change: A CEO's Perspective*,
    44–50
Proxemics, 89–92
    business, role in, 91–92
    defined, 89
    personal zones in, 89–91
Psychographics, 309
Public speaking, 291–343
    after-dinner speech, 301

audience cultural identities, 309
body of, 323–325
central idea of, 323
clincher in, 326
conclusion tc, 325–326
defined, 292
developing the, 313–321
extemporaneous presentation, 335
forecasting, 318
hostile audience, deal with a, in, 338
impromptu presentation, 334
informative briefing, 293
informative speaking, 293–295
introduction to, 321–323
language selection, 310
manuscript presentation, 335
memorized presentation, 335
methods for sequencing, 323–325
modes of presentation, 334–335
motivational speech, 302
orienting material in, 322–323
persuasive speaking, 295–299
physical elements of, 335–339
post-speech analysis, 308, 313
presenting, 333–342
prior speech analysis, 308, 309–312
process speech analysis, 308,
    312–313
professional paper, 294
psychographics, 309
public speaking anxiety, 339–342
purpose statement, 310–312
question-and-answer sessions,
    302–304
restatement, 318
rhetorographics, 309
sales speech, 302
sample speech to inform, 326–328
sample speech to persuade, 328–330
speaker anxiety, 292
speaker inventory form, 331–332
special occasion speeches, 300–304
speech of acceptance, 301
speech of actuation, 296
speech of conviction, 296
speech of introduction, 300
speech of presentation, 301

speech of welcome, 300
spiral, form of, explanation, 323
stage fright. *See* Speaker anxiety
statistics, use of, in, 316
supporting material used in, 315–321
technical report, 293–294
testimony, use of, in, 316
topic selection, 310
visual aids, use of, 337–338
Pupilometrics, 84
Purpose, 8
Purpose statement, 310–312

Quality circles, 18
Question-and-answer sessions,
    302–304
Questions, types of, 193–194
    closed, 193
    discussion, 247
    leading, 194
    mirror, 193
    open, 193
    probe, 194

Receiver, 8
Resume, 201–204, 210–211, 357
    cover letter, 357
    electronically screened, 204
    preparing, 201–204
    sample, 202
Rhetorographics, 309

Sales speech, 302
Schemata, 140
Self-communication, 131–152
    See also Intrapersonal
        communication
Self-concept, 144–145
    spiritual self, 144
    material self, 144
    social self, 144
    physical self, 144
Self-disclosure, 155–156
    defined, 155
Self-fulfilling prophecy, 144
Self-talk, 135, 146

Sender, 8
Sexual harassment, 180–183
    communication about, 182–183
    defined, 181
    EEOC Guidelines on Sexual
        Harassment, 181
Six-step standard agenda, 251–252
Speaker anxiety, 292, 339–342
Speaker inventory, 331
Speech of acceptance, 301
Speech of introduction, 300
Speech of presentation, 301
Speech of welcome, 300
Stage fright. *See* Speaker anxiety
Standard American English, 57–58
    sexism of, 66–67
Stress, 134–138
    coping with, 136–138
    defined, 134
    physiological responses, as factor in,
        135
Supplementary aids, 318, 320–321
    audio aids, 318
    audiovisual aids, 320
    computer-generated aids, 320
    defined, 318
    visual aids, 318
Systematic desensitization, 139

Talk show interview, 225–226
Telecommuters, 22
Teleconferencing, 237
Telephone usage, 158–160
    placing calls, 160
    receiving messages, 158–160
Top-down process of communication,
    16
Total Quality Management (TQM), 7
Transactive process model of
    communication, 11–12

Values, 141
    cognitive complexity, role of in, 141
    cognitive consistency, role of in, 141
    cognitive dissonance, role of in, 141
Verbal communication, 54–75

Verbal markers, 127
Vocalics, 88
Voice mail systems, 160–161
Voting, 249–250
    consensus, 250
    defined, 249
    majority, 250
    part-of-the-whole, 250
    plurality, 250

Written business communication,
        344–366
    ABCs of language, 358
    acceptance of offer, model for, 352
    business letter, model for, 356
    editing of, 364–366
    electronic mail, 360–363
    enhancing the image of, 359–360

executive summary, 357
guidelines for, 355–357
importance of, 345–346
internal memorandum, 353, 354
inverted pyramid structure in, 350
minutes of a meeting, 358
organizational patterns for, 351–357
parallel structure for, 351
preparing a document, 349–350
process of, 346–349
project status report, 353
resume and cover letter, 357
sales proposal, 357
standard application letter, model for,
    352
thank you for an interview, model
    for, 352
writing for the ear, 359

Meet the Authors

ROY BERKO

Roy Berko is a member of the Communication faculty at George Washington University. He was formerly the Associate Director of the Speech Communication Association and has been on the faculties of Towson State University, George Mason University, Pennsylvania State University, and Lorain County Community College. The author of over twenty communication books and editions, he has been the recipient of numerous teaching awards, including being named by the Speech Communication Association as a "Teacher on Teaching." He is the Director of *Communic-aid,* an organizational consulting firm whose clients have included many of the Fortune 500 companies. He has a long history of media appearances discussing communication and business issues.

ANDREW WOLVIN

Andrew Wolvin is a Professor of Speech Communication and former Department Chairperson at the University of Maryland–College Park. With Roy Berko, he has coauthored *Communicating: A Social and Career Focus* and *This Business of Communicating.* He also is coauthor of the books *Listening* and *Perspectives on Listening.* A noted expert on listening in the business organization, he serves as a managerial communication and listening consultant to a number of government agencies and private corporations.

REBECCA RAY

Rebecca Ray is currently Vice President and Manager of Executive Education in the Management Resources and Development Department of Merrill Lynch. Prior to joining Merrill Lynch, she served as a communication consultant designing seminars and training sessions for corporate and individual clients, focusing on presentation skills, behavioral styles, interpersonal communication, interviewing strategies, and sexual harassment from a gender and communication perspective. Ms. Ray has taught at New York University and at Oxford University in England. She is the editor of *Bridging Both Worlds: The Communication Consultant in Corporate America.*